Who Owned Waterloo?

Who Owned Waterloo?

Battle, Memory, and Myth in British History, 1815–1852

LUKE REYNOLDS

OXFORD
UNIVERSITY PRESS

OXFORD
UNIVERSITY PRESS

Great Clarendon Street, Oxford, OX2 6DP,
United Kingdom

Oxford University Press is a department of the University of Oxford.
It furthers the University's objective of excellence in research, scholarship,
and education by publishing worldwide. Oxford is a registered trade mark of
Oxford University Press in the UK and in certain other countries

Published in the United States of America by Oxford University Press
198 Madison Avenue, New York, NY 10016, United States of America

British Library Cataloguing in Publication Data

Data available

Library of Congress Control Number: 2021952891

ISBN 978–0–19–286499–4

DOI: 10.1093/oso/9780192864994.001.0001

Printed and bound in the UK by
Clays Ltd, Elcograf S.p.A.

Links to third party websites are provided by Oxford in good faith and
for information only. Oxford disclaims any responsibility for the materials
contained in any third party website referenced in this work.

For Claire,

for everything.

Acknowledgements

Who Owned Waterloo? started life as my Ph.D. dissertation, and thus my first statement of gratitude must go to my adviser, Timothy Alborn, who gave me the time and guidance to realize that I am, in fact, a cultural historian, and then showed me, both by instruction and example, how to be a good one. He has been unfailingly supportive, has answered my random questions, and still reads my drafts far more quickly than any former student has a right to expect. I also owe a huge debt to my second reader, Benjamin Hett, who has always been willing to provide advice, read a draft, or just chat and listen. In addition, I am grateful to the other two members of my Dissertation Committee, Simon Davis and Robert Johnson of Pembroke College, Oxford, for their advice on turning my dissertation into a manuscript.

Across the time it took to write this book I have been a member (as either a student or faculty) of four academic departments, and I am grateful for the support and advice of all of my colleagues. I owe a particular debt to Marilyn Weber, Alison Kavey, Helena Rosenblatt, and Joel Allen at the Graduate Center; John Jones, Carol Adams, Mary Roldán, Donna Haverty-Stacke, Bernadette McCauley, Angelo Angelis, and Eduardo Contreras at Hunter College; Jennifer Edwards and Adam Arenson at Manhattan College; and Mark Healey and Kathy Erickson at the University of Connecticut.

In researching this project, I have been lucky enough to receive funding from a number of sources. I am deeply grateful to the Graduate Center for funding my work through the Florence J. Bloch Dissertation Fellowship, and two Doctoral Student Research Grants, and to the GC's History Department for a Graduate Teaching Fellowship and a Judith Stein Memorial Fellowship. Outside of the Graduate Center, I must thank the Masséna Society for granting me a Dissertation Research Fellowship, and the North American Conference on British Studies for a Stern Grant. This book necessitated travel to archives in three countries, and would have been a great deal poorer, if not impossible, without the aid of the staffs of the Graduate Center's Mina Rees Library, Hunter College's Leon & Toby Cooperman Library, the New York Public Library, the British National Archives, the British Library, the National Archives of Scotland, the University of Oxford's Bodleian Library, the Library and Archives Canada, McGill University, the University of Southampton's Hartley Library, and others too numerous to name. I must pay particular tribute to Jane Branfield, Archivist to Stratfield Saye House and the Duke of Wellington, who has gone out of her way multiple times not only to find me sources, but also to help me decipher them.

This is also, at least in part, a Covid-19 book, and I would not have been able to write it without the Inter-Library Loan departments of the Graduate Center's Mina Rees Library, Hunter College's Leon & Toby Cooperman Library, and Manhattan College's O'Malley Library. I am also grateful for the enlightened and generous remote research policies of the Cambridge University Library, Brown University's John Hay Library (especially the Anne S. K. Brown Military Collection), and Yale University's Beinecke Rare Book & Manuscript Library as well as the countless unnamed librarians, students, and interns who have digitized the books and newspapers now found in various free and subscription databases around the world.

A number of people have contributed directly to this work, and I would be remiss not to mention them. The members of my reading group, Scott Ackerman, Krystle Sweda, and John Winters, have provided not only encouragement and advice, but also many laughs. I am also grateful to Stephanie Makowski, who found me access to a source no one else could; to Ashley and Robert Wilde-Evans, for providing insider knowledge of Waterloo's 200th anniversary re-enactment; and to both The Armoury of St James's and Charles Graham Architectural Antiques and Fireplaces for granting a historian who randomly contacted you permission to use your images. Speaking of images, I am equally grateful to Lawrence Gullo, who arranged the images of medals in this book, added the route of Wellington's funeral procession to a map of London, and put up with my myriad requests for minute tweaks with grace and charm. I am indebted to *The Journal of Victorian Culture* for giving me the opportunity to explore some of my work on the Waterloo Banquets in article form, and especially to Dr Jane Hamlett and the anonymous reviewers for their comments and suggestions. I also owe a debt of thanks to Gayathri Venkatesan and her team at Straive for their superb work putting the book into production and especially for allowing me to add a final image even after I told them the manuscript was finished.

I am extremely fortunate that I get to work with the editors that I do. Every historian should be lucky enough to work with a developmental editor who is also one of their best friends, and Miranda Dubner has gone out of her way not only to make this book as good as it could be, but also to cheer me on, share my delight, and lessen my frustration on more occasions than I can count. From Miranda, it passed into the hands of Edwin Pritchard, who not only performed magic with all of my formatting but also copyedited it, making it clearer and stronger in the process. Needless to say, any errors that still remain are entirely my own. Nor can too much praise be heaped on Cathryn Steele and her team at Oxford University Press. I do not think Cathryn knew what she was getting into when she agreed to meet me at the American Historical Association's Annual Meeting in January 2020, but despite my constant questions and first-time-author panic, she has cheerfully shepherded me and this book to this point. In the process, she recruited referees whose feedback has made this book much stronger than it otherwise would have been. I am very grateful to each of them.

Finally, there are personal debts to acknowledge. I am very lucky to have friends and family who are vocal in support of what I have chosen to do, and I wish I had the time and space to thank each and every one of you. Despite this, there are those who have gone above and beyond, and must be acknowledged. I am grateful to Sara Robertson for her willingness to function as my base of operations whenever I visit Edinburgh and her tolerance for being dragged to regimental museums. To Audrey Kulas for her constant support. To my late paternal grandfather, Captain George Howard Reynolds, OBE, for helping with the funding of my studies and research trips. To my father, Captain Martyn Reynolds, for first introducing me to this period of British history. To Sana Reynolds, mother extraordinaire, who encouraged me to dedicate my life to teaching and scholarship in the first place and has never since doubted my ability or failed to cheer me up and on. Finally, there is my partner, Claire Sanders, who has supported me every step of the way. She tolerates battle paintings on our apartment walls, a 1796 pattern Heavy Cavalry Sword above the mantlepiece, ridiculous research trips, and a partner who spends far too long grappling with chapters in his office, only to emerge a hollow-eyed and exhausted wreck. I would be a worse scholar and a worse person without her.

Contents

List of Figures   xiii

Introduction: 'The Ever-Memorable Battle of Waterloo'   1

1. 'The most uncomfortable heap of glory that I ever had a hand in':
   Histories and Memoirs   13

2. 'The great English pilgrimage': Battlefield Tourism, Relics, and
   Ownership of the Field   44

3. 'Demonstrations of true British feeling and exultation': Annual
   Commemorations   74

4. 'The fullest instruction on a subject so illustrious': Exhibitions   117

5. 'Grand Military and National Spectacle': Waterloo on Stage
   and Canvas   148

6. 'To commemorate the English character': Monuments
   and Material Culture   175

Epilogue: 'The last great Englishman is low': The Funeral of the
Duke of Wellington   212

Appendix: Military plays and Hippodramas before and after Waterloo   237
Select Bibliography   243
Index   253

List of Figures

1.1 John Burnet, after David Wilkie, *Chelsea Pensioners reading the Gazette of the Battle of Waterloo*, 1831, Rijksmuseum, Amsterdam.   17

2.1 *Plan of Brussels and the country 25 miles to the south. Shewing the situation of the battles of the 16th & 18th of June 1815* (London: Thomas Kelly, 1816) courtesy State Library Victoria.   47

2.2 'The Wellington Tree—Sketched on the Field of Waterloo (1818), The Wellington Tree on the Field of Waterloo', *The Illustrated London News*, 27 November 1852, 469. General Research Division, The New York Public Library. New York Public Library Digital Collections.   59

2.3 Gilt metal oval glazed pendant containing a miniature relief carving of The Tree of Observation, laid down on mother of pearl, the reverse of the closed back inscribed 'Part of the Tree of Observation/Wellington/Waterloo/Halkett's/Gratitude/18th June 1815', London, The Armoury of St James's.   60

2.4 George Jones, *The Village of Waterloo, with travellers purchasing the relics that were found in the field of battle, 1815*, 1821, National Army Museum, London. © National Army Museum/Bridgeman Images.   65

2.5 Illustration from 'The Lion of Waterloo', *The Mirror of Literature, Amusement, and Instruction*, 25 November 1826, no. 224, p. 321. Photo Bodleian Libraries Douce MM 615 (v. 7–8), ill. from p. 32.   72

3.1 William Heath and Thomas McLean, *The Glorious 18th of June*, 1830. Anne S. K. Brown Military Collection, John Hay Library, Brown University, Providence.   91

3.2 *The Royal Gardens Vauxhall* (London: John Grieve, 1841). © The British Library Board Maps Crace Port. 16.66.   95

3.3 Waterloo Banquet Menu, 18 June 1839, 1st Duke of Wellington Misc 18, Stratfield Saye House archive. Translated by Lydia Rousseau, House Steward, Apsley House.   111

4.1 George Cruikshank, A scene at the London Museum Piccadilly, -or- A peep at the spoils of ambition, taken at the Battle of Waterloo—being a new tax on John Bull for 1816, 1816. London, The British Museum, 1859,0316.111 © The Trustees of the British Museum.   125

4.2 Thomas Rowlandson, *Exhibition at Bullock's Museum of Bonaparte's Carriage, Taken at Waterloo*, 1816. The Metropolitan Museum of Art, New York, Harris Brisbane Dick Fund, 1917.   126

4.3   James Scott, after Sir George Hayter, *The Duke of Wellington Visiting the Effigy and Personal Relics of Napoleon*, 1854. London, British Museum, 1872,0309.426 © The Trustees of the British Museum.   132

4.4   'Explanation of the Battle of Waterloo, painted on the largest scale, from drawings taken on the spot by Mr. Henry Aston Barker, (the figured composed and painted by Mr. John Burnet,) now exhibiting in the Panorama, Leicester Square, *Description of the Field of Battle*, 13.' Internet Archive, digitized from the Getty Research Institute.   137

5.1   Royal Amphitheatre Poster from 14 July 1828. Royal Amphitheatre (Astley's), 14 July 1828, The Marcus Stone Collection, London, Victoria & Albert Museum Theatre and Performance, THM/234/8/1, 376. Courtesy of Victoria and Albert Museum, London. Photo by author.   156

5.2   Frontispiece from Pollock's toy theatre version of *The Battle of Waterloo*. Anne S. K. Brown Military Collection, John Hay Library, Brown University, Providence.   159

5.3   *The Field of Waterloo*, exhibited 1818, Joseph Mallord William Turner. Accepted by the nation as part of the Turner Bequest 1856. Photo: Tate.   162

5.4   Thomas Lawrence, *Portrait of the Duke of Wellington, in the dress that he wore, and on the horse he rode at the Battle of Waterloo, 1818.* © Mark Fiennes Archive/Bridgeman Images.   165

5.5   Jan Willem Pieneman, *The Battle of Waterloo*, 1824. Rijksmuseum, Amsterdam.   169

5.6   William Salter, *The Waterloo Banquet, 1836*, 1840, Apsley House, London, © Stratfield Saye Preservation Trust.   171

6.1   After Benjamin Dean Wyatt, *Design for a pyramid commemorating the Napoleonic Wars*, 1815. Royal Collection Trust/© Her Majesty Queen Elizabeth II 2021.   180

6.2   Rudolph Ackermann, *His Royal Highness The Prince Regent's, the Duke of Wellington's, &c. &c. first Visit to Waterloo Bridge on the 18th June, 1817*, 1817. Anne S. K. Brown Military Collection, John Hay Library, Brown University, Providence.   186

6.3   The obverse and reverse dies for the Pistrucci Waterloo Medal. The Royal Mint Museum.   199

6.4   Wellington Door Knocker. Charles Graham Architectural Antiques and Fireplaces, Leicestershire.   202

6.5   Hone and Cruikshank's proposed design for a Peterloo Medal. William Hone and George Cruikshank, 'A Slap at Slop and the Bridge Street Gang', in *Facetiæ and Miscellanies* (London: William Hone, 1827), 36. Duke University Library via archive.org.   208

6.6   *Victory of Peterloo*, William Hone and George Cruikshank, 'A Slap at Slop and the Bridge Street Gang', in *Facetiæ and Miscellanies* (London: William Hone, 1827), 35. Duke University Library via archive.org.   209

7.1 *The Funeral Car of Field-Marshal Arthur, First Duke of Wellington, Album of illustrations of imperial & royal state carriages together with other carriages of deceased statesmen; and the funeral cars of Wellington and Nelson also the four original locomotive engines used on railways in England* (London: Worshipful Company of Coach Makers and Coach Harness Makers, 1899), figure 13. Science, Industry and Business Library: General Collection, The New York Public Library. New York Public Library Digital Collections.   215

7.2 The route of the Duke of Wellington's funeral procession, from Horse Guards Parade to St Paul's Cathedral. Detail from *Reynolds's Map of Modern London* (London: James Reynolds, 1857). The Lionel Pincus and Princess Firyal Map Division, The New York Public Library. Route added by Lawrence Gullo.   217

7.3 Thomas H. Ellis, *Funeral Car of the Late Field Marshal Duke of Wellington*, 1852. London, The British Museum, 1880,1113.2986 © The Trustees of the British Museum.   219

7.4 'Medal of the Late Duke of Wellington, by Pinches', *Illustrated London News*, 20 November 1852, p. 429. General Research Division, The New York Public Library. New York Public Library Digital Collections; The reverse of Medal 35, obverse of Medal 22, and the reverse of Medal 10, James Mudie, *An Historical and Critical Account of a Grand Series of National Medals* (London: Henry Colburn and Co., 1820), Beinecke Rare Book and Manuscript Library, Yale University.   226

Introduction

'The Ever-Memorable Battle of Waterloo'

'Between the Vaudeville and the Concert', reported *The Morning Chronicle* in 1828, 'the Battle of Waterloo was fought over again.'[1] This battle at Vauxhall Gardens was not a rehashing between veterans and armchair generals of the old standard question of whether Napoleon lost the battle by delaying, nor was it a violent debate on whether it was the Anglo-Dutch or Prussian forces who truly won it. Instead, it was an entertainment—an artistic re-enactment of the battle designed specifically for Vauxhall and performed by 'the greatest number of Cavalry and Infantry that ever appeared in any public spectacle'.[2] This grand event, which had prompted Vauxhall to permanently alter its layout when it debuted before packed crowds the previous year, had already become a staple. It was one of the many Waterloo performances, exhibitions, and re-enactments that routinely graced London, often loosely associated with the battle's anniversary on 18 June, but extending throughout the Season. Indeed, the particular performance reported in *The Morning Chronicle* did not take place on 18 June, but on 8 July, during a fete organized by the Duke of Wellington and a number of his circle to benefit Spanish and Italian refugees.[3]

This book explores how ubiquitous and multi-layered Waterloo became in British culture between 1815 and Wellington's death in 1852. It examines events such as Vauxhall's artistic re-enactment while also demonstrating how they became such an established part of the nation's cultural fabric that they were regularly performed and celebrated year-round. Prussia, the Netherlands, Hanover, and Belgium incorporated various commemorations of the battle into their annual calendars, and even France found ways to memorialize the men and the dream of the Hundred Days that they lost there. It was Great Britain, however, that took the commemoration further and actively incorporated the victory into their national identity. Several scholars have demonstrated the role of eighteenth-century warfare in general, and the Napoleonic Wars in particular, in the development of both the British state and the British nation. That development

---

[1] 'Grand Fete at Vauxhall Gardens', *Morning Chronicle*, 9 July 1828, p. 3.
[2] *Morning Post*, 8 July 1828, p. 1.
[3] *Morning Post*, 8 July 1828, p. 1. The *Fete* also received write-ups in London's other papers. 'Vauxhall Gardens', *Morning Post*, 10 July 1828, p. 3; *The Times*, 9 July 1828, p. 3.

Who Owned Waterloo? Battle, Memory, and Myth in British History, 1815–1852. Luke Reynolds, Oxford University Press.
© Luke Reynolds 2022. DOI: 10.1093/oso/9780192864994.003.0001

was neither an accident nor a foregone conclusion but instead a deliberately engineered policy.[4] Waterloo played a meaningful role in the cultural work that preserved that identity and with it, those efforts. The victory, in short, became a crucial part of modern Great Britain's creation myth. Waterloo was also presented as justification for Britain's imperial expansion and position as a global hegemon. It was the final campaign before nearly a century of British ascendancy, and was thus seen as one of the origins, in both definitions of the term, for what became known as the 'Pax Britannica'.[5] Britain had defeated Napoleon, freeing Europe, and had paid for that freedom with the lives of her own sons. Many claimed, therefore, that she had bought with blood the right to expand her empire and act as the world's policeman.[6]

The importance of Waterloo in the nineteenth-century British psyche guaranteed that the victory would be nationalized: as Britain grew in prominence and power, Waterloo was celebrated not just as a military victory by the British army, but as a British victory in the widest definition of the term. It would be commemorated by countless more civilians than soldiers; it would pervade every aspect of civilian culture, and, crucially, many of those celebrations would be curated by civilians, including artists, writers, poets, playwrights, and entrepreneurs. This nationalization took many forms, and various groups and identities within Britain participated in the commemoration of Waterloo in different ways. It is this variety of priorities, remembrances, and celebration that is at the heart of this book, and which prompts its primary question: who owned Waterloo?

To answer this, we must first define what we mean by ownership in this context. *Who Owned Waterloo?* defines ownership as control of the battle's narrative and commemoration, and through that, the curation of Waterloo and the men who fought there in the nation's collective memory. This is, deliberately, a domestic definition of ownership set entirely within the context of Great Britain. The traditional definition of Waterloo ownership—ownership of the valley of Waterloo itself and the international debate over whether the British, Prussian, Dutch, or other allied nations deserve the lion's share of the credit for the defeat of Napoleon—is of interest but is largely discussed through the lens of ownership in

---

[4] Linda Colley, *Britons: Forging the Nation 1707–1837* (New Haven: Yale University Press, 2009), especially 1–9, 196, 327; Holger Hoock, *Empires of the Imagination: Politics, War, and the Arts in the British World, 1750–1850* (London: Profile Books, 2010), especially 13, 361–7; Alan Forrest, *Waterloo* (Oxford: Oxford University Press, 2015); John Brewer, *The Sinews of Power: War, Money and the English State, 1688–1783* (Cambridge, Mass.: Harvard University Press, 1988).

[5] Andrew Porter, *The Oxford History of the British Empire, Volume III: The Nineteenth Century* (Oxford: Oxford University Press, 1999); John Darwin, *Unfinished Empire: The Global Expansion of Britain* (London: Allen Lane, 2012).

[6] Lord John Russell's speech on the evacuation of Spain by the French Army, House of Commons, 18 March 1824, T. C. Hansard, ed., *The Parliamentary Debates*, New Series (London: T. C. Hansard, 1824), X: 1233–4. See also Colley, *Britons*, 1–9; Hoock, *Empires of the Imagination*, 13, 361–7.

the British context.[7] The deliberately domestic definition of ownership employed in this book extends not just to Britain's European allies but to the British Empire. To fully explore the cultural memory of Waterloo in the imperial context would require a work of its own. Therefore, rather than try to make room for it in this one and do it a disservice, the empire has been excluded.

On the evening of 18 June 1815, the British military owned Waterloo. The defeated French had fled the field and were being pursued by the Prussian army, and the British and the allies under their direct control were left, literally, masters of the field. Within days, they began to cede some of that control. The first British visitors to the battlefield arrived on the morning of the 19th and were soon sharing their own experiences with friends in Brussels, Antwerp, and London.[8] The news of the victory arrived in London on the 21st, prompting spontaneous celebrations across the capital and generating, within a week, private fundraising campaigns and interpretations of the battle in the form of new formation dances with only one Waterloo veteran on hand to witness the nation's delight.[9] Within two months, while almost all of the British army was still on the continent, the first history/narrative of the battle was published in London, compiled by Charlotte Waldie, a Roxborough woman who happened to be visiting Brussels with her family when the battle occurred, and whose forty-four-page narrative forms the centrepiece of the work.[10]

Over the next four decades, British ownership of Waterloo was comprehensively nationalized. Within that nationalization, however, various groups established their own claims to certain aspects of the battle and its remembrance. Authors across all strata of British society worked together to ensure that Waterloo was seen as a British victory. Waterloo tourism and relic collecting became a central part of the travel experience of the middle class, as they forged their own version of the eighteenth-century aristocratic grand tour on the newly reopened continent. The annual celebrations that surrounded 18 June anchored the identities of the upper echelons of the army's officer corps, refined the art form of patriotic spectacle, and were embraced in Tory civilian circles as the anniversary of conservatism's triumph over radicalism. Exhibitions and art, in museums

---

[7] For a few examples of modern contributions to that debate, see Timothy Fitzpatrick, *The Long Shadow of Waterloo: Myths, Memories, and Debates* (Philadelphia: Casemate, 2019); Paul L. Dawson, *Waterloo: The Truth at Last, Why Napoleon Lost the Great Battle* (Barnsley: Frontline Books, 2018); Gareth Glover, *Waterloo: Myth and Reality* (Barnsley: Pen & Sword Books, 2014).

[8] Alexander Cavalie Mercer, *Journal of the Waterloo Campaign, Kept Throughout the Campaign of 1815* (Edinburgh & London: William Blackwood and Sons, 1870), I: 345–6.

[9] 'Patriotic Meeting', *Morning Post*, 29 June 1815; 'Waterloo Subscription', *Morning Chronicle*, 30 June 1815; 'For This Week Only. Sadler's Wells', *Morning Chronicle*, 27 June 1815.

[10] *The Battle of Waterloo, Containing the Series of Accounts Published by Authority, British and Foreign, with Circumstantial Details, previous, during, and after the Battle, from a Variety of Authentic and Original Sources, with Relative Official Documents, Forming an Historical Record of the Operations in the Campaign of the Netherlands, 1815. By a Near Observer*, 7th edn (London: J. Booth and T. Egerton, 1815); Gareth Glover, *Waterloo in 100 Objects* (Stroud: The History Press, 2015), 184–5.

and rotundas and on stage and canvas, brought Waterloo to Britain and democ-
ratized the victory, even as they introduced new tensions and cooperation between
veterans and civilian creators and curators. Physical commemorations, whether in
the form of civic structures, the names of streets, towns, and enterprises, or more
individual forms of material culture furthered that democratization, while simultaneously making Waterloo so commonplace that it was stripped of some or all of
its meaning.

Even as the curation of Waterloo's cultural memory was absorbed more and
more into civilian culture, the military found or was thrust into new public roles,
with varying levels of cultural power. Members of the officer corps proved adept at
employing memoirs, artistic patronage, and in leveraging their very presence at
events to shape public perceptions of themselves and the battle, often positioning
themselves as the arbiters of legitimacy. The place of enlisted veterans, however,
was more complex. While some succeeded in retaining their agency through
memoirs or employment as tour guides, others found themselves reduced from
individuals to merely part of the spectacle, hired to add anonymous verisimilitude
to re-enactments, exhibitions, and hippodramas. Many more simply attended.
Most probably did so anonymously, but some, encouraged by offers of free
admission for veterans, donned their uniforms and/or their Waterloo Medal,
unaware or simply not caring that this too made them part of the spectacle.[11]

For every veteran, officer or enlisted, that was documented participating in a
form of commemoration, celebration, or ownership discussed here, many more
simply disappeared into history. Of these, some would have participated privately
or anonymously, but it is likely that others simply did not care. Indeed, there are
areas where it is surprising how insignificant Waterloo ownership proved to be for
the men who actually fought there. While veterans employed eyewitness perspectives and the active voice to emphasize their presence at Waterloo in their
memoirs, the battle typically only represented a small portion of the military
service they sought to record.

Other veterans, along with radical and pacifist civilian groups, saw nothing to
celebrate. In addition to having been a brutal and bloody battle, Waterloo also
functioned as a rallying point and a touchstone for radicals. Here it served the
opposite purpose that it did for conservatives, providing a stark reminder of how
much reform was still necessary, and acting as a rhetorical tool for a variety of
progressive causes. Radicals such as Lord Byron wove allusions to Waterloo into
their criticisms of Britain's army and class systems, while artists such as Joseph
Mallord William Turner eschewed depictions of glory in favour of highlighting

---

[11] Philip Shaw insists that veterans were not aware that their attendance was transactional in this
way. It is more than likely that many of them were fully aware of it and either revelled in the attention
or considered it a price worth paying for free admission to, in Shaw's example, a Waterloo panorama.
Philip Shaw, *Waterloo and the Romantic Imagination* (Basingstoke: Palgrave Macmillan, 2002), 84.

the cost of war. Perhaps the best example of radical ownership of Waterloo came with the St Peter's Field Massacre in 1819. While the participation of Waterloo veterans on both sides is well documented, satirists weaponized a remarkable variety of Waterloo commemorations in the massacre's immediate aftermath, christening it Peterloo and designing monuments and medals to 'celebrate' the government's triumph over radical reform.

While Tories and radicals were the most overt, they were by no means the only groups that co-opted Waterloo to their own ends. Across Great Britain and Ireland, Waterloo celebrations took on profoundly local meanings. Rival towns and cities watched each other's celebrations and measured their own against them, competing in their performative patriotism. Wales, Ireland, and especially Scotland seized on Waterloo commemorations as an opportunity to emphasize their contribution to the Union (and thus their power and voices within it) even as they simultaneously celebrated their own individual achievements within the national victory. Scotland's efforts, which included annual commemorations, panoramas, and memoirs by Scottish soldiers, proved so effective that Lieutenant Colonel Jonathan Leach lamented in his 1831 memoir the popular belief that 'the Scottish regiments ... unaided, defeated the reiterated attacks of the Imperial Legions'.[12]

Waterloo remains one of the most written-about battles in history. In the two centuries since the battle, countless books have appeared arguing every possible conclusion.[13] Re-enactors, grognards, enthusiasts, and historians continue to debate and reinterpret every aspect in books, articles, documentaries, and lectures, at conventions and conferences, in re-enactment bivouacs, and across social media. *Who Owned Waterloo?* is not, however, a book about the Battle of Waterloo. It is a book about Waterloo's collective memory in Great Britain and about the efforts by various groups, between 1815 and 1852, to marry actual memory to that collective memory and thus forge the accepted and acceptable history of Waterloo. While many did so out of pride or personal gain, the legacy of their efforts went beyond personal aggrandizement: because of Waterloo's place in the national identity and creation myth of nineteenth-century Great Britain, the accepted collective memory and history of the battle would, in turn, shape that identity itself. This battle over the memory and history of Waterloo was largely fought within Britain's popular and consumer culture, with everything from memoirs, monuments, rituals, and relics to hippodramas, panoramas, and even

---

[12] Jonathan Leach, *Rough Sketches of the Life of an Old Soldier: During a Service in the West Indies; at the Siege of Copenhagen in 1807; in the Peninsula and the South of France in the Campaigns from 1808 to 1814, with the Light Division; in the Netherlands in 1815; including the Battles of Quatre Bras and Waterloo: With a Slight Sketch of the Three Years Passed by the Army of Occupation in France, &c. &c. &c.* (London: Longman, Rees, Orme, Brown, and Green, 1831), 399.

[13] For an excellent summation up to 2014, see Bruno Colson, 'Waterloo: Two Centuries of Historiography', *International Bibliography of Military History* 34 (2014): 149–70.

shades of blue weaponized in the cause. Fully exploring these efforts places *Who Owned Waterloo?* at the confluence of memory studies and cultural history. This is not new ground. Instead, this book takes established practices in both fields and applies them to a wider study of Waterloo's legacy in Britain than has been attempted before.

Who Owned Waterloo? draws on the memory studies scholarship that explores how the first-hand knowledge that they term 'communicative memory' is transformed by a variety of individual, group, and national efforts into 'collective' or 'cultural memory', a much more enduring but, crucially, curated form of remembrance.[14] Cultural memory provides a level of identity and belonging and is what drove Alfred Bate Richards, a British journalist and barrister, to declare in 1851 that '*we* won Waterloo', despite the fact that he had never served in uniform and had been born in 1820, five years after the battle.[15] While some have challenged the idea of collective or cultural memory (or argued for renaming and re-evaluating it), the idea has been embraced by a growing number of scholars who apply it to the Napoleonic Wars.[16] This book seeks to build on, rather than challenge, these Napoleonic-focused works, but there is an intervention worth noting. Many of them are explicitly transnational in view, seeking to examine the Napoleonic Wars as a shared memory across borders.[17] By contrast, this book is explicitly national in scope and focus, bypassing even the international debates that occurred within Great Britain to concentrate instead on the curation of Waterloo's domestic cultural memory.

In this, *Who Owned Waterloo?* skews towards cultural history, where scholars have demonstrated how the Napoleonic Wars and other displays of state power,

[14] Aleida Assmann, *Cultural Memory and Western Civilization: Arts of Memory* (Cambridge: Cambridge University Press, 2013); Aleida Assmann, 'Transformations between History and Memory', *Social Research* 75, no. 1 (Spring 2008): 49–72; Jan Assmann, 'Communicative and Cultural Memory', in Astrid Erll and Ansgar Nünning, eds, *Cultural Memory Studies: An International and Interdisciplinary Handbook* (New York: De Gruyter, 2008), 109–118. See also Pierre Nora, *Realms of Memory: The Construction of the French Past*, ed. Lawrence D. Kritzman, trans. Arthur Goldhammer (New York: Columbia University Press, 1996–8); Stuart Semmel, 'Reading the Tangible Past: British Tourism, Collecting, and Memory after Waterloo', *Representations* 69 (Winter 2000): 9–37; Jolien Gitbels, 'Tangible Memories: Waterloo Relics in the Nineteenth Century', *The Rijksmuseum Bulletin* 63, no. 3 (2015): 228–57.

[15] Emphasis added. Alfred Bate Richards, *Essays and Opinions* (London: Aylot and Jones, 1851), II: 118; Assmann, 'Transformations between History and Memory', 52, 55–6.

[16] Jay Winter, for example, argues for the use of the term 'historical remembrance' as a way to remove some of the abstract nature of the various definitions of memory, while Alon Confino simultaneously argued for a more rigorous theoretical differentiation between the political, social, and cultural and a wider use of memory itself as an explanatory device. Jay Winter, *Remembering War: The Great War Between Memory and History in the Twentieth Century* (New Haven: Yale University Press, 2006); Alon Confino, 'Collective Memory and Cultural History: Problems of Method', *American Historical Review* 102, no. 5 (December 1997): 1386–403.

[17] Jasper Heinzen, 'Transnational Affinities and Invented Traditions: The Napoleonic Wars in British and Hanoverian Memory, 1815–1915', *The English Historical Review* 127, no. 529 (December 2012): 1404–34; Alan Forrest, Étienne François, and Karen Hagemann, eds, *War Memories: The Revolutionary and Napoleonic Wars in Modern European Culture* (Basingstoke: Palgrave Macmillan, 2012).

Protestant faith, and popular culture were used to forge Britain into a single modern nation with a definable national identity.[18] This book takes Waterloo, which is usually only briefly mentioned in this context, and demonstrates how its memory and commemoration were deliberately designed to reinforce that national identity. It is not alone, of course, in adopting Waterloo as a starting point; several books have looked at Waterloo's legacy (many inspired by the bicentenary in 2015). None, however, has sought to fully address the cultural legacy and question of ownership in the British context.[19] It is also worth noting that many of the cultural histories that address this period in Britain tend to emphasize the radical sides.[20] By reincorporating the conservative nature of a large amount of the culture surrounding military victories this book seeks to readdress that balance.

Waterloo's commemoration, as we will see, did not spring from the Napoleonic Wars fully formed, but evolved over time. As Waterloo's cultural memory became accepted and standardized, its various aspects took on trappings of spectacle in one form or another. This aligns with scholarship of the nineteenth century that has shown that spectacle was used to define a number of portions of its consumers' lives, from their identities as Britons to their homes and entertainments.[21] *Who Owned Waterloo?* demonstrates, however, that forms and uses of spectacle that are traditionally associated with the second half of the nineteenth century (tradition-ally after the 1851 Great Exhibition) emerged earlier. This is particularly true of spectacle employed to further the Victorian fascination with modernity.[22] This is, on the surface, odd. How can the commemoration of a battle that was quickly receding into the past be forward-facing? Recent scholarship, however, has dem-onstrated that the Victorian British ably and enthusiastically used history to define

---

[18] Colley, *Britons*; Hoock, *Empires of the Imagination*.

[19] Forrest, *Waterloo*; Fitzpatrick, *The Long Shadow of Waterloo*; Malcolm Balen, *A Model Victory: Waterloo and the Battle for History* (London: Harper Perennial, 2006); R. E. Foster, *Wellington and Waterloo: The Duke, the Battle and Posterity 1815–2015* (Staplehurst: Spellmount, 2014). Elisa Milkes, 'A Battle's Legacy: Waterloo in Nineteenth Century Britain', Ph.D. dissertation, Yale University, 2002 comes the closest. Indeed, it can be read as a social history version of what this book does in the cultural sphere, examining veterans and widows, the Waterloo Subscription Fund, the Regiments, and local communities.

[20] Marcus Wood, *Radical Satire and Print Culture, 1790–1822* (Oxford: Clarendon Press, 1994); John Gardener, *Poetry and Popular Protest: Peterloo, Cato Street and the Queen Caroline Controversy* (Basingstoke: Palgrave Macmillan, 2011).

[21] Thomas Richards, *The Commodity Culture of Victorian England: Advertising and Spectacle, 1851–1914* (Stanford, CA: Stanford University Press, 1990); Karen Chase and Michael Levenson, *The Spectacle of Intimacy: A Public Life for the Victorian Family* (Princeton: Princeton University Press, 2000); Michael Booth, *Victorian Spectacular Theatre 1850–1910* (Boston: Routledge & Kegan Paul, 1981); Sharon Marcus, 'Victorian Theatrics: Response', *Victorian Studies* 54, no. 3 (Spring 2012): 438–50.

[22] Paul Keen, *Literature, Commerce, and the Spectacle of Modernity, 1750–1800* (Cambridge: Cambridge University Press, 2012).

both their own identities and their own modernity.[23] Waterloo is a perfect example of this: used not only to establish and define national identity, but also to justify and anchor Britain's imperial century.

Where this book diverts from the scholarship on spectacle, however, is with military spectacle. The scholarship of nineteenth-century military spectacle argues that the development of reviews and other military spectacles demonstrates the gradual separation of the military and civilian cultures into performer and spectator and the simultaneous development of the civilian expectation to be entertained.[24] There are several ways, however, that Waterloo complicates this. While the accepted argument that public parades and reviews served as a psychological deterrent against unrest is useful, especially in the context of Ireland and domestic clashes such as St Peter's Fields/Peterloo, it overlooks that the poor behaviour of the soldiers themselves was at least partially to blame for the shift towards spectacle. Simultaneously, we must question whether the participation of Waterloo veterans in these cultural productions had the same effect that the reviews and parades were supposed to have had, or, instead, achieved the opposite result by normalizing and humanizing the military aspects of the spectacle.

The separation of military and civilian cultures is also a central tenet of those works that present the Revolutionary and Napoleonic Wars as the origin point of the modern militarization of society.[25] These works argue that the separation of those cultures was a prerequisite of their location in a hierarchy that sought to imprint military virtues onto civilian life. While there were absolutely divisions between military and civilian life and culture, the borders were permeable and a great deal of the argued influence, in fact, went the other way. David Bell makes a compelling case for the militarization of French society under Napoleon, but his suggestion that it led directly to 'the military's claim of moral superiority' throughout Europe in the nineteenth century does not hold up in the case of post-Waterloo Britain.[26] The outrage directed at the army following the 1821 Waterloo anniversary riot by members of the Foot Guards outside the Marquis of Granby Public House in Westminster discussed in Chapter 3, for example, demonstrates how commemoration of Waterloo complicates such sweeping

[23] Dory Agazarian, 'Buying Time: Consuming Urban Pasts in Nineteenth-Century Britain', Ph.D. dissertation, The Graduate Center, City University of New York, 2019; Raphael Samuel, *Theatres of Memory: Past and Present in Contemporary Culture* (London: Verso, 2012); Lyndsey Rago Claro, 'Pieces of History: The Past and Popular Culture in Victorian Britain, 1837–1882', Ph.D. dissertation, University of Delaware, 2011; Billie Melman, *The Culture of History: English Uses of the Past, 1800–1953* (Oxford: Oxford University Press, 2006).

[24] Scott Hughes Myerly, *British Military Spectacle: From the Napoleonic Wars through the Crimea* (Cambridge, Mass.: Harvard University Press, 1996).

[25] David Bell, *The First Total War: Napoleon's Europe and the Birth of Warfare as we know it* (New York: Mariner, 2007). Myerly is also concerned with militarization, especially as a model for civilian institutions.

[26] Bell, *First Total War*, 243–5, 311–12.

claims.[27] Indeed, instead of the traditional militarization of British culture and society, Waterloo celebration illustrates the opposite: the ceding of British military victories to national ownership.

Who Owned Waterloo? comprises six chapters and an epilogue. While the chapters are thematic in nature, each dealing with a different vector of the expression of ownership of Waterloo, they are organized via a loose chronology. The first two chapters, which explore, respectively, memoirs and histories and battlefield tourism, both begin with the near-immediate aftermath of the battle itself. Simultaneously, the final two chapters, which examine theatrical productions, art, monuments, and various aspects of visual and material culture, are concerned with representations of the battle that are largely still with us. There is, of course, overlap. None of the works, productions, parties, or exhibitions discussed in this book operated in a vacuum, and many interacted in unexpected ways. One of the exhibitions that sought to capitalize on the success of Alex Palmer's Waterloo Museum discussed in Chapter 4, for example, advertised itself in the footnotes of a historical account of Waterloo of the type examined in Chapter 1.[28] In the days before the opening of Waterloo Bridge on 18 June 1817 (Chapter 6), the national press breathlessly reported that Wellington's favourite charger, Copenhagen, had been shipped to London before his master in preparation for the opening ceremony.[29] In fact, Waterloo Bridge's aquatic opening procession had no place for Wellington's horse. Copenhagen had been shipped home so that Sir Thomas Lawrence could see the horse put through his paces at Astley's Royal Amphitheatre before painting him for the 1818 *Portrait of the Duke of Wellington, in the dress that he wore, and on the horse he rode at the Battle of Waterloo* (Chapter 5). Lawrence's equestrian portrait debuted at the same Royal Academy exhibition where Turner displayed his *The Field of Waterloo* (Chapter 5) accompanied a quote from Byron's *Childe Harold's Pilgrimage* (Chapter 2). Finally, in 1849, a group of Nottingham residents closely connected with the Nottingham Wellington Club mentioned in Chapter 3 decided to celebrate the battle's anniversary with a dinner on the battlefield itself, actively participating in the battlefield tourism and performative patriotism discussed in Chapter 2.[30]

This overlap and interaction have forced certain arbitrary decisions. Vauxhall's Waterloo fete, for example, forms one of the centrepieces of Chapter 3. Its great rival, Astley's hippodrama *The Battle of Waterloo* serves the same function in

---

[27] The depiction of officers as handsome but societally dangerous roués in popular novels up to the 1840s demonstrates that a perceived lack of moral superiority was not limited to the immediate post-Waterloo years. See Benjamin Disraeli, *Henriette Temple: A Love Story* (London: Henry Colburn, 1837), I: 112, 120; Lady Charlotte Campbell Bury, *The History of a Flirt, Related by Herself* (London: Henry Colburn, 1840), II: 144.

[28] William A. Scott, *Battle of Waterloo; or, Correct Narrative on that Late Sanguinary Conflict on the Plains of Waterloo* (London: E. Cox and Son, 1815), 172n.–173n.

[29] *Morning Post*, 14 June 1817.

[30] 'Waterloo Day', *Nottinghamshire Guardian*, 21 June 1849, p. 3.

Chapter 5. Readers may wonder, given the rivalry, why they are not in the same chapter. This is because Astley's *Battle of Waterloo* began and ended life as a theatrical production, capable of being performed at any time of year, and only became an annual tradition because of its success. Vauxhall's Waterloo fete, in contrast, was, from the beginning, designed as a form of annual commemoration to celebrate the battle's anniversary, and only took on traditionally theatrical and re-enactment elements to rival Astley's as it evolved.

Chapter 1 examines non-fiction print media such as histories and memoirs. In these works the question of ownership is addressed largely on an international level, with authors of both histories and memoirs striving to emphasize the British, rather than allied, nature of the victory. Beyond that, however, an interesting dichotomy developed, with civilian authors dominating the histories with bird's-eye-view accounts of the battle and campaign, and veterans choosing instead to pen memoirs that eschewed overarching descriptions in favour of personal narratives that, by the very nature of their limited eyewitness scope, emphasized their presence on the battlefield and personal contribution to the victory. The memoirs discussed also demonstrate that, while the decisiveness of Waterloo appealed to many, for these officers Waterloo was just one incident in a much longer and more significant period of war and service.

The battlefield tourism and relic collecting covered in Chapter 2 were crucial to the British rediscovery of the continent following 1815. Although the field saw visitors from every social level that had disposable income, it was of particular significance to Britain's newly modernizing middle class, for whom a trip to the Kingdom of the Netherlands/Belgium and Waterloo was the equivalent of the eighteenth-century's aristocratic grand tour. Battlefield tourism was also inevitably shaped by questions of international ownership. Waterloo saw a continued four-way international skirmish over its ownership between Britain, Prussia, the Kingdom of the Netherlands/Belgium, and France. Thus, Waterloo became a site of British national pilgrimage, which was shaped by poetry, guidebooks, and tourists who were aware that it was just as important to be seen to visit Waterloo as it was to actually visit.

The annual commemorations and various other forms of remembrance that comprise Chapter 3 provide the best example of general and local nationalization of the battle. What started as a shared day of national triumph, where officers and men were feted by civilian society, slowly evolved into a standardized series of fetes, parades, and dinners where military and civilian worlds were deliberately separated. Towns seized the day as another opportunity to outshine their neighbours, while a variety of civilian clubs and venues across the country started hosting their own celebrations, often without the involvement of a single individual who had fought at Waterloo. Nor did the civilian co-option end there. Strictly military events, such as grand reviews and Wellington's Waterloo banquet were claimed as national celebrations and public entertainments by both the press and Britain's crowds. By the time of Wellington's funeral in 1852, 18 June was used as a general day of festivity, often hosting fairs, meetings, and celebrations that had no connection to Waterloo.

Chapter 4 continues the nationalization of commemoration and memory discussed in Chapter 3, but switches focus from the annual commemorations that surrounded 18 June to various public exhibitions. These included several Waterloo museums or exhibits, multiple panoramas, and William Siborne's extensively researched model of the battle. The museums, most famously Bullock's London Museum at the Egyptian Hall in Piccadilly and Madame Tussaud and Sons, drew crowds with artefacts ranging from discarded weapons and pieces of uniforms to Napoleon's coach, which was captured in the French retreat from Waterloo and was put on display in London and throughout Britain. Panoramas across the country offered views of Waterloo in place of relics and found the battle so popular that it was featured into the 1840s. The very success of these exhibitions, however, shines light on the relationship between civilian curation and military legitimacy, as it was the presence of Waterloo veterans that bestowed the appearance of accuracy crucial to popular appeal.

Chapter 5 examines representations of Waterloo in the arts, where the informal approval of veterans at the centre of Chapter 4 took on the more traditional trappings of patronage. Artists such as Sir Thomas Lawrence, Jan Willem Pieneman, and William Salter benefited significantly from the access granted by Wellington and his fellow veterans, while those veterans effectively employed their patronage to shape their depictions and the memory of the battle captured in the resulting paintings. On the stage, Astley's Royal Amphitheatre's phenomenally popular hippodrama *The Battle of Waterloo* took the same approach as the exhibitions discussed previously, burnishing its credentials with reports of attendance by, and thus the approval of, Wellington and other senior military figures.

Chapter 6 completes the shift towards materiality, discussing a variety of physical commemorations including Waterloo Bridge, various forms of commemorative naming, official and unofficial medals, household items, clothing, vegetables, and even snuff. By casting a wider net than surveys of military monuments traditionally engage with, this chapter demonstrates that permanent and semipermanent commemoration in the form of namings and material culture was not only one of the most widespread forms of commemoration but also a virtually uncontested form of nationalization, as Waterloo went from a battle to a bridge, multiple streets, hotels, and businesses. Finally, to demonstrate the ubiquity of Waterloo commemoration in the national conversation, it briefly explores the efforts by satirists to 'commemorate' Peterloo using identical methods, thus further enforcing the link between Waterloo and the St Peter's Field Massacre.

Who Owned Waterloo? concludes with an Epilogue centred around the funeral of the Duke of Wellington in 1852. In the national outpouring of grief that marked Wellington's death, his funeral, and the two months in between, we see a public demonstration of the shared ownership and nationalization of Waterloo and the culmination of the themes examined in this book. Wellington's funeral was a national spectacle in every sense, and it highlights just how firmly entrenched Waterloo was in Britain's national—and civic—identity. The epilogue concludes with a coda discussing the bicentennial in 2015. Between the funeral and the bicentennial, it becomes clear how complicated cultural ownership of Waterloo became and how that cultural legacy is just as significant as its military or political legacy.

1

'The most uncomfortable heap of glory that I ever had a hand in'

Histories and Memoirs

On 30 June 1815, twelve days after the Battle of Waterloo, an advertisement appeared in *The Morning Post*. It announced that the next issue of *Bell's Weekly Messenger* would contain a plan of the battle 'on a large scale'. This plan, the advertisement announced, would 'shew the positions of the Prussians, the English, and the French Forces, and correctly illustrate the Gazette and official accounts'. Not content with merely supplying a visual aid, *Bell's Weekly Messenger* promised it would 'be accompanied with original details, explanatory of the means by which this great victory was obtained'.[1] The speed with which this plan was produced demonstrates how eager the British public was to learn all they could about the battle, as Waterloo mania swept the country. Sensing an opportunity, Britain's authors and publishers leapt to sate the new demand. This chapter examines two periods of significant Waterloo publications: the civilian-authored 'historical accounts' of the battle produced in the months and years immediately following 18 June 1815, and the emergence in the 1830s of a number of memoirs by men of all ranks who had been at Waterloo.

Wrapped up within these publication booms are two aspects of the question of ownership. In the immediate aftermath of Waterloo, civilian historians and the soldiers who had fought there worked together to ensure British ownership of the battle. To this end, both the histories and the original letters and reports they quote are, to one extent or another, dismissive of the Prussian army and both the Dutch and Belgian soldiers under Wellington's command. With the contributions of the other participants dismissed, the role of the British forces is both implicitly and explicitly increased, further justifying British claims of ownership of the victory. By the time of the second publishing phase—the memoir boom of the 1830s and 1840s—the questions of ownership had changed. British ownership of the battle had been sufficiently established to not be in question within the British Isles, but over the preceding fifteen years, those who had fought at Waterloo had seen a diffusion of credit for the victory, diminishing their particular claim on it in

---

[1] *Morning Post*, 30 June 1815, p. 1.

Who Owned Waterloo? Battle, Memory, and Myth in British History, 1815–1852. Luke Reynolds, Oxford University Press.
© Luke Reynolds 2022. DOI: 10.1093/oso/9780192864994.003.0002

favour of a wider ownership not limited to the military sphere. The memoirs that were published in the 1830s can be read, therefore, as an attempt to push back against that diffusion and reinforce the writers' privileged position as the arbiters of Waterloo's cultural memory. They continue the trend of diminishing the efforts of the other allies, while also employing an eyewitness narrative style and the active voice to emphasize the writers' presence on the battlefield and using their lack of a bird's-eye-view historical narrative to prove their bona fides.[2]

Napoleonic Wars memoirs occupy an intriguing place in the history of military memoirs. Located between the re-emergence of the genre in the seventeenth century and its evolution into the popular 'boy's own' adventure stories in the Victorian period, they were heavily influenced by the Romantic tradition. The memoirs of the seventeenth century, inspired by classical texts such as Julius Caesar's *Commentaries on the Gallic War*, tended to be closer in style to histories than memoirs—they were top-down accounts of entire campaigns, with very little personal detail. As the nature of international conflict evolved throughout the seventeenth and eighteenth centuries, however, so too did the style of military memoir. The top-down work focusing on the grand movements of armies across campaigns became the purview of histories, while more memoirs began to appear from lower ranks, often more focused on eyewitness accounts or the minutiae of day-to-day military life.[3] Several memoirs that could be identified as such were printed during the American War of Independence and Revolutionary and Napoleonic Wars, most notably Samuel Ancell's *Circumstantial Journal of the Long and Tedious Blockade and Siege of Gibraltar* (1784) and Robert Ker Porter's *Letters from Portugal and Spain* (1809).[4] The transformation accelerated in line with wider literary trends in the nineteenth century, and scholars have argued that, thanks to its easy and readable style, Captain John Kincaid's *Adventures in the Rifle Brigade in the Peninsula, France, and the Netherlands from 1809–1815* (1830) marks the beginning of the transition from sentimental memoirs in the

---

[2] Their use of the active voice as an explicit claim to action, ownership, and presence presents an intriguing contrast to First World War memoirs, where, as Paul Fussell has argued, veterans of the Western Front used the passive voice to distance themselves from both their actions and the overarching horror of war. Paul Fussell, *The Great War and Modern Memory* (Oxford: Oxford University Press, 1975), 177–8.

[3] For the history of military memoirs, see Alex Vernon, ed., *Arms and the Self: War, the Military, and Autobiographical Writing* (Kent: Kent State University Press, 2005); Neil Ramsey, *The Military Memoir and Romantic Literary Culture, 1780–1835* (Farnham: Ashgate, 2011); Matilda Greig, *Dead Men Telling Tales: Napoleonic War Veterans and the Military Memoir Industry, 1808–1914* (Oxford: Oxford University Press, 2021).

[4] Samuel Ancell, *A Circumstantial Journal of the Long and Tedious Blockade and Siege of Gibraltar: from the 12th of September, 1779 (the Day the Garrison Opened Their Batteries against the Spaniards) to the 23rd Day of February, 1783: Containing an Authentic Account of the Most Remarkable Transactions, in Which the Enemy's Motions, Works, Approaches, Firings, &c. Are Particularly Described* (Liverpool: Charles Wosencroft, 1784); Robert Ker Porter, *Letters from Portugal and Spain, Written during the March of British Troops Under Sir John Moore with a map of the Route, and Appropriate Engravings* (London: Longman, Hurst, Rees, and Orme, 1809).

Romantic Literary tradition to that 'boy's own' adventure genre that came to dominate popular Victorian and Edwardian military writing.[5]

The histories and memoirs discussed here will be familiar to some readers. Like many of the works produced in this period and covering the Napoleonic Wars, they have been used extensively as primary sources. Scholars have studied them to gain insight into battles and daily campaign life, and one will find them listed in the bibliography of almost every history of the Peninsular War. For all of this attention, however, there has been relatively little scholarship that considers these works as cultural artefacts rather than sources. What work has been done has focused exclusively on memoirs and has argued that it was the post-Napoleonic military memoir, influenced by literary romanticism, that developed the sentimental and personal style that would become one of the genre's hallmarks.[6] Crucial to this is the abandonment of the military memoir trope of the accidental author—the bluff old soldier who has picked up his pen without thinking. Instead, these authors, including those discussed within this chapter, not only had clearly defined goals in the writing and the distribution of their work, but also deliberately used the limitations of their eyewitness perspective to reinforce their authority. They were purposeful in deploying their own memories for rhetorical power. In short, they knew precisely what they were doing.[7]

Given the Europe-wide fascination with the Battle of Waterloo, it should come as no surprise that non-memoir narratives of the Battle of Waterloo, largely written by civilians, began appearing almost immediately after the dust settled. These works, usually described by their authors as 'historical accounts', attempted to narrate the battle in a way that would be accessible to civilian readers. For sources, they relied on official publications, correspondence, and informal interviews with soldiers who had been present on the field. These accounts proved extremely popular, and a notable number of them were produced. The two considered here, Charlotte Waldie's *The Battle of Waterloo* published under the pseudonym 'a near observer' in 1815, and William Mudford's 1817 *An Historical Account of the Campaign in the Netherlands in 1815*, can be regarded as representative of the genre.[8]

The first account of the battle to reach British shores was the Duke of Wellington's official dispatch, penned on 19 June from a room in the inn in the

---

[5] Ramsey, *The Military Memoir and Romantic Literary Culture*, chapter 6.

[6] They did this by privileging individual experience, allowing the reader to share the author's sentiments and feel sympathy for them. Ramsey, *The Military Memoir and Romantic Literary Culture*. For a more detailed examination of both the use and analysis of the military memoirs from this period, see Greig, *Dead Men Telling Tales*, 4–11.

[7] Greig, *Dead Men Telling Tales*; Matilda Greig, 'Accidental Authors? Soldiers' Tales of the Peninsular War and the Secrets of the Publishing Process', *History Workshop Journal* 86 (Autumn 2018): 224–44.

[8] For the establishing of Charlotte Waldie's identity, see Gareth Glover, *Waterloo in 100 Objects* (Stroud: The History Press, 2015), 184–5. For other examples, see W. A. Scott, *Battle of Waterloo; or, Correct Narrative of the Late Sanguinary Conflict on the Plains of Waterloo: Exhibiting a Minute Detail*

village of Waterloo (and the reason the battle is known as Waterloo across the English-speaking world).[9] It is a remarkably short document, comprising only four pages when printed as an extraordinary edition of *The London Gazette*.[10] Wellington covers a lot of ground in those four pages. He starts his narrative with Napoleon's invasion on the 15th and closes it in the early hours of the 19th. The description of the battle itself is limited to five paragraphs, with an additional half a page dedicated to naming those officers and regiments that particularly distinguished themselves in the eyes of their general. Wellington centres his narrative on the repeated French infantry attacks on the Chateau of Hougoumont and La Haye Sainte, and the French cavalry attacks on the allied infantry squares, but does not go into much detail, simply stating 'these attacks were repeated till about seven in the evening'. For all its brevity, the Waterloo dispatch is not stinting in its praise. Several British regiments and divisions are named, and Wellington is also complimentary of some of the allies under his command. He notes that the troops of 'the Brunswick corps ... conducted themselves with the utmost gallantry', and makes sure to also mention the Hanoverians. Towards the end of the dispatch, when he is singling out commanders, he also pays tribute to 'General Kruse, of the Nassau service, [who] likewise conducted himself much to my satisfaction, as did ... General Vanhope, commanding a brigade of infantry of the King of the Netherlands'. Wellington also heaps praise on the Prussians, who 'maintained their position with their usual gallantry and perseverance'. Wellington's later reluctance to share credit for his victory with the Prussians has been well documented. In the Waterloo dispatch, however, perhaps because the diplomat in him knew it would be read all over Europe or perhaps because he was still shaken from the previous day, Wellington is more generous. 'I should not do justice to my feelings or to Marshal Blücher and the Prussian army,' he writes in the conclusion of the dispatch, 'if I did not attribute the successful result of this arduous day, to the cordial and timely assistance I received from them.'[11]

Wellington's Waterloo dispatch functioned as the bedrock for the histories published immediately after the battle. Like all copies of the *Gazette* it was publicly available, although because of its short length and extraordinary nature, it cost just

---

of all the Military Operations of the Heroes who Signalized themselves on that Memorable Occasion, opposed to Napoleon Buonaparte, in person: with an authentic memoir of that most extraordinary person; from the beginning, to the end, of his political career (London: E. Cox and Son, 1815); Nelson Bain, *A Detailed Account of the Battles of Quatre Bras, Ligny, and Waterloo: Preceded by a short relation of events, attending the temporary revolution of 1815, in France: and concluding with the immediate political consequences of these decisive victories* (Edinburgh: John Thompson and Co., 1816).

[9] Brian Cathcart, *The News from Waterloo: The Race to Tell Britain of Wellington's Victory* (London: Faber & Faber, 2015); R. E. Foster, *Wellington and Waterloo: The Duke, the Battle, and Posterity 1815–2015* (Stroud: Spellmount, 2014), 78–9.

[10] One page of which is entirely composed of a list of killed and wounded officers. *The London Gazette Extraordinary*, 22 June 1815, number 17028.

[11] *The London Gazette Extraordinary*, 22 June 1815, number 17028, pp. 1213–15.

Figure 1.1 John Burnet, after David Wilkie, *Chelsea Pensioners reading the Gazette of the Battle of Waterloo*, 1831, Rijksmuseum, Amsterdam.

sixpence, as opposed to the standard price of between two and three shillings.[12] It was reprinted extensively and was included in full in both 1815's *The Battle of Waterloo* and Mudford's *An Historical Account of the Campaign in the Netherlands in 1815*. In addition to its justifiable fame as the first official news from Waterloo, it is also well known as the centrepiece of David Wilkie's *The Chelsea Pensioners reading the Waterloo Dispatch*, which was commissioned by Wellington and first debuted at the Royal Academy's summer exhibition of 1822. The painting proved such a hit that, for the first time, a railing had to be installed to protect the painting from the crowds and demand was so high for reproductions that Wilkie received the same amount of money (1,200 guineas) for the right to engrave it as Wellington had paid for the original.[13] Despite the high prices required to recoup the outlay (between three and fifteen guineas, depending on the rarity of the edition), the engraving (Figure 1.1) proved a massive success, no doubt aided by the fact that a proof of it was the centrepiece of Apsley House's Drawing Room decorations for the 1831 Waterloo banquet.[14]

---

[12] *The London Gazette Extraordinary*, 22 June 1815, number 17028, p. 1216; *The London Gazette*, 25 July 1815, number 17044, p. 1532; *The London Gazette*, 26 December 1815, number 17094, p. 2590.

[13] Foster, *Wellington and Waterloo*, 125. Allan Cunningham, *The Life of Sir David Wilkie; with his Journals, Tours, and Critical Remarks on his Works of Art; and a Selection from his Correspondence* (London: John Murray, 1843), II: 73; 'Apsley House', *The London Quarterly Review* 184 (April 1853), 241.

[14] *The Standard*, 20 June 1831, p. 4; *The Times*, 16 July 1831, p. 2.

Between the publication of the extraordinary edition of *The London Gazette* on 22 June and the emergence of the first histories of the battle in August, a British public rendered giddy by patriotic fervour looked to their newspapers for further details of the great triumph. The national and local press, just as eager as their readers, published everything they could get their hands on, including a variety of anecdotes (some of dubious provenance), official reports from the other countries involved as they became available, and a variety of plans of the battle.[15] Particularly prized were letters written by soldiers, extracts from a number of which were published by papers across the country in the months following the battle. Largely penned by enlisted men, this correspondence was not constrained by the same diplomatic niceties as Wellington's official dispatch, and so presented a preview of the claims of British ownership and the dismissal of the efforts of the other allies that would mark the early histories discussed below. Several do not mention the Prussians at all, simply stating that the British flanked the French 'in all directions' and that 'at length Napoleon's army gave way—they fled'.[16] *The Scots Magazine* forged a narrative of the battle out of such extracts for their September 1815 issue that does mention the Prussians, but only as arriving after the British troops had routed the Imperial Guard. Only when the French's 'animal spirits were exhausted, the panic spread, and ... the army was in complete disorder' was 'firing heard on our left; the Prussians were now coming down on the right flank of the French'.[17] Soldiers were also eager to claim glory for their individual regiments: a letter from an officer of the 71st (Highland) Regiment of Foot published in the *Chester Chronicle* insisted that it was their regiment's charge, spurred on by their piper and Major-General Adam, 'was the critical moment that turned the scale of the action, and I do assure you, we made them scamper'.[18]

As thrilling as such accounts of France's 'most complete drubbing' were, they were also necessarily brief, and merely whetted the public's appetite for longer narratives.[19] Thankfully, the British public did not have long to wait. First published in the middle of August 1815, less than two months after the battle itself, *The Battle of Waterloo* was a remarkable achievement considering how quickly it was produced.[20] The work is divided into three parts, the composition of which goes some way to explain how it could have been produced in less than two

---

[15] In addition to the plan mentioned at the beginning of the chapter, see *The Scots Magazine*, 1 September 1815.

[16] 'The Battle of Waterloo: Extract from a native of this city, in the 23rd Royal Welch Fusiliers', *Chester Chronicle*, 11 August 1815, p. 3; 'Battle of Waterloo: Extract from a Letter from a Serjeant in the Royal Artillery Drivers, to his father', *Caledonian Mercury*, 5 October 1815, p. 4.

[17] 'Private Accounts', *The Scots Magazine*, 1 September 1815, 650. Others were more generous. One Scottish cavalry officer 'of rank' informed his father that 'the day was long doubtful, but the fortunate arrival of the Prussians decided it'. 'Battle of Waterloo', *Caledonian Mercury*, 3 July 1815, p. 3.

[18] 'Waterloo', *Chester Chronicle*, 4 August 1815, p. 3.

[19] 'Battle of Waterloo', *Caledonian Mercury*, 3 July 1815, p. 3.

[20] 'In a few days will be published', *The Times*, 9 August 1815, p. 2.

months.[21] The first part comprises personal accounts and descriptions, the longest of which is the forty-four-page narrative by Charlotte Waldie, who also compiled the entire volume.[22] Waldie was a member of the Scottish gentry born in Roxburghshire who was visiting Brussels with family when the campaign occurred, and took the initiative to record her own narrative and put together the volume. She later went on to publish two further anonymous travelogues (one epistolary) and two novels under her married name of Charlotte Eaton between 1817 and 1831.[23] Her family seems to have been artistic in nature, as her younger sister, Jane Watts, also published a travelogue in 1820.[24] Waldie's narrative is split between a personal account of 15–18 June and a general description of the battlefield with extensive references to the two fold-out views of the field included in the volume. The personal account does an excellent job of illustrating the tension experienced by civilians in Brussels and Antwerp during the climactic days of the campaign, as well as showing just how much confusion was produced by the variety of rumours and reports that trickled back from the battlefield. Waldie retreats to Antwerp on 17 June based on repeated news of French victory, and on the 18th received news in Antwerp not only that the allied army had been defeated, but also that Brussels was already in French possession. It was only on the morning of the 19th, 'when fear almost amounted to certainty, when suspense had ended in despair, after a night of misery—that the great, the glorious news burst upon us' of the allied victory.[25]

After briefly describing the joy and relief that swept through Antwerp and Brussels, Waldie turns to her description of the battlefield. The fold-out views of the field are panoramic in nature, and are designed, if joined together, to present a 360-degree view of the valley. The illustrations are subtly numbered, and it is the description of the area represented by each number that forms the structure of the narrative. The author includes a variety of anecdotes and descriptions of the significant actions that took place at each location throughout the day so that, if

---

[21] These descriptions are drawn from the seventh edition, which appears to have been the most common edition to survive.

[22] The Battle of Waterloo, Containing the Series of Accounts Published by Authority, British and Foreign, with Circumstantial Details, previous, during, and after the Battle, from a Variety of Authentic and Original Sources, with Relative Official Documents, Forming an Historical Record of the Operations in the Campaign of the Netherlands, 1815. By a Near Observer, 7th edn (London: J. Booth and T. Egerton, 1815), 1–44.

[23] Narrative of a Residence in Belgium During the Campaign of 1815; and of a Visit to the Field of Waterloo by an Englishwoman (London: John Murray, 1817) ; Charlotte Anne Eaton, Rome in the Nineteenth Century (Edinburgh: Archibald Constable and Co., 1822); Charlotte Anne Eaton, Continental Adventures: A Novel, Founded on the Real Scenes and Adventures of an Actual Tour (London: Sherwood, Gilbert, and Piper, 1827); Charlotte Anne Eaton, At Home and Abroad: Or, Memoirs of Emily de Cardonell (London: John Murray, 1831). She also became a senior partner of her husband's bank, Eaton, Cayley & Co., and ran it from his death in 1834 until her death in 1859.

[24] Jane Waldie, Sketches Descriptive of Italy in the Years 1816 and 1817 With a Brief Account of Travels in Various Parts of France and Switzerland in the Same Years (London: John Murray, 1820).

[25] The Battle of Waterloo, 15–18.

read straight through, one would gain a decent, if not overly chronological, understanding of the battle. Waldie does not entirely abandon her own recollections, and includes in her descriptions of places and events observations from her own visit to the battlefield to emphasize the intensity of the violence.[26] She makes no attempt at a neutral or unbiased view, and closes with a highly patriotic paean to Wellington and the British army who 'wherever the French have appeared as oppressors...have sprung forward as deliverers', to break 'the spell which bound the kingdoms of Europe in ignominious slavery'.[27]

There are a few points worth highlighting in Waldie's account. First, she employs the same style of eyewitness account to establish her bona fides as the military memoirists do later in the chapter. Second, she is extremely complimentary of the Highland regiments, and at one point employs language that makes it sound like they alone faced the might of the French army. This may have contributed, along with letters and newspaper reports, to the belief, so lamented by Lieutenant Colonel Jonathan Leach, that the Highlanders saw the majority of the action at Waterloo. Third, while being openly biased towards the British, Waldie does give credit to the Prussians for their part in the victory, who, according to her, 'had come in at the close of the contest, in time to decide the victory and to share its glory'. Finally, she, like many of the chroniclers and memoirists, discusses the unreliability of portions of the allied army, laying the blame for certain rumours of defeat on 'those dastardly Belgians' who fled through Brussels on 16 June.[28]

The rest of *The Battle of Waterloo* is drawn from a variety of separate sources. The second half of the first part continues the personal narrative theme and comprises a wide variety of accounts from other eyewitnesses and notable officials. These are largely letters, some of which were obtained for Waldie by friends, and some of which were published in newspapers in the aftermath of the battle.[29] The second part is a collection of 'Official Accounts, published by authority', such as Wellington's Waterloo dispatch, Blücher's address to his troops, a variety of allied proclamations, Parliament's official thanks to Wellington, and the French army's account of the battle.[30] All of these, published by the various governments, would have been relatively easy to obtain, but still provided further details. In addition, the appeal of having them translated and bound into a single volume would have been strong, especially to a public succumbing to Waterloo mania. The final part detailed the losses of the various allied armies, the composition of the Army of

---

[26] See her description of the destruction around Hougoumont or the abandoned detritus of war. *The Battle of Waterloo*, 25–6, 41–2.

[27] *The Battle of Waterloo*, 43–4.

[28] *The Battle of Waterloo*, 6, 11, 38. It should be noted that in recent years scholars have sought to rectify this view of the Dutch and Belgian troops. See Veronica Baker-Smith, *Wellington's Hidden Heroes: The Dutch and the Belgians at Waterloo* (Oxford: Casemate Publishers, 2015).

[29] See, for example, *The Battle of Waterloo*, 43, 62.   [30] *The Battle of Waterloo*, 151.

Occupation, officers who were awarded honours for their part in the campaign, biographies of some of the more famous casualties, and a chronology of Wellington's military career. As with part two, almost all of this information could have been obtained easily from a variety of sources, in this case official gazettes, the Annual and Monthly Army Lists, Debrett's Peerage, and other publications and social guides. The appeal was again having it collected in one place and focused entirely on those who had been at Waterloo.

The gamble that the British public would like a single volume that collected all available material on Waterloo paid off. *The Battle of Waterloo* was so popular that it went through four editions in two months, and seven editions in 1815 alone.[31] Each new edition was 'much enlarged and corrected', with the fifth edition adding the translated official French account of the battle.[32] The increasing size and popularity of the volume also drove up the price. The fourth edition was advertised at 7s. 6d. for the boards or 10s. 6d. for the coloured, while the seventh, published only a month later, cost 12s. for the boards or 15s. for the coloured.[33] For those who did not fancy buying a new edition, the publishers also released a supplemental pamphlet, priced only 5s., that would bring any previous edition up to date with the fifth.[34] By the tenth edition, published in 1817, the work had been expanded to two volumes, as it contained a larger collection of accounts as well as 'portraits of Field-Marshals Wellington and Blücher, maps and enlarged plans, view of the field of Waterloo, and thirty-four etchings' by George Jones, later of the Royal Academy.[35] The tenth edition was the standard thereafter until 1852 when, to mark the death of Wellington, an 'enlarged and corrected' eleventh edition was published by the original publisher's son, with added memoirs of Wellington, Blücher, and Napoleon.[36]

Published a year after the eighth edition of *The Battle of Waterloo* in 1817, William Mudford's *An Historical Account of the Campaign in the Netherlands in 1815* spread its narrative net, as the title would imply, far wider. Mudford admits in the work's preface that his original intent was to produce a work akin to 1815's *The Battle of Waterloo* (although he does not mention any other books by name): an 'account to be derived only from the various details which were already before the public', written 'to accompany the plates by which it was to be illustrated'.

---

[31] 'This day is published', *The Times*, 13 October 1815, p. 2; 'To the army', *The Morning Post*, 16 November 1815, p. 1; 'Just published', *The Morning Post*, 19 December 1815, p. 1.

[32] 'To the army', *The Times*, 25 November 1815, p. 1.

[33] 'To the army', *The Morning Post*, 16 November 1815, p. 1; 'Just published', *The Morning Post*, 19 December 1815, p. 1.

[34] 'To the army', *The Morning Post*, 16 November 1815, p. 1; 'To the army', *The Times*, 25 November 1815, p. 1.

[35] *The Battle of Waterloo, also of Ligny, and Quatre Bras, described by the series of accounts published by authority, with circumstantial details. By a near observer*, 10th edn (London: John Booth and T. Egerton, 1817).

[36] *The Battle of Waterloo, with those of Ligny and Quatre Bras, described by eye-witnesses and by the series of official accounts published by authority*, 11th edn (London: L. Booth, 1852).

While considering this, however, Mudford realized that Napoleon's escape from Elba, the Hundred Days, his defeat, and subsequent exile to St Helena contained 'a beginning, a middle, and an end', and was therefore 'susceptible of a distinct relation'. The result is a much longer book than 1815's *The Battle of Waterloo*, with the narrative of Waterloo itself, along with its preliminaries, occupying some seventy pages towards the end of the work's 320 pages.[37]

An Historical Account of the Campaign in the Netherlands in 1815 is not unique in centring its action on Napoleon. The British were fascinated by the emperor and throughout the Revolutionary and Napoleonic Wars he remained a popular subject for every form of media.[38] This fascination, as we will see in Chapter 4, increased after Waterloo, driven not only by a desire to increase the glory of Waterloo by emphasizing the skill and power of the enemy defeated there, but also to further cement British ownership of the victory by emphasizing their ownership of Napoleon himself, now safely relegated to St Helena.[39]

Born in 1782, Mudford trained for a political career. He served as an assistant secretary to the Duke of Kent for a few years, accompanying the duke on a visit to Gibraltar in 1802. Shortly after the visit, however, he decided his skills lay more in writing about politics than engaging directly in them, and he resigned his secretaryship to become a journalist. He cut his teeth as a parliamentary reporter for *The Morning Chronicle*, then one of the leading Whig-identified papers in London, before joining *The Courier* as an assistant editor. In 1817, the same year as he published *An Historical Account of the Campaign in the Netherlands in 1815*, he rose to the editorship of *The Courier*, a post he would hold for over a decade.[40] *The Courier* was an evening paper, and its Tory political alignment more closely matched Mudford's own opinions than the Whiggish *Morning Chronicle*. Those opinions are clearly on display in *An Historical Account of the Campaign in the Netherlands in 1815*. The work is dedicated to Wellington, for 'to whom can a History of the Battle of Waterloo be so appropriately inscribed, as to the illustrious

---

[37] William Mudford, *An Historical Account of the Campaign in the Netherlands, in 1815, under his grace the Duke of Wellington, and Marshal Prince Blücher, comprising the Battles of Ligny, Quatre Bras, and Waterloo; with a Detailed Narrative of the Political Events Connected with those memorable conflicts, down to the Surrender of Paris, and the Departure of Bonaparte for St. Helena* (London: Henry Colburn, 1817), IX: 234–304. It is further supplemented with 41 pages of appendices and 25 plates, most of which are in full colour.

[38] See, for example, William Hazlitt, *The Life of Napoleon Buonaparte* (London: Illustrated London Library, 1803); Lieutenant Sarratt, Royal York Mary-le-bone Volunteers, *Life of Buonaparte* (London: Tegg and Castleman, 1803); W. Burdon, *The Life and Character of Bonaparte, from his Birth to the 15th of August, 1804* (Newcastle upon Tyne: K. Anderson, 1804); Willem Lodewyk Van-Ess, *The Life of Napoleon Buonaparte* (London: M. Jones, 1809); George Moir Bussey, *History of Napoleon* (London: Joseph Thomas, 1811); Pierre Lanfrey, *The History of Napoleon the First* (London: Macmillan and Co., 1886).

[39] For the relationship between the British and Napoleon, both during and after the wars, see Stuart Semmel, *Napoleon and the British* (New Haven: Yale University Press, 2004). See also Appendix.

[40] For more biographical details, see *Oxford Dictionary of National Biography* online, entry William Mudford.

hero who won it?'[41] Mudford compares Wellington to the Duke of Marlborough, and while he admits that the credit for Napoleon's defeat belongs to more than one individual, he does insist that Wellington laid the groundwork.

> You first taught the world that the legions of France were not invincible. It was your great example that infused hope and confidence, where despair and doubt prevailed before. You dissolved the magic spell which held prostrate thrones in vassalage; and every blow you struck for freedom, kindled a patriotic fire in hearts that only dared to wish for liberty. You were the beacon, in that tempestuous night, by whose effulgence, other nations steered their course. At your warning voice they awoke, and armed again for independence.[42]

Beyond idolizing Wellington, Mudford's conservatism is most clearly felt in his nationalism. Throughout his narrative of the battle, he uses possessive and inclusive terms for British forces, referring to 'our regiments' or 'our columns' and describing the army as a whole as 'us'. There is no indication that Mudford is trying to imply, via his choice of words, that he was present at the battle. Rather, his language serves to remind his largely British readership of their relationship to the army, and thus further cement the Britishness of the victory. To this end, he is also dismissive of the Dutch and Belgian troops.[43] On several occasions, he mentions actions taken by allied troops, only to immediately note their failure and defeat. He is particularly dismissive of 'some Belgian infantry, who were placed a little in advance of the 5th division, [who] soon gave way, as the enemy's columns... approached, without presuming to dispute their progress', and of the Cumberland Hussars, 'a foreign regiment, who deemed it quite superfluous that they should engage in the battle'. Mudford even goes so far as to erase the allied portions of the army from the picture at one point, decrying Napoleon's hubris for presuming victory when 'the Duke of Wellington and a British army lay between him and Brussels'. He is, however, largely complimentary of the troops of the King's German Legion (who were technically part of the British army and had served with distinction in the Peninsular War) and Brunswick, who 'behaved with great gallantry, and steadily maintained their position'.[44]

Considering his view of some of the allied troops under Wellington's command, Mudford is surprisingly generous when it comes to the role played by the Prussians. He gives several examples of the good feeling and cooperation between

---

[41] Mudford, *An Historical Account of the Campaign in the Netherlands*, v. Wellington refused permission for the dedication, but either relented or was ignored. Foster, *Wellington and Waterloo*, 92–3.

[42] Mudford, *An Historical Account of the Campaign in the Netherlands*, vi.

[43] He does, however, sing the praises of the Belgian civilians and their kindness and generosity. Mudford, *An Historical Account of the Campaign in the Netherlands*, 247.

[44] Mudford, *An Historical Account of the Campaign in the Netherlands*, 241, 249–50, 272, 274–5, 278, 281, 290 n. 1, 293.

the forces under Wellington and those under Blücher, including Prussian forces cheering British forces and greeting them with renditions of 'God save the King'. Mudford gives full credit to General von Zieten's I Corps' actions against Papelotte, 'which prevented the enemy's right from making any serious efforts against us', and, most definitively, declares that the Prussian capture of Plancenoit broke the enemy's right wing and 'decided the day'. In this view, Mudford differs from his sources. He quotes, in a footnote, 'an officer, who held a high command during the battle', who insisted the Prussians 'suffered us to bear the whole brunt of the battle, and came up just time enough to share the advantage'. In that same footnote, Mudford posits that it may be Prussian guilt that prompted certain behaviour after the battle: 'can it be that any unworthy resentment was felt against us, because a more effectual support was not given that day, to the Prussians? Painful as this supposition is, it derives some support when we remember the reiterated aspersions cast upon the Duke of Wellington by the *Rhenish Mercury*, which professed to speak the sentiments of the Prussian army.'[45]

In keeping with his conservative political views, Mudford reserved his most vociferous criticisms for the French. His scorn was not directed at their martial prowess, for what glory could Britain gain from defeating an unworthy foe? Indeed, he states that 'never did a finer army take the field' than Napoleon's forces at Waterloo, 'for it consisted almost entirely of veteran and highly-disciplined troops, animated too with a spirit of enthusiasm, which may be said to have increased its physical energy'. Mudford's contempt, instead, was for what they were fighting for, which he summed up as 'ambition, perfidy, and despotism', all wrapped up in the person of Napoleon himself. As he notes when discussing the actions of Marshal Ney, the French soldiers, for all their 'thirst for rapine', 'displayed a degree of heroism worthy [of] a better cause'.[46]

Napoleon, for all that he is the centre of Mudford's narrative, is very much the villain of the piece, with Wellington situated as the emperor's opposite in every way. Mudford compares Napoleon to Wellington multiple times, positioning both men as the avatars of their armies. He praises Wellington's 'simple but touching' rhetoric when encouraging his forces to stand, comparing it to 'the turgid stuff with which Bonaparte and his Generals would have striven to animate their men'. Mudford also compares the bravery of these two generals, insisting that Napoleon 'was the first to quit the field of battle, and...ran the fastest', while 'never did ambition, or glory, or duty, inspire a more thorough determination to set life upon every hazard that might win victory, than what animated the Duke of Wellington that day'. *An Historical Account of the Campaign in the Netherlands in 1815* closes with a damning summation of Napoleon's abilities, further emphasizing both his threat and Britain's achievement:

[45] Mudford, *An Historical Account of the Campaign in the Netherlands*, 276 n. 3, 291–5.
[46] Mudford, *An Historical Account of the Campaign in the Netherlands*, 239, 294–6.

With the power to do good, [Napoleon] had the will only to inflict evil...his dominion, like a pestilence, blighted the energies of nature, and his footsteps were tracked by desolation, silence and despair...None dared to speak, who did not dare to encounter dungeons, exile, or death. The blandishments of social intercourse were destroyed, and innocence was no longer the shield of private life. Such was the man, such was the system, such were the calamities, which found their grave on their field of Waterloo; and while we exult in the victory, as a proud addition to our national glory, let us also rejoice for mankind, who that day received their deliverance from our hands.[47]

The advertising for *An Historical Account of the Campaign in the Netherlands in 1815* continued the trends found within it. It was described as an 'important undertaking' and a 'truly NATIONAL WORK'.[48] It did not receive much attention from the popular or literary press, despite being advertised reasonably well.[49] It did, however, gain some traction as the source of extractions for Waterloo anecdotes, most notably a detailed account of the Hon. Colonel Ponsonby that was printed in *The Lancaster Gazette and General Advertiser.*[50] Despite the lack of reviews, it was cited in later works, and was a popular success.[51]

Both works discussed in detail here hint at aspects of Waterloo commemoration that would continue to inform the public's perception of the battle for years to come. The panoramic illustrations of the battlefield in 1815's *The Battle of Waterloo* provided a preview of the grand panoramas of the battlefield discussed in Chapter 4. Waldie's visit to the field in the aftermath of the battle also serves as one of the first examples of Waterloo as a venue for battlefield tourism, which, as demonstrated in Chapter 2, became an expected part of British trips to the Continent. The style of her recollections from the battlefield and explanations of the various significant locations highlighted in the panoramic images can also be seen as an early attempt at the language later employed by successful travel guides. Mudford's *An Historical Account of the Campaign in the Netherlands in 1815* provides no details of a battlefield visit or panorama, its thirty illustrative plates notwithstanding. Its decision to centre the narrative on Napoleon (after the

---

[47] Mudford, *An Historical Account of the Campaign in the Netherlands*, 285, 298–9, 319–20.

[48] Emphasis in original. 'New Works preparing for publication, or lately published, by Henry Colburn, Conduit Street', *The Quarterly Review* 14 (London: John Murray, 1816).

[49] *The London Literary Gazette, and Journal of Belles Lettres, Arts, Sciences, etc.*, 12 June 1819, no. 125, p. 384; *The London Literary Gazette, and Journal of Belles Lettres, Arts, Sciences, etc.*, 19 June 1819, no. 126, p. 400.

[50] 'The Hon. Colonel Ponsonby', *The Lancaster Gazette and General Advertiser, for Lancashire, Westmorland, &c.*, 23 August 1817.

[51] Barclay Mounteney, *An Historical Inquiry into the Principle Circumstances and Events Relative to the Late Emperor Napoleon; in which are investigated the charges brought against the government and conduct of that eminent individual* (London: Effingham Wilson, 1824), 144; Foster, *Wellington and Waterloo*, 239 n. 213.

introduction, Wellington is not mentioned for nearly 100 pages), as discussed above, however, is a prime example of the fascination with Napoleon that swept Britain in the aftermath of the emperor's surrender and second exile.

Despite the overly nationalistic language employed by Mudford and others, Britain held no monopoly on accounts of the Battle of Waterloo or the wider campaign that surrounded it. In 1816 Willem Benjamin Craan, a Brussels-based surveyor and cartographer, published his *Plan du champ de bataille de Waterloo, avec notice historique*. Craan, who was based in Brussels, consulted soldiers who had fought on both sides while preparing his plan, and the resulting map and account was so accurate it earned the approval of both the Prince of Orange, who had commanded the I Corps of the allied army at Waterloo, and his father, William I, while Tsar Alexander I was so taken with it that he presented Craan with a ring as a mark of his respect.[52] The entire thing was translated into English in 1817 by Captain Arthur Gore of the 30th (Cambridgeshire) Regiment of Foot, who had fought and been wounded at Waterloo, but does not seem to have received much attention in Britain.[53] Nor were French pens silent. In 1817, Alphonse de Beauchamp, a former French bureaucrat-turned-historian, famous for his three-volume *Histoire de la Vendée et des Chouans* (1806), which resulted in his banishment by Napoleon, published his two-volume *Histoire des campagnes de 1814 et de 1815*, which dedicated nearly 100 pages to the Waterloo campaign.[54] De Beauchamp's work was known in Britain, and this new opus was advertised there as a 'desirable companion to [Eugêne] Labaume's Campaign in Russia'.[55] A year later, London saw the publication of *The Campaign of 1815*, a narrative of the French side of the campaign, written in English by General Baron Gaspard Gourgaud, who had served as Napoleon's principal orderly officer, and who had followed his exiled emperor to St Helena to serve as his secretary.[56] Prussian authors produced accounts just as quickly as their British, Dutch and Belgian, or

[52] Xavier Heuschling, 'Notice biographique sur Guillaume-Benjamin Craan, auteur du plan de la bataille de Waterloo, etc.', in M. Ch. de Chênedollé, ed., *Bulletin du Bibliophile Belge* (Brussels: J.-M. Heberlé, 1850), VII: 78–82.

[53] 'Battle of Waterloo', *The Times*, 9 January 1817, p. 4; *An Historical Account of the Battle of Waterloo, Fought on the 18th June, 1815. Between the Anglo-Allied Army, under the command of Field Marshal his grace the Duke of Wellington, supported by a part of the Prussian Army commanded by Field Marshal Prince Blücher, of Wahlstadt, and the French Army under the command of Napoleon Bonaparte, intended to explain and elucidate the topographical plan, executed by W. B. Craan, J.U.D. Examining Engineer of the Government Surveys of South Brabant*, trans. Arthur Gore (Brussels: T. Parkin, 1817).

[54] Alphonse de Beauchamp, *Histoire des campagnes de 1814 et de 1815* (Paris: Le Normant, 1817), II: 251–343.

[55] 'Campaigns of 1814 and 1815', *The Morning Chronicle*, 1 July 1816; Eugêne Labaume, *Relation circonstanciée de la campagne de Russie en 1812* (Paris: C. L. F. Panckoucke, 1814).

[56] Gaspard Gourgaud, *The Campaign of MDCCCXV; or, A Narrative of the Military Operations Which Took Place in France and Belgium During the Hundred Days* (London: James Ridgway, 1818); 'Books published this day', *The Times*, 16 January 1819, p. 4.

French counterparts.[57] The most famous Prussian work on the battle, however, would have to wait until 1835, when Carl von Clausewitz's widow, fresh from the success of her husband's *Vom Kriege* or *On War*, published *The Campaign of 1815*.[58] *The Campaign of 1815* is both a history of the overall campaign and a critique of Wellington's actions. When it was published in Britain, it created quite a stir in military circles, and prompted Wellington to write a detailed response in 1842—the only lengthy work he ever produced on the battle.[59]

Having worked with their civilian allies to firmly establish British ownership of Waterloo, at least within the British Isles, the veterans of Waterloo watched as their efforts became too effective. Credit for the victory was no longer just the preserve of the military but became national in scope. The country celebrated the victory, but not, in the eyes of the veterans, the army that won it. The date 18 June was marked in military circles but equally enthusiastically in the civilian sphere. The battlefield itself was a popular tourist destination, but what Britons found there, and in the relics they brought back, was a national pride, not specifically a military one. All these factors, combined with the reduction in Britain's military establishment, and the public relations disasters of events such as the St Peter's Field Massacre, drove several soldiers to intervene directly in this conflict of ownership by writing and publishing memoirs.

These authors used their own experiences to challenge the armchair generals and civilian historians, providing a more intimate history of the battle that was, perforce, centred on the soldiers themselves. While the quarter-century of the Napoleonic Wars produced a remarkable collection of individual primary sources, the memoirs considered here form only a small percentage of the whole. Partially this is due to constraints of time and space, but the paramount consideration is intent. The great majority of individual primary sources now available through the work of scholars were never meant to be published. They comprise personal journals and letters to family and friends. While crucial to our understanding of the Battle of Waterloo and daily military life in the early nineteenth century, they provide little to no insight into the author's feelings on the ownership of Waterloo's memory.[60] Added to this are works published but either limited to

---

[57] For an example of earlier Prussian works, see *Versuch einer militärisch-historischen Darstellung des grossen Befreiungs-Krieges oder Uebersicht der Feldzüge in den Jahren 1813 bis 1815. Dritter Theil, den Feldzug vom Jahre 1815 enthaltend. Mit Planen und Charten* (Weimar: im Verlage des Geographischen Instituts, 1816).

[58] See Vanya Eftimova Bellinger, *Marie von Clausewitz: The Woman Behind the Making of On War* (Oxford: Oxford University Press, 2016).

[59] See Christopher Bassford, Daniel Moran, and Gregory W. Pedlow, trans. and eds, *On Waterloo: Clausewitz, Wellington, and the Campaign of 1815* (CreateSpace Independent Publishing Platform & Clausewitz.com, 2015); Christopher Bassford, *Clausewitz in English: The Reception of Clausewitz in Britain and America 1815–1945* (Oxford: Oxford University Press, 1994).

[60] See, for example, the six volumes of *The Waterloo Archive*, in which Gareth Glover has gathered previously unpublished or exceedingly rare sources on the battle. Four of the six volumes are devoted to the British. Gareth Glover, *The Waterloo Archive, Volumes 1–6* (Barnsley: Frontline Books, 2010–14).

private runs for friends and family or published posthumously. Here again we find sources that are valuable from a military history point of view but that provide little insight into the cultural conflict that emerged after the military victory.[61] Finally, we have accounts focused on the Peninsular War that do not include Waterloo, and which, for obvious reasons, cannot shine light on the issue at hand.[62]

Once these considerations are taken into account, the plethora of memoirs becomes a much more limited pool. Within this selection, this chapter will consider three memoirs that fit the requirements: Captain John Kincaid's *Adventures in the Rifle Brigade in the Peninsula, France, and the Netherlands from 1809–1815* (1830), Lieutenant Colonel Jonathan Leach's *Rough Sketches of the Life of an Old Soldier* (1831), and Quartermaster-Sergeant James Anton's *Retrospect of a Military Life during the Most Eventful Periods of the Last War* (1840). Kincaid's work is the most readable today, as he writes with an easy style and humour, Leach's work is the most pointed in terms of the conflict between military and civilian, and Anton's firmly held beliefs are couched in the deference expected of an enlisted man. It is also worth noting that Kincaid and Leach served together in the 1st battalion of the 95th Rifles, providing us with two versions of the same events during the battle.

It may seem strange that it took between fifteen and twenty years for these memoirs to be produced, but there are multiple reasons for the delay beyond the growing belief in the 1830s that the military ownership of Waterloo needed to be defended. The first and most obvious explanation is that the 1830s was when many soldiers who had served in the Peninsula and at Waterloo were retiring, and writing a memoir seemed an excellent way not only to fill suddenly empty days but also to supplement income. Beyond that, the authors may have been inspired by the success of a number of Peninsular War memoirs that appeared in the 1820s, such as Moyle Sherer's *Recollections of the Peninsula* (1823) or George Gleig's *The Subaltern* (1825).[63] The 1830s also saw the publication of numerous works that brought the Napoleonic Wars back to the forefront of popular culture and may have prompted these memoirs. The first volume of William Napier's *History of the War in the Peninsula and the South of France from the Year 1807 to the Year 1814* appeared in 1828, with subsequent volumes being published to 1840. The thirteen volumes of *The Dispatches of Field Marshal the Duke of Wellington*, edited by Lieutenant Colonel John Gurwood, were also published between 1834 and 1839. In addition to reinforcing popular interest in the Napoleonic Wars, all of these

---

[61] See Alexander Cavalie Mercer, *Journal of the Waterloo Campaign, Kept Throughout the Campaign of 1815* (Edinburgh and London: William Blackwood and Sons, 1870); *The Military Adventures of Charles O'Neil* (Worcester: Published for the Author by Edward Livermore, 1851).

[62] See George Wood, *The Subaltern Officer* (London: Septimus Prowett, 1825); George Robert Gleig, *The Subaltern* (Edinburgh: William Blackwood, 1826).

[63] Neither Sherer nor Gleig fought at Waterloo.

works provided further resources for the would-be authors of memoirs, who were trying to recall and narrate events up to three decades in the past.[64] Finally, these soldiers may have sought to respond to criticisms such as those found in Clausewitz's *The Campaign of 1815*. They may have also taken their inspiration from Wellington himself, whose attitude, especially in regard to the Prussian contribution to the battle, had shifted in the intervening years. Gone was the generous general who attributed 'the successful result of this arduous day, to the cordial and timely assistance I received from' Blücher and the Prussian army.[65] In his place stood the avatar of British military glory, who claimed that the major Prussian achievement had been to arrive in time to 'profit by [the British] victory', and when asked about the French army, simply replied, 'I beat them.'[66]

Despite the difficulties in recollection and the temptation to rely heavily on sources like Wellington's dispatches, there is one characteristic that almost all of these memoirs share in relation to the Battle of Waterloo: they are focused almost exclusively on the action they witnessed. This means that Kincaid's and Leach's narratives are focused on the 95th and, to a certain extent, the wider 5th Division, while Anton limits his to his regiment, the 42nd (Royal Highland) Regiment of Foot (the Black Watch). While this is laudable from the point of view of accuracy, all three had the ability to provide a historically accurate overview of the entire action. They had at their disposal several historical accounts of the full battle, not to mention Wellington's official dispatch. This was, then, a conscious choice on their part. By limiting themselves to their eyewitness accounts, they are separating themselves from the wider civilian histories of the conflict. Their limited views and their use of the active voice are, in fact, their bona fides, proving that they were there, laying claims to their actions, and granting their subsequent opinions the weight of military expertise in the face of a growing civilian Waterloo mania fed on more general and artistic depictions of the battle.

Captain John Kincaid was the second son of a minor Scottish laird with holdings near Falkirk in Stirlingshire.[67] His military experience began with a lieutenant's commission in the North York Militia before transferring to the 95th Rifles in 1809. He first saw active service in the ill-fated Walcheren expedition that same year before sailing with the 95th's first battalion to the Iberian Peninsula in 1810. He served in Wellington's army from that point until the end of

---

[64] Kincaid's *Adventures in the Rifle Brigade* is particularly prized by Peninsular scholars, as its publication date of 1830 means that it is largely untarnished by Napier's *History of the War in the Peninsula*, which became so popular that it effectively homogenized the accounts of many memoirs published after its release. Ian Fletcher, 'Introduction', in John Kincaid, *Adventures in the Rifle Brigade in the Peninsula, France, and the Netherlands from 1809–1815* (Staplehurst: Spellmount, 1998), vii.

[65] *The London Gazette Extraordinary*, 22 June 1815, number 17028, 1215.

[66] Richard Edgcumbe, ed., *The Diary of Frances Lady Shelley, 1818–1873* (New York: Charles Scribner's Sons, 1913), II: 33; Harriet Arbuthnot, *The Journal of Mrs. Arbuthnot, 1820–1832*, ed. Francis Bamford and the Duke of Wellington (London: Macmillan & Co., 1950), I: 234–5.

[67] John Kincaid, *Random Shots from a Rifleman* (London: T. and W. Boone, 1847), 3.

the Peninsular War in 1814, seeing action at several of the more notorious battles and sieges, and rising to the position of battalion adjutant. When news reached Britain of Napoleon's escape and the commencement of what would become the Hundred Days, he was shooting in Scotland, but he joined his regiment in Brussels in time to play an active role in the battles of Quatre Bras and Waterloo. He was promoted to captain in 1826 and sold his commission in 1831. In 1844 he was made exon of the Yeomen of the Guard, and was knighted in 1852 upon succeeding to the rank of senior exon.[68] He was appointed inspector of prisons for Scotland in 1847 and inspector of factories for Scotland and the north of England in 1850. He died in 1862.[69]

Kincaid's first book, *Adventures in the Rifle Brigade in the Peninsula, France, and the Netherlands from 1809–1815* was published in 1830 while he was still serving as a captain in the Rifle Brigade.[70] *Adventures in the Rifle Brigade* is a chronological account of Kincaid's service from 1809 to 1815, beginning with the Walcheren expedition and ending on the morning after the Battle of Waterloo. It is organized by both chapters and date entries but occasionally drops into general anecdote before returning to the main narrative. Kincaid's style lends itself to the occasional anecdote: he writes in a very easy and enjoyable manner and manages to inject moments of humour into an otherwise serious subject. He even manages to find some levity in the bloody Waterloo campaign, to which he dedicates the last fifty pages of his 351-page memoir.[71] The work contains sufficient detail to indicate that Kincaid probably had some rough recollections or notes to draw on (perhaps the records he kept as battalion adjutant), but the only mention Kincaid makes of his sources is in the opening advertisement, when he states that 'in tracing the following scenes, I have chiefly drawn on the reminiscences of my military life...should any errors, as to dates or trifling circumstances, have inadvertently crept into my narrative, I hope they will be ascribed to want of memory, rather than to any willful intention to mislead'.[72]

There are two significant points in Kincaid's recollections that are worth discussing in detail. The first, as discussed in the introduction, is that Kincaid is scrupulous in only relating what he himself saw that day. His description of his position on the morning of the Battle of Waterloo is an excellent example of this: 'Our battalion stood on what was considered the left centre of the position. We

---

[68] Exon is the lowest officer rank in the Yeomen.
[69] For more biographical details, see *Oxford Dictionary of National Biography* online, entry Sir John Kincaid.
[70] The 95th Rifles became the Rifle Brigade in 1816. Kincaid published a follow-up volume, *Random Shots from a Rifleman*, in 1835.
[71] The moment he discovers that his sword has been rusted into its scabbard as a regiment of cuirassiers charges him is written to highlight the madcap lunacy of war, and he describes a column of French infantry headed for his position as 'destined as *our* particular *friends*'. John Kincaid, *Adventures in the Rifle Brigade in the Peninsula, France, and the Netherlands from 1809–1815* (London: T. and W. Boone, 1830), 333, 335–6.
[72] Kincaid, *Adventures in the Rifle Brigade*, vii–viii.

had our right resting on the Namur-road, about a hundred yards in the rear of the farm-house of La Haye Sainte, and our left extending behind a broken hedge, which ran along the ridge to the left. Immediately in our front, and divided from La Haye Sainte only by the great road, stood a small knoll, with a sand-hole in its farthest side, which we occupied, as an advanced post, with three companies.' He then discusses, in slightly less but still authoritative detail, the deployment of the rest of the 5th Division, which 'was formed in two lines; the first, consisting chiefly of light troops, behind the hedge, in continuation from the left of our battalion reserve; and the second, about a hundred yards in its rear. The guns were placed in the intervals between the brigades, two pieces were in the road-way on our right, and a rocket-brigade in the centre.' Finally, Kincaid mentions the 5th Division's neighbours: 'The division, I believe, under General Alten occupied the ground next to us, on the right. He had a light battalion of the German legion, posted inside La Haye Sainte, and the household brigade of cavalry stood under cover of the rising ground behind him. On our left there were some Hanoverians and Belgians, together with a brigade of British heavy dragoons, the royals, and the Scotch [sic] greys.'[73]

Despite having multiple histories of the battle and Wellington's official dispatch at his disposal to fill in the gaps in his knowledge, Kincaid refused to expand further, simply stating 'these were all the observations on the disposition of our army that my situation enabled me to make'. He continues this approach as he describes the day; during lulls in the fight around them, he will mention what he can observe of the rest of the field, noting that 'columns, from the enemy's left, were seen in motion towards Hugamont, and were soon warmly engaged with the right of our army' or 'on our right, the roar of cannon and musketry had been incessant from the time of its commencement; but the higher ground, near us, prevented our seeing anything of what was going on'. Beyond these mentions, however, Kincaid's narrative is limited to the area around the Namur road, La Haye Sainte, and what has become known as the sandpit. The fighting there was intense, and Kincaid highlights several reasons why he did not—and in fact could not—pay attention to the rest of the battle. 'For the two or three succeeding hours there was no variety with us, but one continued blaze of musketry. The smoke hung so thick about that, although not more than eighty yards asunder, we could only distinguish each other by the flashes of the pieces.'[74]

Kincaid's determination to stick to his own eyewitnessed recollections pays off in the climactic moments of the battle, where both the horror of war and the elation of victory seem much more real for the intimacy of the narration. 'I felt weary and worn out,' Kincaid recalls,

---

[73] Kincaid, *Adventures in the Rifle Brigade*, 330–1.
[74] Kincaid, *Adventures in the Rifle Brigade*, 331, 338, 341.

less from fatigue than anxiety. Our division, which had stood upwards of five thousand men at the commencement of the battle, had gradually dwindled down into a solitary line of skirmishers. The twenty-seventh regiment were lying literally dead, in square, a few yards behind us...The smoke still hung so thick about us that we could see nothing. I walked a little way to each flank to endeavor to get a glimpse of what was going on; but nothing met my eye except the mangled remains of men and horses...I had never yet heard of a battle in which every body was killed; but this seemed likely to be an exception.

Then, less than a page after that apocalyptic thought, comes the moment of glory as,

presently a cheer, which we knew to be British, commenced far to the right, and made every one prick up his ears;—it was Lord Wellington's long wished-for orders to advance; it gradually approached, growing louder as it grew near;—we took it up by instinct, charged through the hedge down upon the old knoll, sending our adversaries flying at the point of the bayonet...This movement had carried us clear of the smoke; and, to people who had been for so many hours enveloped in darkness, in the midst of destruction, and naturally anxious about the result of the day, the scene which now met the eye conveyed a feeling of more exquisite gratification than can be conceived. It was a fine summer's evening, just before sunset. The French were flying in one confused mass. British lines were seen in close pursuit, and in admirable order, as far as the eye could reach to the right, while the plain to the left was filled with Prussians.

Kincaid goes on to briefly describe the pursuit of the French, the capture of their baggage train, and the halt of the British advance at dusk, as the Prussians took over the pursuit. He then closes his detailed narrative of the battle by summing it up as 'the last, the greatest, and the most uncomfortable heap of glory that I ever had a hand in'.[75]

Besides providing a singular eyewitness perspective on the battle, Kincaid's treatment of the Prussians also warrants mention. The Prussians feature relatively heavily in Kincaid's account of the Waterloo campaign, considering its eyewitness nature. During the battle for Quatre Bras, he mentions Wellington riding to 'an interview with Blücher, in which they concerted measures for their mutual co-operation'. Later the same day, the 95th are visited by a patrol of Prussian dragoons 'to inquire how it fared with us'. During the Battle of Waterloo itself, Kincaid notes that 'an occasional gun, beyond the plain, far to our left, marked the approach of the Prussians', and he mentions, as quoted above, that the Prussians

---

[75] Kincaid, *Adventures in the Rifle Brigade*, 342–5.

were pouring onto the eastern part of the battlefield as the final charge took place and were instrumental in the ongoing pursuit of the retreating French army. Despite this, however, Kincaid is unshakeable in his insistence that it was the British who won Waterloo. His comment during the battle that they could occasionally hear a gun marking the Prussian advance concludes with the statement, 'but their progress was too slow to afford a hope of their arriving in time to take any share in the battle'.[76]

Kincaid's full thoughts on the nationality of the victory can be found immediately after his narration of the battle, when he allows himself a few pages for rumination on the larger questions presented by 18 June. Chief among these is the 'matter of dispute what the result of that day would have been without the arrival of the Prussians'. He openly acknowledges that 'Lord Wellington would not have fought at Waterloo unless Blücher had promised to aid him with 30,000 men, as he required that number to put him on a numerical footing with his adversary,' but insists that 'the promised aid did not come in time to take any share whatever in the battle'. In pre-emptive response, it seems, to those who would point out that the Prussians arrived in time for the general advance, Kincaid continues, insisting that 'it is equally certain that the enemy had, long before, been beaten into a mass of ruin, in condition for nothing but running, and wanting but an apology to do it'. 'I will ever maintain,' he concludes, 'that Lord Wellington's last advance would have made it the same victory had a Prussian never been seen there.'[77]

Kincaid is equally dismissive of the Dutch and Belgian troops under Wellington's command. After the first French attack, he relates being 'told, it was very ridiculous, at that moment, to see the number of vacant spots that were left nearly along the whole of the line, where a great part of the dark dressed foreign troops had stood, intermixed with the British when the action began'. He continues this thread in his summary. 'Our foreign auxiliaries, who constituted more than half our numerical strength, with some exceptions, were little better than raw militia—a body without a soul, or like an inflated pillow, that gives to the touch, and reassumes its shape again when the pressure ceases—not to mention the many who went clear out of the field, and were only seen while plundering our baggage in their retreat.' In fact, the only foreign troops Kincaid unreservedly praises are the King's German Legion, who fell somewhere between British and foreign troops.[78]

---

[76] Kincaid, *Adventures in the Rifle Brigade*, 314, 319, 338, 344.

[77] Kincaid, *Adventures in the Rifle Brigade*, 346–7.

[78] Kincaid is just as critical of Britain's allies during the Peninsular War. He dismisses the Portuguese as 'creatures of a former age, [who] showed the indolence and want of enterprise which marked them born for slaves'. As for their army, 'as a nation, they owe their character for bravery almost entirely to the activity and gallantry of the British officers who organized and led them'. Kincaid, *Adventures in the Rifle Brigade*, 197, 337, 345–6.

For Kincaid, Waterloo was a British victory, unalloyed by allied aid, and in fact made more difficult by allied delays and incompetence. Even within that British victory, however, Kincaid feels the need to apportion out the glory. He acknowledges the important contribution the British heavy cavalry made at the start of the day but, like many infantrymen before him, criticizes their tendency to overextend themselves until they are 'dispersed or destroyed'.[79] The Royal Artillery served admirably but were handicapped by their relatively low numbers, the disabling fire of their French counterparts, and the proximity of the conflict to their positions. For Kincaid, victory at Waterloo comes down to two things: the infantry and Wellington. 'The British infantry and the King's German Legion', he eulogizes, 'continued the inflexible supporters of their country's honour throughout, and their unshaken constancy under the most desperate circumstances showed that, though they might be destroyed, they were not to be beaten.' Kincaid saves his highest praise, however, for Wellington himself, who, in his view, won the victory with, and despite of, 'all in all, a very bad army'. 'If Lord Wellington had been at the head of his old Peninsula army,' Kincaid insists, 'I am confident that he would have swept his opponents off the face of the earth immediately after their first attack; but with such a heterogeneous mixture under his command, he was obliged to submit to a longer day.'[80]

Adventures in the Rifle Brigade was immediately well received. *The United Service Journal*, Britain's premier military magazine, was equally delighted with both Kincaid and his memoir. The author they praised as 'a capital soldier, a pithy and graphic narrator, and a fellow of infinite jest ... the *beau-ideal* of a thoroughgoing soldier of service'.[81] When it came to the work itself, the *Journal* paid it the compliment of comparing it to Kincaid's old corps, who were arguably the finest skirmishers in the British army.

> The book itself looks part and parcel a Rifleman. Trimly bound in a green jacket, its fire is brisk, desultory, and effective as that of the buoyant corps it fitly represents, every sentence sounding as sharp and searching as the crack of a rifle. Each discharge is a point blank and unerring sketch ... there is nothing extant in the shape of a soldier's journal which, with so little pretension, paints with such truth and raciness the 'domestic economy' of campaigning and the downright business of handling the enemy.[82]

---

[79] Kincaid, *Adventures in the Rifle Brigade*, 345. For a summary of the criticisms levelled by the infantry arm against the British cavalry, and a rehabilitation of the mounted arm, see Ian Fletcher, *Galloping at Everything: The British Cavalry in the Peninsular War and at Waterloo, 1808–15* (Stroud: Spellmount, 2008).

[80] Kincaid, *Adventures in the Rifle Brigade*, 345–6.

[81] 'Adventures in the Rifle Brigade', *The United Service Journal and Naval and Military Magazine 1830* (London: Henry Colburn and Richard Bentley, 1830), I: 478.

[82] 'Adventures in the Rifle Brigade', *The United Service Journal*, I: 478.

In the civilian press, *The Athenæum* lauded it as 'one of the most lively histories of a soldier's adventures which have yet appeared', and had no hesitation in saying that Kincaid's work would 'afford a few hours very agreeable reading; their entire freedom from affectation, will sufficiently recommend them to an extensive class of readers'.[83] *The Edinburgh Literary Journal* declared it an 'excellent and amusing book' which they 'heartily recommended' and took particular delight in Kincaid's glowing opinion of Wellington.[84] *The Cheltenham Chronicle* 'gladly direct[ed] the attention of [their] readers' to *Adventures in the Rifle Brigade*, which they found 'replete with incident and amusing anecdote'.[85] *The Age*'s praise was slightly barbed, noting that 'Kincaid's *Adventures* is written with all the frankness and freedom from study, which bespeaks the gallant soldier.'[86] *The Monthly Magazine* was more generous, simply stating 'his book has one fault, the rarest fault in books, it is too short'.[87]

Perhaps inspired by the success of Kincaid's *Adventures*, Lieutenant Colonel Jonathan Leach, also of the Rifle Brigade, published his own *Rough Sketches of the Life of an Old Soldier* in 1831. Leach was the son of George Leach, a solicitor and naturalist, and Jenny Elford, both of whom came from established and wealthy Devon families. Leach was also the older brother of William Elford Leach, the well-known naturalist.[88] In 1801 Leach obtained a commission in the 70th Regiment of Foot and joined them on the island of Jersey. After nearly a year of garrison duty, the 70th spent a year at Chatham and Shorncliffe under the command of Sir John Moore, who was at that time training Britain's new Light Division, and who introduced to Leach the notions of skirmishing and light infantry. In 1803, Leach sailed for Antigua with the 70th, where he spent two years before being invalided home in 1805. In 1806, he exchanged into the 95th Rifles, a regiment he had become familiar with at Shorncliffe, and in which he would spend the rest of his military career. In 1807 he saw action in Denmark and at the second battle of Copenhagen before returning to Britain. He sailed in 1808 for Portugal. Between 1808 and 1814 he served with the second and then the first battalion of the 95th in the Peninsular War, seeing action at several significant battles. By the commencement of the Waterloo campaign he was a brevet major and third in command of the first battalion of the 95th, which he commanded in the latter part of the battle due to wounds taken by both his superior officers.[89]

---

[83] *The Athenæum Weekly Review* no. 123, 6 March 1830, pp. 130–2.

[84] 'Literary Criticism', *The Edinburgh Literary Journal* no. 70, 13 March 1830, pp. 158–9.

[85] 'Literary and Scientific Intelligence', *The Cheltenham Chronicle and Gloucestershire Advertiser*, 11 March 1830, p. 4.

[86] Quoted in advertising copy in *The Manchester Times and Gazette*, 16 August 1834.

[87] *Monthly Magazine*, April 1830, quoted in advertising copy in John Kincaid, *Random Shots from a Rifleman*, 2nd edn (London: T. and W. Boone, 1847), front advertisement.

[88] Keith Harrison and Eric Smith, *Rifle-Green by Nature: A Regency Naturalist and his Family, William Elford Leach* (London: Ray Society, 2008).

[89] Charles Dalton, *The Waterloo Roll Call with Biographical Notes and Anecdotes* (London: Eyre & Spottiswoode, 1904), 197–8.

Leach continued his service with the 95th as part of the army of occupation, and later served with them in Ireland. He retired from active service in 1821 as a lieutenant colonel.[90]

Leach's *Rough Sketches*, like Kincaid's *Adventures*, is chronological in nature, starting with his joining the 70th in Jersey, and ending with his retirement, although the years after Waterloo are given only very limited space. The foundation on which Leach builds his narrative is the daily journal he kept while on campaign, 'aided by a tolerably fair memory, and some old notes and memoranda'.[91] Rather than breaking up his narrative with general anecdotes as Kincaid did, however, Leach's digressions lean more towards his own opinions, some of which can best be described as rants. Given this difference in style, it is unsurprising that Leach's memoir, while both interesting and informative, is less breezy and entertaining than Kincaid's work. In addition, despite its longer overall length (Kincaid's *Adventures* is 351 pages, Leach's *Rough Sketches* is 411), Leach dedicates less space to both the Waterloo campaign (thirty-nine pages) and the battle itself (thirteen pages) than Kincaid does. Leach's explanation for this is simple. As he writes in the beginning of the chapter dedicated to Waterloo, 'it would be presumptuous in a regimental officer, who was necessarily tied to one spot with his regiment during the whole of the action, to endeavor to throw a light on a subject already so frequently discussed'.[92]

As that explanation would imply, Leach's narrative focuses almost entirely on the experiences of the 95th and the 5th Division. His descriptions are less evocative and detailed than Kincaid's, but the thrust of his recollections matches those of the man who was, at that point, serving as his battalion's adjutant. He notes the same action directed at the Chateau of Hougoumont, blocked from view by the same higher ground, and the same attacks endured by the 95th and their comrades in La Haye Sainte. He too remembers the near destruction of the 27th while in square and is filled with admiration for the King's German Legion's defence of La Haye Sainte. Even his report on the progress of the Prussian advance is remarkably similar, recalling that 'the arrival of the Prussians had been long expected; but the only intimation we had of their approach was the smoke of a distant cannon occasionally seen far on the left'. Where Leach differs from Kincaid is in his interpretation of the importance of the Prussian attack. Rather than maintaining that the French were already beaten, he argues that while the French were on the back foot, they still had some fight in them, and 'that the last

---

[90] It is unclear whether he sold his commission or retired on half-pay. All biographical details are from Jonathan Leach, *Rough Sketches of the Life of an Old Soldier: During a Service in the West Indies; at the Siege of Copenhagen in 1807; in the Peninsula and the South of France in the Campaigns from 1808 to 1814, with the Light Division; in the Netherlands in 1815; including the Battles of Quatre Bras and Waterloo: With a Slight Sketch of the Three Years Passed by the Army of Occupation in France, &c. &c. &c.* (London: Longman, Rees, Orme, Brown, and Green, 1831).

[91] Leach, *Rough Sketches of the Life of an Old Soldier*, vii.

[92] Leach, *Rough Sketches of the Life of an Old Soldier*, 383.

and desperate attack was made by Napoleon with his guard, to annihilate us before the Prussians should arrive to our assistance'. Leach also credits Wellington's decision to order the general advance at least partially to knowledge of the Prussian attack: 'the Prussians were now commencing an attack on the extreme right of the French, which the Duke of Wellington being aware of, and witnessing the immense loss which they had suffered in their last attack, as also their indescribable confusion, ordered a general advance of his whole army, to put the finishing stroke to the work of this bloody day.'[93]

While Leach is content to give some credit for the victory to the Prussians, he does take a stand on the point of ownership of Waterloo. His objection is not to allied military claims, but is instead to civilian encroachment, in the form of criticism of Wellington's actions by 'fire-side and feather-bed tacticians'. 'I have often been heartily tired of, and out of all patience with, the one engrossing question, ever uppermost, and ready to be let fly at any one who happened to have served with the Waterloo army,' he declares, '"pray, sir, was not the Duke of Wellington taken quite by surprise, whilst he was at the Duchess of Richmond's ball at Brussels, by the sudden irruption of Bonaparte's army into Flanders?"' Leach responds to this in two ways. He first informs these critics that every officer in the 5th Division knew that the French army was on the move on 15 June, and there is no way they knew and Wellington did not. He then asks 'these *savans*' if they would have preferred Wellington to gather his army in one place before he knew which route Napoleon was taking, thus risking being bypassed by the French army. 'It is doubtless a pleasant and edifying occupation,' he concludes, 'while sitting by an English fire-side, to criticise and calumniate that commander, who, in spite of his being "taken by surprise," contrived to gain the most splendid and decisive victory ever achieved by the British army or any other.' Having summarily dealt with these critics, he leaves them to nurse their cold shins and their 'half a dozen of port' and continues with his memoirs.[94]

In addition to the question of civilian vs military ownership, Leach addresses where credit should fall within the ranks of those who fought. Unlike Kincaid who demarcates glory via service arm, Leach takes the opportunity to redress what he sees as a national imbalance. He laments that the British popular press seized upon the idea that 'the Scottish regiments were the only people who pulled a trigger on the left of the British position throughout the whole of that protracted struggle, and that they, unaided, defeated the reiterated attacks of the Imperial Legions at that point'. This conviction was further enforced, in his mind, by 'various panoramic exhibitions [that] have also strongly tended to convince the

---

[93] Leach, *Rough Sketches of the Life of an Old Soldier*, 386–93.
[94] Leach, *Rough Sketches of the Life of an Old Soldier*, 379–81. For a more satirical take on the questions 'these *savans*' bombarded returning veterans with, see Captain Withers' story in James White's *Nights at Mess. The Adventures of Sir Frizzle Pumpkin, Nights at Mess, and Other Tales* (Edinburgh: William Blackwood and Sons, 1846), 100–18.

good people of England, that John Bull and Pat were little better than idle spectators on the left of the British position.'[95] Leach therefore takes the opportunity to correct this belief with reference to the 5th Division, which comprised three Highland regiments, one lowland Scottish regiment, and four English regiments.[96] Anyone, he insists, who 'has seen that part of the position which our division occupied, need not be informed that every regiment which composed it must necessarily have been exposed in an equal degree to the repeated attacks of the French; and it was therefore utterly impossible that one regiment should have had a smaller or greater degree of pounding than another'.[97] Leach closes his memoir shortly after addressing this imbalance of glory by expounding at some length on the importance of riflemen and light troops and insisting that light infantry techniques should still be encouraged via organization and training within the British army.

While Leach's work was not as widely reviewed as Kincaid's offerings, it did still receive some positive press. *The United Service Journal* praised its 'animated and rifleman-like character' and declared itself 'indebted to the gallant author for the perusal of one of the most faithful and entertaining volumes which have yet appeared on the fertile subject of the late war'.[98] *The Cheltenham Chronicle*, though it did not review it directly, did consider an extract on military recreation to be of interest to their readers, and so published that excerpt.[99] Leach's feelings on slavery, which he had formed during his time in the Caribbean, also met with the approval of Britain's abolitionists. His thoughts were quoted at length in a letter to the editor of the *North Devon Journal*, where the military nature of the memoir is used to highlight that it is an unbiased eyewitness account, unconnected to the Anti-Slavery Society.[100] A slightly longer version of the same extract was later printed without comment in the *Hereford Journal*.[101]

The final memoir discussed in this chapter, James Anton's *Retrospect of a Military Life during the Most Eventful Periods of the Last War*, was published in 1840, nine years after *Rough Sketches of the Life of an Old Soldier*.[102] Born in Huntly, Aberdeenshire around 1788, Anton enlisted in the militia in 1802 at

---

[95] The hero of the 1824 hippodrama *The Battle of Waterloo* at Astley's, discussed in Chapter 4, was also a member of a Highland regiment. Leach, *Rough Sketches of the Life of an Old Soldier*, 399; J. H. Amherst, *The Battle of Waterloo: A Grand Military Melo-Drama in Three Acts* (London: Duncombe, 1824).

[96] The 79th (Cameron Highlanders), the 42nd (Black Watch), the 92nd (Gordon Highlanders), the 1st (Royal Scots), the 28th (North Gloucestershire), the 32nd (Cornwall), the 44th (East Essex), and the 95th Rifles.

[97] Leach, *Rough Sketches of the Life of an Old Soldier*, 398–9.

[98] 'Rough Sketches of the Life of an Old Soldier', The United Service Journal and Naval and Military Magazine 1831 (London: Henry Colburn and Richard Bentley, 1831), III: 535–6.

[99] 'Literature', *The Cheltenham Chronicle and Gloucestershire Advertiser*, 29 December 1831, p. 4.

[100] J. Bennett, Letter to the Editor, *The North Devon Journal*, 26 April 1832, p. 1.

[101] 'Negro Slavery', *Hereford Journal*, 19 June 1833, p. 1.

[102] Although the date listed on the title page is 1841, Anton's work was sold starting in December 1840. 'A Military Life', *Belfast News-Letter*, 8 December 1840, p. 3.

roughly the age of 14, standing 'at half tiptoe' to meet the height requirement. After eight years in the militia, he and several friends volunteered for a transfer to the 42nd (Royal Highland) Regiment of Foot (the Black Watch). He served for the rest of his career in that storied regiment, eventually rising to the rank of Quartermaster-Sergeant.[103] Notwithstanding Anton's claim that 'few have served so long with less cause to reflect on the hardships of the service', he still occupied a much less privileged position than either Kincaid or Leach, both of whom held commissions.[104]

Anton left the service in 1833 and retired to Edinburgh. There, in Scotland's literary capital, he would almost certainly have been exposed to the various histories and memoirs of the Napoleonic Wars that were published throughout the 1830s. He also found himself surrounded, as he makes clear in the preface of his memoir, by a circle of friends and acquaintances who encouraged his own literary efforts, reading drafts and even editing the proof pages of his manuscript. It was his 'desire to merit the esteem' of these friends, along with 'the good opinion of all who wish to maintain strict discipline in the army', rather than 'to reap any substantial reward for the labour of my pen' that prompted him to publish his memoirs, although any supplement to his 2s. 1d. daily pension must have been welcome. Anton was not starting his literary journey from scratch, however, as he had kept journals throughout his time in uniform. The first two of those journals, possibly uniquely in the records of the Peninsular War, were kept in rhyme. Sadly, Anton chose to model his published memoir on his final journal, which was written in prose, although the final product retains aspects of the lyricism of its original form.[105]

Retrospect of a Military Life, like Kincaid's and Leach's memoirs before it, is chronological in nature, occasionally pausing to delve into an anecdote or ruminate on the wants and needs of the ordinary soldier. While Anton never reaches the level of Leach's rants, he is not shy with his opinions, especially on the subject of military discipline. Unsurprisingly, given his stated motives for penning his memoirs, he is unshakeable in his approval of the army's discipline system, presenting himself in opposition to 'philanthropists who decry the lash' and insisting that flogging is necessary to protect the good men in uniform from the 'despicable demon[s] of discord'. He also takes issue with those same philanthropists who oppose the death penalty for civilian crimes, arguing that abolishing it would somehow be disrespectful of those who 'in obedience to the law have

[103] He held the rank of sergeant at Waterloo.

[104] James Anton, *Retrospect of a Military Life, During the Most Eventful Periods of the Last War* (Edinburgh: W. H. Lizars, 1841), 3, 39; Admission Records for the Royal Hospital Chelsea, 14 August 1833, London, National Archives, WO 23/4, p. 107.

[105] Anton, *Retrospect of a Military Life*, v–vi, 2, 254–6; Admission Records for the Royal Hospital Chelsea, 14 August 1833, London, National Archives, WO 23/4, p. 107.

fought and bled, yet here unpitied die!'[106] Even as he states his opinion, however, Anton never loses sight of that fact that he was an enlisted man and is required to 'know his place'. His statements on discipline are couched with phrases such as 'my opinion may be erroneous, but' and he ends his memoir with the codicil that he is 'aware that I have used more freedom in offering my own opinion on the incidents which have come under my observation, than may be thought justifiable in one of my humble rank and unpretending acquirements.'[107]

Despite its title's claimed limitation to 'the most eventful periods of the last war', the memoir covers Anton's entire thirty-one years in uniform, from 1802 to 1833. Waterloo falls right in the middle of the memoir and is the subject of chapter XIII. While Anton acknowledges the importance of Waterloo, it is very clear that for him, it is simply one more battle in his career, even if the eighteen pages he devotes to it is more space than some other engagements merit.[108] Anton provides a different view of the action from either Kincaid or Leach, combining his own personal recollections with a relatively brief and chronologically compressed overview drawn from several histories, including P. F. F. J. Giraud's account from the French perspective. Anton's longest descriptive passage is, unsurprisingly, given his Scottish blood, devoted to the charge of the British Heavy Cavalry, and especially the 2nd Dragoons (Scots Greys), which swings from fervent national pride to the horrors of war and back again. Even as he and his fellow Highlanders revel in the martial achievements of their countrymen, however, he is careful to emphasize the Britishness of the Union Brigade. '"Glory of Scotland!" bursts spontaneously from the mouth of each Highlander, while rending shouts of "England's" or "Ireland's" glory welcomes the 1st and Enniskillen Dragoons, and echoes along the lines.' This same generosity of spirit is present when Anton mentions the other allied forces. He laments the passing of 'some thousands of brave men, British, Brunswick, [and] Belgic', and while he does not mention the Prussians until the final charge, grants them full credit, noting that 'the hardy Prussians…shared the toils of the hard-fought day'. He is even complimentary of the French, counting their own dead among the brave fallen and declaring that any 'man who brands our foe with cowardice deserves the lie'.[109]

Anton's tendency to slide into more lyrical or dramatic language is on full display throughout his description of Waterloo. He ascribes the rain that soaked the valley on the night before the battle to the anger of the heavens at the allied retreat from Quatre Bras, 'as if the ascending spirits of our fallen companions were imploring the ethereal powers to hurl the bolts of their vengeance in our face, to brand us with cowardice'. Like Kincaid, Anton notes that the sun emerged from

---

[106] It is unclear whether Anton's phrasing is a deliberate reference to the Spartan epitaph at Thermopylae.

[107] Anton, *Retrospect of a Military Life*, 10–12, 205–6, 215–16, 279–81, 394.

[108] The battle of Nivelle, for example, is granted six pages, while Toulouse is awarded ten.

[109] Anton, *Retrospect of a Military Life*, 205, 210–13, 215.

the clouds only at the end of the battle, but while Kincaid simply describes it as a 'fine summer's evening', Anton declares it 'the setting sun of Napoleon's greatness'. Anton's language can sometimes cause confusion (it is, for example, extremely difficult to tell when in the battle something he is describing is occurring and his descriptions of the deaths of Sir Thomas Picton and Sir William Ponsonby and the loss of the Marquess of Anglesey's leg makes it sound as if all three events occurred simultaneously) but it also lends his moments of personal recollection a great deal of power. His description of the night after the battle is particularly evocative, combining harsh realities with the dreams of the common soldier:

> Hail, blessed night! Thou art as welcome to the victorious soldier as rest is to the weary traveller, and thy grateful shade gives to his toils a momentary respite, while deeply immersed in sleep he dreams of all his bygone dangers, and thinks that years have passed since the bloody fray, and that he now sits beside the cheerful hearth, telling the wondrous tale to the listening villagers, while their little urchins cling round his knee and think him a great man: so at least he imagines; till starting in the midst of his supposed narration, he finds himself cold and cheerless on the battle-field.[110]

While not as clear or consistent as Kincaid or Leach in its descriptions of the battlefield, Anton's style is just as effective at establishing his eyewitness bona fides. Like the two rifle officers, he uses that position to grant weight to his own opinions and assertions, especially, as noted, those regarding discipline and punishment. He does not, however, seek to use that same heft to claim or defend a particular stance on the ownership of the battle. Anton's discussions of Britain's allies lack the agenda that is clear in both *Adventures in the Rifle Brigade* and *Rough Sketches of the Life of an Old Soldier*, while the memoir as a whole is missing the obviously well-rehearsed arguments about Wellington's actions and the correct way to distribute the glory of the day. In their place, rather fittingly, we find compassion for the common soldier and his family, phrased in such a way that encouraged his readers to consider not who owned Waterloo, but what was lost in the victory. The 'sense of feeling' of those lying wounded 'still exists, and warns them that death is nigh; their bed, the miry ground; thirst intolerable demands a cooling draught... [but] no drink is here unmixed with blood, no friendly foot steps over this gory field... Death, friendly death, how welcome art thou now!' Thus, 'night passes over the groaning field of Waterloo'. Even as the reader considers the near-apocalyptic sight of a field of victory, Anton turns his pen (and his readers' thoughts) to those waiting at home. 'Ye near relations of those

---

[110] Anton, *Retrospect of a Military Life*, 206, 213, 217–18.

who are stretched lifeless on this field of Europe's freedom, of Britain's glory, does sleep hover round the pillow of your repose? ... Soon, very soon, shall the joyful post appear with the glorious tidings of victory to the arms of Britain, but gloomy tidings he brings to you whose friends lie slain on the field of battle. No answer shall be returned to your letter.'[111]

In perhaps the most striking demonstration of the realities of military life, shortly after recording his thoughts on grief in a moment of victory Anton returns his narrative to the day-to-day realities of the campaign. After Waterloo the 42nd made their way to Paris with the rest of the army before returning to Britain via Calais. They marched the length of England, feted at every halt, eventually returning to Edinburgh, where they were greeted by 'the most distinguished reception that ever a regiment had met with from a grateful country' and were offered, along with access to other celebrations, two days of free admission to the Edinburgh Waterloo Panorama discussed in Chapter 4.[112] The regiment spent the next decade putting down riots and disturbances, first in Glasgow and then in Ireland. In 1825 they were dispatched to the British holdings in the Mediterranean, spending six years as part of the Gibraltar garrison before moving further east to Malta. It was in Malta that Anton's health began to deteriorate. 'Racked with painful stitches, and unable to perform the duties of [his] situation' he was pensioned out in 1833, aged 45, with an official diagnosis of 'chronic rheumatism', and retired, as noted above, to Edinburgh.[113] His memoir was published in the same city seven years later.

Retrospect of a Military Life was immediately well received, with demand driving a second edition within a year of the first. Popular opinion was echoed by the press, which noted with approval Anton's conservative leanings, modest character, and the relative uniqueness of an enlisted memoir. *Chambers' Journal* 'recommend[ed] this little unpretending volume to public notice', declaring that 'animation is indeed carried to poetry in some parts of the narrative'.[114] *The Monthly Review* described it as an 'excellent picture of a common soldier ... welcomed [it] not merely as in some respects a novelty, but as containing an instructive narrative', and highlighted its excellent qualities in a long review. Chief amongst these qualities was the author himself, whose 'perfect feeling of obedience to superior authority, the earnestness with which he regards regularity and strict discipline, and the patience with which he underwent hardships' prompted *The Monthly Review* to 'pronounce the Quarter-master Serjeant to have been made of the best sort of metal that even a Wellington ever commanded'.[115] The *Caledonian*

---

[111] Anton, *Retrospect of a Military Life*, 216, 218.
[112] Anton, *Retrospect of a Military Life*, 252–3.
[113] Anton, *Retrospect of a Military Life*, 394; Admission Records for the Royal Hospital Chelsea, 14 August 1833, London, National Archives, WO 23/4, p. 107.
[114] Quoted in 'A Military Life', *Belfast News-Letter*, 8 December 1840, p. 3.
[115] Article V, *The Monthly Review*, March 1841, 341–3.

Mercury, in a review of the book's second edition in August 1841, expressed delight at the public's 'cordial and encouraging...reception' of 'this unpretending volume' with a 'vein of sterling good sense and honourable feeling [that] runs through the whole narrative'. Seizing on the same themes as *The Monthly Review*, Edinburgh's leading paper praised the work's 'modest and intelligent author', who had taken up residence in their city after his retirement, and recommended the book in particular to young men, for 'while it may be perused with advantage by all ranks and ages, [it] would form a peculiarly attractive and fitting present for youth, that they may see a soldier's life is not a life of indolence and ease'.[116]

Kincaid, Leach, and perhaps most of all Anton succeeded in reminding the British public that there were individuals behind the victory at Waterloo, although it is unclear whether this reminder impacted the balance of ownership claims within the nationalized victory. What is clear is that the various histories and memoirs, along with the other forms of celebration and commemoration discussed throughout this book, did convince the British public that Waterloo was more of a British victory than an allied one, and should be celebrated as such. Many of these works were also commercial successes, most notably 1815's *The Battle of Waterloo* and Kincaid's *Adventures in the Rifle Brigade*, which may have gone some way towards creating a new Victorian style of military memoir and novel.[117] As important as money may have been to retired soldiers, however, the memoirs served another purpose as well: they were a link to their military pasts, not only in the sense of celebrating past glories, but also as a way to ease into their new civilian lives after sometimes decades in uniform while keeping some ties to their previous careers and institutions.

---

[116] 'Literature', *Caledonian Mercury*, 9 August 1841, p. 3.
[117] See Ramsey, *The Military Memoir and Romantic Literary Culture*, chapter 6.

2

'The great English pilgrimage'

Battlefield Tourism, Relics, and
Ownership of the Field

The first tourists arrived at the battlefield of Waterloo before word reached Britain
of the victory. Alexander Cavalié Mercer, a British artillery officer, recorded that
he and his troop had not yet finished breakfast on the morning after the battle
when a carriage arrived from Brussels with civilians determined to 'examine the
field'. One of the tourists, 'a smartly-dressed middle-aged man, in a high cocked-
hat', approached Mercer and his troop 'stepping carefully to avoid . . . polluting the
glossy silken hose that clothed his nether limbs', and asked for details about the
end of the battle. Holding a 'delicately white perfumed handkerchief to his nose'
against the overwhelming odours of war, and looking around in horror at the
bodies, the tourist learned what he could from Mercer before following his
companions towards the Chateau Hougoumont. Mercer deliberately highlights
the contrast between the 'frightful figures' of himself and his men, 'begrimed and
blackened with blood and smoke', sitting on discarded cuirasses and eating their
first meal in three days, and the tourists, one of whom he likens to a Shakespearian
fop, picking their way carefully across the battlefield. For all his sardonic humour,
there is no indication that Mercer was aware that he had witnessed the start of a
tradition that would become an integral part of nineteenth-century British continental tourism.[1]

Waterloo became a touristic phenomenon thanks to a number of factors.
Waterloo's status as a household name and its position within the modern
creation myth of imperial Great Britain guaranteed some interest, but it was its
proximity to Britain, and thus the relative cheapness of getting there, that ensured
a sizeable number of those who wanted to visit, could. The end of the Napoleonic
Wars saw the reopening of the Continent to British travellers, and the Channel
ports suddenly witnessed a large increase in traffic. Some of these travellers were
upper-class, taking the opportunity to reinvigorate the eighteenth-century notion

---

[1] Alexander Cavalie Mercer, *Journal of the Waterloo Campaign, Kept Throughout the Campaign of
1815* (Edinburgh & London: William Blackwood and Sons, 1870), I: 345–6. James Anton, whose
memoir was discussed in Chapter 1, also records tourists arriving the next day 'to pick up some
fragment as a memorial of the battle'. James Anton, *Retrospect of a Military Life, During the Most
Eventful Periods of the Last War* (Edinburgh: W. H. Lizars, 1841), 219.

Who Owned Waterloo? Battle, Memory, and Myth in British History, 1815–1852. Luke Reynolds, Oxford University Press.
© Luke Reynolds 2022. DOI: 10.1093/oso/9780192864994.003.0003

of the 'Grand Tour', but they were joined by a new stratum of middle-class tourists, indulging in opportunities not only for travel itself, but also for the sense of social advancement that came with it.[2] The proximity of the new kingdom of the Netherlands (and Belgium itself, independent after 1830) meant that it was an ideal choice for a continental sojourn, and historians estimate that by the 1830s, between 50,000 and 100,000 Britons a year were making the ferry crossings to Ostend and Antwerp.[3] The fashionableness of Brussels, the prevalence of a British-esque industrial revolution, and the liberal nature of the constitution Belgium adopted in the 1830s gave the trip even more allure, as many Britons saw Belgium as a 'Little Britain'.[4] For those visiting Brussels or planning to, there was immense pressure to visit Waterloo, and it soon became a near-mandatory day trip from the Belgian capital.

The social and patriotic pressure to visit Waterloo shaped how British tourists experienced and interacted with the battlefield. Within a few years of the battle, an accepted way of 'doing Waterloo' emerged, a self-reinforcing homogenization driven by the need of British tourists not just to visit Waterloo, but to be seen to visit Waterloo. That same need drove the flourishing of the relics trade and several distinct forms of performative tourism that, together, lent near-religious fervour to a secular pilgrimage. At their most extreme, British interactions with the field evoked imperialistic ownership as tourists, authors, and guides staked a physical claim to several acres of another European nation's sovereign soil. To explore these interactions more fully, this chapter will follow the same route as British tourists did on an excursion to Waterloo, via a composite narrative journey drawn from a variety of travelogues. It will then examine some of the works and individuals that shaped British expectations, including Walter Scott, Robert Southey, and Lord Byron; the most popular travel guide of the day, John Murray's *A Hand-Book for Travellers on the Continent*; and Sergeant Major Edward Cotton, a veteran of the battle and Waterloo's most famous tour guide. From there it will discuss a variety of relics on display and for sale, from teeth and buttons to the Waterloo Elm and the Marquess of Anglesey's leg, as well as other forms of performative tourism, many of which reinforce the religious similarities. Finally, it will build on the notions of societal pressure, performative tourism, and

[2] James Buzzard, *The Beaten Track: European Tourism, Literature, and the Ways to Culture, 1800–1918* (Oxford: Oxford University Press, 1993); Pieter Francois, 'If it's 1815, This Must be Belgium: The Origins of the Modern Travel Guide', *Book History* 15 (2012): 71–92; Pieter Francois, '"The Best Way to See Waterloo is with your Eyes Shut": British "Histourism", Authenticity and Commercialism in the Mid-Nineteenth Century', *Anthropological Journal of European Cultures* 22, no. 1 (2013): 25–41; Philip Shaw, *Waterloo and the Romantic Imagination* (London: Palgrave Macmillan, 2002), chapter 2.

[3] John Pimlott, *The Englishman's Holiday: A Social History* (London: Faber and Faber, 1947), 189; John Pemble, *The Mediterranean Passion: Victorians and Edwardians in the South* (Oxford: Clarendon Press, 1987), 1.

[4] Francois, '"The Best Way to See Waterloo"', 31.

pilgrimage to address the deliberately created and maintained notion of physical British ownership of the field, despite its location in a different country.

The village of Waterloo is some ten miles from Brussels, and the battlefield another two miles beyond that, and carriages were the easiest and most popular way to get there (see Figure 2.1).[5] Most excursions left in the morning and returned either before or after dinner.[6] Early tourists needed to hire a carriage, with the price ranging from 25 to 30 francs, including gratuity.[7] As it became clear that Waterloo tourism would become a minor industry, shuttle services emerged, including one run by two Englishmen and boasting two British-made four-horse mail coaches, with round-trip tickets costing a more reasonable 5 francs.[8] This particular service boasted staggered departures (the *Warrior* departed at 9 a.m., the *Victoria* at 10 a.m.), stops at all of the fashionable hotels, and a branch service from the village of Mount St John to the Chateau of Hougoumont, so visitors could see the battlefield without tiring or exposing themselves to inclement weather. The mail coaches became so popular that *Bradshaw's Hand-Book* recommended purchasing tickets for whatever day suited 'immediately [upon] arrival in Brussels'.[9]

After boarding their coaches, tourists rode through Brussels and out via the Namur Gate and headed south.[10] The road south was relatively straight, and about 40 or 50 feet wide. Only the centre 10–20-foot strip was paved, however, the rest was a dirt or mud track, depending on the weather.[11] The road was a toll road, with collection points at every league, but most excursions to the field factored the tolls into the overall price for the hiring of a carriage.[12] After passing through Brussels' suburbs, and journeying three or four miles, the road entered the forest of Soignes.[13] The forest, which several visitors, including Byron, link with the better-known Ardennes, was a well-manicured and extensive beech forest, and hemmed in the road tightly on either side. Reactions to the forest varied, from

[5] 'A Visit to Waterloo', *The Pocket Magazine of Classic and Polite Literature* (London: James Robins and Co, 1829), II: 126–7.

[6] Robert Hills departed at 9 a.m., while P. T. Barnum and his companions, in order to be back by their afternoon show, were forced to set out at 4 a.m. Robert Hills, *Sketches in Flanders and Holland; with some account of a Tour Through Parts of Those Countries, Shortly After the Battle of Waterloo; in a Series of Letters to a Friend* (London: J. Haines and J. Turner, 1816), 76; Phineas Taylor Barnum, *Life of P. T. Barnum* (London: Sampson Low, Son, & Co., 1855), 242.

[7] Hills, *Sketches in Flanders and Holland*, 75; Anne Laura Thorold, *Letters from Brussels, in the Summer of 1835* (London: Longman, Rees, Orme, Brown, Green, and Longman, 1835), 272–3.

[8] George Bradshaw, *Bradshaw's Illustrated Hand-Book for Belgium and the Rhine* (London: W. J. Adams, 1853), 40.

[9] Bradshaw, *Bradshaw's Illustrated Hand-Book for Belgium and the Rhine*, 40.

[10] Thorold, *Letters from Brussels*, 273; George Saint George, *A Saunter in Belgium in the Summer of 1835; with Traits, Historical and Descriptive* (London: F. C. Westley, 1836), 362; 'A Visit to Waterloo', *The Pocket Magazine*, 1829, II: 126.

[11] James Simpson, *A Visit to Flanders in July, 1815, Being Chiefly an Account of the Field of Waterloo* (Edinburgh: William Blackwood, 1816), 62.

[12] Thomas Pennington, *A Journey into Various Parts of Europe* (London: George B. Whittaker, 1825), II: 578; Hills, *Sketches in Flanders and Holland*, 75.

[13] The spelling of the forest's name varies from account to account, in all likelihood because most chroniclers only ever heard it spoken. For that reason, this work will use the modern spelling.

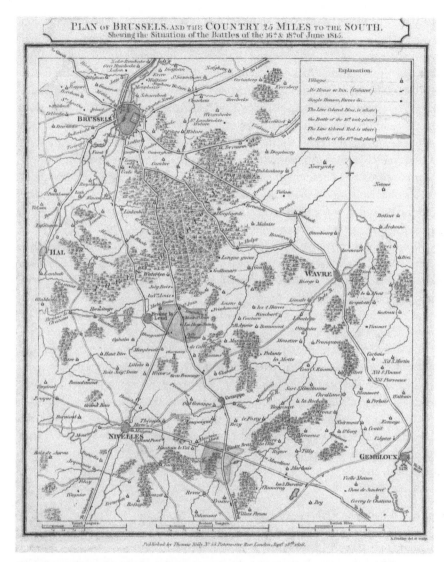

Figure 2.1 *Plan of Brussels and the Country 25 Miles to the South. Shewing the Situation of the Battles of the 16th & 18th of June 1815* (London: Thomas Kelly, 1816) courtesy State Library Victoria.

those who considered it 'delightful' and welcomed its shade to those that declared it 'awful'.[14] For many visitors, the forest presented an opportunity to ruminate on

[14] Wemyss Dalrymple, *The Economist's New Brussels Guide Containing a Short Account of Antwerp Malines, etc.* (Brussels: W. Todd, 1839), 121; William Makepeace Thackeray, *Little Travels and Roadside Sketches* (London: Smith, Elder, & Co., 1879), 332; 'A Visit to Waterloo', *The Pocket Magazine*, II: 126; Simpson, *A Visit to Flanders*, 61.

the past. The wood of the Soignes forest had been commandeered by Napoleon earlier in the war to help build his great invasion fleet at Boulogne, and some could not divorce the forest from the threat of invasion, although they did delight in the fact that the wood that had once built French ships later guarded the back of a British army.[15] Despite the naval implications of Soignes, more visitors were struck by the fact that their army had travelled the same road they were now on. As Charlotte Eaton (née Waldie) noted in 1817, 'it was impossible to retrace without emotion the very road by which our brave troops had marched out to battle ... and by which thousands had been brought back, covered with wounds, in pain and torture'.[16] These emotions were highlighted by visitors' mental images of the chaotic nature of the road during and after the battle, choked with the baggage and the wounded of the allied army. For some time after, the graves of men and horses, and the detritus of war, were clear along the route.[17]

From Soignes, carriages emerged into the village of Waterloo, still two miles from the battlefield itself. Descriptions of the village vary largely depending on when a person visited it. The evolution of Waterloo village is a clear example of how the tourist trade benefited this portion of rural Belgium, and how the area's residents embraced it. Early visitors describe the village as 'naked and wretched', a 'poor, straggling, dirty village', with 'nothing to recommend it' on its own merits.[18] By 1836, however, Murray's *Hand-Book for Travellers* informed its readers that Waterloo had expanded to the point where it was almost joined to Mont St Jean, the hamlet on the edge of the battlefield.[19] Benjamin Silliman, an American who toured Europe in 1851, noted 'many new houses, and among them some beautiful dwellings, have sprung up, evincing a degree of prosperity which is, doubtless, due, in a great measure, to the celebrity conferred by the great battle upon a village formerly of little importance'.[20] The villagers were aware of the benefits of the battlefield, and did their best to take advantage of them. Many earned their living as guides or relic hunters, or by catering to tourists' other needs. They also went

[15] Wood from the Soignes forest had also been used in 'Napoleon's naval schemes at Antwerp'. Simpson, *A Visit to Flanders*, 61; Hills, *Sketches in Flanders and Holland*, 76; James Simpson, *Paris After Waterloo* (Edinburgh: William Blackwood and Sons, 1853), 27.

[16] Charlotte Anne Eaton, *Narrative of a Residence in Belgium During the Campaign of 1815* (London: John Murray, 1817), 248–9. See also 'A Visit to Waterloo', *The Pocket Magazine*, II: 126; Thomas Dyke, *Travelling Mems During a Tour Through Belgium, Rhenish Prussia, Germany, Switzerland, and France, in the Summer and Autumn of 1832: Including an Excursion up the Rhine* (London: Longman, Rees, Orme, Brown, Green, & Longman, 1834), I: 10–11.

[17] Hills, *Sketches in Flanders and Holland*, 77–8; Simpson, *Paris After Waterloo*, 27–8; Simpson, *A Visit to Flanders*, 62–3; Eaton, *Narrative of a Residence in Belgium*, 255–8.

[18] Henry Crabb Robinson, *Diary, Reminiscences, and Correspondence of Henry Crabb Robinson*, ed. Thomas Sadler (Boston: Houghton, Mifflin and Co., 1898), 319; Robert Bell, *Wayside Pictures Through France, Belgium, and Holland* (London: Richard Bentley, 1849), 410; 'A Visit to Waterloo', *The Pocket Magazine*, II: 126.

[19] John Murray, *A Hand-Book for Travellers on the Continent: Being a Guide Through Holland, Belgium, Prussia, and Northern Germany, and Along the Rhine, from Holland to Switzerland* (London: John Murray and Son, 1836), 143.

[20] Benjamin Silliman, *A Visit to Europe in 1851* (New York: G. P. Putnam & Co., 1854), II: 359.

out of their way to maintain the visible links to the past. The villagers did their best to preserve the quartermaster's chalk markings on their doorways, which marked certain houses as the temporary residences of the commanding officers and staffs of the allied army.[21] As the chalk marks inevitably faded over the years, they were replaced by more permanent markers on walls and doors.[22] The inn in the village continued its trade, and many tourists were delighted to take coffee or a meal in the same building where Wellington wrote his Waterloo dispatch.[23]

Waterloo's village church became another focal point for visitors. The church was described as 'elegant, with a handsome dome', and was, thanks to its height, often the first glimpse of the village that travellers had.[24] Its main attraction to tourists, however, was not its picturesque aspect or exterior, but the 'marble tablets to the memory of those who fell in the contest'.[25] These varied in nature, some marked individual deaths while others recorded all the officers of that regiment who fell.[26] More and more of these were erected over time, or replaced as the damp and wear obliterated the names carved into them.[27] The majority of the markers were dedicated to British officers, but some accounts also mention Dutch, German, and French memorials.[28] Having been presented with the first physical evidence of the horrors of the battle in the form of these monuments, tourists then continued on to the actual field of battle, either on foot or once again in their carriages.[29]

Reactions to the field of battle, as with Waterloo village, changed over time. Those who arrived soon after 18 June 1815 were greeted by 'fields then laid waste ... the ground trampled on, and black with thousands of military hats and caps scattered about, and cut in pieces, appearing at a distance like a herd of crows in pursuit of carrion ... bones, and flesh of horses, the dead half-buried', or, shortly after, 'a long line of immense fresh-made graves'.[30] Within two months,

---

[21] Simpson, A Visit to Flanders, 63–4.

[22] John Ashton, Rough Notes of a Visit to Belgium, Sedan, and Paris in September 1870–71 (London: Henry S. King & Co., 1873), 15.

[23] Zachariah Allen, Sketches of the State of the Useful Arts and of Society, scenery, in Great-Britain, France and Holland. Or, The Practical Tourist (Boston: Carter, Hendee & Co. 1833), II: 182; Robinson, Diary, Reminiscences, and Correspondence, 319; Hills, Sketches in Flanders and Holland, 79; John Scott, Journal of a Tour to Waterloo and Paris, in Company with Sir Walter Scott in 1815 (London: Saunders and Otley, 1842), 44.

[24] Bradshaw, Bradshaw's Illustrated Hand-Book for Belgium and the Rhine, 41; Pennington, A Journey into Various Parts of Europe, II: 581–2; Hills, Sketches in Flanders and Holland, 79.

[25] Bradshaw, Bradshaw's Illustrated Hand-Book for Belgium and the Rhine, 41.

[26] Silliman, A Visit to Europe, II: 364–5; Thackeray, Little Travels and Roadside Sketches, 334; Robinson, Diary, Reminiscences, and Correspondence, 319–20.

[27] 'A Visit to Waterloo', The Pocket Magazine, II: 130.

[28] Bell, Wayside Pictures, 410; George Augustus Sala, Waterloo to the Peninsula: Four Months' Hard Labour in Belgium, Holland, Germany, and Spain (London: Tinsley Brothers, 1867), I: 14.

[29] Scott, Journal of a Tour to Waterloo and Paris, 45; Sala, Waterloo to the Peninsula, I: 18; Simpson, A Visit to Flanders, 65.

[30] William Rae Wilson, Travels in Norway, Sweden, Denmark, Hanover, Germany, Netherlands, &c. (London: Longman, Rees, Orme, Brown, and Green, 1826), 533–6; Eaton, Narrative of a Residence in Belgium, 262–3.

most of the discarded matériel of war had been cleaned up, but there were still indications of what had occurred. Henry Crabb Robinson visited on 14 August 1815 and noted that there were still 'arms of trees hanging down, shattered by cannonballs, and not yet cut off. And there were ruined and burnt cottages in many places, and marks of bullets and balls on both houses and trees.'[31] By the end of the decade, however, the battlefield had changed. William Rae Wilson, who visited only a few days after the battle and again in the 1820s, 'could not fail to remark the contrast between its appearance then and at present'. Where before had been a 'field of blood' was now one of 'silent tranquillity ... most of the fields were covered with crops, and the husbandman was moving along slowly with the plough'.[32] There were still signs if one knew where to look. Zachariah Allen spotted skulls still on the field in 1833, and the crops presented their own memorial: 'the fertility of the ground on which the battle was fought increased greatly for several years after it took place. No where were richer crops produced in the whole of Belgium, and the corn is said to have waved thickest, and to have been of a darker colour, over those spots where the dead were interred, so that in spring it was possible to discover them by this mark alone.'[33] By the next decade, however, even those marks had faded. 'There is nothing left of Waterloo,' lamented Robert Bell in 1849, 'you will see nothing in the whole outspread scene but a monotonous, dead level, hardly relieved by an undulation, and dotted only at great intervals with a few trees that have a heart-broken air of funereal loneliness.'[34]

One of the few exceptions to this monotony was the Chateau of Hougoumont, which anchored the changing battlefield to its history just as diligently as it had once anchored the allied right. As such, it quickly became a focus of the tour of the field. 'The most interesting part of the field', reported one account, 'is the Chateau de Huguemont', presenting 'the most evident traces of the effects of war.'[35] Hougoumont had been at the centre of extremely heavy fighting during the battle and had subsequently not been repaired. For British tourists, this added to its charm. Not only did the ruins of Hougoumont stand as testament to the brutal nature of the battle and thus the greatness of the allied victory, but it also appealed to the Victorian mania for ruins in general, bringing Waterloo in line with great

[31] Robinson, *Diary, Reminiscences, and Correspondence*, 319.   [32] Wilson, *Travels*, 533–5.
[33] Allen, *Sketches of the State of the Useful Arts*, II: 184–5; John Murray, *Murray's Handbook for Belgium and the Rhine* (London: John Murray, 1852), 80. This last may be apocryphal. One visitor in 1870 reported that 'the extra fertility it is said to have manifested after the burial of the dead, and the darker spots, real or imaginary, in the corn in those places where the bodies lay thickest—an idea which our great novelist adopted in his "Battle of Life"—must long ago have faded out.' Ashton, *Rough Notes of a Visit to Belgium*, 168–9. There is, however, some evidence that bones from Waterloo were dug up and imported to Britain as fertilizer. See Edward J. Russell, *The Fertility of the Soil* (Cambridge: Cambridge University Press, 1921), 58.
[34] Bell, *Wayside Pictures*, 405–6.
[35] 'A Visit to Waterloo', *The Pocket Magazine*, II: 128–9; Allen, *Sketches of the State of the Useful Arts*, II: 187–8.

classical victories like Marathon.[36] Additionally, Hougoumont allowed tourists to leave their mark on Waterloo. It became customary to write one's name on the walls of the chateau's chapel, a practice encouraged by the fact that a visitor could find the signatures of Byron, Southey, and Wordsworth mixed in with 'millions of names, addresses, and dates in every known language'.[37] George Sala reported that the chapel walls were freshly whitewashed every five years 'but six months afterwards the walls are covered again with names as thick as peas', with some more creative tourists attaching charcoal or pencils to walking sticks or parasols, or mounting ladders borrowed from local farmers, to sign their names up to fifteen feet up the walls.[38] From Hougoumont, tourists usually returned to their carriages and either dined in Waterloo, at the inn at La Belle Alliance on the French side of the valley (and where, per legend and local inscriptions, Wellington and Blücher met), or journeyed back to Brussels itself for their evening meal, content that they had fulfilled their patriotic obligations and 'done' Waterloo.[39]

For all their speed of arrival, the itinerary of those first tourists described by Alexander Cavalié Mercer closely matched what would become the standard. They arrived from Brussels along the same road through the Soignes forest (which must have been an unpleasant drive, considering the amount of baggage and wounded going the other way), passed inevitably through Waterloo village, arrived on the field, examined it briefly, and then made a beeline for the Chateau of Hougoumont.[40] The only thing that would have been lacking were services that catered for the tourist traffic, which would arrive soon after those first tourists.[41]

A number of written works and individuals shaped both the anticipation of the journey to Waterloo and the experience itself. Waterloo attracted its fair share of celebrity guests, and three produced written works which became a part of the battlefield tourism experience. In late July of 1815, Walter Scott embarked on a trip to the continent to visit the battlefield and the allied armies stationed in Paris. Scott was the first celebrity to visit the battlefield, and his trip eventually produced three works: his anonymous epistolary work *Paul's Letters to his Kinsfolk*,

---

[36] Ashton, *Rough Notes of a Visit to Belgium*, 16–18; Bell, *Wayside Pictures*, 405; George Gordon Byron, 'Childe Harold's Pilgrimage', in *The Poetical Works of Lord Byron* (Boston: James R. Osgood and Co., 1874), IV: 167n. See also Stuart Semmel, 'Reading the Tangible Past: British Tourism, Collecting, and Memory after Waterloo', *Representations* 69 (Winter 2000); Francois, '"The Best Way to See Waterloo"'; A. V. Seaton, 'War and Thanatourism: Waterloo 1815–1914', *Annals of Tourism Research* 26, no. 1 (1999): 130–58; John Carman and Patricia Carman, *Battlefields from Event to Heritage* (Oxford: Oxford University Press, 2020).

[37] Sala, *Waterloo to the Peninsula*, I: 22; 'A Visit to Waterloo', *The Pocket Magazine*, II: 128–9; Murray, *A Hand-Book for Travellers on the Continent*, 147; Bell, *Wayside Pictures*, 412–13.

[38] Sala, *Waterloo to the Peninsula*, I: 22.

[39] Bradshaw, *Bradshaw's Illustrated Hand-Book for Belgium and the Rhine*, 43–4; Rajah Ram Chuttraputtee, *Diary of the Late Rajah of Kolhapoor*, ed. Edward W. West (London: Smith, Elder & Co., 1872), 78. See section on British obligations to Waterloo, below.

[40] Mercer, *Journal of the Waterloo Campaign*, I: 345–6.

[41] For an edited narrative of the experience of several of those first tourists, see Louise Allen, *To the Field of Waterloo: The First Battlefield Tourists 1815–1816* (Norfolk: Louise Allen, 2015).

published in 1816; John Scott's *Journal of a Tour to Waterloo and Paris, in Company with Sir Walter Scott in 1815*, published after John Scott's death in 1842; and the purported purpose of the trip, *The Field of Waterloo*, an epic poem published under his own name in 1815. *The Field of Waterloo* was eagerly anticipated, and the *Caledonian Mercury* carried the announcement of its forth-coming publication before Scott had even left Britain, and well before a single word of it had been written.[42] The buzz for the poem was further encouraged by the fact that Scott was donating his profits from the sales of the first edition to the Waterloo Fund. Scott was a proud supporter of the British military. His elder brother and son were both soldiers, and Scott himself, despite lameness from an early childhood bout with polio, was instrumental in the foundation of the Royal Edinburgh Volunteer Light Dragoons, a militia cavalry regiment (whose uniform he wore when he attended a dinner given in Paris by Lord Cathcart in honour of Tsar Alexander I).[43]

Paul's Letters to his Kinsfolk is made up of sixteen letters addressed to Paul's sister Margaret, two cousins, one named Peter and the other simply described as 'The Major', a friend referred to as '——, Esq., of ——', and finally to a friend in the church. Scott uses these varied recipients to address different subjects. To Margaret, he writes of tourism, travel, and general interest; to Peter, continental politics; to the Major and the Reverend, military and religious affairs, respectively; and to Paul's friend ——, Esq., statistics. Waterloo is covered in letters VIII and IX (V–VII discuss Napoleon's advance into Belgium and the other battles of the Waterloo campaign); the first to the Major and the second to Margaret. The letter to the Major, although it starts with a brief description of the journey from Brussels to the field, is, in fact, a well-written and relatively comprehensive narrative of the battle, complete with anecdotes. Scott is almost exclusively concerned with 18 June but does add a few details so that visitors to the battlefield can find locations and thus read his narrative in place.[44] Letter IX, to Margaret, is an account of visiting the battlefield. It touches on many of the traditional facets of narratives of Waterloo tourism, most notably relics and relic hunters, and Paul discusses his purchases and the differences in price between relics purchased on the field, in Brussels, and in Birmingham. Scott purchased his fair share of relics from the field, but the one he (through his avatar Paul) was most fascinated by was a manuscript collection of French songs, 'stained by blood and clay'. It was the palpable authenticity and individuality of the papers that fascinated Scott (as the battlefield letters found by William Rae Wilson discussed later in the chapter

[42] 'In the Press', *Caledonian Mercury*, 31 July 1815, issue 14609, p. 1.
[43] Paul O'Keeffe, General Introduction to *Scott on Waterloo*, by Walter Scott (London: Vintage Books, 2015), 1–10.
[44] Walter Scott, *Paul's Letters to his Kinsfolk*, in *Scott on Waterloo*, 103–37.

fascinated him), and he fills the latter half of his letter to Margaret and its postscript with quoted ballads.[45]

Scott's *The Field of Waterloo* is an epic poem of twenty-three stanzas with an additional six-stanza conclusion. Scott drew from his own experiences visiting the battlefield and supplemented it with details obtained from his guides and various witnesses he met in Paris, including Wellington himself. The poem was finally published in October of 1815, and, despite great public anticipation, was widely lambasted by critics. *The Critical Review*, in a six-page excoriation, dismissed it as 'absolutely the poorest, dullest, least interesting composition' Scott had yet produced, and noted his 'obvious and incessant . . . alliterative imitation of Lord Byron'.[46] They dismissed the usefulness of the poem for educational purposes, noting that the official gazette was far more informative, and even negatively compared the poem's style to Wellington's 'modest dispatches'.[47] Britain's literati joined in *The Critical Review*'s drubbing, with Thomas, Baron Erskine penning perhaps the most damning condemnation:

> On Waterloo's ensanguined plain
> Lie tens of thousands of the slain;
> But none, by sabre or by shot,
> Fell half so flat as Walter Scott.[48]

For Scott, fully aware of the vast suffering and loss of life endured by Waterloo's 'tens of thousands', that quatrain must have cut particularly close to the bone. He redeemed his reputation somewhat by reminding his public that he was donating his share of the profits to the Waterloo Fund, but when the British public looked to him as a battlefield guide, it was his anonymous *Paul's Letters to his Kinsfolk* that they chose, not his signed epic poem.

Following on Walter Scott's heels in September 1815 came Britain's Poet Laureate, Robert Southey. Southey had begun his literary career as a radical but had gradually become more conservative. By the time he left for the Continent, his politics were relatively close to Scott's, although in Southey's case tinged by a virulent strain of anti-Gallicism (and especially anti-Bonapartism).[49] Southey's politics are on full display in his 1816 composition, *The Poet's Pilgrimage to Waterloo*. Composed entirely in sestains, the poem is divided into two sections, 'A journey to the scene of war' and an allegorical condemnation of French politics

---

[45] Walter Scott, *Paul's Letters to his Kinsfolk*, in *Scott on Waterloo*, 137–54.

[46] 'Scott's Field of Waterloo', *The Critical Review* Series V: II: 5 (November 1815): 459.

[47] 'Scott's Field of Waterloo', *The Critical Review* Series V: II: 5 (November 1815): 459.

[48] Thomas Erskine, quoted in John Lord Campbell, *The Lives of the Lord Chancellors and Keepers of the Great Seal of England* (Philadelphia: Blanchard and Lea, 1851), VI: 518.

[49] Shaw, *Waterloo and the Romantic Imagination*, 33–4, also chapter 3; David Eastwood, 'Robert Southey and the Meaning of Patriotism', *Journal of British Studies* 31, no. 3 (July 1992): 265–87; Carl Woodring, 'Three Poets on Waterloo', *The Wordsworth Circle* 18, no. 2 (Spring 1987): 54–7.

'from Mirabeau to Buonaparte'.[50] In addition to condemning the French Revolution and the empire that followed it, Southey uses the poem to justify Britain's primacy not only through the nation's martial victories but also through its moral enlightenment.[51] It is the first part of Southey's pilgrimage, however, that concerns us. Starting with the Channel crossing, Southey guides his readers from Ostend to Brussels and onwards to the battlefield. The work explicitly reinforces British experiences and expectations in several ways. First, Southey's route, not only from Ostend to Brussels but also from Brussels to 'the field of blood', echoes the route discussed at the beginning of this chapter—the route taken by most British visitors.[52] Southey travels through Soignes to the village of Waterloo, pays his respects at the Waterloo church, and then ventures on to the battlefield, exploring in turn Hougoumont, La Haye Sainte, and La Belle Alliance.[53] Second, Southey deliberately ties Waterloo to the great battles of the past, arguing that it is only rivalled by Platea and Tours.[54] Finally, through the poem's title and its language, Southey is at least partially responsible for Waterloo's enshrinement as a near-religious experience for the British, who travelled there with the same reverence as continental pilgrims who visited Catholic holy sites.

Not to be outdone by Scott and Southey, Lord Byron visited Waterloo in May 1816 on his way to summer with Percy Shelley in Switzerland and included his thoughts on the battle and the field in the third canto of his *Childe Harold's Pilgrimage*. All three poets shared a sympathy for those who had fallen in the battle, but from there, their views diverge quite strikingly. Southey was growing more conservative as time went on. Scott was a lifelong Tory and a general supporter of the British army and its goals. Byron, by contrast, was a vocal supporter of Napoleon, and viewed the third canto of *Childe Harold's Pilgrimage* as an opportunity to respond to the celebratory poems of Scott and others. The choice to continue his epic work in this way is significant—it was *Childe Harold* that propelled Byron towards literary celebrity, and its third canto (which at this point had been awaited for four years) was sure to command a wide audience. Byron makes several deliberate choices to highlight his views. The most significant is that he does not mention the Duke of Wellington, although he does mention the Duke of Brunswick and his own cousin, Frederick Howard, who died at the battles of Quatre Bras and Waterloo respectively. Byron's 'coverage' of the battle is not focused on glory or the deeds of the many catapulted to fame by the conflict, but on those who fell. 'Stop!' declares the poet, quoting the Roman satirist Juvenal, 'for thy tread is on Empire's dust.' He takes the opportunity of the

---

[50] 'Argument' in Robert Southey, *The Poet's Pilgrimage to Waterloo* (London: Longman, Hurt, Rees, Orme, and Brown, 1816).

[51] Eastwood, 'Robert Southey and Patriotism', 276–7; Woodring, 'Three Poets on Waterloo', 55.

[52] 'The Field of Battle' in Southey, *The Poet's Pilgrimage*, sestain I.

[53] 'The Field of Battle', in Southey, *The Poet's Pilgrimage*, sestains I–LV.

[54] 'Flanders', in Southey, *The Poet's Pilgrimage*, sestains I–IV.

Duchess of Richmond's ball, held in Brussels on the evening of 15 June, to highlight the contrast between the joys of living and the sudden descent into death:

> Last noon beheld them full of lusty life,
> Last eve in Beauty's circle proudly gay,
> The midnight brought the signal sound of strife,
> The morn the marshalling in arms,—the day
> Battle's magnificent stern array!
> The thunder-clouds close o'er it, which when rent
> The earth is cover'd thick with other clay,
> Which her own clay shall cover, heap'd and pent,
> Rider and horse,—friend, foe,—in one red burial blent.

For all his contrarian viewpoint, however, Byron still adheres to some of the standard tropes of visiting and describing Waterloo. He mentions the Soignes forest (although he folds it into the larger Ardennes forest) waving above the allied troops 'her green leaves, | Dewy with nature's tear-drops as they pass, | Grieving, if aught inanimate e'er grieves, | Over the unreturning brave,—alas!' He also comments on the lack of discernible features and monuments on the field, noting that 'no colossal bust | Nor column trophied for triumphal show' mark the battle. Where he does differ from many is that he feels this is appropriate; 'the moral's truth tells simpler so, | As the ground was before, thus let it be.' The stanzas of *Childe Harold* that concern Waterloo are not as rabidly pro-Napoleon as some other chroniclers (although he does refer to the field as 'the grave of France'), but instead give off a resigned bitterness concerning what the battle achieved for all its terrible losses. This is best summed up by the end of stanza 17, where Byron questions whether the only beneficial thing to come out of Waterloo was an increased wheat crop: 'How that red rain hath made the harvest grow! | And is this all the world has gained by thee, | Thou first and last of fields! king-making Victory?' This is a theme he would return to years later in *Don Juan* when, while addressing the Duke of Wellington directly, he demanded, 'And I shall be delighted to learn who, | Save you and yours, have gained by Waterloo.'[55]

For all that Byron sympathized with the French and Napoleon, his work became one of the standards to read before visiting Waterloo and even to refer to while visiting. One guidebook, written by a veteran of the battle, acknowledged

---

[55] George Gordon Byron, *Childe Harold's Pilgrimage: A Romant* (Philadelphia: W. A. Leary & Co., 1852), canto 3: stanzas 17–31, 103–8; George Gordon Byron, *Don Juan* (London: C. Daly, 1852), canto 9: stanza 4, 249; for an example of a pro-Napoleon view of Waterloo, see Orlando Williams Wight, *Peoples and Countries Visited in a Winding Journey Around the World* (Detroit: Raynor & Taylor, 1888), 396; for more on Byron and Waterloo, see Shaw, *Waterloo and the Romantic Imagination*, 165–91; Semmel, 'Reading the Tangible Past'.

that Byron's romanticism might not be for everyone and recommended that 'the more staid traveller' rely on Scott's *Letters* and a map, while leaving Byron to young lady visitors.[56] The most popular guidebook, John Murray's *A Hand-Book for Travellers on the Continent*, sought to appeal to all, including a map of the field and extensive quotations from both Byron and Southey. John Murray III, the well-known London publisher, first produced his *Hand-Book* in 1836 to address 'the want of any tolerable English Guide Book for Europe north of the Alps'. It was organized by region and by city 'hubs' within those regions, as well as by various routes between those hubs. From the beginning, Waterloo was included as a part of Route 25, which outlined the journey from Brussels to Aix La Chapelle, via Waterloo, Namur, Liège, and Spa. The description of Waterloo—both the village and the field—fills some seven pages. The coverage is detailed and written in a clear manner, and landmarks are numbered so they can be found on the accompanying map. The *Hand-Book* quotes extensively from other sources, both poetry and travel narratives. In structure and order, it closely resembles the traditional layout. It starts with Soignes forest, before discussing the village and the church, the field, La Haye Sainte, La Belle Alliance, and finally, Hougoumont. This further cemented that order as the 'correct' order to narrate a visit to Waterloo.[57]

Murray's *Hand-Book* was so popular it became the basis for a franchise, with guides being produced for London and a variety of British counties, all the way out to India, Burma, and Ceylon. Waterloo continued to be included in reprints of *A Hand-Book for Travellers on the Continent*, as well as *Murray's Handbook for Belgium and the Rhine*. William Makepeace Thackeray heartily endorsed the *Hand-Book* in his *Little Travels and Road-Side Sketches*, stating the delight and instruction he had obtained from 'my guide, philosopher, and friend', and noting that 'every English party I saw had this infallible red book in their hands, and gained a vast deal of historical and general information from it'.[58] John Ashton, who visited Waterloo with a party of strangers, recounted that one of the group was 'a spinster of mature years, wearing spectacles and carrying a large guide book, to which she was constantly referring', and who, when their guide was showing them around the battlefield, was 'constantly checking him off by Murray'.[59]

Other visitors, rather than simply using Murray as their guide or employing the *Hand-Book* to check their local guides, looked to the book for advice on finding a reliable one. While the first two editions simply warned that travellers would be

[56] Henry R. Addison, *A Rough Sketch of the Field at Waterloo* (Brussels: Belgian Company of Booksellers, 1842), 10–11.
[57] John Murray, *A Hand-Book for Travellers on the Continent: Being a Guide Through Holland, Belgium, Prussia, and Northern Germany, and Along the Rhine, from Holland to Switzerland* (London: John Murray and Son, 1838).
[58] Thackeray, *Little Travels and Roadside Sketches*, 333; *Hand-Book for Travellers on the Continent*, 151–8.
[59] Ashton, *Rough Notes of a Visit to Belgium*, 14–18.

'assailed' by a profusion of guides, from 1839 on the *Hand-Book* had no hesitation in recommending 'Edward Cotton, late sergeant-major in the 7th hussars ... as the best guide to the field of Waterloo'.[60] Cotton might have been designed for the role. Described as an 'active and intelligent man' who kept his 'full military stature' well into his retirement, he had fought in the battle as a trooper in the 7th Hussars.[61] After rising to the rank of sergeant-major, he had retired and taken up residence in the village of Mount St John around 1835, where he promptly founded a Waterloo museum and established himself as a tour guide.[62] Despite claims from rival Belgian guides that he had not fought in the battle itself and had been ignorant of the campaign until he arrived in Mount St John, Cotton soon became 'the crack guide' in the eyes of his countrymen (it is unclear whether Belgian claims that he was hopelessly biased towards the British were ignored or actively helped establish him).[63]

Cotton's standard tour of the field, which was accompanied by a narrative hailed for its 'energy and animation', rather than 'the parrot eloquence' of a recitation, did its part to further reinforce the standard way of 'doing Waterloo'. Starting at his museum, he would conduct visitors to the top of the Lion Mound, located along what had once been the allied ridge (discussed later in the chapter). From this position, he would 'reconnoitre the most important posts in a bird's-eye view of the field from Mount Saint John, and then fixing upon the spot from whence [Wellington] surveyed the field on the 18th of June', would narrate the campaign. Having taken his audience from the Congress of Vienna to the rout of the French on the evening of the 18th, he would conduct them off the mound and on to Hougoumont.[64]

Sergeant-Major Cotton died on 22 June 1849 and was buried, per his wishes, in Hougoumont's orchard, alongside a number of British soldiers who fell defending the chateau.[65] He left behind two legacies: his Waterloo Museum and his guide-book and narrative of the battle, *A Voice from Waterloo*, first published in 1847. Taken together, along with his decade-and-a-half as a guide, these represent one of the most significant efforts to curate the memory of Waterloo undertaken by an enlisted veteran. What is even more noteworthy, especially in light of the efforts by veteran officers discussed in Chapters 4 and 5, is that he was not challenged in his efforts. Indeed, veteran officers, from Lt General Sir Hussey (later 1st Baron) Vivian to Colonel John Gurwood (Wellington's private secretary) wrote letters

---

[60] *Hand-Book for Travellers on the Continent*, 142; John Murray, *A Hand-Book for Travellers on the Continent: Being a Guide Through Holland, Belgium, Prussia, and Northern Germany, and Along the Rhine, from Holland to Switzerland* (London: John Murray and Son, 1839), 151.

[61] Bell, *Wayside Pictures*, 405; 'Waterloo and its Guide', *Leicester Chronicle*, 22 September 1849, p. 4.

[62] Edward Cotton, *A Voice from Waterloo* (London: B. L. Green, 1849), vii.

[63] 'Travellers' Wonders in Belgium', *Morning Post*, 22 April 1839, p. 2; 'Notes of a Tourist', *Northampton Mercury*, 27 February 1847, p. 4.

[64] 'Waterloo and its Guide', *Leicester Chronicle*, 22 September 1849, p. 4.

[65] *Sheffield Independent*, 14 July 1849, p. 5.

and sent gifts to demonstrate their approval of Cotton and his efforts.[66] Such encomiums, when combined with the sergeant-major's own 'soldierly knowledge and veracity', go a long way towards explaining why, when Cotton presented Robert Bell with some bones he claimed were from one of Waterloo's casualties, the usually cynical Bell 'implicitly believed him'.[67]

Cotton was not alone in offering relics for both display and sale. Indeed, all the guides and travel narratives of Waterloo discussed the profusion of relics and the industries that grew up around them. These can loosely be divided into two types: visitation and collection, and each is worth exploring. Visitation relics are relics located on site that were visited rather than purchased. In this, they closely resemble saints' relics from the Roman Catholic tradition, and indeed, form a crucial part of the similarities between secular British pilgrimage to Waterloo and religious Catholic pilgrimage to the major religious centres of Europe. As with saints' relics, the visitation relics of Waterloo were linked with individuals, in this case, the Duke of Wellington and the Marquess of Anglesey.

The Duke of Wellington's relic was not of his body, but was a tree permanently associated with him. The Wellington Tree was an elm, positioned on the British ridge near where the Namur road crossed a country lane, where, according to several accounts of the battle, Wellington oversaw the beginning of his triumph. Despite several other accounts arguing that the duke had too much tactical sense to place himself out in the open, the tree, and the spot, had become associated with Wellington. Whether or not Wellington took advantage of its shade on 18 June, the tree was an ideal location for tourists to survey the battlefield for the first time. Because of its location on the side of the main road, it was also one of the first landmarks that visitors encountered when they arrived on the field from Waterloo village and was thus often used as a reference point. The site of the tree and its position on the allied ridge is the first point in Murray's *Hand-Book* to be identified by number on the map.[68]

The Wellington Tree was not well treated. It was 'mutilated and stripped by relic hunters' and 'carried off piece-meal' (Figure 2.2).[69] Pieces were kept as simple relics, or carved into works of art, such as a 'Gratitude Pendant', which held a portion of the elm carved into an image of the elm itself (Figure 2.3).[70] Eventually what was left was cut down and sold to John George Children, a former militia officer and Librarian of the British Museum, who happened to be on the battlefield

---

[66] Cotton, Voice from Waterloo, 270–3; *Catalogue of the Late Sergeant-Major Cotton's Waterloo Library and Museum* (Brussels: Combe & Vane Weghe, 1872).

[67] Bell, *Wayside Pictures*, 405–6.

[68] *Hand-Book for Travellers on the Continent*, 153–4; Thorold, *Letters from Brussels in the Summer of 1835*, 276–9; Barnum, *Life of P. T. Barnum*, 243–4.

[69] *Hand-Book for Travellers on the Continent*, 154; Wilson, *Travels*, 533n.

[70] Another piece was carved into a miniature sword blade and fitted into a miniature gold commemorative sword. See Miniature commemorative sword believed to have belonged to Lord Raglan, 1818 (c), London, National Army Museum, NAM. 2014-05-8-1.

Figure 2.2 'The Wellington Tree—Sketched on the Field of Waterloo (1818), The Wellington Tree on the Field of Waterloo', *The Illustrated London News*, 27 November 1852, 469. General Research Division, The New York Public Library. New York Public Library Digital Collections.

Figure 2.3 Gilt metal oval glazed pendant containing a miniature relief carving of The Tree of Observation, laid down on mother of pearl, the reverse of the closed back inscribed 'Part of the Tree of Observation/Wellington/Waterloo/Halkett's/Gratitude/ 18th June 1815', London, The Armoury of St James's.

the day the farmer was removing it.[71] Children commissioned Thomas Chippendale Jr to make two chairs from the wood, one for the prince regent and one for himself (which he later gifted to Wellington), as well as several other keepsakes.[72] The popular rumour that he had 'transferred [the Wellington Tree] to his own garden in England' so incensed Children that he wrote a letter in his own defence to *The Times* arguing that the farmer was going to cut the tree down anyway, as the relic hunters had killed it, and were trampling so much of his corn crop in their effort to get to it, 'that the produce of half an acre of land was annually lost in consequence'.[73] Unworked pieces of 'arbor Vellingtoniensis', as the *Royal Cornwall Gazette* christened it, were valued as relics, but the wood was also 'hacked and twisted...into toothpicks and snuff-boxes' and 'different devices', to be 'retained as a memorial of the battle'.[74] Even after it had been removed, guidebooks and visitors' accounts continued to use the spot where the Wellington Tree had stood as a landmark to orient visitors to the battlefield, and usually commented in passing on the sad story of the fate of the tree.[75]

The other visitation relic worth discussing in detail is the Marquess of Anglesey's leg. Anglesey, then known as the Earl of Uxbridge, commanded the allied cavalry at Waterloo, and led the charge of the heavy cavalry (comprising the Household Brigade and the Union Brigade), which routed the French I Corps, captured the eagle of the *45éme ligne*, and was later immortalized in part by Elizabeth Thompson's 1881 painting *Scotland Forever!* One of the last cannonballs fired by the French guns in the battle shattered his right knee, and his leg was amputated several hours after the battle.[76] Uxbridge was made the Marquess of Anglesey a few weeks after the battle, and served in various government positions,

[71] 'The Lion of Waterloo', *The Mirror of Literature, Amusement, and Instruction*, 25 November 1826, no. 224, p. 321; *Hand-Book for Travellers on the Continent*, 154; Anna Atkins, *Memoir of J. G. Children, Esq.* (London: John Bowyer Nichols and Sons, 1853), 193–4.

[72] The Duke of Rutland was gifted enough of the wood to have his own chair made, while his mother, the Dowager Duchess of Rutland, received a piece that she had turned into an inkstand. Geoffrey de Ballaigue, 'The Waterloo Elm', *Furniture History* 14 (1978): 14–18; *Berrow's Worcester Journal*, 24 November 1825; 'Friday's Post', *The Ipswich Journal*, 26 November 1825; 'Miscellaneous', *Royal Cornwall Gazette, Falmouth Packet & Plymouth Journal*, 26 November 1825; Waterloo Elm Inkstand, The Armoury of St. James's, <https://armoury.co.uk/collections/antiques/products/the-waterloo-elm-inkstand-1820>.

[73] The letter was never sent. John George Children to the Editor of *The Times*, 30 September 1818, reproduced in Atkins, *Memoir of J. G. Children*, 193–4; 'The Lion of Waterloo', *The Mirror of Literature, Amusement, and Instruction*, 25 November 1826, no. 224, p. 321; 'Friday's Post', *The Ipswich Journal*, 26 November 1825.

[74] 'Miscellaneous', *Royal Cornwall Gazette, Falmouth Packet & Plymouth Journal*, 26 November 1825; Dyke, *Travelling Mems*, I: 11–12; Wilson, *Travels*, 533n.

[75] 'The Lion of Waterloo', *The Mirror of Literature, Amusement, and Instruction*, 25 November 1826, no. 224, p. 321; *Hand-Book for Travellers on the Continent*, 154; Wilson, *Travels*, 533n.; Dyke, *Travelling Mems*, I: 11–12; Thorold, *Letters from Brussels in the Summer of 1835*, 276–9.

[76] According to military legend, Uxbridge was riding next to Wellington when it occurred. 'By God, sir, I've lost my leg!' he exclaimed, at which point Wellington supposedly glanced away from the telescope he was using to survey his victory and replied, 'By God, sir, so you have!' George Charles Henry Victor Paget Anglesey, *One-Leg: The Life and Letters of Henry William Paget, First Marquess of Anglesey* (New York: Morrow, 1961), 149.

including Master-General of the Ordnance and Lord-Lieutenant of Ireland, until his death in 1854.[77] His leg, however, much in the manner of numerous Catholic saints, had a longer career than he did. The leg was amputated at the house of M. Paris, 214, Chaussée de Bruxelles, who buried it in his garden 'decorously within a coffin, under a weeping willow', and 'placed over it a handsome tomb' bearing the following inscription:

> Here lies the Leg of the illustrious and valiant Earl Uxbridge, Lieutenant-General of His Britannic Majesty, Commander in Chief of the English, Belgian and Dutch cavalry, wounded on the 18 June 1815 at the memorable battle of Waterloo, who, by his heroism, assisted in the triumph of the cause of mankind, gloriously decided by the resounding victory of the said day.[78]

214, Chaussée de Bruxelles was located opposite the church in the village of Waterloo, and so became a must-see stop on the Waterloo tour, traditionally directly after visiting the church. Visitors witnessed the room and bloody chair where the leg was amputated, the gravesite, and were shown a boot that, it was claimed, the leg had been wearing when it was amputated. The house (and perforce the leg) remained in the Paris family, and by 1849, when Robert Bell visited, he was shown around by a 'coarse Titanesque woman' who related 'extravagant legends of both leg and boot, for the delectation of the *gobe-mouche* English who flock here in crowds to visit them'.[79] It was most likely the same woman who was described by P. T. Barnum when he visited six years later, and who, upon his request, sold both him and his travelling companion, Sherwood Stratton, strips of the 'original boot' roughly three inches long by one inch wide for a couple of francs. Her willingness to mutilate this historical relic 'without hesitation' must lead us to the same conclusion that it led Barnum to, that 'this must have been about the 99,867th boot that had been cut up as the "Simon pure" since 1815'.[80]

It was not just average tourists who visited the Marquess's leg. In 1821, while on a continental tour, George IV visited Waterloo, with Wellington himself acting as his tour guide. The king remained quiet and subdued throughout, neither asking his tour guide any questions nor giving any sign that the battlefield affected him in any way, until Wellington led him to the small garden behind 214, where, upon sighting the monument to Anglesey's leg, 'he burst into tears'.[81] A few years after

[77] He walked using the first articulated artificial limb ever realized. *Oxford Dictionary of National Biography* online, entry Henry William Paget, first Marquess of Anglesey.
[78] *Hand-Book for Travellers on the Continent*, 152; 'The Marquis of Anglesea's Leg', *The Morning Chronicle*, 19 August 1817; 'Marquis of Anglesey's Leg', *Notes And Queries*, 3rd Series, II, 27 September 1862, 249.
[79] Bell, *Wayside Pictures*, 411.   [80] Barnum, *Life of P. T. Barnum*, 242.
[81] Philip Guedalla, *Wellington* (New York: Harper & Brothers, 1931), 330; Christopher Hibbert, *George IV: Regent and King, 1811–1830* (London: Allen Lane, 1973), 229; Dalrymple, *The Economist's New Brussels Guide*, 121.

this visit, George IV's example was followed by the King and Princess of Prussia, although there is no record whether they joined their tears to His Britannic Majesty's.

Not everyone was as taken with the leg as George IV. Murray's *Hand-Book* noted 'the absurdity of the thing', and Robert Bell declared it a 'strange union of the ludicrous and the tragical. It was a thought worthy of Cervantes to build a tomb to the glory of the Marquis of Anglesey's leg.'[82] The periodical *Notes and Queries* recorded that beneath the grand epitaph quoted above, someone had added, 'Here lies the Marquis of Anglesey's limb; | The Devil will have the remainder of him.'[83] Thackeray, in his *Little Travels and Roadside Sketches*, took the opportunity to point out the inherent classism in Britain's commemoration of the battle. Describing Waterloo church, the author wondered 'why was not every private man's name written upon the stones in Waterloo Church as well as every officer's? . . . if the officers deserved a stone, the men did. But come, let us away to drop a tear over the Marquis of Anglesea's leg!'[84]

While the visitation relics were 'must-see' items, it was the collection relics that provided the visitor with both a tangible link to the battlefield and the social cachet at home of having been there.[85] Collection relics took a remarkable variety of forms and ranged from objects so ordinary that it was only their origin that made them special to frankly gruesome memento mori. The Wellington Tree and the boots of the Marquess of Anglesey are all worth mentioning again here, as they were visitation relics that became collection relics. They are also fine examples of ordinary objects that became noteworthy because of their origin. The scrap of leather that Barnum purchased or the pieces of the Wellington tree that visitors hewed off were, in and of themselves, merely scraps of leather and wood, but because of their origins, like splinters sold as pieces of the 'true' cross, they were prized as relics. Heman Humphrey, the president of Amherst College who visited Europe in 1835, brought away, as his only relic of the field, 'a piece of charcoal

---

[82] *Hand-Book for Travellers on the Continent*, 152; Bell, *Wayside Pictures*, 410–11.

[83] 'Marquis of Anglesey's Leg', *Notes and Queries*, 3rd Series, II, 27 September 1862, 249.

[84] Thackeray, *Little Travels and Roadside Sketches*, XVI: 336. Anglesey's leg was not the only military limb to be treated in such a manner. The arm of Confederate general Thomas 'Stonewall' Jackson took on a similar hint of the reliquary. See Robert Krick, 'The Mortal Wounding of Stonewall Jackson', in Gary Gallagher, ed., *Chancellorsville: The Battle and Its Aftermath* (Chapel Hill: University of North Carolina Press, 1996); James Robertson, *Stonewall Jackson: The Man, the Soldier, the Legend* (New York: Macmillan, 1997); Wallace Hettle, *Inventing Stonewall Jackson: A Civil War Hero in History and Memory* (Baton Rouge: Louisiana State University Press, 2011). For battlefield tourism and relics in the American context, see Thomas A. Chambers, *Memories of War: Visiting Battlegrounds and Bonefields in the Early American Republic* (Ithaca, NY: Cornell University Press, 2012); Joan E. Cashin, ed., *War Matters: Material Culture in the Civil War Era* (Chapel Hill: University of North Carolina Press, 2018).

[85] See Semmel, 'Reading the Tangible Past'; Leora Auslander and Tara Zahra, eds, *Objects of War: The Material Culture of Conflict & Displacement* (Ithaca, NY: Cornell University Press, 2018); Susan Pearce, 'The *Matériel* of War: Waterloo and its Culture', in John Bonehill and Geoff Quilley, eds, *Conflicting Visions: War and Visual Culture in Britain and France, c.1700–1830* (Aldershot: Ashgate, 2005), 207–26.

from the ruins of the farm house of Hugomont'.[86] The chateau's chapel provided perhaps the most sacrilegious of the relics—the hands, feet, and nose from a statue of the Virgin Mary, along with the body of the infant Christ she once held.[87] The farm was also the source of some of Waterloo's least obvious relics; in addition to the charcoal, visitors would collect oats from the chateau's fields, or be sold sticks from its wood as mementoes.[88] As mentioned above, Hougoumont also allowed for performance tourism, in the form of visitors signing their names on the whitewashed walls of the chapel, and this led to the collecting not of a relic of the Battle of Waterloo, but of a relic of the tourism that the battle produced. Visiting the chapel, the anonymous author of a report in *The Pocket Magazine of Classic and Polite Literature* 'anxiously sought for [the signature] of Lord Byron, whose stanzas alone were enough to make Waterloo immortal; and the guide pointed out to me an excavation in the stone where it had been, but from whence some selfish and unfeeling Englishman had removed it!'[89] Robert Bell encountered the same gap, and declared it 'an act of sacrilege' akin to 'the spoliation of the Elgin marbles'.[90]

The nature of the relics that visitors carried away from Waterloo, and their experience in obtaining them, depended largely on when they visited the battle-field. Wilson visited the field on 21 June 1815, three days after the battle had taken place, and encountered 'masses of papers, books, cartouch-boxes, drum heads, figures of eagles, crucifixes, scabbards, sheaths of bayonets, torn clothes, shattered muskets, [and] fragments of military dresses'.[91] Because of his prompt arrival, Wilson obtained several relics not available to later visitors, in the form of letters written to soldiers who perished on the field.[92] By the time Waterloo tourism became popular, the dead had been buried and the vast majority of the detritus of war had been picked up. Some relics could still be found on the field by chance, especially smaller items exposed by farming practices. Thomas Dyke recorded that 'bones, bullets, trappings, and various military ornaments meet the eye in every direction upon the newly-ploughed lands', and that he and his companions 'picked up several mementos'.[93] As time went by, however, fewer relics were found by tourists on the battlefield, and visitors turned to the local relic hunters.

The relic hunters of Waterloo are another inevitable part of a visit to the battlefield and are mentioned in almost every account. Murray's *Hand-Book* called

[86] Heman Humphrey, *Great Britain, France, and Belgium* (New York: Harper & Brothers, 1838), II: 337–8.

[87] Sala, *Waterloo to the Peninsula*, I: 21.

[88] Thackeray, *Little Travels and Roadside Sketches*, XVI: 336; Ashton, *Rough Notes of a Visit to Belgium*, 18.

[89] 'A Visit to Waterloo', *The Pocket Magazine*, II: 128–9.   [90] Bell, *Wayside Pictures*, 412–13.

[91] Wilson, *Travels*, 533–6.

[92] While he kept the letters, he did write to those who had written them to tell them the fate of the addressees. It was, in several cases, the first news they had heard of those individuals. Wilson, *Travels*, 533n.

[93] Dyke, *Travelling Mems*, I: 11–12.

them 'a set of harpies...a numerous horde who infest the spot', while Humphrey noted 'it is almost impossible to shake them off'.[94] George Jones, the well-known battle painter, who visited the field immediately after the battle itself, clearly recognized that they were going to become a permanent fixture; in addition to multiple studies of the battle he immortalized the village of Waterloo, complete with villagers selling relics to British tourists (Figure 2.4). They became famous enough that Anne Katherine Elwood, when visiting Thebes, compared the souvenir sellers there to Waterloo's, recording that the Elwoods had 'scarcely...come to anchor, ere we were beset by wild-looking natives, offering necklaces, scarabaei, and other curiosities for sale, with the same eagerness with which the Waterloo people bring relics to travellers'.[95] Relics came in many forms, but the most common were metal military objects: brass eagles, cap badges, buckles from shoes, bags, and boxes, uniform buttons, and of course, spent bullets, cannon

Figure 2.4 George Jones, *The Village of Waterloo, with travellers purchasing the relics that were found in the field of battle, 1815*, 1821, National Army Museum, London. © National Army Museum/Bridgeman Images.

---

[94] *Hand-Book for Travellers on the Continent*, 151, 158; Humphrey, *Great Britain, France, and Belgium*, II: 337–8.
[95] Anne Katherine Elwood, *Narrative of a Journey Overland from England, By the Continent of Europe, Egypt, and the Red Sea, to India* (London: Henry Colburn and Richard Bentley, 1830), I: 183.

balls, and shell fragments.[96] While most sellers concentrated on these smaller items, larger finds were also available. The most popular of these were helmets and cuirasses stripped from dead cavalrymen, although pistols and sabres were also sold.[97] The inherently martial aspect of these items was often expanded on, as Zachariah Allen discovered when a young relic hunter, 'supposing we were Englishmen, pressed us to purchase a six-pound cannon shot; and by way of enhancing the value of his merchandize, observed, as he held it out to us, that it had killed a Frenchman'.[98]

In addition to metallic and wooden souvenirs, a variety of more grisly relics emerged from the battlefield. The same ploughs that turned up buttons and cap badges also turned up bones and skulls, and many of these were collected by visitors or offered up for sale.[99] The fame of a person, if they could be identified, added to the lustre of such relics. Sir Walter Scott, a great admirer of the prize fighter John Shaw, who died at Waterloo serving as a corporal in the 2nd Life Guards, had his body exhumed from its original resting place near La Haye Sainte and returned to Britain. He had the rest of the body buried, but kept Shaw's skull in his library at Abbotsford, where it remains to this day.[100] For others, however, the motivation was more personal. The widow of Captain George Holmes of the 27th (Inniskilling) Regiment of Foot clearly desired a true memento mori of her late husband, who had been shot in the back, the bullet damaging a vertebra on its way into his chest cavity. She had his body macerated (boiled), and the damaged vertebra and bullet removed. They were subsequently varnished, and she had the bullet coated in silver and the vertebra modified to include a small silver-gilt container, the lid of which was engraved with the word 'Waterloo' inside a laurel wreath and a pile of weapons behind a drum, helmet, and trumpet.[101]

One of the great ironies of the relic mania that emerged from Waterloo is that one of the most common sets of relics, which would have been fitting memento mori, were used for practical purposes rather than collecting or memorializing the battle. False teeth, made from teeth extracted from corpses and then mounted in a base carved from ivory, became popular in the eighteenth century, but with the turn of the nineteenth century, and especially with the 50,000 casualties of Waterloo, all located relatively close to Britain, they became even more popular. Rather than teeth taken from poor corpses that had died of old age and a variety of

---

[96] Humphrey, *Great Britain, France, and Belgium*, II: 337–8; Allen, *Sketches of the State of the Useful Arts*, II: 189; *Hand-Book for Travellers on the Continent*, 148–9.

[97] Robinson, *Diary, Reminiscences, and Correspondence*, 319; Hills, *Sketches in Flanders and Holland*, 97; Barnum, *Life of P. T. Barnum*, 243–4.

[98] Allen, *Sketches of the State of the Useful Arts*, II: 189.

[99] *Hand-Book for Travellers on the Continent*, 158; Dyke, *Travelling Mems*, I: 11–12; Bell, *Wayside Pictures*, 405–10.

[100] Gareth Glover, *Waterloo in 100 Objects* (Stroud: The History Press, 2015), 133–5.

[101] Glover, *Waterloo in 100 Objects*, 178–9.

other maladies, teeth taken from battlefield casualties were extracted from young and fit men, whose demise, in most cases, did not impact the quality of their teeth. Zachariah Allen witnessed a skeleton uncovered by workmen during a visit to the battlefield in 1833. The workmen 'began diligently to extract the teeth, and immediately brought me a handful of them for sale. The guide observed to me that whilst the teeth were fresh and in good order, they formed a considerable article of trade to supply the English and French dentists.'[102] Dentists across Britain, as well as in Europe, began to advertise dentures made from 'Waterloo Teeth' or 'Waterloo Ivory'. Henry Crabb Robinson, only just back from a trip to Waterloo himself, had a Waterloo tooth fitted by a dentist in Norwich in January 1816, and was promised by the dentist that the Waterloo tooth would 'outlast twelve artificial teeth'.[103] The appeal was not the cachet of the battlefield or the association with Britain's glory, but the quality of the teeth. The teeth became so popular that the term became eponymous. Teeth taken from casualties of the Crimean War, or even imported from the US Civil War, were still advertised and sold as Waterloo Teeth.[104]

Teeth were not the only items that sometimes held only a dubious connection to Waterloo. The demand for relics of all kinds inevitably led to the exhaustion of the items found on the battlefield, and thus a rise in the business of creating fake relics. Ann Thorold, who visited the battlefield in 1835, reported that the demand for buttons was so great that

> there existed a manufactory at Liege to supply the numerous visitors with the wished-for prize, who, in the plenitude of their joy, liberally rewarded the vendor. This farce has had its day; and now, in offering a button, they remark to you, 'This is a real one; the manufactured button has the eagle's head turned the other way.' Ever ready to think ourselves the lucky wight, we walk on with a singularly contented countenance, inwardly resolving to detect the authenticity of the treasures of those friends who have previously visited the spot, when to our dismay another button is offered, with the eagle's head exactly in the opposite direction, the fellow swearing his the true, ours the manufacture; our dreams vanish, our pride sinks, but we pocket the button.[105]

---

[102] Allen, *Sketches of the State of the Useful Arts*, II: 189.

[103] Robinson, *Diary, Reminiscences, and Correspondence*, 327.

[104] Semmel, 'Reading the Tangible Past', 9; Glover, *Waterloo in 100 Objects*, 257–9. Teeth were not the only physical remains extracted from Waterloo used for a useful purpose. Sir Charles Bell, a military surgeon who treated wounded men on the field, took home a French soldier's skull, sliced by sabre cuts, and used it as a teaching aid for trainee surgeons in the various hospitals in which he served. Upper Skull, Surgeons' Hall Museums, <https://museum.rcsed.ac.uk/the-collection/key-collections/key-object-page?objID=2719&page=5>; Skull Sliced by Sabre Cuts, 200 Objects of Waterloo, Waterloo 200, <http://waterloo200.org/200-object/skull-sliced-by-sabre-cuts/>. See also note 33.

[105] Thorold, *Letters from Brussels in the Summer of 1835*, 279–80.

Several months after his own visit to Waterloo, P. T. Barnum made the same unfortunate discovery, when, on a visit to Birmingham, he 'made the acquaintance of a firm who manufactured to order, and sent to Waterloo, barrels of "relics" every year. At Waterloo these "relics" are planted, and in due time dug up, and sold at large prices as precious remembrances of the great battle'. He noted sourly that his own purchased relics 'looked rather cheap after this discovery'.[106] It may very well have been knowledge of the same firm and practice that led Thackeray to remark that the fields of Waterloo grew 'not only oats, but flourishing crops of grape-shot, bayonets, and legion-of-honour crosses, in amazing profusion'.[107] The Waterloo guide books warned against such fakes. Murray's *Hand-Book* cautioned travellers that 'when the real articles fail, the vendors are at no loss to invent others, so that there is little fear of the supply being exhausted'.[108] The warnings often fell on deaf ears, however, as the desire to own a relic of the battlefield outweighed many visitors' common sense. 'If you have sufficient credulity', noted Robert Bell, 'you may imagine yourself standing here surrounded by associations which will put you back some four-and-thirty years of your life.'[109] The trade, and the flow of gullible tourists, continued, to the point where, some fifty-five years after the battle, John Ashton recorded that his group 'were assailed by the relic-vendors, who pressed us to buy the usual things... The guide books tell you these things are spurious, but a very cursory examination inclined us to the opinion that most of them are genuine.'[110]

Crowds of relic hunters, all vying for attention and ingenious fakes, often 'aged' with the genuine dirt of Waterloo, were not the only inconveniences that British tourists faced on their visit to the field. Robert Hills, who visited the field shortly after the battle, had his carriage stopped on its return to Brussels 'by sentinels, whose business it was to search for, and take away, any weapons or armour which might have been found therein'. These guards, Hills noted, were stationed at barricades right before the gates of Brussels, but did not, in any way, warn outgoing travellers that purchases made at the battlefield would be confiscated. Nor was Brussels the only place where this occurred; a friend of Hills had three cuirasses seized by customs officers at the port of Ostend.[111] The lack of other reports of this nature as tourism boomed seems to indicate that, once the majority of relics were minor items such as buttons, bullets, and shako and cap badges, and once fake relics replaced real ones, the authorities abandoned this search and

---

[106] Barnum, *Life of P. T. Barnum*, 248.

[107] Thackeray, *Little Travels and Roadside Sketches*, XVI: 336.

[108] *Hand-Book for Travellers on the Continent*, 158.   [109] Bell, *Wayside Pictures*, 405–10.

[110] Ashton, *Rough Notes of a Visit to Belgium*, 15. Relic hunters/vendors were not the only people trying to take advantage of tourists. In 1817, a junior officer used his service at Waterloo to endear himself to a group of British tourists travelling to Brussels before selling one of them a forged bill on the British Linen Company and then robbing another of £100 and various accessories. 'Forgery and swindling', *The Morning Post*, 4 September 1817.

[111] Hills, *Sketches in Flanders and Holland*, 101.

seizure policy and let the trade flourish. The outrage expressed by Hills and his compatriots, however, brings us to the final, crucial, characteristic of British tourism to Waterloo: ownership.

On 31 July 1815, James Simpson, a British lawyer, mounted the carriage he had hired in Brussels for the occasion and instructed his coachman to take him to Waterloo. '"Oui, Monsieur l'Anglais" [the coachman] answered, with a smack of whip and an emphasis, which shewed that he felt that conducting Englishmen *there*, was conducting them to their own proper domain.'[112] The coachman, in all likelihood originally from Brussels or the surrounding area, almost certainly felt no such thing, but did feel a fondness for the gold that flowed from British visitors drunk on national pride. For the British, however, Simpson's statement would not have seemed strange at all: it summed up their feelings on the field perfectly. Waterloo may have been located in another country on the Continent, but it was British blood that had soaked it and British arms that had won it: it was the British who owned Waterloo.

This conviction of ownership emerged in two notable ways: first, widespread outrage when another power dared to alter the battlefield and, second, the overwhelming social pressure to visit the field. The first is best demonstrated by the British reaction to the Lion's Mound. Completed in 1826, the Lion's Mound stands 140 feet high and boasts a circumference of roughly 1,700 feet.[113] At its top is a stone pedestal on which stands an iron lion, the heraldic symbol of the kingdom of the Netherlands, facing France with 'a bold and triumphant look' and one paw on a globe.[114] The inscription simply reads '18th June, 1815.'[115] The mound, which took several hundred men and horses six years to complete, is centred on the point of the allied line where the Prince of Orange was wounded.[116]

Unsurprisingly, there were numerous British objections to the Lion's Mound. Of these, the most common was that the mound had significantly altered the topography of the battlefield. As active farmland and a popular tourist destination, the topography of Waterloo was, in fact, ever changing, but those were gradual and inevitable changes. The addition of a giant conical mound was another matter altogether, and was regarded by many Britons as a 'kind of sacrilege which they

---

[112] Simpson, *A Visit to Flanders*, 60.

[113] Several contemporary accounts place the height at 200 or 225 feet. 'The Lion of Waterloo', *The Mirror of Literature, Amusement, and Instruction*, 25 November 1826, no. 224, p. 321; Henry Watkins Allen, *The Travels of a Sugar Planter, or, Six Months in Europe* (New York: John F. Trow, 1861), 118–19; Silliman, *A Visit to Europe*, II: 362; Thorold, *Letters from Brussels in the Summer of 1835*, 276–7.

[114] Allen, *Travels of a Sugar Planter*, 118–19.

[115] Contemporary accounts claim that the lion is cast out of captured French cannon. Silliman, *A Visit to Europe*, II: 362; Thorold, *Letters from Brussels in the Summer of 1835*, 276–7.

[116] Allen, *Sketches of the State of the Useful Arts*, II: 188–9; Murray, *A Hand-Book for Travellers on the Continent*, 155; John M. Cobbett, *Letters from France* (London: Mills, Jowett, and Mills, 1825), 267–8.

will not soon forget, nor forgive'.[117] The mound itself was not the only topographical sacrilege, however, for all that earth had to have come from somewhere, and the Dutch-Belgian workers had taken it from the allied ridge, 'so as to reduce the most commanding point of Wellington's position to dead level'.[118] This completely changed the field, to the point where 'until you are aware of this circumstance, the idea arises that from that spot the field of battle could not be distinctly surveyed'.[119] Many viewed this change as a deliberate attempt by the Dutch to raise the Prince of Orange by diminishing Wellington, 'the earth on which the hero [Wellington]'s foot rested, now contributes to a monument of victory too proud to be sullied by another's tread'.[120] The outrage was not just reserved for Wellington's honour, but extended to all of Britain's hallowed dead. As one travelogue commented, 'there is bad taste in thus seeking to glorify one particular wound amidst so many instances of devotedness to death'.[121] This criticism was made more legitimate by the fact that the mound contained the remains of several hundred soldiers of all nationalities, whose original graves were disturbed during the monument's construction, and who were now a part of the 'watchtower of death'—a 'great sepulchral mound' that seemed to honour only one wound.[122] The story that Wellington, upon visiting Waterloo after the erection of the mound, exclaimed, 'they have spoilt my battlefield', is apocryphal, but many who did visit the site lamented the mound as 'an ill imagined excrescence'.[123]

Not everyone objected to the mound. Robert Macnish, a Scottish surgeon, declared that the pyramid was 'exceedingly striking' and 'partakes in no small degree of the sublime'.[124] Dyke, even as he objected to the mound's topographical sacrilege, begrudgingly admitted that 'as a work of art the monument is very fine'.[125] For many, the very size of the mound was its best feature. It was climbable by a spiralling road, later replaced by a more direct but challenging flight of steps. Braving those stairs, however, provided access to a 'panorama of the whole view in a moment or two, without any embellishment from the imagination, or any vain flourishes of nationality'.[126] Murray's Hand Book declared the mound 'by far the

---

[117] Humphrey, *Great Britain, France, and Belgium*, II: 338.
[118] Humphrey, *Great Britain, France, and Belgium*, II: 338.
[119] Thorold, *Letters from Brussels in the Summer of 1835*, 277.
[120] Thorold, *Letters from Brussels in the Summer of 1835*, 277; Sala, *Waterloo to the Peninsula*, I: 25.
[121] Mary Boddington, *Slight Reminiscences of the Rhine, Switzerland, and a Corner of Italy* (London: Longman, Rees, Orme, Brown, Green, and Longman, 1834), I: 30.
[122] Murray, *A Hand-Book for Travellers on the Continent*, 155; Silliman, *A Visit to Europe*, II: 362; Humphrey, *Great Britain, France, and Belgium*, II: 339; Sala, *Waterloo to the Peninsula*, I: 13–14.
[123] Wellington, in fact, never visited the battlefield after the mound's construction. The anecdote probably originated in chapter 7 of Victor Hugo's *Les Miserables*. J. Paine, 'Links with the Iron Duke', *United Empire* 19, no. 3 (March 1928), 139; Boddington, *Slight Reminiscences*, I: 30. George Sala goes on for nearly a page about the mound's and lion's ugliness. Sala, *Waterloo to the Peninsula*, I: 24.
[124] D. M. Moir, *Tales, Essays, and Sketches, by the Late Robert Macnish, LL.D.* (London: Henry G. Bohn, 1844), II: 452.
[125] Dyke, *Travelling Mems*, I: 12–13.   [126] Bell, *Wayside Pictures*, 407–8.

best station for surveying the field', and multiple accounts agree.[127] The view even redeemed the mound in the eyes of some. Humphrey, who visited Waterloo shortly after the mound was completed, admitted that his first instinct was to object to the mound's reshaping of the battlefield. When he climbed to the top, however, and saw 'what a perfect map lies spread out before you the whole scene of action ... I confess I was glad the pyramid had been raised, even at whatever expense of military taste.'[128]

Complaints about Dutch monuments aside, the most obvious manifestation of perceived British ownership was the sheer number of British tourists that visited the battlefield. Although no official numbers were kept, several anecdotal sources seem to indicate that, at least up until the 1850s, the British were the most numerous visitors.[129] The British were also, as discussed above, the most likely to purchase relics. (Many of which, in later years, were manufactured in Britain to begin with.) This domination of the tourist trade was partially a result of one of the internal manifestations of British-perceived ownership: an obligation to visit. British tourists, visiting the Continent, felt enormous pressure to visit Waterloo. It became the quintessential secular pilgrimage, and religious language was often employed to reinforce that idea. George Sala, as he departed Brussels for the field, remarked that he had 'commenced the great English pilgrimage', and noted that Waterloo church, despite its Catholic nature, was, 'to the English pilgrim, second only in reverent interest to St. Paul's and Westminster Abbey'.[130] Other visitors reserved their awe for the field itself. One author described a 'pilgrimage to its plains ... to tread upon soil, consecrated by British heroism'.[131] Thomas Pennington agreed, declared the 'ground hallowed with the ashes of our gallant countrymen', and walked it 'with slow and solemn steps'.[132] The *Leicester Chronicle* insisted that 'it would be heresy to come to Brussels and not to go' to Waterloo, while another article discussing the Belgic mound even published an illustration of the mound and the battlefield that, in its use of light and perspective, bears a striking resemblance to religious imagery (Figure 2.5).[133]

Just as important as visiting Waterloo, or possibly even more so, was being seen to visit Waterloo. Ann Laura Thorold noted several reasons for visiting the battlefield, including 'old England's glory, pride in the living, or sorrow for the

---

[127] Murray, *A Hand-Book for Travellers on the Continent*, 154–5; Silliman, *A Visit to Europe*, II: 362; Thorold, *Letters from Brussels in the Summer of 1835*, 278; Harriman, *Travels and Observations*, 331–2; Sala, *Waterloo to the Peninsula*, I: 23.

[128] Humphrey, *Great Britain, France, and Belgium*, II: 338.

[129] In the 1850s, Americans seem to have become the prevalent tourists. Silliman, *A Visit to Europe*, II: 359–60; Ashton, *Rough Notes of a Visit to Belgium*, 13–14; Bradshaw, *Bradshaw's Illustrated Hand-Book for Belgium and the Rhine*, 40.

[130] Sala, *Waterloo to the Peninsula*, I: 4, 11.

[131] 'A Visit to Waterloo', *The Pocket Magazine*, II: 126.

[132] Pennington, *A Journey into Various Parts of Europe*, II: 579.

[133] Belgium, *Leicester Chronicle*, 20 October 1838, p. 1; 'The Lion of Waterloo', *The Mirror of Literature, Amusement, and Instruction*, 25 November 1826, no. 224, p. 321.

Figure 2.5 Illustration from 'The Lion of Waterloo', *The Mirror of Literature, Amusement, and Instruction*, 25 November 1826, no. 224, p. 321. Photo Bodleian Libraries Douce MM 615 (v. 7–8), ill. from p. 32.

dead', but presented as the most compelling reason 'because every one goes; because you cannot stand proof against the repeated questions, on your return, "Of course you saw Waterloo?" because you cannot encounter the faces of astonishment at your feebly answered "No."'[134] Much as all roads once led to Rome, in the nineteenth century the known truth was that 'every one visits Waterloo', and they were then expected to talk about it when they got home.[135] This became so expected that Thackeray, ever eager to buck tradition, stated in his *Little Travels and Roadside Sketches* 'I thought to myself... what a fine thing it will be in after-days to say that I have been to Brussels and never seen the field of Waterloo.' The pressure was too great, however and, growing bored with Brussels, he 'jingled off at four miles an hour for Waterloo'. We have mentioned Thackeray's reactions to Waterloo church and Anglesey's leg, but even he, cynic that he was, was moved by the power of the field within the collective British psyche, and declared, four pages after his admission that he intended not to go,

[134] Thorold, *Letters from Brussels in the Summer of 1835*, 271–2.
[135] 'A Visit to Waterloo', *The Pocket Magazine*, II: 126.

Well, though I made a vow not to talk about Waterloo either here or after dinner, there is one little secret admission that one must make after seeing it. Let an Englishman go and see that field, and he *never forgets it*. The sight is an event in his life; and, though it has been seen by millions of peaceable *gents*—grocers from Bond Street, meek attorneys from Chancery Lane, and timid tailors from Piccadilly—I will wager that there is not one of them but feels a glow as he looks at the place, and remembers that he, too, is an Englishman.[136]

Waterloo's power almost scared him. 'It is a wrong, egotistical, savage, unchristian feeling, and that's the truth of it. A man of peace has no right to be dazzled by that red-coated glory, and to intoxicate his vanity with those remembrances of carnage and triumph.'[137] But it was that power that drove the battlefield's tourism industry and ensured the battle's place in British collective memory.

---

[136] Thackeray, *Little Travels and Roadside Sketches*, XVI: 336.
[137] Thackeray, *Little Travels and Roadside Sketches*, XVI: 336.

3

'Demonstrations of true British feeling and exultation'

Annual Commemorations

The first truly public annual commemoration of the Battle of Waterloo was a riot.[1] On 5 June 1816 both *The Morning Chronicle* and *The Times* ran notices that 'on the 18th instant, all the troops in the Metropolis and its vicinity will have a grand field day on Wimbledon Common, in commemoration of the battle of Waterloo'. The review, the reports maintained, would be attended by the prince regent, the Duke of York in his capacity as commander-in-chief, and 'all the General Staff in town and its vicinity'. The field day captured enough public interest that enterprising pleasure boat companies offered a special hire service from Westminster Bridge to Putney for the occasion.[2] There was only one problem: no such field day was planned.[3] Instead, every enlisted Waterloo veteran of the Royal Horse Guards and the Foot Guards gathered for an outdoor dinner on tables laid along the Long Walk of Windsor Park, where they were served 'plenty of roast beef, plum pudding, porter, &c., and each man had a pint of wine presented to him' by a local wine merchant.[4] The Duke of York made his way to Windsor to grace the event, and later attended a grand dinner given by the officers of the Foot Guards to the officers of the Royal Horse Guards (Blue) in the Windsor Barracks Riding House, which had been decorated with laurel and the regimental colours for the occasion.[5] Fifteen miles to the east, unaware that the Guards were busy with their own revels, thousands of Londoners, 'many of whom were in a state of

---

[1] Portions of this chapter first appeared in Luke Reynolds, 'Serving His Country: Wellington's Waterloo Banquets, 1822–52', *Journal of Victorian Culture* 23, no. 2 (2018): 262–78. doi:10.1093/jvcult/vcx015. © 2018 Leeds Trinity University.

[2] *Morning Chronicle*, 5 June 1816; *The Times*, 5 June 1816, p. 3; *Morning Chronicle*, 14 June 1816.

[3] *The Cheltenham Chronicle and Gloucestershire Advertiser* blamed the misunderstanding 'partially [on] a *hoax*, and partially [on] an interested expedient'. *The Cheltenham Chronicle and Gloucestershire Advertiser*, 20 June 1816, p. 3.

[4] 'Anniversary of the Battle of Waterloo', *Morning Chronicle*, 19 June 1816, p. 3.

[5] On the 17th the officers of the Royal Horse Guards (Blue) had hosted the officers of the Foot Guards at the Cavalry Barracks. 'Anniversary of the Battle of Waterloo', *Morning Chronicle*, 19 June 1816, p. 3. There were also other celebratory dinners at the Windsor Town Hall and the Thatched-house Tavern. *The Times*, 19 June 1816, p. 3. The Duke of York subsequently caught a cold, which was blamed on his having sat 'in the draught from two windows' during the dinner. 'The Duke of York', *Caledonian Mercury*, 27 June 1816.

Who Owned Waterloo? Battle, Memory, and Myth in British History, 1815–1852. Luke Reynolds, Oxford University Press.
© Luke Reynolds 2022. DOI: 10.1093/oso/9780192864994.003.0004

intoxication', assembled on Wimbledon Common. Disappointed at the lack of a show, 'among other outrages...the mob set fire to the heath'.[6] News of this disturbance reaching London, they finally got their martial display, as a detachment of cavalry were dispatched to disperse the crowds and prevent any further destruction.[7]

Despite such an inauspicious start, 18 June became a notable date in the British social calendar. This chapter explores how Waterloo commemorations were standardized over time and examines several celebrations that became annual traditions, such as Vauxhall Garden's fete and Wellington's Waterloo banquet. It also charts the nationalization of the celebrations from something explicitly military to a day of general revelry. 'Waterloo Day', as it was eventually christened, became a national holiday or saint's day, hosting such non-martial events as the opening of a railway and a large livestock market. In many towns and cities, the day also became openly political, as various Tory and Conservative societies embraced the victory and its hero, Wellington, as symbols of the divine righteousness of conservatism and a bulwark against the growing calls of the radical reformers.

Waterloo was a watershed: the last time a battle, rather than an entire conflict, was singled out for remembrance—and the final time remembrance truly took the form of uncomplicated, triumphant celebration.[8] Toasts were, of course, drunk in silence to 'the memory of those who fell', but even the moments of silence at Apsley House—let alone the raucous fetes at Vauxhall—were a far cry from the sombre laying of wreaths of poppies at the Cenotaph that mark Remembrance Day traditions in the twentieth and twenty-first centuries.[9] The Crimean War (1853–1856) saw the beginning of the shift to a new, all-encompassing, and much more solemn form of remembrance that eventually became a fundamental part of British culture after the First and the Second World Wars. For thirty-seven years, without any victories of equal magnitude to supplant it, Waterloo's annual commemoration remained necessary to British military and national identity.

---

[6] *Royal Cornwall Gazette*, 22 June 1816; 'Postscript', *The Cheltenham Chronicle and Gloucestershire Advertiser*, 20 June 1816, p. 3.

[7] 'Postscript', *The Cheltenham Chronicle and Gloucestershire Advertiser*, 20 June 1816, p. 3; *Royal Cornwall Gazette*, 22 June 1816; *Hereford Journal*, 26 June 1816, p. 4.

[8] This overall trend, arguably, can be seen as part of both the wider democratization of war and the fading importance of decisive set-piece battles. Stephanie Markovits, *The Crimean War in the British Imagination* (Cambridge: Cambridge University Press, 2009); Trevor Royle, *Crimea: The Great Crimean War, 1854–1856* (New York: Palgrave Macmillan, 2000), III: 5. See also Ian F.W. Beckett, 'Military Commemoration in Britain: A Pre-History', *Journal of the Society for Army Historical Research* 92, no. 370 (Summer 2014): 147–59. It should be noted, however, that despite the disasters of the Crimea, war in general was celebrated and glorified in some portions of British life up to 1914. See Michael Paris, *Warrior Nation: Images of War in British Popular Culture, 1850–2000* (London: Reaktion Books, 2000), chapter 1.

[9] 'The Waterloo Banquet', *The Times*, 19 June 1851, p. 5.

In that time, it became the apogee of military celebration, and shaped the traditions of commemoration itself.[10]

Everything discussed in this chapter sought to commemorate Waterloo in one way or another. This goal differs from those of the various memoirs and histories and the mania for relic hunting discussed in previous chapters, as well as some of the exhibitions discussed in the next chapter, where the aim was more to recreate Waterloo than to remember it. This distinction is particularly noteworthy when it comes to issues of participation and scope, where it simultaneously widens and narrows the field. By attending a military parade or review, a rural sports day, or Vauxhall's Waterloo fete, any Briton could remember Waterloo, even if they had not been alive in 1815, thus accelerating and strengthening the transition from communicative to cultural memory.[11] The Waterloo banquet and other gatherings of veterans, however, deliberately excluded civilians and younger soldiers in an effort to preserve the sanctity of their communicative memory and thus their positions as the owners and arbiters of Waterloo's cultural memory. To complicate matters even further, however, even the most elite events were transformed, by onlookers and the press, into national spectacles to be observed by those outside them, thus again widening the reach of events rendered worthy of attention by their limited guest lists.[12] They provided an anchor to that battle and the quarter-century of war that preceded it, a conflict which played a crucial role in the development of a national identity and served as the moral and

[10] This means this chapter fits neatly into the scholarship on invention of tradition, while building on it by providing Waterloo as a detailed case study for the developments discussed in, for example, Eric Hobsbawm and Terence Ranger, eds, *The Invention of Tradition* (Cambridge: Cambridge University Press, 2013); David Cannadine, *Aspects of Aristocracy: Grandeur and Decline in Modern Britain* (New Haven: Yale University Press, 1994); David Cannadine, *Ornamentalism: How the British Saw Their Empire* (Oxford: Oxford University Press, 2001).

[11] Much has been made of the outwardly egalitarian nature of Britain's pleasure gardens but, as recent scholarship has shown, hidden costs and late hours meant regular attendance was unavailable to the lower middle and working classes until the 1840s. That said, attendance was still open to a much larger percentage of the population than had been at Waterloo, including the entire female portion of the upper middle and upper classes. Peter Borsay, 'Pleasure Gardens and Urban Culture in the Long Eighteenth Century', in Jonathan Conlin, ed., *The Pleasure Garden, from Vauxhall to Coney Island* (Philadelphia: University of Pennsylvania Press, 2013), 49–77; Jonathan Conlin, 'Vauxhall Revisited: The Afterlife of a London Pleasure Garden, 1770–1859', *Journal of British Studies* 45, no. 4 (October 2006): 718–43. For the egalitarian promise of pleasure gardens, see John Brewer, '"The Most Polite Age and the Most Vicious": Attitudes Towards Culture as a Commodity, 1660–1800', in Ann Bermingham and John Brewer, eds, *The Consumption of Culture, 1660–1800: Image, Object, Text* (London: Routledge, 1997), 341–61; David Solkin, *Painting for Money: The Visual Arts and the Public Sphere in Eighteenth-Century England* (New Haven: Yale University Press, 1992); Penelope J. Corfield, *Vauxhall and the Invention of Urban Pleasure Gardens* (London: History and Social Action Publications, 2008).

[12] This complicates the top-down interpretation of spectacle emphasized by some scholars. See Scott Hughes Myerly, *British Military Spectacle: From the Napoleonic Wars Through the Crimea* (Cambridge, Mass.: Harvard University Press, 1996); Thomas Richards, *The Commodity Culture of Victorian England: Advertising and Spectacle, 1851–1914* (Stanford, CA: Stanford University Press, 1990); Paul Keen, *Literature, Commerce, and the Spectacle of Modernity, 1750–1800* (Cambridge: Cambridge University Press, 2012).

rhetorical basis for British hegemony. As noted in the book's Introduction, that development was no accident, and Waterloo commemoration played a significant part in its continual evolution.[13]

Simultaneously, however, many of these events were profoundly local. British towns paid attention to what their neighbours were doing and were determined not to be left behind. Even towns that did not host balls, sports days, or dinners marked the day 'by the display of flags, firing of guns', the ringing of church bells, 'and other demonstrations of true British feeling and exultation'.[14] Just as many of the activities and events discussed across the chapters of this book provided individuals with a myriad of options for performative nationalism, Waterloo's annual commemoration offered local polities the same opportunity. Many, just as they did with the naming of infrastructure discussed in Chapter 6, seized the chance. There were, of course, local motivations beyond the simple display of performative nationalism. In Ireland, and especially Dublin, military-themed celebrations such as the various reviews in Phoenix Park allowed the Anglo-Irish elite to demonstrate by their presence their commitment to the Union while the British army, much as it had done in occupied France, 'clothe[d] the iron fist of occupation in the velvet glove of spectacle'.[15] Ireland's relationship with Waterloo was further complicated by the number of Irish and Anglo-Irish soldiers who had fought in the battle, most notably Wellington himself.[16] Across the Straits of Moyle, Scotland had its own motivations for what Elisa Milkes dubbed its 'precociousness in Waterloo commemoration'.[17] Scotland recognized in the battle a dual opportunity to celebrate Scottish achievements—the capture of the Eagle of the 45th *Régiment d'Infanterie de Ligne* by the 2nd Dragoons (Scots Greys), the parts played by Highland Regiments—while simultaneously further

[13] Linda Colley, *Britons: Forging the Nation 1707–1837* (New Haven: Yale University Press, 2009), 1–9, 196, 327; Holger Hoock, *Empires of the Imagination: Politics, War, and the Arts in the British World, 1750–1850* (London: Profile Books, 2010), 13, 361–7; R. E. Foster, *Wellington and Waterloo: The Duke, the Battle and Posterity 1815–2015* (Staplehurst: Spellmount, 2014); Alan Forrest, *Waterloo* (Oxford: Oxford University Press, 2015).

[14] 'Bath, Wednesday 23 June', *Bath Chronicle and Weekly Gazette*, 24 June 1819, p. 3. See also 'Southampton', *Salisbury and Winchester Journal*, 21 June 1819, p. 4; 'News', *Leeds Intelligencer*, 18 June 1821, p. 3; *Westmorland Gazette*, 23 June 1821, p. 3; *Lancaster Gazetter*, 21 June 1823, p. 3; Cheltenham, *Morning Post*, 29 June 1825; *Newcastle Courant*, 23 June 1827; *York Herald*, 24 June 1837, p. 7; *Bristol Mercury*, 19 June 1841, p. 8.

[15] Luke Reynolds, '"There John Bull might be seen in all his glory": Cross-Channel Tourism and the British Army of Occupation in France, 1815–1818', *Journal of Tourism History* 12, no. 2 (2020): 154; Christine Haynes, *Our Friends the Enemies: The Occupation of France after Napoleon* (Cambridge, Mass.: Harvard University Press, 2018); Myerly, *British Military Spectacle*.

[16] For one example of this complicated relationship, see P. F. Garnett, 'The Wellington Testimonial', *Dublin Historical Record* 13, no. 2 (June–August 1952): 48–61.

[17] Elisa Milkes, 'A Battle's Legacy: Waterloo in Nineteenth Century Britain', Ph.D. dissertation, Yale University, 2002, 370.

emphasizing their crucial place in the United Kingdom and making a case for greater influence.[18]

Alongside local interests were political and religious ones. Waterloo was celebrated by a large number of conservative organizations, who sought to make 18 June a political as well as national victory. The most obvious explanation for this is the permanent association of Waterloo with Wellington, who combined in himself both the avatar of British victory and one of the patron saints of British conservatism. The association of Waterloo with conservatism went beyond this, however, as the victory at Waterloo, and in the Napoleonic Wars in general, was inherently conservative. A new radical threat, in the form of first Revolutionary and then Napoleonic France, was beaten back by a coalition of old-regime states, thus preserving the status quo. Simultaneously, many saw it as a Protestant victory over the old Catholic enemy; a triumph won, in part, by Britain's adherence to the true faith.[19]

This presented a challenge to Catholics, Radicals, Whigs, and later Liberals who wished to commemorate the victory. For some, Waterloo commemoration presented the opportunity to weaponize the association for their own benefit. While the best example of this is the efforts by satirists in the aftermath of Peterloo discussed in Chapter 6, it was also a strategy embraced by Irish Catholics, who used Wellington's Irish birth and the preponderance of Irish men in the ranks to call for Catholic Emancipation.[20] More common, however, was the urge to lessen or remove Wellington's presence in their commemorations, emphasizing instead the national aspects of the victory.[21]

The news of the victory at Waterloo reached London on 21 June 1815, three days after the battle. It was carried by Major Henry Percy, aide-de-camp to the Duke of Wellington, who, along with his own experiences of the battle, bore Wellington's Waterloo dispatch and the two French Eagles that had been captured on the field.[22] Percy, who had been on the road since being handed Wellington's dispatch, first delivered the news to Earl Bathurst, Secretary of State for War,

---

[18] Scotland was also at the forefront of contributions to the Waterloo Fund and in the creation of a National Monument. See Milkes, 'A Battle's Legacy', chapters 4 and 6. Instead of regimental colours, Napoleonic French infantry carried eagle battle standards.

[19] Some went so far as to claim that the domestic misfortunes endured by Britain in the immediate aftermath of the war were God's punishment for the restoration of the Catholic regimes of Europe. See John Pye Smith, *The Sorrows of Britain* (London: Josiah Conder, 1817), 16–17.

[20] Colley, *Britons*, 333.

[21] Barbara Barrow, '"The Waterloo of Democracy against Despotism": Chartist Internationalism and Poetic Repetition in the Labourer, 1847–48', *Victorian Periodicals Review* 48, no. 4 (Winter 2015), 511–30; George Gordon Byron, *Don Juan* (London: C. Daly, 1852). See also Chapter 6 and Robert Poole, *Peterloo* (Oxford: Oxford University Press, 2019).

[22] Percy was the fifth son of Algernon Percy, Earl of Beverley, and grandson of Hugh Percy, Duke of Northumberland. For the details of Percy's journey, see Brian Cathcart, *The News from Waterloo: The Race to Tell Britain of Wellington's Victory* (London: Faber & Faber, 2015), chapters 4, 7, and 11; Reginald Colby, *The Waterloo Despatch: The Story of the Duke of Wellington's Official Despatch on the Battle of Waterloo and its Journey to London* (London: Her Majesty's Stationary Office, 1965).

before continuing on to St James's Square, where the prince regent was attending a party. Clad in the same bloodstained uniform he had worn at the battle and at the Duchess of Richmond's ball that had preceded it, he interrupted the party to lay the Eagles and the news at the feet of the prince regent. He was rewarded the next day with a promotion to lieutenant colonel and the Order of the Bath.[23]

Lieutenant Colonel Percy received another, less tangible reward for his three-day journey: he was the only Waterloo veteran to be in the capital for the preliminary and spontaneous celebrations of victory.[24] The days after Waterloo marked a high point for the army's reputation in Britain. Spontaneous celebrations and illuminations emerged across the capital in the days following the arrival of the news.[25] Within a week, meetings were held in the City to establish a Waterloo Relief Fund, both houses of Parliament voted official thanks, and theatrical gala evenings, new formation dances, and new songs were being dedicated to the victory.[26] The men who actually fought at Waterloo missed this outpouring, as they were still in France and Belgium. They received their own celebrations in the form of dinners for general officers and multiple reviews and levees in and outside Paris, many attended by allied monarchs, but the only British civilians present at those events were tourists.[27]

Even as the first spontaneous celebrations spread, *The Times* called for more organized and sober commemoration in the form of a day of national 'thanksgiving to Almighty God', 'Divine providence, and...those whom that gracious Providence has raised up to be a protection to their country and mankind'.[28] The prince regent agreed and three days later ordered the Archbishop of Canterbury to 'prepare a Form of Prayer and Thanksgiving to Almighty God' which would then be printed and distributed throughout England, Wales, and Ireland.[29] The prayer, which came in at a restrained 161 words, reflected the fact

---

[23] Forrest, Waterloo, 54; Cathcart, *The News from Waterloo*, 233–5.

[24] Although he left shortly after to return to Wellington's army. Cathcart, *The News from Waterloo*, 247.

[25] Cathcart, *The News from Waterloo*, 237–56.

[26] 'Patriotic Meeting', *Morning Post*, 29 June 1815; 'Waterloo Subscription', *Morning Chronicle*, 30 June 1815; House of Commons debate on Thanks to the Duke of Wellington, Prince Blücher, and the Allied Armies, 23 June 1815, Historic Hansard vol. 31, columns 980–9; House of Lords debate on Thanks to the Duke of Wellington, Prince Blücher, and the Allied Armies, 23 June 1815, Historic Hansard vol. 31, columns 971–7; *Morning Chronicle*, 27 June 1815; *Morning Post*, 27 June 1815, p. 1. The compositions kept coming, see *Morning Post*, 21 July 1815, p. 1; *Morning Post*, 28 July 1815. For the Waterloo fund, see Milkes, 'A Battle's Legacy', chapter 4.

[27] Reynolds, '"There John Bull might be seen in all his glory"', 139–55; Haynes, 'Our Friends the Enemies'; Huw Davies, 'The Legacy of Waterloo: War and Politics in Europe in the 19th Century', in Nick Lipscombe, ed., *Waterloo: The Decisive Victory* (Oxford: Osprey, 2014), 345–75. Walter Scott attended a levee in addition to the dinner mentioned in the previous chapter. Paul O'Keeffe, general introduction to *Scott on Waterloo*, by Walter Scott (London: Vintage Books, 2015), 10–11; Diary of Lord R. E. H. Somerset, 1815–17, Bodleian Library Special Collections, Bodleian Library, University of Oxford.

[28] 'London, Monday, 26 June 1815', *The Times*, 26 June 1815, p. 3.

[29] 'At the Court of Carlton-House', *The London Gazette*, 1 July 1815, issue 17032, p. 1273. It was printed in English and Welsh, Milkes, 'A Battle's Legacy', 171 n. 76.

that the fate of Europe was still in flux by beseeching 'merciful God, that the result of this mighty battle, terrible in conflict, but glorious beyond example in success, may put an end to the miseries of Europe, and staunch the blood of nations' while blessing 'the Allied Armies with thy continued favor'.[30]

Written to be read 'at morning and evening service, after the General Thanksgiving' and alongside a more traditional sermon, the archbishop's prayer left it up to individual clergy whether they would address Waterloo in more detail.[31] Several soon realized that a sermon was the most logical way to encourage contributions to the Waterloo Fund and advertisements for and reports of such sermons began appearing in papers across the country in late July, often proudly noting how much money was collected.[32] The preaching of such sermons went from precocious displays of local charity and performative patriotism to royal command on 17 August when the prince regent issued instructions that a letter should be circulated by the Archbishops of Canterbury and York 'to...their several provinces' instructing 'Ministers in each parish [t]o effectually excite their parishioners to a liberal contribution'.[33] The result was a large number of Waterloo Fund Sermons, many of which were eventually published.[34]

The Waterloo Fund Sermons represented, for many Britons, their first experience of the collective commemoration of the battle and they serve as a preview of many of the themes discussed in this chapter.[35] Despite explicitly calling for donations to the Waterloo Fund, a charity that centred veterans and their dependants,

---

[30] *A Form of Prayer and Thanksgiving to Almighty God* (London: George Eyre and Andrew Strahan, 1815), Beinecke Rare Book and Manuscript Library, Yale University; *The Battle of Waterloo; or, a Faithful and Interesting History of the Unparalleled Events Connected Therewith* (Manchester: J. Gleave, 1818), 452.

[31] *Form of Prayer and Thanksgiving to Almighty God*, title page.

[32] £80 was collected in Hertford and a single sermon in Winchester generated over £30. *Morning Post*, 21 July 1815, p. 1; 'Sunday's Post', *Norfolk Chronicle*, 29 July 1815, p. 1; 'Winchester', *Salisbury and Winchester Journal*, 31 July 1815, p. 4.

[33] 'At the Court of Carlton-House', *The London Gazette*, 19 August 1815, issue 17053, p. 1693. While Scottish churches were not subject to the instruction, the General Assembly of the Church of Scotland adopted a similar one almost immediately, worded to include and encourage dissenter congregations. Milkes, 'A Battle's Legacy', 172.

[34] T. F. Bowerbank, *A Sermon preached in the Parish Church of Chiswick, Middlesex, on Sunday, July 30, 1815* (Chiswick: C. Whittingham, 1815); Edward Patteson, *A Sermon Delivered in the Parish Church of Richmond in Surrey, on Sunday the 30th Day of July, 1815* (London: F. C. and J. Rivington, 1815); Peter Roe, *A Sermon Preached in the Episcopal Chapel of Harrogate, Sunday, July the 30th, 1815* (Dublin: John Jones, 1815); Daniell Mathias, *Waterloo Subscription: A Sermon, to Recommend the Same* (London: Rivingtons, 1815); Henry Cotes, *Another Mite for Waterloo* (Newcastle: E. Charnley, 1815); Proctor Robinson, *A Sermon, Preached in the St. Edmund's Church, Dudley, on Sunday, August 20, 1815* (Dudley: John Rann, 1815); Powell Samuel Criche, *Sermon, Preached for the Benefit of the Waterloo Sufferers* (Bristol: Wm. Major, 1815); John Sympson Sergrove, *A Sermon...For the Benefit of the Sufferers at Waterloo* (London: Sherwood, Neely, and Jones, 1815); John Vickers, *A Sermon...In Aid of the Waterloo Subscription* (Norwich: Bacon, Kinnebrook, and Co., 1815).

[35] For a detailed exploration of the Waterloo Fund Sermons, and especially their use of the image of suffering, see Milkes, 'A Battle's Legacy', chapter 4. For British event sermons in general, see John Wolffe, 'British Sermons on National Events', in Robert H. Ellison, ed., *A New History of the Sermon: The Nineteenth Century* (Leiden: Brill, 2010), 181–206.

the sermons' language actively promoted a national definition of ownership. It was Britain's special role as a divinely favoured nation, they argued, that had caused God to grant victory to Wellington and his men.[36] Waterloo, therefore, had been earned by every Briton, with their Protestant faith and their rejection of revolution and immorality. They praised the courage of the men who had fought there, but Waterloo was unquestionably 'a victory in which the arm of God was wonderfully conspicuous'.[37] Unsurprisingly, given this theme, many of the sermons, like the annual Waterloo commemorations that followed them, were also openly conservative, praising Britons' love of law, order, the constitution, and the status quo.[38] 'We fear God,' declared the Reverend Proctor Robinson, 'we look up with awe to Kings, with Affection to Parliaments; with Duty to Magistrates; with Reverence to Priests; and with Respect to Nobility.'[39] Finally, although some made sure to mention Blücher and the Prussians, it was clear that Waterloo was a British victory and that they were the ones truly responsible for peace and 'the deliverance of Europe'.[40]

Even as sermons for Waterloo and its victors were being preached up and down the country, more earthy celebrations were also emerging. The Devon seaside resort of Exmouth threw a ball and a celebratory dinner was given by the Old Soldiers' Club of Bury.[41] Bath's Sydney Gardens (a pleasure garden akin to London's Vauxhall) hosted a Grand Gala on 23 August that anticipated many of the features that became associated with Vauxhall Garden's Waterloo fetes, including themed musical performances and a firework show that boasted depictions of HMS *Bellerophon* with Napoleon on board and, in an attempt to tie the triumph of Waterloo to the War of 1812, emblems 'of France and America overpowered by the Royal Standard of Great Britain'.[42] *The Chester Chronicle* lamented in late October that 'the greatest victory which History records, [had] been celebrated in every principal city and town in the United Kingdom' except their own.[43] This oversight was corrected by the inaugural dinner of the Waterloo Club on 23 October , possibly the first Waterloo Club to be explicitly connected to a conservative political identity.[44] The date 18 January 1816 was designated a day of 'General Thanksgiving to Divine Providence on the re-establishment of Peace

---

[36] Cotes, *Another Mite for Waterloo*, 11–13; Robinson, *A Sermon*, 16–18; Bowerbank, *A Sermon*, 8–10.

[37] Criche, *Sermon*, 11–12.

[38] Mathias, *Waterloo Subscription*, 5–7; Criche, *Sermon*, 7–9; Vickers, *A Sermon*, 9–10.

[39] Robinson, *A Sermon*, 7.

[40] Cotes, *Another Mite for Waterloo*, 13; Robinson, *A Sermon*, 14–15; Mathias, *Waterloo Subscription*, 15–18; Criche, *Sermon*, 11–12.

[41] *Trewman's Exeter Flying Post*, 6 July 1816, p. 4; *Bury and Norwich Post*, 12 July 1815, p. 2.

[42] All of the evening's profits went to the Waterloo Fund. *Bath Chronicle and Weekly Gazette*, 17 August 1815, p. 3.

[43] 'Dinner—Battle of Waterloo', *Chester Chronicle*, 27 October 1815, p. 3.

[44] Toasts were drunk to 'the Immortal Wellington; may he prove as serviceable to the interests of Great Britain in the Cabinet, as he has been in the field', to 'the principles of a Pitt', and the ability of Britain's 'happy constitution' to withstand 'the plea of political reformation'. 'Dinner—Battle of Waterloo', *Chester Chronicle*, 27 October 1815, p. 3.

in Europe', and was marked with special prayers 'in all the churches throughout the kingdom'.[45] In the capital, the day was selected as the ideal one for the formal deposit of the Eagles taken at Waterloo in the Chapel Royal, Whitehall, escorted by a company of the 1st Foot (Grenadier) Guards made up entirely of Waterloo veterans. The service of thanksgiving at the Chapel Royal featured a sermon by William Howley, Lord Bishop of London, and was attended by 'a considerable number of persons of fashion and of distinction in public life', including His Royal Highness the Duke of York, 'several other naval and military officers, [and] many elegant and distinguished females'. Howley's sermon, which echoed many of the themes of the earlier Waterloo Fund Sermons, was somewhat upstaged however, when, apparently without official sanction, the sergeants carrying the French Eagles lowered them to the ground before the colours of the Grenadier Guards, prompting 'loud huzzas' from the august company.[46]

Five months after the Eagles were ensconced in the Chapel Royal, the first anniversary of the battle was celebrated. In addition to the Brigade of Guards' Windsor dinner and the field day turned riot on Wimbledon Common, a variety of celebrations presented themselves to the *ton*. The Dutch ambassador gave an entertainment for the diplomatic set in honour of the anniversary, which was attended by the Russian and Spanish ambassadors as well as Robert Stewart, Viscount Castlereagh, then Foreign Secretary.[47] *The Morning Chronicle*'s 'Mirror of Fashion' also noted a 'numerous party of fashionables' that evening, while the Argyle Rooms hosted a 'Grand Vocal and Instrumental Concert' in honour of the victory, at which would be debuted 'a Grand Military Symphony, entitled "The Battle of Waterloo;" and a Hymn for four voices, addressed to the Shades of the Brave, and dedicated to the Waterloo Men'.[48] Outside London, it was roughly this model that was followed. Edinburgh offered a double bill of entertainments. Forty-nine of the city's most influential men, including three marquesses and six earls, served as stewards for a sumptuous public dinner with tickets priced at a steep one guinea each.[49] Those same men acted as patrons for a slightly less elite Grand Fete and Ball, which boasted the band of the Sixth Dragoon Guards, timed

[45] *The Bury and Norwich Post*, 24 January 1816. Churches across the kingdom had already heard sermons preached in support of the Waterloo Fund. Edward Patteson, *A Sermon Delivered in the Parish Church of Richmond in Surrey, on Sunday the 30th Day of July, 1815, In Behalf of the Families of Those who Fell, Or Were Disabled' in the Battle of Waterloo* (London: Rivingtons, 1815); Daniell Mathias, *Waterloo Subscription: A Sermon, to Recommend the Same* (London: Rivingtons, 1815); Henry Cotes, *Another Mite for Waterloo: A Sermon* (Newcastle: Edward Walker, 1815); Powell Samuel Criche, *A Sermon, preached for the benefit of the Waterloo Sufferers* (Bristol: William Major, 1815).

[46] *The Bury and Norwich Post*, 24 January 1816; *Morning Chronicle*, 13 January 1816; *Morning Post*, 13 January 1816; William Howley, *A Sermon, Preached on Thursday, January 18, 1816* (London: T. Bensley and Son, 1816).

[47] 'Anniversary of the Battle of Waterloo', *Morning Chronicle*, 19 June 1816, p. 3.

[48] 'Anniversary of the Battle of Waterloo', *Morning Chronicle*, 19 June 1816, p. 3; *Morning Chronicle*, 18 June 1816, p. 1.

[49] *Caledonian Mercury*, 13 June 1816, p. 1.

to commence after the conclusion of the dinner.[50] Ipswich likewise hosted a dinner and ball, while in Liverpool 'the demonstrations of satisfaction, usual on the return of memorable days, were manifested'.[51] In Derby and Inverness a more democratic spirit prevailed. In Derby, the True Blue Club gave a dinner to the NCOs and enlisted veterans of the 73rd (Perthshire) Regiment of Foot, while in Inverness 'the Provost, Magistrates, and many of the respectable inhabitants of the town' did the same for a party of NCOs and privates from the 42nd (Royal Highland) Regiment of Foot (The Black Watch).[52] Meanwhile in Bury St Edmunds they simply cut out the middleman and every soldier of the 13th Light Dragoons received 2s. from a town subscription (further supplemented by another shilling each from their colonel), and 'several of the innkeepers gave them a gratuitous dinner'.[53]

'The second anniversary of the glorious and most important battle of Waterloo' in 1817 continued the trend.[54] In London, however, the stakes were somewhat raised by the public opening of Waterloo Bridge on 18 June (see Chapter 6). Hoping to outshine the efforts of the Foot Guards the previous year, the Royal Horse Guards (Blue) threw a 'magnificent *Fete Champetre*...at [the Riding House in] Windsor, in commemoration of the battle of Waterloo...to the whole of the fashionable world'.[55] The fete boasted three military bands that provided music for dancing from 11 p.m. until 5 a.m., interrupted at 1 a.m. by a sit-down supper for 1,000 guests at tables decorated by trophies of Wellington's campaigns.[56] Both the prince regent and the Duke of Wellington were in attendance, with the future George IV holding court in the ballroom from within the campaign tent of the Tipu Sultan, which had been captured at the 1799 siege of Seringapatam at which Wellington, then simply Colonel Arthur Wellesley, had been present.[57]

Despite the magnificence of the Windsor fete, the 'whole of the fashionable world' were spoiled for choice when it came to amusements on the evening of the anniversary.[58] Almack's also threw a 'splendid *Fete*' 'in a style of unexampled

---

[50]   Tickets for the fete were 5s. each. *Caledonian Mercury*, 15 June 1816, p. 1.

[51]   *The Bury and Norwich Post*, 19 June 1816; *Liverpool Mercury*, 21 June 1816.

[52]   *The Derby Mercury*, 13 June 1816. The same democratic spirit did not quite make it to the *Caledonian Mercury*, who seemed almost surprised that the soldiers behaved themselves, noting with approbation that 'they seemed properly to appreciate their well earned laurels, and to consider the medal which they wear, not only an honourable badge of their distinguished bravery, but as a not less marked pledge for their general good conduct'. Inverness, *Caledonian Mercury*, 22 June 1816.

[53]   'Battle of Waterloo', *The Bury and Norwich Post*, 26 June 1816.

[54]   *Royal Cornwall Gazette, Falmouth Packet & Plymouth Journal*, 14 June 1817.

[55]   'Other Parties', *Morning Post*, 9 June 1817, p. 3.

[56]   'Windsor, June 19', *Morning Post*, 20 June 1817, p. 3; 'The Mirror of Fashion', *Morning Chronicle*, 20 June 1817, p. 3; 'Other Parties', *Morning Post*, 9 June 1817, p. 3.

[57]   'Almack's Ball', *Morning Post*, 20 June 1817, p. 3; 'Windsor, June 19', *Morning Post*, 20 June 1817, p. 3.

[58]   In addition to those discussed, there were London celebrations held at Croydon Barracks, the Pulteney Hotel, and the Ordnance Office. 'Other Parties', *Morning Post*, 9 June 1817, p. 3; *Morning Chronicle*, 20 June 1817; 'Festivities in the Past Week', *Morning Post*, 23 June 1817.

magnificence' attended by over thirty of Britain's titled aristocracy, the ambassadors of Sardinia and Spain, a number of other 'fashionables', and the officers of the First and Second Regiments of the Life Guards.[59] Slightly more modest than the fete in Windsor, the dancing at Almack's only lasted until 4:30 a.m.[60] For those who preferred to spend the evening outside, Vauxhall Gardens offered a 'splendid Fete, in celebration of this great National Event'.[61] Vauxhall had served as a patriotic space for nearly a century and, drawing on that tradition and especially a grand celebration of Vittoria in 1813, Vauxhall pulled out all the stops for Waterloo.[62] Most notably, their trademark illuminations were on full display. 'The south side of the Gardens', reported The Morning Post, 'presented, in blazing letters, "Wellington" and "Waterloo," and a bust of the hero in the centre; the whole surrounded by a splendid border of lamps, representing laurels. In other parts of the gardens were His Grace's arms,' and other 'emblems and devices appropriate to the occasion'.[63] Although Vauxhall could not rival Almack's for titled heads, they were not wanting for attendees. The Morning Post informed their readers on 20 June that they had 'seldom seen the Gardens more crowded, or an assemblage distinguished, in a greater degree, for rank, fashion, and elegance'.[64]

Outside the capital, celebrations largely revolved around what the Westmorland Gazette described in 1818 as 'plenty of old English cheer': food, drink, and an atmosphere of 'utmost harmony and conviviality'.[65] Dinners were thrown by or in celebration of Waterloo veterans in Truro, Bury St Edmunds, and Canterbury.[66] A public dinner was held in Salisbury, while in Lyndhurst 18 June was chosen as the date for the Lyndhurst Amusements 'in commemoration of that glorious day'.[67] The Lyndhurst Amusements are also worth noting as the advertisement announcing them is one of the first times 18 June is described as 'Waterloo Day', a term that would become more common as certain annual celebrations became standard.[68]

For the next few years, celebrations followed the models set in 1816 and 1817, with dinners, dancing, and public amusements.[69] The year 1819 saw the debut of a

---

[59] 'Almack's Ball', Morning Post, 20 June 1817, p. 3; 'Almack's Ball', Morning Post, 13 June 1817, p. 3.

[60] 'Almack's Ball', Morning Post, 20 June 1817, p. 3.   [61] Morning Post, 18 June 1817, p. 1.

[62] A Brief Historical and Descriptive Account of the Royal Gardens, Vauxhall (London: Gye and Balne, 1822), 8–10; Eleanor Hughes, 'Guns in the Gardens: Peter Monamy's Paintings for Vauxhall', in Conlin, The Pleasure Garden, 78–99; Conlin, 'Vauxhall Revisited', 725.

[63] 'Vauxhall', Morning Post, 20 June 1817, p. 3; Morning Post, 18 June 1817, p. 1.

[64] Those present included His Royal Highness the Duke of Cumberland, the Hungarian Prince Esterházy, and the French ambassador. 'Vauxhall', Morning Post, 20 June 1817, p. 3.

[65] Westmorland Gazette, 20 June 1818, p. 3; 'Winchester', Salisbury and Winchester Journal, 21 June 1819, p. 4.

[66] 'Truro, Friday, June 20', Royal Cornwall Gazette, 21 June 1817, p. 2; The Bury and Norwich Post, 25 June 1817.

[67] The Salisbury and Winchester Journal, 16 June 1817, p. 4.

[68] The Salisbury and Winchester Journal, 16 June 1817, p. 4.

[69] See, for example, Westmorland Gazette, 20 June 1818, p. 3; 'Winchester', The Salisbury and Winchester Journal, 22 June 1818, p. 4; 'London', Morning Post, 17 July 1818, p. 3; Stamford Mercury,

rural sports day at Winterslow Hut in commemoration of the battle and the inaugural dinner of the Ludgershall Waterloo Friendly Society. Lasting into the 1820s, the Winterslow Hut amusements featured such sporting delights as wrestling, single stick matches (a form of duelling involving cudgels), donkey racing, and 'singing for snuff by old women'.[70] The Waterloo Friendly Society's less energetic commemoration, which usually involved a sermon, a dinner, and a small parade, outlasted Winterslow Hut's offering, and was still going in the mid-1830s.[71] The debacle on Wimbledon Common was not repeated, but there were several planned and successful military reviews and inspections.[72] In 1821, however, two events, one planned and one an accident, reshaped Waterloo commemoration.

On 18 June 1821, a party of private soldiers and NCOs from the Foot Guards were celebrating the anniversary in the Marquis of Granby public house in Westminster when an altercation broke out, apparently over a spoiled game of marbles. The altercation turned into a riot which left several injured and one civilian dead from a fractured skull. Five soldiers were eventually tried in the Old Bailey, where two were found guilty of manslaughter and the other three were acquitted.[73] The coroner's jury, which rendered a verdict of wilful murder and remanded the case to the attention of the Old Bailey, also requested that the coroner take the much rarer step of addressing a letter to the Duke of York, the commander-in-chief, expressing 'their regret that during the two last anniversaries of the battle the drunken and disorderly conduct of the soldiers... had excited considerable alarm'.[74] The Duke of York's military secretary, Sir Herbert Taylor, responded, assuring the coroner, the jury, and, by extension, the citizens of London that the commander-in-chief was 'most anxious to check any excesses committed by the soldiers, and to enforce order and peaceable conduct in their

25 June 1819, p. 3; 'Selkirkshire', *Caledonian Mercury*, 1 July 1819, p. 4; 'Salisbury, Monday June 5, 1820', *The Salisbury and Winchester Journal*, 5 June 1820, p. 4; 'Waterloo Club—Paisley', *Glasgow Herald*, 23 June 1820, p. 4.

[70] 'Salisbury', *The Salisbury and Winchester Journal*, 21 June 1819, p. 4; 'Salisbury, Monday June 5, 1820', *The Salisbury and Winchester Journal*, 5 June 1820, p. 4; *The Salisbury and Winchester Journal*, 11 June 1821, p. 4; *The Salisbury and Winchester Journal*, 17 June 1822, p. 4; *The Salisbury and Winchester Journal*, 16 June 1823, p. 4.

[71] 'Salisbury, Monday, June 26, 1826', *Salisbury and Winchester Journal*, 26 June 1826, p. 4; 'Salisbury, Monday, June 25', *Salisbury and Winchester Journal*, 25 June 1827, p. 4; 'Salisbury, Monday June 23, 1828', *Salisbury and Winchester Journal*, 23 June 1828, p. 4; 'Salisbury, Monday June 22, 1829', *Salisbury and Winchester Journal*, 22 June 1829, p. 4; 'Local Intelligence', *Salisbury and Winchester Journal*, 30 June 1834, p. 2.

[72] *Leeds Intelligencer*, 21 June 1819, p. 3; 'Mirror of Fashion', *Morning Chronicle*, 19 June 1820, p. 2.

[73] 'The Late Riot in Westminster', *Morning Post*, 27 June 1821, p. 3; 'Sunday and Tuesday's Posts', *Bath Chronicle and Weekly Gazette*, 28 June 1821, p. 2; *Bury and Norwich Post*, 4 July 1821, p. 4; 'The Late Riot in the Almonry', *Morning Post*, 4 July 1821, p. 3; 'Old Bailey—The Late Fatal Riot in Westminster', *Morning Chronicle*, 25 July 1821, p. 3; 'Old Bailey, July 25', *Liverpool Mercury*, 27 July 1821, p. 8; 'Westminster Sessions, Thursday, Oct. 18', *Morning Post*, 19 October 1821, p. 3.

[74] *Bury and Norwich Post*, 4 July 1821, p. 4; 'The Late Riot in the Almonry', *Morning Post*, 4 July 1821, p. 3.

intercourse with all classes of his Majesty's subjects', and suggesting that it was perhaps because the two battalions of Foot Guards which had fought at Waterloo were 'distributed in quarters, and not placed in barracks, where they would have been more within the reach of due and close control'.[75]

Even as the riot was spilling out of the Marquis of Granby, a new tradition was being inaugurated on the other side of Green Park. The year 1821 marked the first year that Wellington hosted what would become the Waterloo banquet.[76] Limited that year to between thirty and forty of Wellington's closest comrades and officers of the Royal Horse Guards (Wellington was the regiment's colonel), the banquet evolved into the definitive military commemoration of the anniversary, hosted by the duke for over three decades.[77]

The combination of the Westminster Riot and the debut of the Waterloo banquet marked an unofficial turning point in Waterloo commemorations. In the following years, a segregation of celebrations began to occur along both the civil/military divide and class lines. Within the military, no doubt encouraged by a high command eager to avoid another Westminster Riot, commemorative events were designed to limit civilian contact on and around 18 June. Private dinners replaced public balls, with the transition being led by various groups of veterans/pensioners.[78] Societies of Pensioners paraded and dined on 18 June regularly in Worcester, London, and Wilton, proudly wearing their Waterloo Medals.[79] Where public events occurred, they took the form of parades and reviews, all of which encouraged less interaction with the general populace.[80] In 1822, 1823, 1825, and 1835 the Guards regiments on duty paraded with sprigs of laurel in their caps/helmets, as well as on their colours.[81] In 1824 the 1st Foot (Grenadier) Guards held a 'grand field day in Hyde Park', complete with 'all the new evolutions

---

[75] 'The Late Riot in the Almonry', *Morning Post*, 4 July 1821, p. 3.

[76] 'Fashionable World', *Morning Post*, 18 June 1821, p. 3. Julius Bryant states that the tradition began in 1820, but neither I nor R. E. Foster can find any mention of such an event in the press. Julius Bryant, *Apsley House: The Wellington Collection* (London: English Heritage, 2015), 20; R. E. Foster, 'Food for Thought: The Waterloo Banquet', *The Waterloo Journal* 35, no. 2 (Summer 2013): 13. Furthermore, on 18 June 1820, Wellington attended the Marchioness of Salisbury's Confersazione. *Morning Post*, 20 June 1820, p. 3.

[77] The *Morning Post* gives the total attendees at 42, while Wellington's clerk at the Ordnance Office, W. Holdernesse, who witnessed portions of this first banquet, puts the number at 34. It is also from the list of guests he recorded that we know that invitations were not limited exclusively to officers of the Royal Horse Guards. *Morning Post*, 18 June 1821, p. 3; *Morning Post*, 21 June 1821, p. 3; 18 June 1821 entry, Journal of W. Holdernesse, 1st Duke of Wellington Personal Correspondence/Holdernesse, Stratfield Saye House archive.

[78] *Morning Post*, 18 June 1824; *Caledonian Mercury*, 28 June 1827.

[79] Worcester, *Berrow's Worcester Journal*, 19 June 1823, p. 3; *Berrow's Worcester Journal*, 24 June 1824; *Berrow's Worcester Journal*, 23 June 1825; *Berrow's Worcester Journal*, 21 June 1827; 'Waterloo Grand Dinners', *Morning Post*, 20 June 1825; 'Mirror of Fashion', *Morning Chronicle*, 20 June 1825; 'Local Intelligence', *Salisbury and Winchester Journal*, 25 June 1832, p. 3.

[80] For private military dinners, see *Caledonian Mercury*, 29 June 1827; 'Home News', *Berrow's Worcester Journal*, 30 June 1836, p. 4.

[81] 'Waterloo Day', *Morning Post*, 19 June 1822, p. 3; 'The Mirror of Fashion', *Morning Chronicle*, 19 June 1822, p. 3; 'The Battle of Waterloo', *Morning Post*, 19 June 1823, p. 3; *The Times*, 20 June 1825,

and field exercise' and a public salute of Apsley House as they marched past.[82] The grand field days or reviews were periodically repeated. In 1836 William IV, the Prince of Orange, Wellington, and over 120 officers reviewed three regiments of the Foot Guards, three regiments of the Household Cavalry, two regiments of lancers, and a selection of artillery.[83] Two years later and ten days before her coronation, Victoria reviewed a selection of troops in Hyde Park on Waterloo Day.[84] Wellington also continued to hold his banquet, which as early as 1823 was already being referred to by the press as 'his annual grand dinner'.[85]

On the civilian side, the separation of Waterloo commemoration from military commemoration accelerated. More events appeared that claimed a military theme but lacked military guests. At the same time, one of the unintended consequences of the military's poor behaviour and subsequent retreat into private events was to further cede ownership of Waterloo to the nation as a whole. The removal of Waterloo's military guardians freed the civilian population to eschew the military theme altogether and celebrate Waterloo as a purely national event. Occasional or regular public dinners with no military guests reported were hosted in the Liverpool suburb of Crosby, Liverpool itself, Bury, Maldon, Ipswich, York, Windsor, Winchester, Bristol, Chester, Blandford, Andover, Ludlow, Retford, Lancaster, and Salisbury.[86] In 1823 the parish church of Stoke-by-Nayland hosted its 'annual meeting of amateurs in Sacred Music', 'in commemoration of the victory of Waterloo', while Norfolk chose the eve of the anniversary as their Guild-Day and the inauguration of their chief magistrate.[87] In 1824 The Times sardonically noted that a crowded and popular 'Grand Military Fete and Masquerade' in London's King's Theatre was 'called military, we presume, upon

p. 2; 'Miscellaneous', *Trewman's Exeter Flying Post*, 23 June 1825; 'Army and Navy', *Lancaster Gazetter*, 27 June 1835, p. 2. The tradition of the laurel on Waterloo Day lasted to at least 1849. 'The Army', *Morning Chronicle*, 19 June 1849, p. 7.

[82] The Waterloo veterans involved in the field day also wore laurel. 'The Memorable Eighteenth of June', *Morning Post*, 19 June 1824.

[83] 'Grand Review in Hyde Park', *The Times*, 16 June 1836, p. 3; 'Waterloo Day', *Lancaster Gazetter*, 25 June 1836, p. 1.

[84] 'The Court, Coronation, &c', *Exeter and Plymouth Gazette*, 16 June 1838, p. 4.

[85] 'Miscellaneous Epitome', *Norfolk Chronicle*, 28 June 1823, p. 4.

[86] 'Varieties, Local', *Liverpool Mercury*, 21 June 1822, p. 6; *Bury and Norwich Post*, 26 June 1822, p. 2; 'The Eighteenth of June', *Liverpool Mercury*, 20 June 1823, p. 8; 'Bury', *Bury and Norwich Post*, 25 June 1823, p. 2; 'Sporting', *Yorkshire Gazette*, 19 July 1823, p. 3; 'Windsor', 18 June *Morning Post*, 20 June 1825; *Morning Post*, 22 June 1827; 'Winchester', *Hampshire Telegraph and Sussex Chronicle*, 22 June 1829; 'Salisbury, Monday June 22, 1829', *Salisbury and Winchester Journal*, 22 June 1829, p. 4; 'Winchester', *Hampshire Telegraph and Sussex Chronicle*, 22 June 1829; 'Sons of Paradise', *Bristol Mercury*, 23 June 1832, p. 3; 'Waterloo Day', *Chester Chronicle*, 22 June 1838, p. 3; 'Local Intelligence', *Salisbury and Winchester Journal*, 18 May 1835, p. 3; 'Local Intelligence', *Salisbury and Winchester Journal*, 17 June 1839, p. 3; 'Andover', *Salisbury and Winchester Journal*, 24 June 1839, p. 4; 'Ludlow Odd Fellows' Society', *Hereford Journal*, 23 June 1841, p. 3; 'Retford', *Stamford Mercury*, 23 June 1848, p. 2; 'Anniversary of Waterloo', *Westmorland Gazette*, 23 June 1849, p. 2; 'Retford', *Stamford Mercury*, 25 June 1852, p. 2.

[87] 'Bury', *Bury and Norwich Post*, 25 June 1823, p. 2; 'Guild-Day. Tuesday, June 17', *Norfolk Chronicle*, 21 June 1823, p. 2.

the principle of *Lucus a non lucendo*; for there were but two military uniforms in the room'.[88] In 1827 *The Morning Post*, reported that the Subscription Balls at the Cheltenham Assembly Rooms had celebrated the anniversary 'with a profuse display of variegated lamps and festoons of laurel, with the other customary ensignia of festival and rejoicing' but do not mention a single officer in attendance.[89] Nor is there a record of any officers attending the 'Grand Shinny Match' in Copenhagen Fields, London, that the Society of True Highlanders decided was the ideal way to commemorate the anniversary in 1841.[90]

The open association of the anniversary with the conservative cause also accelerated. The Chester Waterloo Club may have been the first to openly identify 18 June with conservative politics, but they were soon joined by the Norwich Waterloo Club, the Stockport Loyal Wellington Club, the Salisbury and South Wilts Conservative Society, the Nottingham Constitutional Club, the Nottingham Wellington Tory Club, the Carlisle Conservative Association, and an unnamed conservative society in Fordingbridge.[91] Nor was this politicization limited to England. In 1839 William McKendrick wrote to Wellington to seek the duke's permission to found the 'Glasgow Wellington Club' which would meet every 18 June and 'admit members only of good character and of similar conservative opinions'.[92] Sir John Hope was a member of a similar club in Edinburgh, and the surviving toast cards from their Waterloo dinners (which took place in 1835, 1836, and 1838) all show an equal dedication to conservative politics and Protestantism, with toasts being drunk to the 'success of the conservative cause', 'the immortal memory of William Pitt', and 'the Conservative Members of the House of Commons'.[93] Many of these gatherings also openly allied the causes of conservatism and Protestantism, with toasts to 'Protestant Ascendancy' and 'The

---

[88] 'King's Theatre', *The Times*, 25 June 1824, p. 3. '*Lucus a non lucendo*' is a form of illogical argument which claims that two items are related because of their opposite nature.

[89] 'Cheltenham, June 22', *Morning Post*, 25 June 1827, p. 3.

[90] Shinny is a form of street hockey. The match was followed by a dinner. *Morning Post*, 16 June 1841, p. 1.

[91] 'Dinner—Battle of Waterloo', *Chester Chronicle*, 27 October 1815, p. 3; 'Constitutional Association', *Westmorland Gazette*, 2 June 1821, p. 1; 'Battle of Waterloo', *The Lancaster Gazette and General Advertiser*, 25 June 1825; 'Eighteenth of June', *Morning Post*, 25 June 1825; 'Stockport Wellington Club', *Standard*, 22 June 1827, p. 1; 'Twelfth Anniversary of the Battle of Waterloo', *Standard*, 25 June 1827; 'Salisbury', *Salisbury and Winchester Journal*, 23 June 1834, p. 4; 'Conservative Meetings', *Morning Post*, 23 June 1835, p. 6; 'Grand Conservative Festival at Nottingham', *Derby Mercury*, 24 June 1835, p. 3; 'Colonel Chatterton's Triumph', *Nottinghamshire Guardian*, 20 December 1849, p. 1; 'Provincial', *Blackburn Standard*, 1 July 1835, p. 2. There is some evidence that the Nottingham Wellington Tory Club was often referred to simply as the Nottingham Wellington Club. See 'Papal Aggression', *Nottinghamshire Guardian*, 14 November 1850, p. 8.

[92] William McKendrick to Wellington, 12 August 1839, Hartley Library, University of Southampton, MS 61 Wellington Papers, WP2/61/98.

[93] These were not the only toasts; each dinner boasted over 20 toasts. Printed Toast Cards for Waterloo Dinners, 1835, 1836, and 1838, Sir John Hope, 31 Moray Place, National Records of Scotland, Edinburgh, GD253/187/6. For the relationship between Wellington, Waterloo, and Scottish conservatism, see J. E. Cookson, 'The Edinburgh and Glasgow Duke of Wellington Statues: Early Nineteenth-Century Unionist Nationalism as a Tory Project', *The Scottish Historical Review* 83, no. 215 (April 2004): 23–40.

Church as by law established' given alongside those to the heroes of Waterloo and conservative politics.[94] Wellington, although he clearly approved of conservative politics, did not go out of his way to endorse or encourage these banquets. His reply to William McKendrick is noncommittal, and there is no record of his reply to another Glaswegian club requesting an autographed letter from him to crown their own Waterloo celebrations.[95]

In more rural areas, the civilian delights of the rural sports day at Winterslow Hut continued and were joined by a number of rural balls and amusements.[96] Oakham threw an outdoor tea party and dance in 1823, but the most successful rural entertainment was Alresford's Dance on the Nythe.[97] Also known as the Waterloo Maying, the Dance on the Nythe was a two-day event each year, held on the common next to Old Alresford Pond.[98] Under the patronage of Baron and Lady Rodney, 'a handsome and spacious bower was erected' with a full band and small boats to bring revellers across Old Alresford Pond.[99] The boats were constantly kept busy, as reports from the 1820s state that over 200 'highly respectable' couples were often on the dance floor at once, 'surrounded by crowds of merry spectators'.[100] The event was clearly a highlight of the local social calendar, with 'all the beauty and fashion of the neighbourhood grac[ing] the scene', 'highly gratified with their amusement' and behaving with 'the utmost decorum'.[101] The only recorded military presence was a former trooper of one of the Light Dragoon regiments who would provide entertainment by 'running about with a wheelbarrow blindfolded', an amusement at which he apparently showed remarkable skill.[102]

---

[94] 'Anniversary of the Battle of Waterloo', *Morning Post*, 28 June 1827, p. 4; *The Times*, 21 June 1845, p. 8; Printed Toast Cards for Waterloo Dinners, 1835, 1836, and 1838, Sir John Hope, 31 Moray Place, National Records of Scotland, Edinburgh, GD253/187/6.

[95] Wellington to William McKendrick, draft reply, 1839, Hartley Library, University of Southampton, MS 61 Wellington Papers, WP2/61/98; John Thomas to Wellington, 13 June 1839, Hartley Library, University of Southampton, MS 61 Wellington Papers, WP2/59/101.

[96] *The Salisbury and Winchester Journal*, 17 June 1822, p. 4; *The Salisbury and Winchester Journal*, 16 June 1823, p. 4. Winterslow Hut prompted imitators, most notably at Petersfinger and the Somerset town of Wellington. 'Bath, Wednesday June 23', *Bath Chronicle and Weekly Gazette*, 24 June 1819, p. 3; *Salisbury and Winchester Journal*, 11 June 1821, p. 4; 'Salisbury', *Salisbury and Winchester Journal*, 16 June 1823, p. 4; 'Salisbury', *Salisbury and Winchester Journal*, 13 June 1836, p. 4; 'Salisbury', *Salisbury and Winchester Journal*, 17 June 1839, p. 4.

[97] 'Oakham, June 20', *Stamford Mercury*, 27 June 1823, p. 3, 'Winchester', *Hampshire Telegraph and Sussex Chronicle*, 22 June 1829.

[98] A maying is the celebration of May Day, traditionally held on 1 May every year. In a particularly patriotic move, the towns around Winchester decided to move their annual May Day celebration to 18 June to mark Waterloo. See 'Winchester, June 13', *Morning Post*, 13 June 1825; 'Dance on the Nythe', *Morning Post*, 27 June 1825; 'Winchester', *Hampshire Telegraph and Sussex Chronicle*, 22 June 1829.

[99] 'Dance on the Nythe', *Morning Post*, 27 June 1825; 'Southampton, June 25', *Morning Post*, 27 June 1826.

[100] 'Dance on the Nythe', *Morning Post*, 27 June 1825; 'Winchester', *The Salisbury and Winchester Journal*, 23 June 1823, p. 4; 'Southampton, June 25', *Morning Post*, 27 June 1826.

[101] 'Winchester', *The Salisbury and Winchester Journal*, 23 June 1823, p. 4; *Hampshire Telegraph and Sussex Chronicle*, 25 June 1827; 'Dance on the Nythe', *Morning Post*, 27 June 1825.

[102] *A Narrative of the Life of Richard Titheridge, a Native of Alresford, Better Known in Winchester and Southampton by the Name of Dickey Dung Prong, Formerly a Light Dragoon in the British Army. To which is Added, an Account of the Murder of His Father, about Sixty-two Years Ago* (London: John Fletcher, 1835), 8.

There were, of course, exceptions. In 1826 Colonel Horner and the officers of the North Somerset Yeomanry Cavalry gave a 'grand gala...at Sydney Gardens' in Bath complete with illuminations, an imitative triumphal arch, a transparency depicting the charge of the 2nd Dragoons (Scots Greys), and a variety of performances. The event and 'the fineness of the weather attracted a very numerous assemblage', who were 'afforded the highest gratification'.[103] Two years later Colonel Ross and the officers of the 4th (Royal Irish) Dragoon Guards attended a Waterloo ball in Exeter after the entire regiment 'paraded the streets in their full equipment, and lent the ball the regimental band.[104] In 1850, the 28th (North Gloucestershire) Regiment of Foot threw a grand ball in Portsmouth in celebration of the day and receiving new colours.[105]

While physical separation and the limitation of interactions to more carefully choreographed events significantly reduced disturbances such as the Westminster Riot, they could not completely overcome the dangers of the heady mix of victory and alcohol. In 1823 a group of Dragoons broke every window in the Duke of Wellington Public House in Canterbury when, after drinking heavily in celebration of the battle, they involved themselves in a massive brawl with a group of tradesmen.[106] Three years later a veteran of the 42nd (Royal Highland) Regiment of Foot (The Black Watch) summed up the views of many serving and former soldiers when he explained to a magistrate that he 'must get drunk' upon the anniversary of Waterloo and, as he had not retreated before the French at Waterloo, he refused to do so before a watchman or magistrate.[107] While there is no record of whether he was ever arraigned for drunkenness again, the sight of veterans overindulging on 18 June became common enough that in 1830 the 'portrait and military painter' William Heath produced a satirical print condemning such excesses (Figure 3.1).[108] Scathingly entitled *The Glorious 18th of June*, the print does not show the apotheosis of Britain's glory or even a grand review or dinner, but instead two drunken cavalry officers staggering arm in arm. Their jackets undone, trousers unstrapped, headwear askew, and belts, pouches, and swords hanging haphazardly from their arms and necks they lurch from one celebration to another, jovial faces beaming and the Waterloo Medal shining proudly from at least one of their breasts.[109]

---

[103] 'Bath, June 24', *Morning Post*, 27 June 1826; Sydney Gardens hosted another Waterloo Gala in 1840, with no mention of officers being present. *Bath Chronicle and Weekly Gazette*, 18 June 1840, p. 3.
[104] *Exeter and Plymouth Gazette*, 31 May 1828, p. 3; *Exeter and Plymouth Gazette*, 21 June 1828, p. 2.
[105] 'Naval Intelligence', *The Times*, 15 June 1850, p. 8.
[106] Thankfully, on that occasion no one was killed. *Morning Post*, 23 June 1823, p. 4.
[107] 'A Waterloo Relic', *Hampshire Chronicle*, 26 June 1826, p. 2.
[108] Lawrence Binyon, *Catalogue of Drawings by British Artists and Artists of Foreign Origin Working in Great Britain, Preserved in the Department of Prints and Drawings in the British Museum* (London: Trustees of the British Museum, 1900), II: 301.
[109] The area where the hussar's medal would be worn is covered by his pelisse.

THE GLORIOUS 18 OF JUNE

Figure 3.1 William Heath and Thomas McLean, *The Glorious 18th of June*, 1830. Anne S. K. Brown Military Collection, John Hay Library, Brown University, Providence.

It soon became clear to Horse Guards and regimental commanders, however, that such public displays (whether in the flesh or in print) were only slightly less damning than the Westminster Riot, and reports of drunk and disorderly conduct around the anniversary disappeared.[110] With this better behaviour and the further segregation of events along both military/civilian and class lines came a switch in how the public perceived the military's role in Waterloo commemoration. In the years immediately following the battle, its veterans were at the heart of the commemorations, and the celebrations were as much for them as they were expressions of general national joy. As time went on, however, many Waterloo veterans, especially enlisted men, went from being centred in the celebrations to merely appearing as set dressing within them. This led to civilian society co-opting the military's commemorations, viewing them as spectacles for the nation's entertainment. Wellington's Waterloo banquet, as we shall see, captured the imagination of the entire nation and the popular press went out of their way to

---

[110] It is likely that the drunkenness continued, but in private.

cover it as a national and historical event. This trend was not limited to the rarefied air of Apsley House, however. In 1822 *The Morning Post* reported that 'the concourse of people assembled' to observe the laurel-decked Waterloo Day inspection parade 'was immense', and they were well entertained by the spectacle and the regimental bands.[111] At the grand review in 1836 'crowds of well-dressed persons' appeared as early as 8 in the morning (the event began at 11), 'and in the course of the morning every window that could command a view, and the very house tops, were occupied with anxious spectators'.[112] A more routine inspection of the Foot Guards regiments on Waterloo Day in 1841 still attracted 'several hundreds of the nobility, ladies, gentlemen, &c.'[113] Regimental bands were known to give concerts around 18 June, and military manoeuvres on the anniversary also attracted large crowds in Dublin in 1829, 1835, 1838, and 1849, Chatham in 1833, Devonport in 1844, and Portsmouth in 1850.[114] The trend was even more pronounced in private entertainments. Astley's Royal Amphitheatre's hippo-drama *The Battle of Waterloo* (which debuted in 1824 and is discussed in detail in Chapter 5) advertised that it employed veterans in its battle scenes while various galleries, museums, and panoramas offered free admission on 18 June to any veteran who wore his Waterloo Medal.[115] While these were, on the surface, laudable gestures, the former reinforced the notion that veterans were part of the spectacle, and the latter actively attempted to recruit veterans for verisimilitude.

From 1821 on, two events rose to the forefront of annual Waterloo commem-oration. One, unsurprisingly, was the Waterloo banquet hosted by Wellington himself. The other was the Vauxhall Waterloo fete. There is a temptation to regard pleasure gardens as an eighteenth-century phenomenon that somehow survived into the nineteenth century. Part of this image is driven by Vauxhall's own success-ful attempt to market itself as an oasis of Georgian London in the bustling Victorian metropolis.[116] More recent scholarship has examined and looked beyond the pleasure garden's manufactured 'Old Vauxhall' image, however, to demonstrate that pleasure gardens in general and Vauxhall in particular continued to reinvent

---

[111] 'Waterloo Day', *Morning Post*, 19 June 1822, p. 3.

[112] 'Waterloo Day', *Lancaster Gazetter*, 25 June 1836, p. 1.

[113] The inspection was prior to them assuming their duties as the guards of the Buckingham Palace. 'Waterloo Day', *Standard*, 19 June 1841, p. 2.

[114] *Morning Post*, 20 June 1825; 'The Army', *Morning Chronicle*, 23 June 1829; 'Launch of the Waterloo', *The Times*, 19 June 1833, p. 5; 'Army and Navy', *Lancaster Gazetter*, 27 June 1835, p. 2; 'Army and Navy', *Lancaster Gazetter*, 30 June 1838, p. 1; 'Grand Review in Devonport', *The Times*, 22 June 1844, p. 7; 'Anniversary of the Battle of Waterloo', *Freeman's Journal*, 19 June 1849, p. 2; 'Naval Intelligence', *The Times*, 19 June 1850, p. 6.

[115] See Chapters 4 and 5. 'The Waterloo Museum', *Morning Post*, 18 November 1815, p. 3; *Caledonian Mercury*, 22 June 1820, p. 3; *Norfolk Chronicle*, 29 September 1821, p. 2; 'Anniversary of the Battle of Waterloo', *Morning Post*, 14 June 1825, p. 1; *Morning Post*, 15 June 1825, p. 3; Philip Shaw, *Waterloo and the Romantic Imagination* (Basingstoke: Palgrave Macmillan, 2002), 84; Milkes, 'A Battle's Legacy', 371–2.

[116] Conlin, 'Vauxhall Revisited', 735–43.

themselves and remained popular throughout the nineteenth century.[117] Vauxhall's Waterloo fetes have received only token attention from scholars but serve as a prime example of that determination to innovate and the popularity that came with it. With Waterloo, Vauxhall took what had up until that point been a largely inchoate collection of spectacles around the country and shaped them into an art form. In the early years, when Vauxhall's crowds were its chief spectacle, the fete emphasized them with illuminations, music, and other entertainments that encouraged perambulation and socializing. As the tastes of London's crowds moved towards more Victorian definitions of spectacle and theatricality, the fete also adapted, shifting from highlighting its immersive ambience to staging re-enactments where guests were palpably an audience. Finally, as Vauxhall made a virtue of its anachronism and became 'Old Vauxhall', its history and bona fides were further polished by the annual commemoration of one of the Regency's defining moments. The result was a tradition that lasted from 1817 until 1850 and would fundamentally alter the layout of the gardens.[118] The Waterloo fetes proved so successful that one night was often not enough for the populace, and they were regularly held on multiple days around the anniversary, sometimes extending into July.[119]

Located in the neighbourhood of Kennington on the south side of the Thames, Vauxhall Gardens had been one of London's premier outdoor enter-tainments since the days of Samuel Pepys.[120] Known for fireworks, musical performances, outrageous architecture, romantic assignations, and, of course, illuminations, Vauxhall was popular enough that its location influenced the location of the Huntley Ferry and Vauxhall Bridge.[121] Although theoretically open to anyone who could pay the entrance fee (which was 3s. 6d. through the 1820s and rose to 4s. after that), Vauxhall had several invisible barriers to entry: transportation costs, the price of suitable clothes, and the pressure to purchase expensive food and drink once inside.[122] In addition to strict financial concerns

[117] Rachel Cowgill, 'Performance Alfresco: Music-Making in London's Pleasure Gardens', in Conlin, ed., The Pleasure Garden, 100–26; Lee Jackson, Palaces of Pleasure: From Music Halls to the Seaside to Football. How the Victorians Invented Mass Entertainment (New Haven: Yale University Press, 2019), 121–2; Conlin, 'Vauxhall Revisited'.

[118] 'Vauxhall Gardens', The Times, 19 June 1850, p. 4; 'The Last of Vauxhall', The Era, 17 July 1859, p. 11.

[119] The first Waterloo fete in 1817 was held at least twice. Morning Post, 18 June 1817, p. 1; Morning Post, 19 June 1817, p. 1; 'Royal Gardens, Vauxhall', The Times, 25 July 1827, p. 2; 'Repetition. Royal Gardens, Vauxhall', The Times, 9 July 1828, p. 2.

[120] For a general history of Vauxhall, see David Coke and Alan Borg, Vauxhall Gardens: A History (New Haven: Yale University Press/Paul Mellon Centre for Studies in British Art, 2011); Jackson, Palaces of Pleasure, chapter 5; William B. Boulton, Amusements of Old London (New York: Tabard, 1970), II: 1–41; A Brief Historical and Descriptive Account of the Royal Gardens, Vauxhall; Richard D. Altick, The Shows of London (Cambridge: The Belknap Press, 1978), chapters 7 and 23.

[121] When the bridge opened, the Vauxhall Gardens advertisements included it as one of the attractions. 'The Mirror of Fashion', Morning Chronicle, 24 July 1816, p. 3.

[122] Borsay, 'Pleasure Gardens and Urban Culture', 65–7; 'Vauxhall-Gardens', The Times, 5 June 1841, p. 8.

were temporal ones. Vauxhall was best experienced after dark and ran late. In 1827 the Surrey magistrates sought to limit this by mandating that the fireworks start no later than 11 p.m. Vauxhall's proprietors responded by simply postponing the concert until after the fireworks, thus further extending the evening.[123] Waterloo's anniversary was also more often than not on a weeknight. To truly enjoy the Waterloo fete one not only needed money for transportation, clothing, entrance, and food and drink, but also the luxury of not having to be anywhere early the next morning. This further limited the attendance to London's fashionable set.

The fetes in 1818, 1819, and 1820 closely followed the pattern set in 1817, with illuminations, music, and a rope performance from the well-known tightrope walker Madame Saqui, the evening concluding 'with a superbly brilliant discharge of fire-works'.[124] In 1821 Vauxhall's proprietors seized on the anniversary as the perfect event with which to open for the London season after a complete redecoration, promising 'a number of appropriate Emblems and Devices...with an unusual variety of attractive Novelties', three bands, a *tableau mouvant*, and fireworks that 'will exceed in splendour and variety all former Seasons'.[125] The next few years followed that model (although the price reverted to the standard admission of 3s. 6d., rather than staying at the 5s. 6d. that was charged in 1821), with martial music and illuminations serving to highlight Vauxhall's non-Waterloo attractions such as the Heptaplasiesoptron and the cosmoramas, both answers to the growing popularity of panoramas.[126] The 1823 fete, for example, featured the 'Military, Concert, Scotch, and Pandean Bands...perform[ing] several Pieces of Martial Music, and the Vocal Performers will sing several Military Songs'. While the Illuminations were bolstered by '10,000 additional lamps, in Military and other Devices, causing the Gardens to have a more than usual brilliant appearance'.[127] In 1824, in response to competition from the new *Battle of Waterloo* hippodrama at Astley's and the peristrephic panorama of Waterloo at the Spring Gardens, Vauxhall upped the ante again.[128] The number of additional lamps went from 10,000 to 12,000, and they were arranged to form the words

---

[123] 'Vauxhall-Gardens', *The Times*, 5 June 1827, p. 3.

[124] *The Times*, 18 June 1818, p. 2; *Morning Chronicle*, 18 June 1819, p. 1; *Morning Post*, 19 June 1820, p. 1.

[125] The fireworks promised to recreate the eruption of Mount Vesuvius. *Morning Chronicle*, 18 June 1821, p. 3.

[126] *The Times*, 18 June 1819, p. 2; *Morning Chronicle*, 18 June 1821, p. 3; *Morning Post*, 18 June 1822, p. 1; *Morning Chronicle*, 19 June 1822, p. 3; *Morning Chronicle*, 18 June 1823, p. 3. The Heptaplasiesoptron was a display of seven mirrors in a semi-hexagon which, when lit, displayed 'several illuminated revolving pillars and palm-trees, twinning serpents, and a fountain of real water'. *A Brief Historical and Descriptive Account of the Royal Gardens, Vauxhall*, 19; Jackson, *Palaces of Pleasure*, 123. A cosmorama is a collection of circular or near-circular perspective pictures, usually of landmarks. *Descriptive Catalogue of the Cosmorama Panoramic Exhibition* (London: A. A. Paris, 1825).

[127] *Morning Chronicle*, 18 June 1823, p. 3. The claims of additional lamps became so common that satirists of the gardens took to using them as a running joke. Conlin, 'Vauxhall Revisited', 738.

[128] See Chapters 4 and 5.

'"Wellington," and "Waterloo"...[and illuminate] a transparent portrait of the hero'.[129] The fireworks took the form of St George and the Dragon and Wellington's name once again, with the legend 'Long may he live' suspended beneath it, while, in direct response to Spring Gardens' peristrephic panorama, a new piece was added to the cosmoramas, 'painted expressly for the occasion, representing the Battle of Waterloo'.[130] The gambit paid off, as *The Times* reported that 'the company was numerous and respectable, comprising many persons of fashion'.[131]

The Vauxhall Waterloo fete reached its apogee of spectacle in 1827. Under the direction of Charles Farley of the Theatre Royal, Covent Garden, the area around the Fireworks Tower was cleared to create a multi-acre natural stage.[132] On this new open plot, known until Vauxhall closed in 1859 as the Waterloo Ground (Figure 3.2), 'an exact Representation of the Field of Battle, with the various Buildings of the Farm-houses, La Belle Alleance [*sic*], Hougomont, &c.... [was]

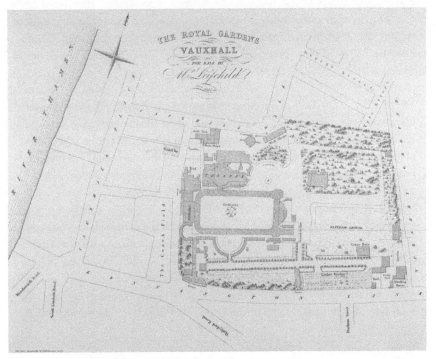

Figure 3.2 *The Royal Gardens Vauxhall* (London: John Grieve, 1841). © The British Library Board Maps Crace Port. 16.66.

---

[129] *Morning Post*, 19 June 1824.
[130] *Morning Post*, 19 June 1824; 'Vauxhall Gardens', *The Times*, 19 June 1824, p. 5.
[131] 'Vauxhall Gardens', *The Times*, 19 June 1824, p. 5.
[132] 'The Mirror of Fashion', *Morning Chronicle*, 4 June 1827; 'Vauxhall Gardens', *Morning Post*, 19 June 1827.

erected in the same relative situations as on the Plains of Waterloo'.[133] While they were clearing the foliage from the new Waterloo Ground, the proprietors of Vauxhall laid underground gas pipes. Using these, they illuminated the action with 'great bodies of fire of various colours', blew up artillery wagons, and, at the climax of the action, 'set fire' to the Chateau Hougoumont.[134]

On this purpose-built and illuminated dance floor of Ares 'upwards of a 1000 Soldiers', 'most...selected from troops actually engaged in the battle' supplemented by John Cooke and his equestrian team from the Royal Amphitheatre, Liverpool, put on a spectacle that the *Morning Post* declared was 'one of the most grand and extraordinary perhaps ever witnessed in this country'.[135]

The 1827 fete was a direct response to Astley's *Battle of Waterloo*. Rumours circulated that Vauxhall would hire Andrew Ducrow, Astley's chief equestrian, and his team for the event.[136] Instead, they hired Cooke, Ducrow's chief competition, declaring his stud of horses 'unrivalled'.[137] Aware that their audience would also inevitably compare the spectacle to Astley's hippodrama, they laced their advertisements with snide comments about the superior accuracy of any outdoor depiction. Fresh from their success on the 18th, the proprietors of Vauxhall crowed in *The Morning Chronicle, The Morning Post,* and *The Times* on 20 June that

The new Grand Spectacle of the *Battle of Waterloo*, produced for the first time on Monday evening, has created a sensation and effect totally unprecedented. The immense resources of the Royal Gardens—resources possessed by no other place of public amusement—have enabled the Proprietors to achieve what has hitherto been considered an impossibility—the giving a true and animated picture of the terrific progress of a great National Battle, with all its attendant casualties, and sublime and imposing effects. The vastness of the space the Proprietors are enabled to devote to this extraordinary Spectacle, for the unrestrained evolutions of Cavalry and Infantry—the realities and advantages their scene of action affords them, of actual hill, plain, wood, and building, correctly placing before the eyes of the spectators these heroic glories of which all have heard, and in which all are interested, fully realize all that has been recorded in Classical History of the immense arenas of the Greeks and Romans...the various awful

[133]   *The Examiner,* 17 June 1827, p. 15.
[134]   *The Examiner,* 17 June 1827, p. 15; 'Vauxhall Gardens', *The Times,* 20 June 1827, p. 2.
[135]   'Vauxhall Gardens', *Morning Post,* 19 June 1827; *The Examiner,* 17 June 1827, p. 15.
[136]   *Berrow's Worcester Journal,* 7 June 1827.
[137]   This rumour has led to the incorrect belief that the 1827 Vauxhall fete incorporated portions of J. H. Amherst's *Battle of Waterloo*. Brenda Assael, *The Circus and Victorian Society* (Charlottesville: University of Virginia Press, 2005), 51. There is the slight possibility that some of Ducrow's riders were recruited as auxiliaries, but there is no indication of a more formal agreement. *The Examiner,* 17 June 1827, p. 15. Two years before, however, the two organizations had cooperated, and Astley's performances had concluded for a time with 'a Pot Pourri After-Entertainment, called Vauxhall at Astley's'. 'Royal Amphitheatre', *Morning Chronicle,* 16 June 1825.

and electrical tableaus, occurring in different parts of the progress of the Battle of Waterloo, chiefly executed by troops actually engaged in that tremendous contest, excited no less astonishment than delight in the spectators, and were crowned at the close with the universal acclamations of approbation of as numerous and brilliant an assemblage as ever graced the Royal Gardens with their presence.[138]

Boasting aside, certain members of the press were not persuaded by the benefits of the outdoor re-enactment. *The Examiner* questioned 'how far this necessarily very expensive entertainment will answer the object of its projectors, seems to us doubtful. Astley satiates curiosity as to horses, and, like all theatrical representations of battles, almost everything else is unavoidably a noisy representation of nothing.'[139] *The Standard* was even more damning, simply concluding 'as a piece of action and spectacle it is far inferior to that exhibited at Astley's last season'.[140] All of the reviews, however, admitted that Vauxhall's fete was a success when it came to attendance. 'These Gardens', reported *The Times*, 'presented the fullest attendance of visitors on Monday evening which we ever remember to have witnessed,' and even *The Standard* admitted that the re-enactment, 'in combination with the other wonders of Vauxhall ... [will] dazzle the sight and affect the imagination of Londoners for a time'.[141]

The Standard proved correct, and the public flocked to Vauxhall. After a hugely successful opening night the spectacle was repeated on Wednesday, 20 June, when *Berrow's Worcester Journal* reported they again 'drew an immense crowd', but that 'the public expectation has not been answered to the full extent'.[142] Repeat performances followed through to the end of August, attracting not only a large portion of London but also such notable figures as the Prince of Leiningen, His Royal Highness the Duke of Gloucester, the Duke of Sussex, and members of the court of the Queen of Württemberg.[143] Wellington himself graced the event on the night of 12 July, and, according to Prince Hermann von Pückler-Muskau, 'laughed heartily at his representative'.[144] Wellington may have been laughing, but others

---

[138] *Morning Chronicle*, 20 June 1827, p. 3; *Morning Post*, 20 June 1827, p. 3; *The Times*, 20 June 1827, p. 2.

[139] 'Vauxhall Gardens', *Examiner*, 24 June 1827, p. 11.

[140] 'Vauxhall', *Standard*, 19 June 1827, p. 1.

[141] 'Vauxhall Gardens', *The Times*, 20 June 1827, p. 2; 'Vauxhall', *Standard*, 19 June 1827, p. 1.

[142] 'Vauxhall', *Berrow's Worcester Journal*, 21 June 1827.

[143] *Morning Chronicle*, 23 June 1827; 'Mirror of Fashion', *Morning Chronicle*, 14 July 1827; *Morning Post*, 7 August 1827; 'Miscellaneous', *Trewman's Exeter Flying Post*, 6 September 1827; Pamphlet advertising the King's Birthday Gala at Vauxhall, 13 August 1827, London Play Places 8 (23f), John Johnson Collection, Bodleian Library, University of Oxford; Vauxhall Gardens Advertisement, 27 August 1827, London Play Places 8 (22c), John Johnson Collection, Bodleian Library, University of Oxford; Vauxhall Gardens Advertisement, 1827, London Play Places 8 (22d), John Johnson Collection, Bodleian Library, University of Oxford.

[144] Hermann von Pückler-Muskau, *Tour in England, Ireland, and France, in the Years 1826, 1827, 1828, and 1829* (Philadelphia: Carey, Lea, & Blanchard, 1833), 157. His letter dated 12 July (156–8) contains a detailed description of the performance.

were completely taken in by the scenery and the soldiers. None more so than Albert Smith, the author, playwright, and mountaineer, who saw the spectacle when he was 12. Twenty years later he recalled that 'the entire evening was to me one scene of continuous enchantment. The Battle of Waterloo was being represented on the firework-ground, and I could not divest myself of the idea that it was a real engagement I was witnessing... When I stood years afterwards on the real battle-field I was disappointed in its effect. I thought it ought to have been a great deal more like Vauxhall.'[145]

There was one other area where Vauxhall's 1827 re-enactment was accurate: noise. In theory the re-enactment was accompanied by a *Waterloo Cantata* composed by Henry Bishop, then the pleasure gardens' musical director.[146] In reality, the overriding soundscape was one of gunfire and explosions. When, in May of the following year, rumours began to circulate that Vauxhall was preparing to either revive last year's show or perhaps use the same system to recreate the recent allied naval victory at Navarino, 'an old Under-Sheriff' in the area wrote an excoriating letter to *The Times* insisting that 'the noise of the exhibition of the battle of Waterloo could only be compared to the cannonading of a town'.[147] Under different circumstances, the proprietors of Vauxhall, pushing their claims of accuracy, would probably have been delighted to hear that their performance 'conveyed through an extensive and thickly-peopled district the exact effect of artillery and platoon firing', but not when it came attached to accusations of 'disgusting orgies of lust and drunkenness, and the deliberate robbing of industrious workers and the sick of their rest, and the dying of the peace in their final moments'.[148]

In deference to local pressure and very probably the extreme cost of 1827's show, the fete was slightly scaled back in 1828.[149] Even as the advertisements insisted that the 1828 Gala would be 'on the most magnificent and extensive scale ever witnessed in these Gardens', and reassured readers that 'The Battle of Waterloo, which last season excited so much interest, will be represented... it being understood that the Public fully expect that this Grand National Spectacle will then form part of the Amusements', changes were under way. Neither Charles Farley nor John Cooke returned, but instead 'Large Bodies of Soldiers, Horse and Foot, will be engaged, under the direction of Mr. Ducrow, who will bring into Action his Stud of highly-bred Horses, and his whole Equestrian Company will

---

[145] Albert Smith, 'Vauxhall', in Albert Smith, ed., *Gavarni in London: Sketches of Life and Character, with Illustrative Essays by Popular Writers* (London: David Bogue, 1849), 92.

[146] Cowgill, 'Performance Alfresco', 119.

[147] 'National Morals', *The Times*, 21 May 1828, p. 3.

[148] 'National Morals', *The Times*, 21 May 1828, p. 3. The popularity of Vauxhall's Waterloo fete had caused a slight increase in crime. 'Police', *The Times*, 20 June 1827, p. 3.

[149] Several papers noted the expense of the spectacle. 'Vauxhall Gardens', *Jackson's Oxford Journal*, 23 June 1827; 'Vauxhall Gardens', *The Examiner*, 24 June 1827, p. 11.

attend the Gardens after the performance at the Amphitheatre.'[150] The performance still contained (much to the horror, no doubt, of 'an old Under-Sheriff') 'the
various attacks of infantry and cavalry, the blowing up of an ammunition wagon,
and the view of the Chateau of Goumont in flames' but the boasts of 1,000
soldiers, as well as the claim that most of the performers were veterans, were
missing.[151] In an effort to obtain that same verisimilitude, the Gardens offered a
demonstration of a 'real Congreve War Rocket' which was securely fastened to a
stake 'and thus ignited, will shew the intensity of its powers of burning' without
the danger of setting Kennington or Lambeth ablaze.[152] Despite the insistence of
The Morning Post that 'the spectacle formed as grand and terrific a picture...as
could well be presented to the public', something was lacking.[153] Perhaps it was the
fact that, no matter what the proprietors of Vauxhall did, they could not compete
with royal pomp.

In 1828, the most significant Waterloo celebration was a regatta on the Thames,
held by the Duke of Clarence (later William IV), then the Lord High Admiral, to
mark the battle. The regatta, which featured a rowing race centred, rather fittingly,
on Waterloo Bridge and boasting a total of 23 sovereigns in prize money, drew the
ceremonial barges of several of the City's guilds and attracted not only Wellington
and an elite crowd of senior army and naval personnel, but also aristocrats and
several ambassadors, including Prince Polignac, then representing France at the
Court of St James's.[154] Consequently the grandest of Vauxhall's 1828 Waterloo
performances took place not on 18 June, but twenty days later on 8 July, as part of
a 'grand dress fete for the benefit of the Spanish and Italian refugees'. Given that
the organizational committee boasted Lord Fitzroy Somerset, then military secretary, who lost his right arm at Waterloo, and was presided over by Wellington
himself, and that tickets cost a full sovereign, Vauxhall pulled out all the stops. The
advertisements insisted that 'by special desire, the celebrated grand spectacle of
the Battle of Waterloo will be performed...the whole embracing the greatest
number of Cavalry and Infantry that ever appeared in any public spectacle', while
The Morning Post declared the spectacle 'revived with increased splendour'.[155]
Despite Wellington's approval (his arrival in Field Marshal's uniform to the
strains of 'See, the Conquering Hero Comes' was so distracting it apparently
denied the vaudeville entertainment an audience), the 1828 Vauxhall Battle of

[150] *Morning Post*, 18 June 1828, p. 2; *Morning Chronicle*, 18 June 1828, p. 3.
[151] 'Vauxhall Gardens', *Morning Post*, 19 June 1828, p. 3; 'Vauxhall Gardens', *Morning Chronicle*,
19 June 1828, p. 2.
[152] *Morning Post*, 18 June 1828, p. 2; *Morning Chronicle*, 18 June 1828, p. 3.
[153] 'Vauxhall Gardens', *Morning Post*, 19 June 1828, p. 3.
[154] 'Waterloo Regatta', *The Times*, 19 June 1828, p. 6; 'The Regatta', *Morning Chronicle*, 19 June
1828, p. 2.
[155] *Morning Post*, 8 July 1828, p. 1; 'Vauxhall Gardens', *Morning Post*, 10 July 1828, p. 3.

Waterloo closed early on 11 July, sabotaged by the revival, on 14 July, of Astley's *Battle of Waterloo*.[156]

In 1829 Astley's began their tradition of reviving *The Battle of Waterloo* for the anniversary and rather than contest the field, Vauxhall's Waterloo fete returned to its roots, honouring the victory with music and illuminations rather than re-enactments and flames.[157] This became the standard at Vauxhall. The year 1833 saw the debut of the 'Waterloo Waltzes', which *The Times* declared 'ought to be heard by all lovers of martial music', while in 1836 the crowds were entertained by the band of the Coldstream Guards.[158] The twentieth anniversary of the battle in 1835 was bathed in light, 'an absolute galaxy of artificial stars' with an 'immense grand military trophy composed of' 'no less than 13,500 lamps. Besides this brilliant display there was a sprinkling of halberds and muskets (in lamps), ranged along the walks, and pictures of soldiers bivouacking, and flags, and banners, of every colour and country, decorating the trees'.[159] In 1838 one end of the large quadrangle was dominated by 'a portrait of the Duke of Wellington in bronze-coloured lamps, surrounded with wreaths of laurel in green lamps'.[160] Whatever musicians and performers were in residence at that time performed, often adding some form of military piece or theme, and they were supplemented by more explicitly martial music and further decorations.[161] In this, Vauxhall set the standard. The King's Theatre, Haymarket, on the days around the anniversary, would add a fourth act to their musical selections comprising 'Beethoven's celebrated Battle Symphony, composed in celebration of the Battle of Waterloo, with appropriate scenery, decorations, &c., and drama-tized expressly for this occasion. The whole to conclude with the National Anthem "God save the King."'[162] The Prague Minstrels, who were performing at the Egyptian Hall, Piccadilly, during the fifteenth anniversary of the battle in 1830, announced to potential audience members that 'in commemoration of the Battle of Waterloo, their popular piece under that name, with a new movement,

---

[156] 'Grand Fete at Vauxhall Gardens', *Morning Chronicle*, 9 July 1828, p. 3; *Morning Chronicle*, 14 July 1828, p. 2; *Morning Post*, 14 July 1828, p. 1. At the end of the season Vauxhall threw a Grand Union Gala which attempted 'to combine in one Grand Fete the splendid Attractions of all the Galas of the Season' including the Waterloo fete, but it is unclear how much of the Waterloo fete made it into this smorgasbord of spectacle. *Morning Chronicle*, 26 August 1828, p. 2; *Morning Post*, 29 August 1828, p. 2.

[157] *The Times*, 18 June 1829, p. 2; 'Vauxhall Gardens', *Morning Post*, 20 June 1829.

[158] 'Vauxhall', *The Times*, 18 June 1833, p. 6; 'Vauxhall Gardens', *The Times*, 18 June 1836, p. 3.

[159] 'Vauxhall', *The Times*, 20 June 1835, p. 5; 'Royal Gardens, Vauxhall', *Morning Post*, 20 June 1835, p. 3.

[160] 'Vauxhall Gardens', *The Times*, 19 June 1838, p. 5.

[161] 'Royal Gardens, Vauxhall', *The Times*, 17 June 1836, p. 4; 'Vauxhall Royal Gardens', *The Times*, 17 June 1823, p. 2.

[162] In fact, Beethoven's Battle Symphony, also known as Wellington's Victory, was actually com-posed in 1813 and honoured the victory at Vittoria, not Waterloo. 'King's Theatre', *The Times*, 19 June 1830, p. 2; 'King's Theatre, Haymarket', *The Times*, 17 June 1830, p. 2.

and also the Duke of Wellington's Grand March, will be performed throughout the present week'.[163]

Vauxhall made one final attempt to balance re-enactment and illumination in 1849. They recruited 'a body of military, amounting in all to 400 men ... under the command of veterans who had fought in the battle which the occasion was intended to commemorate'.[164] Rather than attempt a full re-enactment with only 400 men, however, they were presented as part of a multimedia display christened 'the Vauxhall Battle-piece' or the 'Waterloo Battle *Fete*'.[165] The soldiers paraded, manoeuvred, and fired muskets and cannons in time with music produced by a 400-instrument band, the heart of which was the full band of the Royal Artillery. The marching and aural spectacle were matched with a firework display designed to create '"splendid representations from the regions of light and fire, commemorative of the great battle-field". Rockets were sent off into the air, and blue lights burnt, and brilliant devices exhibited in surprising abundance. It terminated with a transparency of the Duke of Wellington at Waterloo, and with an interesting display of the electric light, which was thrown on the military deploying across the ground. The effect', *The Standard* concluded, 'was very striking.'[166] The Vauxhall Battle Piece was performed only once more, on 25 June, when the Duke of Wellington escorted his daughter-in-law, Lady Douro, and, according to observers, 'enjoyed it all'.[167] Despite this encomium, Vauxhall returned to its usual entertainments.[168]

The next year, 1850, was the last that Vauxhall explicitly celebrated the anniversary of Waterloo. The fete boasted the usual fireworks and illuminations, but the only advertised special entertainment was a 'colossal tableau, illustrative of this memorable day'.[169] Even lacking specific martial entertainments, the evening was a success, 'attended by a vast concourse of company' including Wellington's son, the Marquess of Duoro.[170] Despite this, in 1851 the proprietors of Vauxhall ended a thirty-three-year tradition by turning their swords to ploughshares. They threw open their doors on 18 June not for a grand military gala, but instead for a 'grand horticultural *fete*', with £225 in prizes and no entrance fees.[171]

---

[163] 'The Prague Minstrels', *The Times*, 19 June 1830, p. 1.
[164] 'Vauxhall Gardens', *Standard*, 19 June 1849, p. 3.   [165] *Morning Post*, 23 June 1849, p. 1.
[166] 'Vauxhall Gardens', *Standard*, 19 June 1849, p. 3.
[167] John Forster, *The Life of Charles Dickens* (London: Chapman & Hall, 1870), II: 100. Forster claims Wellington visited Vauxhall on 29 June, but by then the gardens were no longer performing the Waterloo Battle-piece and had instead reverted to their traditional entertainments. *Morning Post*, 29 June 1849, p. 1.
[168] *Morning Post*, 23 June 1849, p. 1; *Morning Post*, 25 June 1849, p. 1.
[169] *Morning Chronicle*, 18 June 1850, p. 1. *The Times* declared that the tableau showed good taste. 'Vauxhall Gardens', *The Times*, 19 June 1850, p. 4.
[170] 'Vauxhall Gardens', *The Times*, 19 June 1850, p. 4.   [171] *Morning Post*, 16 June 1851, p. 1.

Even as the grand horticultural fete was in full swing at Vauxhall, preparations were being made on Piccadilly for Wellington's Waterloo banquet.[172] Since 1821, the banquet had continued to grow in size, stature, and media coverage even as other Waterloo commemorations ebbed and flowed. It had become such a staple of London society that, when, in January 1853, only a few months after the death of the Duke of Wellington, his son opened Apsley House to the public for a day to commemorate his father, one of *The Times*'s most pressing questions concerned the annual gathering:

> In the picture gallery the annual Waterloo Banquet was held, and though it must be confessed that for such a purpose this long and narrow apartment was by no means well adapted, yet to the visitor this fact is its chief attraction. For upwards of 30 years did the Duke here assemble around him the chiefs with whom he fought his last battle, and here, as time rolled on, he found himself among the last of that distinguished band of veterans, the greatest spared longest to witness the permanence of his own fame. When the next 18th of June comes round who will be worthy to preside over the surviving representatives of that army which conquered at Waterloo?[173]

The Waterloo banquet was held at Apsley House from 1821 until 1852.[174] Throughout the years, it varied in size and how much popular attention it received, but the event remained an all-male formal dinner with a guest list comprising exclusively veteran officers of the battle, the reigning sovereign (or, in the case of Victoria, her consort Prince Albert), and, on occasion, the ranking ambassador of an allied nation.[175] In theory, this limited the potential guest list to some 1,770 men. Analysis of guest lists from nineteen Waterloo banquets, however, shows that only an elite 207—a little under 12 percent—ever received an invitation.[176]

---

[172] For the full details of the banquet, see Luke Reynolds 'Serving His Country: Wellington's Waterloo Banquets, 1822–1852', *Journal of Victorian Culture* 23, no. 2 (2018): 262–78.

[173] 'Apsley House', *The Times*, 7 January 1853, p. 5.

[174] As discussed earlier, the 1821 banquet was only for officers of the Royal Horse Guards. In 1822, Wellington opened the guest list to encompass his command staff. 'The Mirror of Fashion', *Morning Chronicle*, 19 June 1822, p. 3.

[175] Foster, 'Food for Thought', 13.

[176] 18 June 1821 entry, Journal of W. Holdernesse, 1st Duke of Wellington Personal Correspondence/Holdernesse, Stratfield Saye House archive; 1828/1829 Waterloo Banquet Guest List, 1st Duke of Wellington Misc 18, Stratfield Saye House archive; 1840 Waterloo Banquet Guest List, 1st Duke of Wellington Misc 18, Stratfield Saye House archive; 1841 Waterloo Banquet Guest List, 1st Duke of Wellington Misc 18, Stratfield Saye House archive; Waterloo Banquet at Apsley-House, *The Times*, 20 June 1836, p. 5; 'The Waterloo Banquet', *The Belfast News-Letter*, 26 June 1838; 'The Waterloo Banquet', *Morning Chronicle*, 19 June 1849; and reports on the Waterloo Banquet in *The Times*, 20 June 1839, p. 6; 19 June 1841, p. 5; 20 June 1842, p. 6; 20 June 1843, p. 5; 19 June 1844, p. 5; 19 June 1845, p. 5; 19 June 1846, p. 8; 21 June 1847, p. 8; 20 June 1848, p. 8; 19 June 1849, p. 5; 19 June

There is remarkably little scholarship on the Waterloo banquet, but what there is argues that the emergence of the banquet into the public sphere in 1821 marks a general warming to the army in the softening of the immediate post-war radicalism.[177] While this is broadly true, it overlooks the fact that the banquet presented a socially acceptable alternative to the drunken riots that the Westminster coroner's jury had objected to in 1821. Nor does it explain the enduring allure of the affair, as the growth of the banquet, both in attendance and press coverage, indicates that the event increased in its popularity over its thirty-one-year history. In fact, the emergence of the banquet was not driven by the softening of post-war radicalism, but instead developed to provide several proactive benefits. The banquet served three primary functions in those thirty-one years. For those who attended, it was a celebration of their military achievements, both past and present, allowing them to bask in the glory of 1815 in a publicly acceptable way. For the British army in general, despite the elite nature of the banquet itself, it functioned as a grand celebration in miniature—a surrogate for national acclaim and a pinnacle event, from which all other Waterloo celebrations drew both pomp and legitimacy. For the nation, the Waterloo banquet functioned as a conduit back to Waterloo itself, providing context and a sense of permanence even as national commemorations of the victory continued to evolve. In short, even as other celebrations and memories of Waterloo and the Napoleonic Wars faded, the Waterloo banquet increased in importance, both for those old soldiers who donned their uniforms and medals to dine in splendour, and those who flocked to Hyde Park Corner to witness the external portions of the event or read about it in ever-increasing media coverage.

The banquet was an inherently conservative event, in both the political and more broadly cultural sense. While Wellington did not steep it in the explicit Toryism of its various civilian imitators, his position as the avatar of conservative politics meant that any celebration of him and his achievements carried with it a conservative angle. In 1841 that conservative association led Prince Albert, a staple at the Waterloo banquets, to withdraw his RSVP five days before the event, stating that 'my going to your dinner one or two days previous to a dissolution of Parliament might be misconstrued into a party demonstration'.[178] From a foreign

---

1850, p. 5; 19 June 1851, p. 5; 19 June 1852, p. 8. An attempt to create a master invitation list in late 1841/early 1842 indicated that 150 officers who were regular invitees were still alive. Army List, 1st Duke of Wellington Misc 18, Stratfield Saye House archive.

[177] Foster, 'Food for Thought'; Rory Muir, *Wellington: Waterloo and the Fortunes of Peace, 1814–1852* (New Haven: Yale University Press, 2015), 184. On the Waterloo banquet in general, see Foster, *Wellington and Waterloo*, 131, 158–60; Forrest, *Waterloo*, 109; Muir, *Wellington: Waterloo and the Fortunes of Peace*, 184, 274, 559; N. P. Dawnay and J. M. A. Tamplin, 'The Waterloo Banquet at Apsley House, 1836, by William Salter', *Journal of the Society for Army Historical Research* 49, no. 198 (Summer 1971): 63–76.

[178] Prince Albert to Wellington, 13 June 1841, Hartley Library, University of Southampton, MS 61 Wellington Papers, WP2/77/20. Not all felt that way, however. Sir George de Lacy Evans, Radical MP for Rye and later Westminster and one of the most progressive generals in the British army, was a regular guest at the banquets, especially after 1847.

policy perspective, the multinational nature of the banquet table's trappings highlighted by the event, and the praise of certain allied nations, presented a material endorsement of the European Congress system and the balance-of-power approach championed by Lord Castlereagh and Wellington at the Congress of Vienna long after the system had outlived its usefulness. On the domestic side, hero worship of Wellington and his officers provided a gateway into conservative thought for many who would not otherwise have considered it: many who flocked to Hyde Park Corner to cheer Wellington and his officers owed their vote to the 1832 Representation of the People (Great Reform) Act, a piece of legislation that Wellington and the majority of his officers opposed. While Britain may have been the most democratic of the major allies, the Napoleonic Wars were still a victory for conservatism and the status quo over radicalism and change. It is unclear how many of those at Hyde Park Corner distinguished that particular victory from the more general one over Britain's old enemy, but it is safe to assume that some did. To the extent that the Waterloo banquet informed other celebrations of the battle, it enabled the officers to control the narrative. That control was crucial to their use of Waterloo as a calling card and badge of honour in their own lives and careers, and to the use of the battle as a conservative touchstone.[179]

The 18th of June was a busy day at Apsley House. Wellington's carefully cultivated permanent association with the victory at Waterloo meant that, for those acquainted with him, the best way to mark the day was to call on its victor. *The Times* in 1850 listed 178 individuals of note who had come to pay their respects including representatives of the royal family, several allied countries, the aristocracy, the clergy, the army and navy, Parliament, 'and others far too numerous to mention'.[180] For those who did not know Wellington personally or resided too far away to call, congratulations in writing served the same purpose. For several days surrounding 18 June each year, Wellington routinely received congratulations on his victory. These included brief notes from friends and acquaintances and congratulations appended to letters concerning other business.[181] Wellington also received an extensive amount of unsolicited correspondence from admirers. Some contained merely their best wishes, or requests for his autograph dated 18 June, but others were more imaginative. Several included poems inspired either by Wellington or the battle, bound volumes (including a

---

[179] Barrow, '"The Waterloo of Democracy against Despotism"'.

[180] 'The Waterloo Banquet', *The Times*, 19 June 1850, p. 5; 'The Waterloo Banquet', *The Times*, 20 June 1848, p. 8.

[181] See, for example, Duke of Gordon to Wellington, 17 June 1833; Marquess Wellesley to Wellington, 18 June 1841; Ernest Augustus, King of Hanover to Wellington, 18 June 1842; Colonel Gurwood to Wellington, 18 June 1842; Sir James Graham to Wellington, 18 June 1843, Hartley Library, University of Southampton, MS 61 Wellington Papers, WP2/4/63, WP2/77/35, WP2/89/2–3, WP2/89/5, WP2/105/40.

dictionary), and on one notable occasion, a turtle.[182] At least one entrepreneur sought to capitalize on both Wellington's patronage and the potential for a captive audience presented by the dinner. In 1836 the Cornwall engineering firm of J. George and Son sent Wellington the plans for a steam war chariot with a request that he lay the plans 'on the table at the Grand Waterloo Dinner, after the cloth is removed' so that 'the Great Generals [present] will have an opportunity of [judging]...the utility of the invention'.[183] Wellington, who had no desire to see his annual celebration inundated with military inventions, directed J. George and Son to apply directly to the Master General of the Ordnance (at that point Sir Richard Hussey Vivian, who was, in fact, on the guest list for that night's banquet).[184]

While Wellington was inundated with well-wishers, notes, and gifts, the staff of Apsley House were preparing for the banquet. The banquet took place in three locations over the three decades it was held. From 1821 until 1828, the banquet was held in the state dining room in the north-eastern corner of Apsley House, which could seat between fifty and sixty guests.[185] In 1829, partially because of the ongoing construction of the picture gallery and partially for convenience, Wellington, then Prime Minister, held the banquet in 10 Downing Street.[186] There is no evidence that anyone objected to this extremely martial gathering taking place in Britain's premier political address, although there are some indications that the more politically savvy guests saw attendance as implicit support for Wellington's efforts towards Catholic Emancipation.[187] In 1830, the banquet first took place in its new permanent home, the newly finished picture gallery that occupies the entire western end of the first floor of Apsley House. Wellington had the gallery purpose built to allow him to host grand formal occasions, from balls to the banquet. The room could seat eighty-five comfortably

[182] Richard Dannelly Davy to Wellington, 16 June 1836; Maria Matthews to Wellington, 17 June 1845; Revd John Prowett to Wellington, 18 June 1837; Sir John Edmund de Beauvoir to Wellington, 18 June 1844; Lieutenant Edmund Peel to Wellington, 16 June 1836; Duke of Rutland to Wellington, 18 June 1838; James Knowles to Wellington, 18 June 1837; Isaac Niblett to Wellington, 14 June 1843, Hartley Library, University of Southampton, MS 61 Wellington Papers, WP2/40/106, WP2/130/133, WP2/46/121, WP2/121/24, WP2/40/107, WP2/52/43, WP2/46/120, WP2/105/12. The turtle prompted a rare reply from Wellington.
[183] J. George & Son to Wellington, 18 June 1836, Hartley Library, University of Southampton, MS 61 Wellington Papers, WP2/40/118–119.
[184] Wellington's draft reply to J. George & Son to Wellington, 18 June 1836, Hartley Library, University of Southampton, MS 61 Wellington Papers, WP2/40/118–119; 'Waterloo Banquet at Apsley-House', The Times, 20 June 1836, p. 5.
[185] Bryant, Apsley House, 20–2; Foster, 'Food for Thought', 13.
[186] 'The Duke of Wellington's Grand Dinner', Morning Post, 19 June 1829.
[187] Duke of Clarence to Duke of Wellington, 18 June 1829, Hartley Library, University of Southampton, MS 61 Wellington Papers, WP1/1026/1. 1829 was the last time we have a record of Charles Gordon-Lennox, Duke of Richmond receiving an invitation. Richmond was the leader of the Ultra-Tories who, outraged over Wellington's support for Catholic Emancipation, joined with Earl Grey's Whig government in 1830. It seems likely that, in response, Wellington had him permanently struck from the guest list. There is no record of if he attended the 1829 banquet, but it is doubtful. 1828/9 Waterloo Banquet Guest List, 1st Duke of Wellington Misc 18, Stratfield Saye House archive.

and drew inspiration from the most fashionable halls in Europe, including yellow silk damask walls and mirrored window shutters designed to bring a little bit of Versailles to Hyde Park.[188] The paintings that gave the gallery its name, while not wholly martial in nature, still served to remind the viewer of Wellington's achievements. The majority of the paintings were from the Spanish Royal Collection; 165 paintings rescued from Joseph Bonaparte's baggage train by British soldiers after the battle of Vittoria and formally given to Wellington by King Ferdinand VII in 1816.[189]

The service for the banquet was traditionally a gold service formerly owned by the Duke of York, which sometimes alternated with a silver set gifted by Don John, King of Portugal.[190] The size of the table could be expanded or contracted depending on the number of guests expected, but whatever the size the table was laid to completion, as empty seats were preferable to gaps in the service.[191] The table was built around two 12-foot-high candelabras, the gift of Tsar Alexander of Russia, each carved from a solid block of marble, and, thanks to their weight of 1.25 tonnes, permanent fixtures in the gallery.[192] The centre of the table was dominated by 'the magnificent silver plateau presented to the Duke by the King of Portugal, 27 feet long, and 4 feet wide' and decorated with a 'hundred trophies', supplemented in later years with equestrian statues of Wellington and Napoleon designed by Count D'Orsay.[193] The Russian candelabras were rein-forced by three more in gold, the gift of the citizens of London, shaped as foot soldiers, each wearing the uniform and carrying the standard of one of the allied nations that fought at Waterloo.[194] The final touch on the table was the porcelain dessert set from the King of Prussia, which completed the Grand Alliance of table decorations.[195] Each piece represented 'some engagement or general officer engaged in it; the service containing the whole series of his grace's victories in India, the Peninsula, and at Waterloo.'[196] Taken as a whole, the effect of the table was imposing and political. Even thirty years after the creation of the formal Great Powers system, Wellington's table represented his conservative backing for Castlereagh's vision—a gilded embodiment of the Congress of Vienna.

---

[188] Harriet Arbuthnot, *The Journal of Mrs. Arbuthnot, 1820–1832*, ed. Francis Bamford and the Duke of Wellington (London: Macmillan & Co., 1950), II: 336–7, plate 15.

[189] Bryant, *Apsley House*, 16–17.

[190] 'Waterloo Banquet at Apsley-House', *The Times*, 20 June 1836, p. 5; 'The Waterloo Banquet at Apsley-House', *The Times*, 19 June 1841, p. 5; 'The Waterloo Banquet', *The Times*, 20 June 1843, p. 5.

[191] *Morning Post*, 20 June 1836, p. 5.

[192] 'Apsley House', *The Times*, 8 August 1835, p. 7; *The Mirror of Literature, Amusement, and Instruction* (London: J. Limbird, 1837), XXIX: 159–60.

[193] 'The Waterloo Banquet', *The Times*, 20 June 1843, p. 5; 'The Waterloo Banquet', *The Times*, 19 June 1846, p. 8; 'The Waterloo Banquet', *The Times*, 19 June 1850, p. 5; 'The Waterloo Banquet', *The Times*, 19 June 1852, p. 8.

[194] 'Apsley House', *The Times*, 8 August 1835, p. 7; *Mirror of Literature*, XXIX: 159–60.

[195] 'The Waterloo Banquet', *The Times*, 20 June 1843, p. 5.

[196] *Mirror of Literature*, XXIX: 159.

If the main table represented the Continent with its network of alliances and battlefields, the oaken buffet and sideboard were solidly British.[197] At its centre rested the Wellington Shield, commissioned in 1814 by the Merchants and Bankers of London. While inspired by John Flaxman's famous Achilles' Shield, designed for George IV, the Wellington shield was in fact designed by Thomas Sothard and made by Benjamin Smith in silver gilt and deadened gold. The central boss depicts Wellington and his generals riding in triumph over a French standard while an allegorical representation of fame crowns him with laurels. Surrounding the central boss are scenes from Wellington's career from the victory at Assaye in 1803 to the confirmation of his dukedom in 1814.[198] The details on the shield attracted so much attention from visitors that in 1822 Wellington commissioned James Deville, a well-known local lamp maker, to design and install a mount in the sideboard that allowed the shield to be inclined and rotated at the viewer's will.[199] The Wellington Shield was flanked by two more candelabra, also made by Smith, designed to look like stylized trees laden with the fruit of victory with trophies and weapons laid at their bases. One is surmounted by a figure of Victory supported by an English Grenadier, a Scottish Highlander, and an Irish Light Infantryman, each holding their national flag, while the other features a Portuguese civilian, an Indian Sepoy, and a Spanish Guerrilla capped by the figure of Fame.[200] Despite the fact that the Wellington Shield was designed in 1814 and thus does not depict Waterloo, and was only inspired by Flaxman's Achilles' Shield, visitors and the press routinely still referred to it as Flaxman's Achilles' or Waterloo Shield.[201] The descriptions of the room found in various newspapers demonstrate some bias in this area, always making sure to mention the 'splendid Achilles shield' even if only providing a general description of the rest of the plate and decorations.[202]

As stories of the banquet and its lavish setting spread through newspapers across the country, so too did public curiosity. The elite and inherently limited nature of the guest list, combined with the media coverage, intrigued Britons across all levels of society. Some sought to bypass the guest list and gain admission to the event itself as 'a spectator to witness the assembling of your Grace's Guests at Apsley House' or 'to see the Conqueror of the great Napoleon surrounded by the gallant spirits whom his genius conducted to victory'.[203] These requests were

---

[197] 'Apsley House', The Times, 8 August 1835, p. 7.

[198] 'The Wellington Shield', The Saturday Magazine, 1 March 1834, 81–3.

[199] Another rotation device was constructed for the Shield's display cabinet, where it was rotated by a handle. Bryant, Apsley House, 22–4.

[200] 'The Wellington Shield', The Saturday Magazine, 1 March 1834, 83.

[201] 'Waterloo Banquet at Apsley-House', The Times, 20 June 1836, p. 5; 'The Waterloo Banquet at Apsley-House', The Times, 19 June 1841, p. 5; 'The Waterloo Banquet', The Times, 20 June 1842, p. 6.

[202] 'Waterloo Banquet at Apsley House', Standard, 20 June 1836.

[203] Thomas Smyth to Wellington, 11 June 1846, Hartley Library, University of Southampton, MS 61 Wellington Papers, WP2/143/72; 'Persevere' to Wellington, 19 June 1837, Hartley Library, University of Southampton, MS 61 Wellington Papers, WP2/46/123; B. R. Haybon to Wellington, 16 June 1840, Hartley Library, University of Southampton, MS 61 Wellington Papers, WP2/69/29.

always denied, but in the 1830s it became common to admit select groups during the day to 'see the Waterloo plate laid out, in preparation for the Waterloo dinner'.[204] Individuals and groups applied in writing to Wellington or his secretaries to request admission.[205] Although open to a wider population than the banquet itself, entry to view the plate was still limited to rarefied social circles. For those unknown to Wellington or his secretaries letters of introduction were required and permission for admission had to be obtained in advance.[206] Requests for admission became so regular that lithographed tickets were produced, with blanks for the individual's name, the number of people in the group, and the signature of one of Wellington's secretaries or some other individual with the power of admittance.[207] *The Times* informed their readers in 1836 that 'a large number of the nobility' had been admitted via these tickets to view 'the tables as set out for the entertainment, in the Waterloo Gallery'.[208] *The Morning Post* the same year recorded that 'every part of the spacious apartment...constantly crowded with a succession of elegant company...From twelve o'clock at noon until three company were constantly entering into, and departing from, Apsley House.'[209] By 1839 requests had become so common that Wellington stopped the practice temporarily, and *The Chartist* reported that 600 people had, by this action, been denied entry.[210] It is unclear how long the ban continued, but there are multiple requests for admission in the Wellington papers from after that date.[211]

Those who did not gain admission, but still wanted to experience some small part of the evening, could join the crowds that gathered outside the gates of Apsley House in the hours before the dinner. The size of the gathering varied per year, but on several occasions it blocked Piccadilly or would have, if not for the efforts of the Metropolitan Police.[212] The make-up of the crowd varied. The majority were average London pedestrians, described by the papers simply as 'respectable', but, as *The Times* noted, the crowd 'was not confined to the middle classes': horsemen and 'the carriages of the nobility' were scattered throughout the crowd.[213] Some of

---

[204] E. G. Sievers to Wellington, 16 June 1834, Hartley Library, University of Southampton, MS 61 Wellington Papers, WP2/11/23.

[205] Wellington to H. Tucker, 16 June 1838, Hartley Library, University of Southampton, MS 61 Wellington Papers, WP2/52/39.

[206] Count Kielmansegge to Wellington, 8 June 1846, Hartley Library, University of Southampton, MS 61 Wellington Papers, WP2/143/55.

[207] Passes to see the Waterloo dinner table, Hartley Library, University of Southampton, MS 69 Christopher Collins Papers, MS69/2/42–3.

[208] 'Waterloo Banquet at Apsley-House', *The Times*, 20 June 1836, p. 5.

[209] *Morning Post*, 20 June 1836, p. 5.   [210] 'Waterloo Banquet', *The Chartist*, 23 June 1839.

[211] B. R. Haybon to Wellington, 16 June 1840, Hartley Library, University of Southampton, MS 61 Wellington Papers, WP2/69/29; Count Kielmansegge to Wellington, 8 June 1846, Hartley Library, University of Southampton, MS 61 Wellington Papers, WP2/143/55.

[212] 'Waterloo Banquet', *The Chartist*, 23 June 1839; 'Waterloo Banquet at Apsley House', *Standard*, 20 June 1836; 'The Waterloo Banquet', *The Times*, 20 June 1843, p. 5.

[213] 'Waterloo Banquet at Apsley House', *Standard*, 20 June 1836; 'The Waterloo Banquet', *The Times*, 19 June 1846, p. 8; 'The Waterloo Banquet', *The Times*, 19 June 1844, p. 5.

those in attendance must have hoped that the golden light of glory shining from the windows and doorway of Apsley House would illuminate them. Many wore military uniforms and decorations (the Earl of Cardigan was spotted in 1846), and those who wore the Waterloo Medal, as was noted of one Chelsea pensioner, 'displayed not a little *amour propre*'.[214] For those who sought some favour or acknowledgement, manoeuvring for position was required to obtain the ideal spot: 'there were many noblemen and gentlemen on horseback who took up their position on the western side of the eastern entrance-gate—a position which commanded the recognition of those distinguished officers entitled to join the festive board of the noble and gallant Duke'.[215] Those distinguished officers were not above a little acknowledgement and jockeying themselves, and as they arrived, many in open-topped carriages (when the June weather allowed it), their popularity was judged by the volume of the crowd's cheers. John Byng, Earl Strafford; Alexander Fraser, Lord Saltoun; Sir Harry Smith; and Prince Castelcicala were all popular, but the perennial favourites were Sir Henry Hardinge, the Marquess of Anglesey, King William IV, Prince Albert, and the Duke of Wellington himself, who emerged from the house to welcome the king or prince consort.[216]

Having alighted from their carriages and acknowledged the crowd, guests made their way into Apsley House past the Band of the Grenadier Guards (Wellington was their colonel) and into the salon for pre-dinner drinks.[217] The royal guests were traditionally the last to arrive (shortly after 7). They would be greeted three times before they even entered Apsley House, first by the crowd, next by Wellington himself, and finally by the band, who would mark that moment either with the national anthem or, sometimes in the case of Prince Albert, the Coburg March.[218] Dinner would be announced between 7:30 and 8, whereupon Wellington and his royal guests would head the procession into the gallery for the meal.

Despite being the stated purpose of the evening, the food itself played a decidedly secondary role at the Waterloo banquet. Only one menu from the three decades of banquets survives, and the newspaper reports of the evening,

---

[214] 'The Waterloo Banquet at Apsley House', *The Times*, 19 June 1841, p. 5; 'The Waterloo Banquet', *The Times*, 19 June 1846, p. 8; 'The Waterloo Banquet', *The Times*, 21 June 1847, p. 8; 'The Waterloo Banquet', *The Times*, 19 June 1850, p. 5.

[215] 'The Waterloo Banquet', *The Times*, 20 June 1843, p. 5.

[216] 'The Waterloo Banquet', *The Times*, 20 June 1843, p. 5; 'The Waterloo Banquet', *The Times*, 19 June 1844, p. 5; 'The Waterloo Banquet', *The Times*, 19 June 1846, p. 8; 'The Waterloo Banquet', *The Times*, 20 June 1848, p. 8; 'The Waterloo-Banquet', *The Times*, 19 June 1849, p. 5; 'The Waterloo Banquet', *The Times*, 19 June 1850, p. 5; 'The Waterloo Banquet', *The Times*, 19 June 1851, p. 5; 'The Waterloo Banquet', *The Times*, 19 June 1852, p. 8; 'Waterloo Banquet at Apsley House', *Standard*, 20 June 1836.

[217] See, for example, 'The Waterloo Banquet at Apsley House', *The Times*, 19 June 1841, p. 5; 'The Waterloo Banquet', *The Times*, 21 June 1847, p. 8; 'The Waterloo Banquet', *The Times*, 19 June 1851, p. 5.

[218] For the band playing the national anthem, see 'The Waterloo Banquet', *The Times*, 19 June 1846, p. 8; for the Coburg March, see 'The Waterloo Banquet', *The Times*, 19 June 1850, p. 5.

which are particularly extensive in the later years, do not mention the food at all.[219] It was the food's role to highlight the service, rather than the other way around, and to provide a justification for the sit-down nature of the celebration. Despite its neglect by history and the press, the food produced by the Apsley House kitchens was sumptuous. The menu from the 1839 Banquet records five courses, supplemented by three different sets of four removes, and two side table services over the course of the dinner (Figure 3.3).[220] Dinner began with two soup options, after which diners were presented with a four-option fish course, supplemented by four meat removes.[221] This was followed by a course of twenty-four entrées which heavily favoured fowl, but included lamb, rabbit, pasta, and rice dishes. After that came four roasts, again supplemented by four cold removes and four flying plate removes—items such as soufflés, fondues, and cheeses, served rapidly because of their time-sensitive nature. Finally came twenty-four entremets, both sweet and savoury, supplemented by a sweet side table service.[222] Throughout the meal, the band, which had moved from the foyer to an adjacent room, provided music.[223] Considering the explicit patriotic overtones of the event, it is worth noting that the menu still maintained a heavy continental influence in both food and style, and that the 1839 menu itself is in French.[224]

Once the dinner was over, what many recognized as the most important part of the evening could begin: the toasts. These were not simply the raising of glasses but presented opportunities for acknowledgement on both sides. The toasts consisted of short speeches (often interrupted by cheers and shouts) by the individual giving the toast and subsequently by the one 'returning thanks'.[225] The unwavering order of the toasts reflected the implicit hierarchy built in to the British army.[226] The first toast was always to the sovereign, followed, in later years, by one to Prince Albert, who would, at the culmination of his thanks,

---

[219] The closest is a mention in passing, such as this example from the 1851 *Times* report of the evening: 'The banquet, which included every luxury, being over, and desert having been placed on the table...' 'The Waterloo Banquet', *The Times*, 19 June 1851, p. 5.

[220] 'Waterloo Banquet Menu', 18 June 1839, 1st Duke of Wellington Misc 18, Stratfield Saye House archive.

[221] Removes are additional dishes within a course, added after the originals are removed. In this case, the four fish dishes are placed on the table, and when diners have been served, the fish dishes are removed and replaced with four meat dishes which can be eaten separately or together with the fish, but are still considered to be part of the same course. Dan Jurafsky, *The Language of Food: A Linguist Reads the Menu* (New York: W. W. Norton & Co., 2014), 25.

[222] All of the details of the menu are drawn from the Waterloo Banquet Menu, 18 June 1839, 1st Duke of Wellington Misc 18, Stratfield Saye House archive.

[223] For a sample playlist, see 'The Waterloo Banquet', *The Times*, 20 June 1843, p. 5; 'The Waterloo Banquet', *The Times*, 21 June 1847, p. 8.

[224] This was perhaps due to the fact that Wellington's cook was French. Bryant, *Apsley House*, 22; Waterloo Banquet Menu, 18 June 1839, 1st Duke of Wellington Misc 18, Stratfield Saye House archive.

[225] With the exception of 1850, when Wellington requested that there be no cheering so as not to disturb a sick friend staying with him. 'The Waterloo Banquet', *The Times*, 19 June 1850, p. 5.

[226] For detailed descriptions of the order and wording of the toasts, see 'The Waterloo Banquet', *The Times*, 20 June 1842, p. 6; 'The Waterloo Banquet', *The Times*, 19 June 1846, p. 8; 'The Waterloo Banquet', *The Times*, 19 June 1850, p. 5.

Menu for the 1839 Waterloo Banquet

Turtle Soup		Spring Soup	

Four Fish Dishes

Turbot with Lobster Sauce	Dover Sole Fillets au Veloute	Trout in Genevoise Sauce	Matelotte of Eels

Four 'Removes'

Fat Chicken a la Régence	Ham with Madeira	Beef Fillets a la Jardinière	Veal (Calves) Head en Tortue

Twenty-Four Entrees

Two Supreme of Fowls with Truffles	Two Ducklings Fillets with Garden Peas
Two Pigeon Fillets a la Maréchale	Two Lamb Cutlets a l'Italienne
Two Glazed sweetbread of Veal with Asparagus	Two Young Rabbits a la Toulouse
Two Quenelles of Fowls a la Béchamel	Two Chicken a la Reine, a la Chivry
Two Tendons of Veal with Macédoine	Fillets of Fowls a la Orly with Tomato Sauce
Warm Pate a la Financière	Macaroni Timbale a la Milanaise
Casserole of Potatoes with Blanquette of Fowls	Casserole of Rice a la Reine

Escalopes of Young Leveret with mushrooms

Four Roasts

Poulardes	Pricked Leverets	Pricked Leverets

Four Cold 'Removes'

Loaf of Game in Jelly	Biscuit with Chantilly	Pheasant Pâté	Baba in Madeira Wine

Four Removes 'Flying Plates'

Vanilla Soufflé	Cheese Fondue	Lemon Soufflé	Ramequins of Parmesan

Twenty Four Entremets

Two Fruit Salads	Two Charlottes of Strawberries
Two Vanilla Creams	Two Garnished Pinapple Jellies
Two Garnished Plover Eggs in Aspic	Apple Nougat
Glazed Genoese Cakes	D'Artois of Apricots
Merengued Fanchonettes	Crayfish with Wine Champagne
Two Garden Peas a la Française	Two French Beans a la Maitre d'Hotel
Two Artichokes a la Barigoule	Two Asparagus with Butter Sauce

Lobsters Salad

Side Table First Service	Side Table Second Service
Two Vol au Vent with Béchamel	Two Apple Tarts
Two Croquettes of Fowls au Veloute	Goosberry Tart
Two Haunch of Venison	Currants Tart
Roast Beef	Cabinet Pudding
Saddle of Roasted Mutton	Rice Pudding
Rice with Consommé	Fried Whitting

Figure 3.3 Waterloo Banquet Menu, 18 June 1839, 1st Duke of Wellington Misc 18, Stratfield Saye House archive. Translated by Lydia Rousseau, House Steward, Apsley House.

propose a toast to the Duke of Wellington. Wellington would then give 'the army that fought the battle of Waterloo', followed, in silence, by 'the memory of those who fell'.[227] After glasses had been recharged, Wellington would, in strict hierarchical order, toast the cavalry, the Guards, and the infantry of the line, before acknowledging the artillery, staff, engineers, and, traditionally last, the Prussians. In some cases, toasts to other allies or branches of service (such as the medical staff) would be made based on those in attendance.[228]

The toasts, however, went beyond the general honour of each officer hearing their arm of the service acknowledged. Wellington, in toasting each branch, would pick an officer or two to represent them, both in honour and in response. Some

---

[227] 'The Waterloo Banquet', *The Times*, 19 June 1851, p. 5. The wording of these two toasts is nearly identical every year.

[228] The presence of Prince Castelcicala, for example, would generally inspire a toast to 'the foreigners who fought in the British army at Waterloo'. 'The Waterloo Banquet', *The Times*, 19 June 1850, p. 5.

officers served in this role regularly. The Marquess of Anglesey, for example, almost always represented the cavalry, which he had commanded at Waterloo, while Wellington usually used the toast to the Prussian Army to acknowledge Sir Henry Hardinge, who had served as the British liaison to Blücher's forces. For the regular line infantry, which represented the lion's share of the Waterloo officers, Wellington had more freedom to pick, and he usually used it as a way to highlight an officer he felt worthy of attention. 'The noble and gallant Duke', *The Times* reported in 1850, dedicated the next toast 'to "the line," a portion of the army that greatly exhibited the courage and determination of the British soldier. He thought there was an officer present who had rendered great services in the line—Sir Colin Halket.'[229]

The speeches having been concluded, the guests returned to the saloon for tea and coffee and more informal conversation.[230] The banquet usually broke up between 10 and 11, often with Wellington and guests making their way on to other events.[231] In 1828 Wellington and His Royal Highness the Duke of Clarence spent nearly half a day together, first at the Waterloo Regatta, where Wellington was His Royal Highness's guest, then at Apsley House, where His Royal Highness was Wellington's guest, and finally at the Grand Ball at Almack's, where they joined a sizeable portion of the *ton*.[232] A decade later in 1838, when Queen Victoria was hosting a ball at Buckingham Palace on Waterloo Night, the entire gathering was invited to move from banquet to ball, an invitation that 'his Grace and several of his gallant visitors' accepted.[233]

There are several possible explanations for the general British public's level of interest in and enthusiasm for such an elitist military gathering, and for the way that interest and enthusiasm only increased as the year of the actual battle receded. The first was sheer national pride: Waterloo had been, as *The Times* in 1851 put it, the 'crowning achievement of our national arms', the moment that had cemented Britain's role as the global hegemon of the nineteenth century.[234] The second was the Victorian mania for hero worship. The veterans of the Napoleonic Wars and Waterloo in particular made excellent candidates for the status of 'great men' as explored by Thomas Carlyle and his contemporaries.[235] This presented an

---

[229] 'The Waterloo Banquet', *The Times*, 19 June 1850, p. 5.

[230] See, for example, 'The Waterloo Banquet', *The Times*, 19 June 1852, p. 8.

[231] In 1851 Wellington attended a social reunion and in 1852 two different receptions after the banquet. 'The Waterloo Banquet', *The Times*, 19 June 1851, p. 5; 'The Waterloo Banquet', *The Times*, 19 June 1852, p. 8.

[232] 'Waterloo Regatta', *The Times*, 19 June 1828, p. 6; *Morning Post*, 20 June 1828, p. 3; 'Almack's Grand Ball', *Morning Post*, 20 June 1828, p. 3.

[233] Marquess Curyingham to Wellington, 17 June 1838, Hartley Library, University of Southampton, MS 61 Wellington Papers, WP2/52/41; 'The Waterloo Banquet', *Belfast News-Letter*, 26 June 1838; 'The Duke of Wellington's Waterloo Banquet', *Standard*, 19 June 1838.

[234] 'The Waterloo Banquet', *The Times*, 19 June 1851, p. 5.

[235] Thomas Carlyle, *On Heroes, Hero-Worship, and the Heroic in History* (London: James Fraser, 1841); Ralph Waldo Emerson, *Representative Men: Seven Lectures* (Boston: Phillips, Sampson, and Company, 1850).

intriguing contradiction however, as one facet of Carlyle's arguments is that his 'Great Men' stand, by their actions or intellect, above the majority and can speak for more than just themselves. This played directly into the idea of association with the Waterloo banquet, the Waterloo Men, and Hyde Park Corner as a gateway to conservatism—letting those 'Great Men' (especially Wellington and his conservative allies) speak for one.[236] The cult of hero-worship also fed the Victorian fondness for self-improvement and self-aggrandizement, for, as scholars have pointed out, one must believe in 'great men' if one wishes to become a great man.[237] This tension between hopeful and actual self-made 'Great Men' of the new Victorian mould (often self-made through industry), and more traditionally politically and militarily minted 'Great Men' kept the debate going, and the coverage of the Waterloo banquets provided a suitable venue. Association with these men, whether through touring the Apsley House picture gallery, gathering outside on the evening of the banquet, or merely reading about it in the popular press, allowed association with some small measure of their achievements and greatness.[238]

The third explanation, which combines aspects of the first two, is that the celebration of Waterloo provided an anchor, as the century continued, to the twenty-five years of war that had significantly shaped Britain, internally and externally. In the inevitable nationalization of the victory, its celebrations— including elite affairs such as the banquet—were slowly co-opted into events of national remembrance. In 1839 *The North Wales Chronicle* argued that the traditional description of the banquet as 'annual' should be replaced by 'national'.[239] Two years later, *The Times* noted that the celebration had 'become of historical interest, not only to this country, but to Europe in general'.[240] The passing of time became an integral part of reporting the banquet, with later reports opening with an honour-roll of those veterans who had died in the past year.[241]

[236] David R. Sorensen, Introduction to *On Heroes, Hero-Worship, and the Heroic in History*, by Thomas Carlyle (New Haven: Yale University Press, 2013), 1–16; Owen Dudley Edwards, ' "The Tone of the Preacher": Carlyle as Public Lecturer in On Heroes, Hero-Worship, and the Heroic in History', in Thomas Carlyle, *On Heroes, Hero-Worship, and the Heroic in History*, ed. David R. Sorensen and Brent E. Kinser (New Haven: Yale University Press, 2013), 199–208; Sara Atwood, ' "Leading human souls to what is best": Carlyle, Ruskin, and Hero-Worship', in Carlyle, *On Heroes* (2013), 247–57; Brent E. Kinser, 'Thomas Carlyle, Social Media, and the Digital Age of Revolution', in Carlyle, *On Heroes* (2013), 272–81.

[237] Walter E. Houghton, *The Victorian Frame of Mind: 1830–1870* (New Haven: Yale University Press, 1985), 310–14.

[238] Houghton, *Victorian Frame of Mind*, chapter 12; Cornelia D. J. Pearsall, 'Burying the Duke: Victorian Mourning and the Funeral of the Duke of Wellington', *Victorian Literature and Culture* 27, no. 2 (1999): 365–93; Stuart Semmel, 'Reading the Tangible Past: British Tourism, Collecting, and Memory after Waterloo', *Representations* 69 (Winter 2000): 9–37.

[239] 'Waterloo Banquet', *The North Wales Chronicle*, 25 June 1839.

[240] 'The Waterloo Banquet at Apsley House', *The Times*, 19 June 1841, p. 5.

[241] See, for example, 'The Waterloo Banquet', *The Times*, 19 June 1851, p. 5; 'The Waterloo Banquet', *The Times*, 19 June 1852, p. 8.

What is more telling, however, is that to the press, the advancement of time made the subject more worthy of reporting, not less. As *The Times* put it in 1842: 'as upwards of a quarter of a century has elapsed since that glorious victory ... it yearly becomes of additional interest, not only to those moving in the military circles, but to the nation at large'.[242] Hero worship, history, and self-celebration were all individually popular in Victorian Britain; the combination of all three by the Waterloo banquet provided too heady a mix to be ignored.

While the general populace and the majority of the press were in favour of the Waterloo banquet, the celebration was not universally popular. In 1831, during the controversy over the Great Reform Act, a mob throwing stones at Apsley House targeted the picture gallery in particular, presumably at least partially because of its association with the banquet.[243] The next year, on the anniversary of Waterloo, Wellington himself was attacked on his way home from the Bank of England and had to finish his journey with an escort of 100 policemen.[244] That same year Bristol's Sons of Paradise, a society that dined together every year on the anniversary, drank their customary health to Wellington 'not with the "usual honours," but almost with apathy; while every allusion to reform was loudly cheered'.[245] Conservatives also occasionally took advantage of the anniversary to criticize Wellington. In the aftermath of the passing of the Roman Catholic Relief Act of 1829, the conservative paper *The Westmorland Gazette* reported that on the anniversary 'no ensign waved over any of [Kendal's] public buildings'. 'Had the hero of that bloodstained day fallen in the arms of victory,' they maintained, 'the laurel would have bloomed long green and fresh over his tomb, and the tears of his affectionate country would have bedewed his grave; but *now* another fate awaits him from posterity. We presume this ceremony in honour of *him* will be omitted in other places as well as in Kendal.'[246]

Other critics held the banquet up as a sign that the British army had been fighting the same battle for nearly forty years and had failed to move with the times. In 1852, in response to the resurgence of France under Louis Napoleon (soon to become Emperor Napoleon III) a letter to the Editor of *The Times* lambasted '"Horse Guards"' for having been 'asleep since 1815 and has only awoke once every June, to assist at the Waterloo banquet'.[247] The army's high command, the letter continued, 'has outdone Alexander, for only "thrice he routed

---

[242] 'The Waterloo Banquet', *The Times*, 20 June 1842, p. 6.   [243] Arbuthnot, *Journal*, II: 432.

[244] 'Attack upon the Duke of Wellington', *Bristol Mercury*, 23 June 1832; Letter to the Editor, *The Times*, 19 June 1832, p. 3.

[245] The Chairman took the opportunity to note that 'though the merit of that individual as a soldier must be acknowledged by all ... it could not but be admitted that there were other points of his conduct which could never be applauded by the friend of his country'. 'Sons of Paradise', *Bristol Mercury*, 23 June 1832, p. 3.

[246] 'The Gazette', *The Westmorland Gazette*, 20 June 1829, p. 2.

[247] Letter to the Editor from 'An Englishman', *The Times*, 24 January 1852, p. 5.

all his foes, and thrice he slew the slain"; while it has performed that capital operation six-and-thirty times'.[248]

The sumptuousness of the banquet also drew criticism. The radical newspaper *The Chartist* reported in 1839 the case of 'a Waterloo man, who was in the thickest of the fire, and received two wounds in the engagement [who] passed by Apsley House dinnerless and pennyless on the 18th of June, and saw the men whom he had enabled to win the battle assembling to luxuriate upon gold plate ... Could not a WATERLOO MAN,' the paper concluded, 'dine off of his "glory"?'[249] *The Bristol Mercury* took a similar approach, noting that while the gold plate the officers would be dining off was a gift of George IV, it was paid for by the British public, a 'small circumstance the Duke and his guests would do well to recollect, when they shall meet in celebration of their gold-plated military orgies'.[250]

Many of the most vocal criticisms of the annual banquet came from beyond the borders of Britain. The French press, unsurprisingly, took issue with the celebration of their defeat, accusing the British of living in the past and glorifying war. (*The Times* responded to this accusation by pointing out that the French continued to celebrate the anniversary of Austerlitz (a battle ten years older than Waterloo) every year on 2 December.[251]) Nor was it just the French press who were insulted. Two years after Wellington's death, *The New York Daily Times* advanced the opinion that the alliance between Britain and France occasioned by the Crimean War would not have been possible had Wellington still been alive and hosting his annual dinner, noting 'in the present year, friendly as England is with France, there would have been much that is ungracious or even insulting, in keeping up this braggadocio festival'.[252]

By Wellington's death in 1852, the anniversary of Waterloo had been commemorated by countless public and private dinners, by parades, reviews, re-enactments, regattas, balls, and various sporting events. It had been marked by toasts given by the British sovereign, by serried ranks of veterans bedecked in laurel, and by 'a match of single-stick played for a good old cheese'.[253] As time passed, however, and as the segregation of military and civilian events became the norm, 18 June also took on the qualities of a bank holiday, when people expected the day off because they'd always had it, or when events were held because they always had been. The date saw the opening of canals and the launch

---

[248] The line of poetry the letter quotes is, rather fittingly, from 'Alexander's Feast' by John Dryden (1697), which describes a victory banquet. Letter to the Editor from 'An Englishman', *The Times*, 24 January 1852, p. 5.

[249] It is interesting to note that in the same issue *The Chartist* published a relatively positive report on the banquet itself. 'A Waterloo Man', *The Chartist*, 23 June 1839.

[250] 'The "Service of Gold Plate"', *Bristol Mercury*, 23 June 1832.

[251] 'Express from Paris', *The Times*, 25 June 1846, p. 7; 'The Ordinary Antagonism of the French Journals', *The Times*, 29 June 1846, p. 4.

[252] 'The Anglo-French Union', *The New York Daily Times*, 8 July 1854, p. 4.

[253] *Salisbury and Winchester Journal*, 11 June 1821, p. 4.

of steam-packets lacking even a cursory connection to Waterloo.[254] This trend is arguably best demonstrated by the Somerset town of Shepton Mallet, which decided that the ideal way to commemorate the battle was with a cattle fair. It ran from 1828 into the 1850s and, in its heyday, attracted well over 500 attendees along with cattle, horses, sheep, and pigs.[255] No mention is made in any report, however, of any festivities that occurred during or alongside the fair that made even passing allusion to the battle that gave it its name. The Waterloo banquet and Vauxhall's fete, along with other annual celebrations in more than name, were forced to do the heavy lifting when it came to anchoring the date to the events of 1815 and thus providing a venue for actual commemoration and remembrance. Veterans remained crucial to that anchoring, even as they were transformed from actors in history to actors upon a stage. In the next chapter, we will see how those same veterans used many of the same tools—most notably their presence—to influence how Waterloo was experienced and remembered in various exhibitions that were not tied to a single day of the year, but instead remained popular year-round.

---

[254] *Westmorland Gazette*, 23 June 1821, p. 3; *Liverpool Mercury*, 24 June 1825.

[255] 'Bath, Wednesday June 27', *Bath Chronicle and Weekly Gazette*, 28 June 1827, p. 3; 'Salisbury', *Salisbury and Winchester Journal*, 2 June 1828, p. 4; 'Bath, Wednesday June 25', *Bath Chronicle and Weekly Gazette*, 26 June 1828, p. 3; *Trewman's Exeter Flying Post*, 6 November 1828, p. 3; *Bath Chronicle and Weekly Gazette*, 23 June 1831, p. 3; *Bristol Mercury*, 22 June 1833, p. 3; *Bath Chronicle and Weekly Gazette*, 26 June 1834, p. 3; 'Salisbury', *Salisbury and Winchester Journal*, 13 June 1836, p. 4; *Salisbury and Winchester Journal*, 28 June 1841, p. 3; 'From Our Correspondents', *Bristol Mercury*, 15 June 1850, p. 8.

4

'The fullest instruction on
a subject so illustrious'

Exhibitions

In a letter to *The Morning Post* printed in late July 1815, a reader identified only as
'T' suggested that, in order to raise money for the Waterloo Fund, the government
should allow 'the public exhibition of Napoleon Bonaparte, amongst those other
specimens of untamed ferocity and savage cunning which at present embellish his
Majesty's Tower of London'.[1] While such an idea was more reminiscent of the
triumphs of imperial Rome than the salons of imperial London, T was not wrong
in their assumption that the former emperor would draw a crowd. Indeed, they
were clearly inspired by the crowds that flocked to Devon's Tor Bay in the hope
of catching a glimpse of Bonaparte, then ensconced on HMS *Bellerophon*.[2]
Bonaparte was not, of course, destined for the Tower, but instead for St Helena,
the tiny volcanic island in the South Atlantic that had for over a century and half
served as a supply port for the East India Company. In the absence of the man
himself, London's entrepreneurs instead turned to the artefacts of his reign and,
above all, the battle that ended his ambitions.

Public exhibitions themed around Waterloo and the French Wars rivalled
Waterloo Day celebrations as the way most of the British population experienced
and remembered Waterloo. As Chapter 2 demonstrated, Waterloo immediately
became a tourist attraction and even pilgrimage site for Britons who, by visiting
the battlefield and engaging in various forms of performative tourism (such as
bringing home a relic or signing their name on the walls of Hougoumont's
chapel), could link themselves to history and Britain's glory. Despite its proximity
to the United Kingdom, however, a trip to Waterloo was still time consuming and
costly for the majority of Britons. The exhibitions discussed in this chapter
provided a chance to 'visit' Waterloo and experience the triumph through its relics
for a fraction of the price of a continental trip and without having to leave the

---

[1] 'Exhibition of Bonaparte', *Morning Post*, 29 July 1815, p. 3.
[2] 'Bonaparte at Torbay', *The Times*, 27 July 1815, p. 3. For a comprehensive history of Britain's
relationship with Napoleon, see Stuart Semmel, *Napoleon and the British* (New Haven: Yale University
Press, 2004). See also David Cordingly, *Billy Ruffian: The Bellerophon and the Downfall of Napoleon*
(London: Bloomsbury, 2003), 259–66. The crowds got even bigger after the *Bellerophon* sailed for
Plymouth.

Who Owned Waterloo? Battle, Memory, and Myth in British History, 1815–1852. Luke Reynolds, Oxford University Press.
© Luke Reynolds 2022. DOI: 10.1093/oso/9780192864994.003.0005

comforts of London or the other cities of the British Isles. This democratization of experience proved wildly popular throughout the first half of the nineteenth century, inspiring national and international tours, special events, and forming the foundation of several fortunes. Exhibitions, and especially the various panoramas, are one of the forms of Waterloo commemoration most explored by scholars; nearly every work concerned with the memory and legacy of Waterloo, Wellington, or visual culture in nineteenth-century Britain discusses some aspect of these exhibitions.[3] Almost all of this scholarship examines these exhibitions through the more traditional lens of ownership: as attempts by the British to claim sole ownership of the victory to the exclusion of the Prussians and even the allies under Wellington's direct command. Rather than rehashing these arguments, this chapter will largely concentrate on the other vector of ownership: ownership and curation by civilians rather than the military within Britain itself, and the questions of accuracy and legitimacy accompanying that particular form of nationalization of memory.

This approach requires engagement with the cultural study of spectacle and museology.[4] Built on the notion that the nineteenth century saw a seismic shift in how visual culture, spectacle, and artefacts were experienced, scholars have argued that what was created simply as a form of spectacle to be observed for entertainment was deliberately transmogrified into an educational form of entertainment designed equally to shape the behaviour of the visitor and to inform their worldview. Starting traditionally in the mid-nineteenth century, and almost always anchored in one way or another by the Great Exhibition of 1851, this scholarship argues that the public museum was designed to modernize not just Britain, but

[3] Richard D. Altick, *The Shows of London* (Cambridge: The Belknap Press, 1978); Timothy Fitzpatrick, *The Long Shadow of Waterloo: Myths, Memories, and Debates* (Oxford: Casemate, 2019); Alan Forrest, *Waterloo* (Oxford: Oxford University Press, 2015); Elisa Milkes, 'A Battle's Legacy: Waterloo in Nineteenth Century Britain', Ph.D. dissertation, Yale University, 2002; Rory Muir, *Wellington: Waterloo and the Fortunes of Peace, 1814–1852* (New Haven: Yale University Press, 2015); R. E. Foster, *Wellington and Waterloo: The Duke, The Battle and Posterity, 1815–2015* (Staplehurst: Spellmount, 2014); Neville Thompson, *Wellington After Waterloo* (London: Routledge & Kegan Paul, Ltd, 1986); Philip Shaw, *Waterloo and the Romantic Imagination* (Basingstoke: Palgrave Macmillan, 2002), chapter 2; Susan Pearce, 'The *Matériel* of War: Waterloo and its Culture', in John Bonehill and Geoff Quilley, eds, *Conflicting Visions: War and Visual Culture in Britain and France, c.1700–1830* (Aldershot: Ashgate, 2005), 207–26; Gillen D'Arcy Wood, *The Shock of the Real: Romanticism and Visual Culture, 1760–1860* (New York: Palgrave, 2001), chapter 3. Siborne's model has also received some scholarly attention. See Malcolm Balen, *A Model Victory: Waterloo and the Battle for History* (London: Harper Perennial, 2006) or Peter Hofschroer, *Wellington's Smallest Victory* (London: Faber & Faber, 2005), although it should be noted that Hofschroer is virulently anti-Wellington and the work is best read with knowledge of that bias.

[4] This field is also heavily influenced by Michel Foucault, Pierre Bourdieu, and Asa Briggs. See Michel Foucault, 'Of Other Spaces', *Diacritics* 16, no. 1 (Spring 1986): 22–7; Michel Foucault, *The Order of Things* (New York: Vintage, 1994); Pierre Bourdieu, 'The Forms of Capital', in John G. Richardson, ed., *Handbook of Theory and Research for the Sociology of Education* (Westport, Conn.: Greenwood Press, 1986); Tony Bennett, *The Birth of the Museum: History, Theory, Politics* (London: Routledge, 1995); Asa Briggs, *Victorian Things* (Chicago: University of Chicago Press, 1989).

Britons.[5] While the timeframes of most of the exhibitions discussed here pre-date those under discussion in these works, the Waterloo exhibitions fit neatly into this model. The collection and display of the relics of Waterloo and Napoleon demonstrate not only the later impetus to use spectacle to disarm threat, but also that the display of such items further emphasized Britain's primacy.[6] Building on that, the various Waterloo panoramas, much like James Wyld's giant model of the earth (also located in Leicester Square), the Great Exhibition, the British Museum, and the South Kensington Museum, physically centred the world on the United Kingdom and emphasized the totality of British achievement.[7]

Where the Waterloo exhibitions diverge from mid- to late nineteenth-century public museums, however, is in their audience. Because one of the chief vectors of analysis in this chapter, and indeed this book, is the civil/military divide, it is tempting to view these two blocs as separate from each other but unified within themselves. This is inaccurate. Both the military and civilian blocs had internal divides whose relationships to Waterloo also shifted over time. Within the military, this is best demonstrated by the evolution of their involvement in the effort to legitimize public exhibitions. For the Waterloo Museum of 1815, it was enough to hire wounded enlisted veterans as staff. By the time we arrive at William Siborne's model, however, it is what the officers say that matters, a shift he himself tacitly endorsed by only interviewing officers when researching his model. On the civilian side the question comes down to who precisely made up the British public that flocked to these exhibitions. There are indications that Waterloo exhibitions had more cross-class appeal than other entertainments of the age. For the last two weeks of its display in Glasgow in November 1816, 'tradespeople and children' could purchase tickets for Howe's panorama of Waterloo at half price—sixpence as opposed to one shilling.[8] Nor was this demand limited to Glasgow. The noted diarist Fanny Anne Burney recorded a conversation with a panorama exhibitor in the early 1840s where the man claimed that the Waterloo panorama was the only exhibit to ever provoke excitement in 'mechanics'.[9]

Despite this appeal, however, we are still some way from John Ruskin's dream of 'large educational museums in every district of London, freely open every day,

[5] Barbara J. Black, *On Exhibit: Victorians and Their Museums* (Charlottesville: University Press of Virginia, 2000); Lara Kriegel, *Grand Designs: Labor, Empire, and the Museum in Victorian Culture* (Durham, NC: Duke University Press, 2008); Robert Aguirre, *Informal Empire: Mexico and Central America in Victorian Culture* (Minneapolis: University of Minnesota Press, 2004); Kayla Kreuger McKinney, 'Collecting Subjects/Objects: The Museum and Victorian Literature 1830–1914', Ph.D. dissertation, West Virginia University, 2015.

[6] Black, *On Exhibit*, 11; Aguirre, *Informal Empire*, introduction and chapter 1.

[7] Aguirre draws a direct line between Barker's Waterloo panorama and the creation of imperial subjects. Aguirre, *Informal Empire*, 41; Black, *On Exhibit*, chapter 1; Kriegel, *Grand Designs*.

[8] A. D. Cameron, *The Man Who Loved to Draw Horses: James Howe 1780–1836* (Aberdeen: Aberdeen University Press, 1986), 32.

[9] Margaret S. Rolt, ed., *A Great-Niece's Journals: Being Extracts from the Journals of Fanny Anne Burney (Mrs. Wood) from 1830 to 1842* (Boston: Houghton Mifflin, 1926), 308.

and well lighted and warm at night, with all furniture of comfort, and full aids for the use of their contents by all classes'.[10] Admission to the various exhibitions discussed here ranged between one and two shillings. Average daily wages for a craftsman between 1815 and 1850 were roughly 3s. 8d., while for an unskilled labourer they were 2s. 4d.[11] Like the Waterloo fete at Vauxhall, this made the exhibitions affordable in theory but in reality the preserve of the burgeoning middle class and above. When this chapter discusses the civilian audience for these exhibitions, therefore, it is not claiming that Waterloo exhibitions, for all of their national appeal, pre-empted the wider democratization of the Great Exhibition or South Kensington Museum's Bethnal Green Branch or circulating museum programme by several decades.[12] It should also be noted that there are indications that even the limited expansion of the paying public, driven by interest in Waterloo and Napoleon, was too democratic for some.

While Waterloo exhibitions may have had certain inherent advantages when it came to attracting visitors, not all of them were a success. There were various short-lived rivals to the better-known Waterloo Museum, most notably the Waterloo Exhibition on St James's Street.[13] From 1823 to 1824 the Waterloo Rooms, 'the most fashionable lounge' on Pall Mall, tried to lure customers by displaying 'the so much admired White Barb Horse (and Charger) of the late Emperor Napoleon'.[14] Finally, as discussed at the end of the chapter, there was William Siborne's model. Several factors set the successful exhibitions apart from the unsuccessful ones. First, Waterloo exhibitions, like all forms of popular entertainment, required a certain level of showmanship. Alex Palmer, William Bullock, and the Messrs Marshall, as we shall see, all had something of the showman about them and knew how to appeal to a crowd. Barker's Leicester Square panorama provided that same showmanship in its very design, with customers entering via a dark hallway and staircase that suddenly thrust them into brilliant, 360-degree spectacle.[15]

This use of spectacle and wider appeal prompts the question: how did these exhibitions differ from the annual commemorations (and especially Vauxhall) discussed in the previous chapter? For a start, while neither the commemorations discussed in the previous chapter nor the exhibitions discussed in this one were as accessible as the circulating museums of the second half of the nineteenth century,

---

[10] Quoted in Black, On Exhibit, 6.

[11] Gregory Clark, 'The Conditions of the Working Class in England, 1209–2004', Journal of Political Economy 113, no. 6 (December 2005): 1325.

[12] Kriegel, Grand Designs, chapters 3 and 5.

[13] William A. Scott, Battle of Waterloo; or, Correct Narrative on that Late Sanguinary Conflict on the Plains of Waterloo (London: E. Cox and Son, 1815), 172n.–173n.

[14] This was, presumably, his favourite warhorse, Marengo, captured at Waterloo. Admittance was the standard 1s. The Examiner, 22 February 1824, p. 16; Gareth Glover, Waterloo in 100 Objects (Stroud: The History Press, 2015), 153–5.

[15] Shaw, Waterloo and the Romantic Imagination, 85–6.

the exhibitions were, by design, more accessible than either Vauxhall or the Waterloo banquet. At their most successful, exhibitions were open seven days a week for months on end; their admission fees were lower than Vauxhall and came without the hidden costs; they did not go as far into the night as Vauxhall's fetes; and they toured the country. Secondly, these exhibitions sought to explicitly recreate Waterloo, something that the annual commemorations, with the notable exception of Vauxhall's re-enactments, did not attempt. Finally, and crucially, these exhibitions sought to use spectacle to do more than simply entertain; they sought to educate. For Vauxhall, it was enough for their Waterloo fete to dazzle. Accuracy was a bonus, but not required. For the exhibitions discussed in this chapter, however, spectacle alone was not enough: they also needed to be historically accurate.

Legitimacy and the appearance of accuracy could make or break an exhibition. As it was the presence of military men that provided that legitimacy, Waterloo veterans, in this case very much still spiritually led by the Duke of Wellington, retained some ownership of the memory of Waterloo and shaped how it was remembered by the wider British public. Thus, it was their definition of accuracy, rather than what had actually occurred, that mattered. This adds a crucial dimension to the relationship between civilian curation and military presence: by incorporating military men into their exhibitions, either as part of the exhibitions themselves or as part of the paying audience, civilian curators legitimized their events and representations of Waterloo in the eyes of the paying public.

This chapter will examine multiple exhibitions divided into two categories: relics and representations. Relic exhibitions were collections of physical items with provenance that could be traced back to the battle itself. This includes Palmer's Waterloo Museum, with its selection of weapons and detritus collected from the field, and the various exhibitions centred around Napoleon's carriage. Representation exhibitions were centred not on items collected from the battlefield, but instead on depictions of it either on canvas or in the form of lead soldiers. While they were themselves physical in nature, they held no direct physical connection to the battle. Both categories had their advantages and disadvantages. Relic exhibitions, if collected correctly, have their legitimacy baked in, thus guaranteeing the perception of accuracy. Relic exhibitions guaranteed the perception of accuracy, but were limited by their scope and the availability of the product. There were only so many relics of the field, and entrepreneurs like Palmer and Bullock were not only competing with each other, but also with amateur collectors of the type discussed in Chapter 2. In contrast, representation exhibitions were infinitely reproducible, in the same way that traditional oil paintings of the battle would be. The disadvantage came with that flexibility. Lacking the anchor of physical items, these exhibitions lived or died on the appearance of accuracy.

Alex Palmer of 20 St James's Street, the 'celebrated' 'Cutler to his Majesty', seems to have hit upon the idea of purchasing and displaying curiosities as a way to lure people into his shop; offering to show his collection for free 'for the gratification of the visitants' in exchange for the 'purchase of some trifling article in his line of business'.[16] This appears to have been his motivation when, less than two months after the Battle of Waterloo, he made a decision that would briefly propel him out of the cutlery business and into museum management. While visiting Paris in late July, Palmer attended the sale of a variety of items from Bonaparte's wardrobe, now the property of Francois Durand, *Maitre de Garde de Robe*. Recognizing the lure of a collection that included several of the former emperor's ceremonial outfits, two of his swords, the belt of the Grand Marshal of France, and the stars of a variety of military and chivalric orders, Palmer bought the lot and began to make plans to bring it back across the Channel to a victorious Britain.[17] Already aware that the legitimacy of such items would be crucial to their appeal, Palmer requested, and received, a letter written and signed by Durand, guaranteeing the provenance of the items.[18] He also purchased from British and Prussian soldiers in Paris a number of medals of the *Légion d'Honneur* and 'an infinity of crosses, [in] iron, silver, [and] gold'.[19]

Palmer returned to London in August and embarked on his original plan to 'form a curious exhibition...*gratis*'.[20] That plan soon changed. From a free gimmick designed to lure customers into his St James's Street premises Palmer soon realized he had the foundations of an independent enterprise. Two months later the *Morning Post* reported that he had again returned from another purchasing trip to the Continent with 'an incalculable number of articles' and multiple paintings and was looking for 'premises sufficiently capacious' to display his collection.[21] Palmer found those premises at 97 Pall Mall, formerly the site of the Star and Garter Tavern, and opened the Waterloo Museum to the public on 17 November 1815, with admission costing 1s. 6d.[22] The museum was divided into two rooms, the Armoury, or Cuirassiers' Hall, and the Grand Saloon, and at the time of the museum's catalogue's printing (presumably for the opening in November) boasted some 185 objects or collections.[23] Of these, roughly one-third

[16] 'Napoleon Bonaparte's Wardrobe', *Morning Post*, 9 August 1815, p. 3; *Kent's Directory for 1803* (London: R. and H. Causton, 1803), 150.

[17] The only thing he was unsuccessful in his attempts to buy was Napoleon's coronation regalia as Emperor of France, the highlight of which was a purple velvet imperial robe studded with bees. Durand insisted 'they belong in France'. 'Napoleon Bonaparte's Wardrobe', *Morning Post*, 9 August 1815, p. 3.

[18] 'Napoleon Bonaparte's Wardrobe', *Morning Post*, 9 August 1815, p. 3.

[19] 'Napoleon Bonaparte's Wardrobe', *Morning Post*, 9 August 1815, p. 3.

[20] *Morning Post*, 22 August 1815, p. 3.   [21] *Morning Post*, 25 October 1815, p. 3.

[22] 'The Waterloo Museum', *Morning Post*, 18 November 1815, p. 3; *Catalogue of the Waterloo Museum, 97, Pall Mall. Established in the Year 1815* (London: J. Lowe, 1815) ; *Morning Post*, 29 April 1816, p. 1.

[23] Some of the catalogue entries are for multiple items such as 'three pioneers' axes'. *Catalogue of the Waterloo Museum*, 3, 7; 'The Waterloo Museum', *Morning Post*, 18 November 1815, p. 3.

were directly linked to Waterloo, while the balance was made up by paintings, items associated with Napoleon, his family, his marshals, and imperial or Revolutionary France in general.[24]

While the legitimacy of Napoleon's items had been established by Durand's letter and other items purchased from French officials would very probably have been likewise documented, Palmer chose to emphasize the veracity of his Waterloo relics in two different ways. First, the language employed in the various catalogue descriptions of such items deliberately emphasized their proximity to the carnage. In this vein we find entries for a French infantryman's cap which had 'received five cuts from the sabre of an English Dragoon'; a grenadier of the Imperial Guard's coat, 'pierced with musket balls, five of which had entered his body'; a cuirass holed by grape shot; a trumpet of the Imperial Guard 'so battered that it bears but small resemblance of its original shape'; shell fragments with horse hair still stuck to them; and two cannon balls found in Hougoumont, 'one of which killed Capt. Crawford and eight men of the Guards'.[25] Such descriptions, paired with the damaged nature of many of the items on display (there were so many 'bayonets taken from the field, some of them broken, and much injured in the contest [along with] various trappings and broken swords, also found on the field' that they did not even rate a numbered entry in the catalogue), helped to highlight the chaos of the battle and possibly transport visitors from Pall Mall to the field of battle, providing the desired link to the victory.[26] In 1816, Samuel Butler, who had visited the museum in preparation for a visit to the field itself, delightedly recorded that he had found the wall damaged by a round shot he had 'seen . . . in the Waterloo Museum'.[27]

Second, Palmer employed, as museum staff, disabled veterans who, in the words of the *Morning Post*, 'were . . . deprived of their limbs in that ever-memorable conflict'.[28] Pre-empting Vauxhall's use of enlisted veterans by a decade, this is a reversal of the more traditional military attendance used to legitimize civilian owned and curated commemorations of Waterloo that nonetheless achieved the same end. Although it accomplished the laudable result of providing a few recently wounded and discharged soldiers with a new way to earn their livelihood, this hiring choice effectively turned the veterans into living exhibits. Visitors could marvel at the vast array of implements of violence before turning to see the results on the flesh of their countrymen. As with the

---

[24] *Catalogue of the Waterloo Museum.*
[25] *Catalogue of the Waterloo Museum*, 3, 4, 5, 20. There is a chance that the same cuirass was featured in an exhibition of relics organized to celebrate Waterloo's 75th anniversary in 1890. 'The Waterloo Exhibition', *Morning Post*, 2 January 1890, p. 6; 'Waterloo', *The Era*, 11 January 1890, p. 7.
[26] *Catalogue of the Waterloo Museum*, 6.
[27] Samuel Butler, 'A Visit to the Field of Waterloo in July 1816 and Short Tour in Belgium & France', quoted in Milkes, 'A Battle's Legacy', 375.
[28] 'The Waterloo Museum', *Morning Post*, 18 November 1815, p. 3.

catalogue descriptions and condition of the displays, the proximity to violence was deliberately invoked to increase verisimilitude.

The Waterloo Museum proved successful enough that Palmer kept journeying across the Channel to add to the collection.[29] In 1817 the guidebook *Walks Through London* noted that the museum collection had recently been supplemented by nine new paintings and that 'the collection of trophies from the field of Waterloo has also received considerable addition'.[30] The guide highly recommended the museum, noting that it was 'an ornament to the metropolis, and a lasting monument to the triumph of our arms'.[31] Despite this encomium the museum closed the same year and its collections were auctioned off on 13 and 14 March 1817.[32]

Patrons who sought further relics of the battle and Napoleon's downfall could find them on Piccadilly, only a short walk north of Palmer's space on Pall Mall. It was there that Bullock's London Museum at the Egyptian Hall offered the chance to see the crown jewel of relic exhibitions: Napoleon's carriage.[33] Captured by the Prussians on the evening of Waterloo, Napoleon's military carriage and its contents made their way up the chain of command to General Blücher, who promptly shipped it to Britain as a gift for the prince regent. The future George IV, despite his desire to tie himself to the victory (see Chapters 5 and 6), had no use for the carriage and sold it to William Bullock for £2,500.[34] Bullock, with the same impresario's instincts that had already made his museum a success, hired Napoleon's coachman of ten years, a Dutchman by the name of Jean Hornn, who had been left for dead when the carriage was captured but survived at the cost of his right arm, to become a living part of the exhibit (along with several of the coach's horses) and threw the exhibit open to the public in the first week of January 1816, with an admittance price of one shilling.[35] The carriage, which was dark blue and gilt and, appropriately, bullet-proof, Hornn, the horses, Napoleon's

[29] This was probably helped by a series of articles in the *Morning Post* highlighting portions of the collection. See 'The Waterloo Museum', *Morning Post*, 4 December 1815, p. 3; 'The Waterloo Museum', *Morning Post*, 8 December 1815, p. 3; 'The Waterloo Museum', *Morning Post*, 5 January 1816, p. 3.

[30] David Hughson (Edward Pugh), *Walks Through London, Including Westminster and the Borough of Southwark, with the Surrounding Suburbs* (London: Sherwood, Neely, and Jones, 1817), II: 270.

[31] Hughson (Pugh), *Walks Through London*, II: 270.

[32] In January 1817, the price of admission was reduced to 1s. to try to boost attendance. *Morning Post*, 21 January 1817, p. 2; *Morning Post*, 11 March 1817, p. 4; *Morning Chronicle*, 13 March 1817, p. 4. It seems at least some of Palmer's collection ended up in Christie's 'Grand Exhibition of Military Antiquities' housed at Pall Mall's Gothic Hall and subsequently at the Royal Armoury in Haymarket. See 'Replies. Sotton's Waterloo Museum', *Notes and Queries* 11 September 1909, series 10, vol. XII, 210–11.

[33] For a more detailed history of William Bullock and the Egyptian Hall, see Aguirre, *Informal Empire*, chapter 1; Aleck Abrahams, 'The Egyptian Hall, Piccadilly, 1813–1873', *The Antiquary* 42 (February 1906): 61–4; Altick, *The Shows of London*, chapter 18.

[34] Abrahams, 'The Egyptian Hall', 62; Altick, *The Shows of London*, 239–40.

[35] *Morning Post*, 2 January 1816, p. 1; *Morning Post*, 26 February 1816; *The Leeds Mercury*, 2 March 1816; Joseph Farington, *The Farington Diary*, ed. James Grieg (London: Hutchinson & Co., 1923), VIII: 88; Altick, *The Shows of London*, 239–40; Abrahams, 'The Egyptian Hall', 63.

camp bed, travelling case, and its luxurious contents proved to be the smash hit of the season.[36] Drawn by the chance to see something that had participated in both the Russian and Waterloo campaigns, the legitimacy of which was guaranteed by both Hornn and the prince regent, 10,000 people a day flocked to Piccadilly.[37]

This level of popularity brought its own detractors. George Cruikshank and Thomas Rowlandson caricatured the crush that resulted, depicting exaggerated British stereotypes crawling all over the carriage while dozens try to squeeze inside like a Regency version of phonebooth stuffing (Figures 4.1 and 4.2). Both Cruikshank and Rowlandson, much like James Gilray's *Buonaparte 48 hours*

Figure 4.1 George Cruikshank, A scene at the London Museum Piccadilly, -or- A peep at the spoils of ambition, taken at the Battle of Waterloo—being a new tax on John Bull for 1816, 1816. London, The British Museum, 1859,0316.111 © The Trustees of the British Museum.

---

[36] In late January Bullock also added Napoleon's gold and diamond snuff box. *Morning Post*, 29 January 1816. For a detailed description of the carriage, see J. Norris Brewer, *London and Middlesex; or, an Historical, Commercial, & Descriptive Survey of the Metropolis of Great-Britain* (London: J. Harris, 1816), V: 643–53.

[37] Altick, *The Shows of London*, 240–1. The Exhibition catalogue that Bullock produced included, along with a suitably patriotic narrative, the account of the carriage's capture by Major Baron von Keller of the Prussian army, extracts from a number of letters to and from Prince Blücher that reference the carriage, and Hornn's affidavit, sworn before Sir Matthew Wood, Lord Mayor of London, that the coach was Napoleon's and had been used in the Russian Campaign. *A Description of the Costly and Curious Military Carriage of the Late Emperor of France, Taken on the Evening of the Battle of Waterloo* (London: William Bullock, 1816).

EXHIBITION AT BULLOCK'S MUSEUM OF BONEPARTES CARRIAGE TAKEN AT WATERLOO.

Figure 4.2 Thomas Rowlandson, *Exhibition at Bullock's Museum of Bonaparte's Carriage, Taken at Waterloo*, 1816. The Metropolitan Museum of Art, New York, Harris Brisbane Dick Fund, 1917.

after landing! thirteen years earlier, use crude depictions of their countrymen to register their disdain for their behaviour, if not their cause. The scenes are unquestionably triumphal in nature, but in all three prints the only person depicted with any respect is Bonaparte himself (Cruikshank and Rowlandson include busts of the former emperor, while the centre of Gilray's print, famously, is the severed head of the then First Consul of the French Republic).[38] Despite the madding crowds, several notable society figures attended the exhibition. John Pratt, First Marquess Camden, 'and a number of distinguished characters' visited in late February 1816 and spoke at length to Hornn.[39] Lord Byron, already a noted fan of Bonaparte, was so taken by the carriage that he had a replica made that replaced Napoleon's campaign necessities with a library and full dinner service. He used it in his various European tours and may have been in it when he visited Waterloo in May 1816.[40] Joseph Farington, the landscape painter, visited on the final day of the Exhibition's London run, 24 August 1816. He seems to have been more taken with Hornn than the carriage but did note in his diary that 'such has

[38] See Linda Colley, *Britons: Forging the Nation 1707–1837* (New Haven: Yale University Press, 2009), chapter 7.
[39] *Morning Post*, 26 February 1816.
[40] Leslie Marchand, *Byron: A Biography* (New York: Alfred A. Knopf, 1957), II: 603, 661, 718, 791, 813; Altick, *The Shows of London*, 241n.

been the Public Curiosity in London to see this Carriage that upwards of 220,000 persons have paid to be admitted to see it'.[41]

From London, Bullock took the carriage and its entourage on tour. Its first stop was Frogmore Cottage in Windsor, where Queen Charlotte, two of her daughters, the Princesses Augusta, Elizabeth, and her niece Princess Sophia of Gloucester received a private tour and a demonstration of Hornn's driving through Windsor.[42] Having received the royal blessing, the carriage travelled onward to Maidenhead, then 'to Bristol, from thence to Dublin; and afterwards to Edinburgh'.[43] It proved to be equally popular outside the capital. In a letter written later in life to the journalist William Jerdan, Bullock sardonically ascribed nearly supernatural powers to the carriage, which, he noted, 'gave me the power of accomplishing, in a few months, what, with all his talents, riches, and armies, [Napoleon] could never succeed in doing; for in that short period I over-ran England, Ireland, and Scotland, levying a willing contribution on upwards of 800,000 of his Majesty's subjects; for old and young, rich and poor, clergy and laity, all ages, sexes, and conditions, flocked to pay their poll-tax, and gratify their curiosity by an examination of the spoils of the dead lion.'[44] Between London and the rest of the British Isles, it is estimated that he made £35,000 on the carriage, quattuordecupling his original investment of £2,500.[45]

By late 1818, Bullock had decided that the carriage and its associated collections had made him all the money they could within the British Isles and that the next logical step was an international tour focused on India or America. Not keen on travelling that far or for that long, he offered the entire collection up for sale in November of 1818, noting that in London the carriage 'has been visited by nearly half a million of persons; and, is presumed, would be equally attractive in India or America'.[46] Bullock sold the four carriage horses in a separate auction hosted by Tattersall's Repository, the well-known horse auction house. A large crowd gathered on 30 November 1818 to witness the sale of the four brown geldings, who were introduced by Mr Tattersall as 'Bony the First, Second, Third, and Bony the Last'.[47] The four horses were sold to different individuals, and together netted 73 guineas, while the harness, including the postilion's saddle, fetched another £2 14s.[48] While the horses were snapped up, no would-be international impresario

---

[41] Farington, *The Farington Diary*, VIII: 88.

[42] 'Windsor, Aug. 27', *The Times*, 28 August 1816, p. 3.

[43] 'Windsor, Aug. 27', *The Times*, 28 August 1816, p. 3; Farington, *The Farington Diary*, VIII: 88. We also know it visited Brighton. The gap in London's collection of exhibitions was almost immediately filled by Bonaparte's 'Pleasure Carriage' which went on show at the Bartholomew Fair at half the admission price of the London Museum. Altick, *The Shows of London*, 241.

[44] William Jerdan, *The Autobiography of William Jerdan* (London: Arthur Hall, Virtue, & Co., 1852), II: 87.

[45] Abrahams, 'The Egyptian Hall', 63.   [46] *The Times*, 30 November 1818, p. 1.

[47] 'Sale of Buonaparte's Horses', *Chester Chronicle*, 4 December 1818, p. 3.

[48] *Morning Chronicle*, 1 December 1818, p. 3; 'Sale of Bonaparte's Horses', *Caledonian Mercury*, 5 December 1818, p. 2.

could be found to bring Napoleon's carriage to India or America. The coach was still in Bullock's possession in June 1819 and was eventually sold to a coachmaker for a relatively paltry £168.[49]

Even as Bullock was trying to sell Napoleon's coach, he was converting his largest asset, the Egyptian Hall, from a museum to a general exhibition space. With the Egyptian Hall now playing host to a variety of collections from locations as diverse as Lapland and Mexico, it seemed that Waterloo relic exhibitions were a thing of the past, replaced by the panoramas discussed later in this chapter.[50] Physical exhibitions of Waterloo's figures and relics, however, would undergo a revival in the 1830s at the hands of perhaps the longest-lived popular exhibition company in London: Madame Tussaud and Sons. Starting in 1835 with a 'group of ten figures of the great men of the late war', the collection grew to encompass Napoleon's coach (and a number of accessories that accompanied it, acquired in 1842), and the 1843 Shrine of Napoleon.[51]

Madame Tussaud's most established link to the Revolutionary and Napoleonic Wars was the proprietress herself. The former art tutor to Louis XVI's sister, Madame Tussaud was briefly imprisoned and due to be executed as an enemy of the people before her sentence was commuted in exchange for her using her talents to capture the death masks of the freshly guillotined and other notable figures (on both sides) of the French Revolution. These likenesses formed the base of her impressive collection of waxworks, which she began to display for a fee.[52] Invited to exhibit her collection at London's Lyceum Theatre during the brief peace of Amiens in 1802, she was trapped in Great Britain by the resumption of hostilities in 1803 and became a staple touring exhibition across the British Isles. In 1835, apparently sold on remaining in Britain, she and her sons took up residence in what would become their permanent home the next year: the Baker Street Bazaar.[53]

In addition to individual figures and relics (such as the blade of one of the guillotines used during the Terror), Madame Tussaud's favoured groups of figures in tableau (a practice they still use in their museums today).[54] These tableaux often featured groups of individuals by theme, rather than recreating a documented

[49] Abrahams, 'The Egyptian Hall', 63; Altick, *The Shows of London*, 241.

[50] Aguirre, *Informal Empire*, chapter 1.

[51] 'Madame Tussaud', *Morning Post*, 21 May 1835, p. 4.

[52] Along with the collection she inherited from her teacher/mentor, Philippe Curtius, a Swiss physician. For a complete biography of Madame Tussaud, see Kate Berridge, *Madame Tussaud: A Life in Wax* (New York: Harper Collins, 2006); Pamela Pilbeam, *Madame Tussaud and the History of Waxworks* (London: Hambledon and London, 2003). She also wrote an edited autobiography that was published in 1838. Marie Tussaud, *Madame Tussaud's Memoirs and Reminiscences of France, Forming an Abridged History of the French Revolution*, ed. Francis Hervé (London: Saunders and Otley, 1838).

[53] *Morning Post*, 19 March 1835, p. 1; Pilbeam, *Madame Tussaud*, chapter 5.

[54] John Theodore Tussaud, *The Romance of Madame Tussaud's* (New York: George H. Doran Company, 1920), 90–1.

event from history, and such was the case for the first new group debuted in the Baker Street Bazaar in the spring of 1835, 'a splendid group of ten figures of the great men of the late war'.[55] The group, anchored by Wellington and Napoleon, also contained Admiral Nelson; Prince Blücher; French Marshals Murat, Ney, and Bernadotte; Alexander I of Russia; Francis II of Austria; and Frederick William III of Prussia, all dressed in uniform.[56] *The Morning Post* were effusive in their praise for the new tableau. They particularly praised the main attractions, noting that 'Napoleon and Wellington seem but to want motion to be life itself', but concluded their review by declaring the entire group 'one of Madame Tussaud's most happy efforts . . . seen to great advantage in the great room of the Bazaar'.[57]

One reason Wellington's depiction was so lifelike was that he had posed for it himself.[58] A notable fan of the wax museum, Wellington was one of the first visitors to their new permanent home in Baker Street, had a standing order for the museum to 'let him know whenever a new figure of exceptional interest was added to the Exhibition', and is the only non-royal listed by name as a patron on the cover of Madame Tussaud's 1851 catalogue.[59] This patronage benefited both parties. Wellington, as he had done with Sir Thomas Lawrence and Jan Willem Pieneman and would do with William Salter (see Chapter 5), used his presence and influence to ensure that his likeness was not only accurate but also dignified and met with his approval—a semi-permanent rebuttal in wax to the inherently temporary criticisms levied at him just three years earlier in response to his opposition to the 1832 Representation of the People (Great Reform) Act. Madame Tussaud's, in turn, received the public approval of the ultimate arbiter of military legitimacy: no one would question the accuracy of Tussaud's Napoleonic and Waterloo-themed items with Wellington's name listed on the cover of the catalogue. Tussaud's, as Salter would in the years following, also received access to Wellington's circle. The 1851 catalogue notes that the likenesses of the Marquess of Anglesey and Lord Hill were both taken from in-person sittings, something that would have been much easier to arrange with a letter of introduction from Wellington.[60]

Madame Tussaud and Sons continued to build on their success, adding representations of politicians, European royals, and other 'public characters', including the newly crowned Victoria I.[61] The addition of George IV's splendid coronation

[55] 'Madame Tussaud', *Morning Post*, 21 May 1835, p. 4.

[56] 'Madame Tussaud', *Morning Post*, 21 May 1835, p. 4.

[57] 'Madame Tussaud', *Morning Post*, 21 May 1835, p. 4.

[58] *Biographical and Descriptive Sketches of the Distinguished Characters which compose the Unrivalled Exhibition of Madame Tussaud and Sons* (London: Madame Tussaud and Sons, 1851), 3. Hereafter cited as *Madame Tussaud's 1851 Catalogue*.

[59] Tussaud, *The Romance of Madame Tussaud's*, 117–18; *Madame Tussaud's 1851 Catalogue*, cover.

[60] *Madame Tussaud's 1851 Catalogue*, 4.

[61] 'Madame Tussaud's Exhibition', *Morning Post*, 8 November 1836, p. 3; 'Public Amusements', *Morning Chronicle*, 18 August 1837, p. 2; Tussaud, *The Romance of Madame Tussaud's*, 118.

robes in 1841 reinforced the idea that the past would still draw as good a paying crowd as the present, and so the museum leapt, the next year, at the opportunity to acquire Napoleon's famed carriage.[62] According to Tussaud family legend, Madame Tussaud's eldest son Joseph was on London Bridge when he heard another pedestrian state that a carriage they were admiring was nothing compared to Napoleon's. Joseph engaged the man in conversation, and it was subsequently revealed that the legendary vehicle was owned by Robert Jeffreys, a coach manu-facturer on Gray's Inn Road.[63] Joseph immediately negotiated the purchase of the carriage and returned to the museum, full of ideas of how to introduce Napoleon's Carriage to a new generation of Londoners.[64]

Much like Bullock had, the Tussauds supplemented the carriage with a variety of other items connected with the late emperor and with them opened a new set of rooms in March 1843.[65] For only sixpence in addition to the museum's base admission price of 1s., visitors could experience ' "The Shrine of Napoleon, or Golden Chamber," the Room containing the Carriage taken at Waterloo, the Table of Marshals, and Chamber of Horrors'.[66] Given that the purchase of the relics and the decoration of the new rooms had cost somewhere between £5,000 and £13,000, sixpence seems generous, but Madame Tussaud's most likely made up some of the expense of the new rooms by selling souvenir programmes for the new exhibit that included a narrative of the carriage's capture, a summary of the Battle of Waterloo, a copy of Bullock's catalogue, and the Waterloo dispatches and biographical details of Wellington, Napoleon, and Blücher.[67] Lured by the advert-isements and determined to prove the legitimacy of the bold claim stated in the exhibition catalogue that 'everything connected with the late Emperor Napoleon belongs to British history', Londoners flocked to the new rooms, led by Prince Albert, who visited within two weeks of their opening.[68] *The New Monthly Belle*

---

[62] *Morning Post*, 3 May 1841, p. 1; *Morning Post*, 15 March 1843, p. 1; Tussaud, *The Romance of Madame Tussaud's*, 120–6. Altick gives the date of purchase as 1843, which is when the carriage went on display. Altick, *The Shows of London*, 241.

[63] It is unclear whether this is the same coachmaker that Bullock had sold the coach to. According to John Theodore Tussaud's family history of Madame Tussaud's, Jeffrey's had taken the carriage 'in part payment for a bad debt'. Tussaud, *The Romance of Madame Tussaud's*, 121.

[64] Tussaud, *The Romance of Madame Tussaud's*, 120–3.

[65] *Morning Post*, 15 March 1843, p. 1.

[66] *The Military Carriage of Napoleon Buonaparte, taken after the Battle of Waterloo* (London: Madame Tussaud and Sons, 1843), 24; *Morning Post*, 15 March 1843, p. 1; *Morning Post*, 13 May 1843, p. 1.

[67] The commemorative catalogue printed for the opening puts the cost at between £5,000 and £6,000. The 1862 Madame Tussaud and Sons' Catalogue claims that the new rooms, inclusive of their content, cost 'nearly £13,000'. *Military Carriage of Napoleon Buonaparte*, 24; *Biographical and Descriptive Sketches of the Distinguished Characters which compose the Unrivalled Exhibition and Historical Gallery of Madame Tussaud and Sons* (London: G. Cole, 1862), 22. Hereafter cited as *Madame Tussaud's 1862 Catalogue. Madame Tussaud's 1851 Catalogue*, 23.

[68] *Military Carriage of Napoleon Buonaparte*, 24; 'Court Circular', *The Standard*, 28 March 1843, p. 2; *Morning Post*, 15 March 1843, p. 1; *Morning Post*, 13 May 1843, p. 1; *The Era*, 23 July 1843, p. 4; *Morning Chronicle*, 29 July 1843, p. 6; *The Era*, 30 July 1843, p. 4.

Assemblée was especially taken with the expansion, noting that it encompassed 'the rise and fall of Majesty—the alpha and omega of greatness', and that it 'reflect [ed] the highest credit on the judgement and good taste of Madame Tussaud and her sons'.[69]

Besides claiming British ownership of the entirety of Napoleon's life, the exhibition catalogue made the much more reasonable claim that 'relics, when authenticated, bring the period to which they belong immediately to the imagination'.[70] Such a claim, of course, along with the success of the new rooms, rested on the authentication of the relics. Joseph Tussaud had ensured that, when he purchased the carriage, he also purchased proof of its provenance. In addition to acquiring the affidavit that Jean Hornn had sworn in 1816 before the Lord Mayor of London, letters went out to the coachmakers of continental Europe and 'it was certified...that M. Simon, of Brussels, built the carriage, and that most of the contrivances for economizing space and ensuring comfort and convenience were suggested by the emperor himself and his second wife, Marie Louise; also that this was the carriage which had picked up Napoleon on his retreat to Paris after the burning of Moscow'.[71] The inclusion of Bullock's original catalogue also reinforced the provenance, as did extracts from several letters written by Blücher and other Prussian officers that mentioned the carriage.[72] As for the other relics that accompanied the carriage, Madame Tussaud's reassured its guests that they had passed from the late emperor to his brother, Prince Lucien Bonaparte, and were 'affirmed before Masters in Chancery'.[73] For those who were particularly distrustful, certificates of authenticity were available for examination.[74] In total, ten of the twenty-nine pages of the souvenir catalogue of the exhibition are either partially or fully dedicated to proving the legitimacy of the collection.

In addition to the letters, certificates, and affidavits, Madame Tussaud and Sons had the implicit backing of Wellington, which further reinforced their claims to legitimacy. Wellington remained a frequent visitor to the museum throughout the rest of his life, posing again for a waxwork in 1852.[75] His favourite models, according to John Theodore Tussaud, 'being those of Queen Victoria and the dead Napoleon'.[76] He visited the Shrine of Napoleon (which featured the dead emperor lying in state on his camp bed, dressed in his favourite Chasseurs uniform, his feet covered by a replica of the riding cloak he wore at the battle of Marengo) so often that Joseph Tussaud suggested in 1852 that he be painted

[69] 'Madame Tussaud's Exhibition', *The New Monthly Belle Assemblée* 19 (August 1843): 125.
[70] *Military Carriage of Napoleon Buonaparte*, 24.
[71] Tussaud, *The Romance of Madame Tussaud's*, 123–6.
[72] *Military Carriage of Napoleon Buonaparte*, 7–16.
[73] *Military Carriage of Napoleon Buonaparte*, 24.
[74] *Military Carriage of Napoleon Buonaparte*, 24.   [75] *Madame Tussaud's 1862 Catalogue*, 15.
[76] Tussaud, *The Romance of Madame Tussaud's*, 118.

paying his respects. The artist Sir George Hayter and Wellington both liked the idea, and the resulting painting was the last Wellington ever sat for.[77] Completed three months after Wellington's death, the painting showed the duke in his preferred civilian garb of a blue coat and white trousers, slightly stooped with age, paying his respects to his great rival. The painting was displayed in Madame Tussaud's until it was destroyed in a fire in 1925, but a hugely popular mezzotint of it was produced by James Scott in 1854, several copies of which still exist (Figure 4.3).[78]

Madame Tussaud's was, understandably, quite proud of the Duke of Wellington's patronage, and went out of their way to honour him in kind. In 1844, the year following the debut of the Napoleon Rooms, Wellington's portrayal in the museum was also upgraded. He was removed from the 'great men of the late war' group and was given pride of place in a new tableau of Victoria and Albert offering Wellington 'the honours he so well deserves, surrounded by Sovereigns in

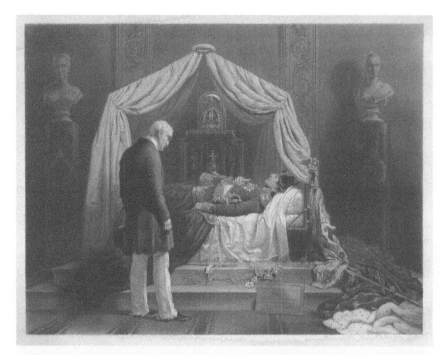

Figure 4.3 James Scott, after Sir George Hayter, *The Duke of Wellington Visiting the Effigy and Personal Relics of Napoleon*, 1854. London, British Museum, 1872,0309.426 © The Trustees of the British Museum.

[77] Tussaud, *The Romance of Madame Tussaud's*, 154–5.
[78] Tussaud, *The Romance of Madame Tussaud's*, 155; 'Waxworks Fire', *The Times*, 20 March 1925, p. 11.

amity with England, supported by the great Characters of the day'.[79] The tableau contained eighteen figures, including Victoria, Albert, and Wellington, along with Nicholas I of Russia, Frederick William IV of Prussia, and four of Wellington's companions-in-arms, Viscount Gough, Viscount Hardinge, the Marquess of Anglesey, and Lord Hill.[80]

Madame Tussaud's continued to amass Napoleonic relics, including the coat Napoleon wore when he was elected first consul and two more carriages: the barouche he used while in exile on St Helena and the state carriage built for his coronation as the King of Italy in 1805.[81] All three, along with Hayter's painting, a large number of waxworks, and a significant portion of the museum's relics, were destroyed in a fire in 1925.[82]

While the relics offered by the various Waterloo and Napoleonic exhibitions provided the material connection to Waterloo so touted by Madame Tussaud's, representation exhibitions offered a different way to experience the victory from within the British Isles.[83] Without the implicit tactile promise of relics, represen-tation exhibitions instead plunged their guests into the heart of the battle, using a variety of display tricks to bring Waterloo to life in Britain. Authenticity and legitimacy were crucial to the success of representation exhibitions. Lacking the direct physical connection to Waterloo that could be found in relics, representa-tion exhibitions relied on claims of accuracy and the presence of veterans to prove their bona fides. Those bona fides boosted ticket sales across the spectrum, but they were especially critical given representation exhibitions' status as educational diversions. That success cut both ways. Napoleon's coach, at the end of the day, told a viewer nothing about how the battle had unfolded besides its eventual victor; it served as an anchor to a scene that was painted not by the relics in that room, but by histories, memoirs, paintings, and plays. Inaccuracy in a hippodrama or a painting could be dismissed as artistic licence, but panoramas and Siborne's model claimed to be accurate representations of the day. We have already seen in Chapter 1 how panoramas contributed to the assumption that the Highland

[79] *Madame Tussaud's 1851 Catalogue*, 3; 'Madame Tussaud', *Morning Post*, 21 May 1835, p. 4; 'Whitsuntide Amusements', *Morning Post*, 27 May 1844, p. 5. The 'great men of the late war' was reworked to show 'the Allied Monarchs... offering to Napoleon the kingdom of France, as it was under Louis XIV... which he refuses'. Wellington was replaced by Napoleon's favourite Mameluke. *Madame Tussaud's 1851 Catalogue*, 6–8.

[80] Also included were Espartero, Regent of Spain; Wellington's brother the Marquess of Wellesley; and his staunch political ally Sir Robert Peel. *Madame Tussaud's 1851 Catalogue*, 3–5.

[81] Tussaud, *The Romance of Madame Tussaud's*, 139–42; *Madame Tussaud & Sons' Exhibition Catalogue Containing Biographical & Descriptive Sketches of the Distinguished Characters Which Compose Their Exhibition and Historical GalleryM* (London: Madame Tussaud & Sons, 1880), 35; H. M. Forbes, 'The Napoleonic Centenary: The Greatest Collection of Napoleon Relics in the World', *The Sphere* (7 May 1921): 138–9.

[82] Two-thirds of the exhibits were destroyed. 'Waxworks Fire', *The Times*, 20 March 1925, p. 11; 'Madame Tussaud's', *The Times*, 25 March 1925, p. 11; Ben Weinreb, Christopher Hibbert, Julia Keay, John Keay, *The London Encyclopaedia* (London: Macmillan, 2008), 294.

[83] *Military Carriage of Napoleon Buonaparte*, 24.

regiments saw the majority of the action on the left side of the allied position. Ensuring that representation exhibitions were representative of the memory of Waterloo they wanted preserved was therefore just as crucial to the British military as legitimacy was to the ticket sales of the civilian curators.

The first type of representation exhibitions, panoramas, exploded into popularity in the late eighteenth century.[84] Developed by Robert Barker, an Irish-born portrait painter based in Edinburgh in 1787, the panorama (or 'la nature à coup d'œil', as he originally dubbed it) was a 360-degree painting that was designed to be viewed from the centre. Lit by cunningly concealed skylights and designed so that visitors could not see the top or bottom of the canvas, Barker's panorama was so effective that nautical paintings reportedly caused seasickness.[85] Barker held a patent on the panorama until 1801, during which time he built the first permanent panorama rotunda in London's Leicester Square.[86] It proved to be such a hit that in 1795 he added another, smaller viewing chamber above the first, thus allowing him to display two views, one comprising almost 1,000 square metres of canvas, and the other 250 square metres.[87] Other artists and entrepreneurs took note of the success and when Barker's patent expired in 1801, panoramas sprang up across Great Britain. As the popularity of panoramas increased through the first decade of the nineteenth century, more and more artists and managers looked to the Revolutionary and Napoleonic Wars for inspiration. These views of battles and sieges, significantly larger and more awe-inspiring than anything that could be found outside a theatre, entertained as well as educated, and scholars have argued that they served the same function that newsreels would a century later.[88]

Barker's Leicester Square panorama, the grand doyenne of 360-degree spectacle, was twice beaten to the punch when it came to Waterloo.[89] In October of 1815 it was announced in the *Caledonian Mercury* that a wooden rotunda was being erected at the east end of York Street in Edinburgh to display the new

[84] See Altick, *The Shows of London*, chapter 10; Stephan Oettermann, *The Panorama: History of a Mass Medium*, trans. Deborah Lucas Schneider (New York: Zone Books, 1997); Hubert J. Pragnell, *The London Panoramas of Robert Barker and Thomas Girtin* (London: London Topographical Society, 1968); Scott Wilcox, 'The Panorama and Related Exhibitions in London', M.Litt. thesis, University of Edinburgh, 1976; Shaw, *Waterloo and the Romantic Imagination*, chapter 2; Dietrich Neumann, 'Instead of the Grand Tour: Travel Replacements in the Nineteenth Century', *Perspecta* 41 (2008): 47–53.

[85] Wood, *The Shock of the Real*, 103. Altick, *The Shows of London*, 132–4; Milkes, 'A Battle's Legacy', 370.

[86] The building still exists, on Leicester Place. It is now, somewhat ironically, the Roman Catholic Church of Notre Dame de France.

[87] Scott Wilcox, 'Panorama'. Grove Art Online. 2003; Accessed 9 July 2020. <https://doi.org/10.1093/gao/9781884446054.article.T065087>.

[88] Milkes, 'A Battle's Legacy', 370; Altick, *The Shows of London*, chapter 13. See also Ian F.W. Beckett, *British Military Panoramas: Battle in the Round, 1800–1914* (Warwick: Helion & Company, forthcoming 2022).

[89] Altick notes that to Londoners the Leicester Square panorama 'was "*the* panorama," just as the Royal Academy's annual show was "*the* exhibition"'. Altick, *The Shows of London*, 136.

'Grand Panorama of Waterloo' painted by James Howe, the well-known Scottish animal painter.[90] The panorama, which was probably managed by Messrs Marshall, a father–son team of Edinburgh entrepreneurs, opened on 1 November 1815, to coincide with Edinburgh's Music Festival and was such a success that Howe added another panorama, of equal size, depicting the battle of Quatre Bras two days before Waterloo, and the management started offering 5s. season tickets to cater to returning guests.[91] Given its popularity, its status as the first panorama of Waterloo, its point of origin in Edinburgh, and that its artist was a Scot, it is very possible this is the panorama that contributed to the general belief that the Highland regiments won Waterloo. Despite that rather dubious claim, the accuracy of Howe's panorama was being touted in advertisements even before it opened. The public would find, in the rotunda, 'a correct View of the Ground, with every particular circumstance of the battle, as collected by [James Howe] on the spot, from the principal Officers, both British and Foreign, who were in the battle'.[92] Early in 1816, the management sought to further emphasize the military connection, and thus the accuracy of the panorama, by offering free admission to all soldiers who had fought in the battle.[93] The *Caledonian Mercury* backed up the claims of authenticity, informing its readers on the occasion of the opening of the Quatre Bras panorama that the addition 'renders the panorama complete, and affords a full view of the transactions of these memorable days'.[94] The complete panorama ran in Edinburgh to June 1816, when it was packed up and moved to a similar wooden rotunda in Glasgow.[95] It met with equal success there, running until November 1816 and attracting 600 visitors per day.[96]

Following closely on the heels of Howe's Edinburgh panorama, two Waterloo panoramas opened in London, each under the management of one of Robert Barker's sons. At the turn of the nineteenth century, Robert Barker's eldest son, Tomas Edward Barker, partnered with the panorama artist Ramsay Richard Reinagle to open a new panorama to rival his father's, this time on the Strand. When Robert Barker died in 1806, then, it was his younger son, Henry Aston Barker, who took over the Leicester Square panorama in partnership with his

[90] *Caledonian Mercury*, 26 October 1815, p. 1; *Caledonian Mercury*, 3 February 1816, p. 1. For James Howe, see Cameron, *The Man Who Loved to Draw Horses*.

[91] A single ticket cost 1s. Given that the panorama was displayed in a wooden building in an Edinburgh winter, the advertisements also assured the public that the building was heated by warm air from 'Patent Stoves'. *Caledonian Mercury*, 30 October 1815, p. 3; *Caledonian Mercury*, 30 November 1815, p. 1; *Caledonian Mercury*, 10 June 1816; 'Panorama of Waterloo', *Caledonian Mercury*, 10 June 1816; Milkes, 'A Battle's Legacy', 371; Erkki Huhtamo, 'Penetrating the Peristrephic: An Unwritten Chapter in the History of the Panorama', *Early Popular Visual Culture* 6, no. 3 (November 2008): 220.

[92] *Caledonian Mercury*, 26 October 1815, p. 1; *Caledonian Mercury*, 28 October 1815, p. 1.

[93] *Caledonian Mercury*, 3 February 1816, p. 1.

[94] 'Panorama of Waterloo', *Caledonian Mercury*, 10 June 1816.

[95] *Caledonian Mercury*, 10 June 1816; 'Panorama of Waterloo', *Caledonian Mercury*, 10 June 1816.

[96] Cameron, *The Man Who Loved to Draw Horses*, 13, 32; Milkes, 'A Battle's Legacy', 371.

father's apprentice John Burford.[97] The Strand panorama could never catch up to the Leicester Square panorama's name recognition. It suffered from financial difficulties in 1806/1807 and was, by the end of 1815, on its last legs.[98] Despite this, it managed to open its Waterloo panorama on 30 January 1816, nearly two months before its rival in Leicester Square.[99] Henry Aston Barker, however, had the last laugh. When the Leicester Square Waterloo panorama opened in late March it was an instant success and generally considered to be the most popular panorama ever displayed in the rotunda.[100] Recognizing that there was not room in London for two Waterloo panoramas, Tomas Edward Barker took the Strand Waterloo panorama on tour in the summer of 1816, exhibiting it for nearly a month in a field in Exeter.[101] The patronage of the citizens of Devon was not enough to save him, however, and he subsequently sold the Strand panorama to Henry Aston Barker and John Burford, who ran the two rotundas as one concern.[102]

One of the reasons that it took until late March 1816 for Henry Aston Barker to open his Waterloo panorama in Leicester Square was that he understood the importance of accuracy and took his time to achieve it. Like Howe, he travelled to Waterloo to sketch the field of battle, and included in the guide that could be purchased for sixpence at the Rotunda the following reassurance: 'Mr. H. A. Barker respectfully informs the Public that, in order to give a correct Representation of the Battle of Waterloo, he went to Paris, and, from the officers as Head-quarters, procured every possible Information on the Subject.'[103] The final painting, executed by John Burnet, reflected the effort, depicting over seventy individuals, locations, and moments (Figure 4.4).[104] The legitimacy of the Leicester Square Waterloo panorama was further burnished by the presence of a large number of army officers in their crowds. Felix MacDonogh, *The Literary Gazette*'s society writer, identified five military archetypes that could be found at the panorama. There was the old general, who was so taken with the scene that his companions worried they 'should have to pass the night on the field of battle, or to bivouac somewhere in the neighbourhood'; the helpful officer who is happy to act

[97] In addition to name recognition, the Leicester Square panorama had the notable advantage that both Henry Aston Barker and John Buford were painters, while Tomas Edward Barker was not. Altick, *The Shows of London*, 137.

[98] Altick, *The Shows of London*, 137.   [99] *Morning Post*, 29 January 1816, p. 1.

[100] *The Times*, 25 March 1816, p. 1; Milkes, 'A Battle's Legacy', 372–3.

[101] *Trewman's Exeter Flying Post or Plymouth and Cornish Advertiser*, 18 July 1816; *Trewman's Exeter Flying Post or Plymouth and Cornish Advertiser*, 8 August 1816.

[102] Altick, *The Shows of London*, 137.

[103] *Description of the Field of Battle, and Disposition of the Troops engaged in the Action, fought on the 18th of June, 1815, near Waterloo; Illustrative of the Representation of that great Event in the Panorama, Leicester-Square* (London: J. Adlard, 1816), 13.

[104] For an academic exploration of the experience of the Leicester Square Waterloo panorama, see Shaw, *Waterloo and the Romantic Imagination*, 85–91.

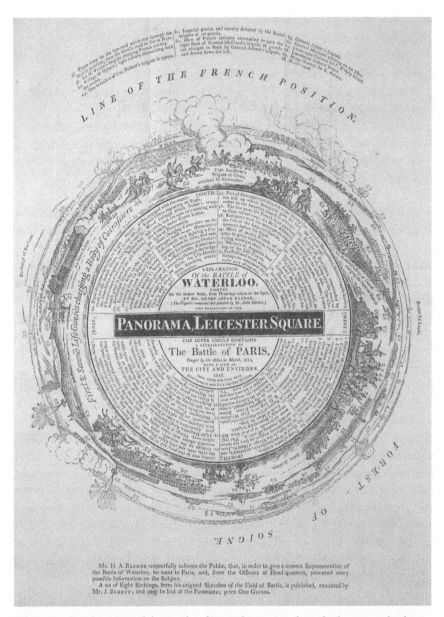

Figure 4.4 'Explanation of the Battle of Waterloo, painted on the largest scale, from drawings taken on the spot by Mr. Henry Aston Barker, (the figured composed and painted by Mr. John Burnet,) now exhibiting in the Panorama, Leicester Square, *Description of the Field of Battle*, 13.' Internet Archive, digitized from the Getty Research Institute.

as a guide to civilian visitors; the 'Exquisite *militaire*' fop, impressed by the accuracy of the spectacle, almost despite himself;

> the military spectator, who had been an actor in the scene, and who, pride beaming in his countenance, yet wrapt in silence, looked on the representation of that awful and eventful reality,—or the garrulous but worthy veteran, who saw his own deeds of arms live again in the pictured story, and who, bereft of an arm, or of a leg, and leaning on a friend, indulged in the gratifying account of what his country owed him, whilst, 'Thrice he routed all his foes, And thrice he slew the slain.'[105]

With its accuracy and legitimacy guaranteed, and its spectacle never in doubt, the Leicester Square Waterloo panorama became the smash hit of the season. Less than two months after it opened, the crush drove Barker and Burford to erect an 'elevated stage' in the centre of the viewing platform, which, as they announced in *The Times*, guaranteed that 'every object can be seen without inconvenience, as the spectators in the back are raised so as to look over the heads of those in front'.[106] Felix MacDonogh, in addition to cataloguing the military visitors, recorded that 'there were groups of all classes' among the patrons, while a panorama exhibitor later recollected that it was one of the few pieces to attract all Britons, due to its status as 'a *national* subject [that] was sure to interest all ranks'.[107] The Waterloo panorama was the main attraction at the Leicester Square rotunda from March 1816 until early May 1818, when it was sent to Edinburgh for display.[108] For those who wanted to experience it even after that, the Rotunda offered a series of eight etchings by Burnet, based on Barker's original sketches. These could be enjoyed individually but were also designed, when joined together, to create a personal miniature panorama. The *Annals of the Fine Arts* pronounced it 'a novelty most interesting and useful', while also praising the artistry and accuracy of both the views and the etchings.[109] Between the 1s. admission price, sixpence for the guide, and a full guinea for the etchings, the panorama made its proprietors over £10,000 in the first few months, and when Barker retired in 1822 it was generally considered that it was his Waterloo panorama profits that allowed him to do so.[110]

---

[105] 'Sketches of Society. The Hermit in London, or Ketches of English Manners, No. VIII. The Waterloo Panorama', *The Literary Gazette, and Journal of Belles Lettres, Arts, Politics, Etc.*, 29 August 1818, no. 84, p. 556–7.

[106] *The Times*, 13 May 1816, p. 1.

[107] 'Sketches of Society', *The Literary Gazette, and Journal of Belles Lettres, Arts, Politics, Etc.*, 29 August 1818, p. 557; Rolt, *A Great-Niece's Journals*, 308.

[108] *The Times*, 25 March 1816, p. 1; *The Times*, 30 April 1818, p. 1; *Caledonian Mercury*, 5 October 1818, p. 1.

[109] Review of New Prints, *Annals of the Fine Arts* (London: Sherwood, Neely, and Jones, 1817), I: 94–5.

[110] *The Times*, 25 March 1816, p. 1; *Description of the Field of Battle*, cover, 13; Oettermann, *The Panorama*, 111; Rolt, *A Great-Niece's Journals*, 308; Milkes, 'A Battle's Legacy', 373.

Much like Astley's Royal Amphitheatre's hippodrama, *The Battle of Waterloo*, discussed in Chapter 5, the Leicester Square Rotunda periodically revived the Waterloo panorama. They exhibited it from October 1820 to March 1821 and debuted a new painting from the original sketches in 1842 after it was discovered that the original had been ruined by damp.[111] The 1842 edition continued to attract military support, receiving a visit from the Marquess of Anglesey shortly after it opened.[112] It also garnered a glowing review in *The Times*, which noted that Waterloo 'will never lose its interest with Englishmen, and which, though nearly 27 years have elapsed since the event took place, still possesses attractions to draw the British public'.[113] *The Times* praised the panorama's accuracy, reporting that 'the picture is illustrative of the written accounts of the battle, and conveys a good notion of the events of the day.... it is one', they concluded, 'that everybody should see'.[114]

As popular as 360-degree panoramas were, however, they required special buildings and vast amounts of space to display properly. Towns without rotundas (or, as in Exeter, a convenient field) were denied this new form of spectacle until, shortly before Waterloo, the same Messrs Marshall who were probably about to finance Howe's traditional panorama in Edinburgh developed a solution.[115] Christened the peristrephic panorama, these were effectively a giant scroll of canvas on two rollers. The rollers would be positioned vertically some distance apart and turned simultaneously, thus creating a moving picture. Not only were these easier to travel with, but they also did not require a specialized building for their display, meaning they could tour smaller towns or smaller venues in larger cities. While they lacked the full immersive feel of traditional panoramas, they were better suited to displaying narratives, and proved to be extremely popular.[116]

Waterloo panoramas, especially those managed by the Messrs Marshall, helped to cement the legitimacy of peristrephic panoramas as both a form of spectacle

---

[111] *Morning Chronicle*, 4 October 1820, p. 1; *Morning Chronicle*, 21 March 1821, p. 1; 'Panorama of the Battle of Waterloo', *The Times*, 22 March 1842, p. 6; *The Times*, 29 March p. 1. In all probability it was the 1820 run which Wellington visited (both Altick and Shaw note that he approved of it, and advertising for the panorama in 1852 mentions his attendance), as during the first run he was largely in France fulfilling the duties of commander of the Allied army of occupation. Altick, *The Shows of London*, 222; Shaw, *Waterloo and the Romantic Imagination*, 83; *The Illustrated London News*, 13 November 1852, p. 407.

[112] 'Court Circular', *The Times*, 15 April 1842, p. 5. The 1842 revival also received a visit from the boys of the Royal Military Asylum. 'Court Circular', *The Times*, 24 June 1842, p. 6.

[113] 'Panorama of the Battle of Waterloo', *The Times*, 22 March 1842, p. 6.

[114] 'Panorama of the Battle of Waterloo', *The Times*, 22 March 1842, p. 6.

[115] Huhtamo has found mention of the Marshalls displaying a peristrephic panorama of 30 miles of the River Thames in Dublin as early as 5 April 1815. Huhtamo, 'Penetrating the Peristrephic', 232 n. 5.

[116] See Erkki Huhtamo, *Illusions in Motion: Media Archaeology of the Moving Panorama and Related Spectacles* (Cambridge, Mass.: The MIT Press, 2013); Huhtamo, 'Penetrating the Peristrephic', 219–38; Altick, *The Shows of London*, chapter 15.

and education.[117] In 1816, they displayed their 'Grand Historical Peristrephic Painting of the ever-memorable Battles of Ligny, and Waterloo' in Dublin, beginning a nearly decade-long tour that would encompass Manchester, Leeds, Hull, Newcastle, Edinburgh, Glasgow, Aberdeen, Bury, Norwich, Stamford, Bath, Exeter, Portsmouth, London, and even make its way across the Atlantic to New York.[118] The more narrative nature of the exhibition required set performance times, rather than the open admission and self-guided experience favoured by the 360-degree panoramas, but even this could be an advantage.[119] Higher prices (2*s.* as opposed to 1*s.*) were charged for better seats and, because only a set portion of stage had to be lit, they could, unlike the rotundas, offer 'brilliantly illuminated' evening shows.[120] In addition, peristrephic panorama managers, especially the Messrs Marshall, did all they could to enhance the more theatrical potential of the moving image. A full military band accompanied the display, which the *Morning Post* declared 'gives a noble effect, and heightens the idea to realize itself', and there are indications that at least some shows featured a narrator.[121] In Edinburgh, a bagpiper was hired to 'play appropriate airs' whenever the Highland regiments were displayed.[122] The novelty was also emphasized. 'This Panorama being upon an entirely novel construction', advertisements stentoriously informed readers, 'the Proprietors think it necessary to state, that it is not the one from Leicester-square, London'.[123] The greatest advantage, however, came in the form of flexibility. Because peristrephic panoramas were, quite literally, unrolled before the eyes of their patrons, it was a lot easier to add new scenes and details to them than it was to traditional panoramas. The purchasable narration/description (which they christened *The Waterloo Catalogue*) from the Marshalls' 1816 Dublin show lists seven scenes, starting with 'Napoleon Bonaparte and Staff, with the French

---

[117] Later peristrephic panoramas were advertised as from the same producers as the Waterloo panorama. *Bury and Norwich Post*, 16 October 1822, p. 2; *Bristol Mercury*, 18 August 1823, p. 2; *Hampshire Telegraph and Sussex Chronicle*, 21 June 1824.

[118] *Description of Messrs. Marshall's Grand Historical Peristrephic Painting of the ever-memorable Battles of Ligny, and Waterloo!* (Dublin: William Henry Tyrrell, 1816); *Description of Messrs. Marshall's Grand Historical Peristrephic Painting of the ever-memorable Battles of Ligny and Waterloo* (Manchester: M. Wilson, 1817); 'Leeds, Saturday, April 19', *Leeds Mercury*, 19 April 1817; *The Hull Packet and Original Weekly Commercial, Literary and General Advertiser*, 2 September 1817; *Newcastle Courant*, 11 September 1819, p. 1; *Caledonian Mercury*, 22 June 1820, p. 3; *Glasgow Herald*, 17 November 1820, p. 3; *Aberdeen Journal*, 14 March 1821, p. 2; *Bury and Norwich Post*, 4 July 1821, p. 2; *Norfolk Chronicle*, 1 September 1821, p. 3; *Stamford Mercury*, 1 March 1820, p. 3; *Bath Chronicle and Weekly Gazette*, 24 October 1822, p. 3; *Trewman's Exeter Flying Post*, 6 March 1823, p. 4; *Hampshire Telegraph and Sussex Chronicle*, 20 October 1823, p. 3; *The Examiner*, 7 December 1823, p. 15; *Caledonian Mercury*, 21 February 1825; *Morning Herald*, 31 August 1840, p. 3; Altick, *The Shows of London*, 429n. It should be noted that they had other peristrephic panoramas touring simultaneously, especially in the later years.

[119] Depending on the size of the city, the Marshalls displayed theirs between four and six times per day. *Caledonian Mercury*, 22 June 1820, p. 3; *Norfolk Chronicle*, 1 September 1821, p. 3.

[120] *Stamford Mercury*, 1 March 1820, p. 3; *Trewman's Exeter Flying Post*, 6 March 1823, p. 4.

[121] *The Leeds Mercury*, 14 June 1817; 'The Theatre', *Morning Post*, 23 December 1823, p. 3.

[122] *Caledonian Mercury*, 22 June 1820, p. 3.

[123] *Bath Chronicle and Weekly Gazette*, 31 October 1822, p. 2.

Army' on 16 June and ending with a group of French prisoners on 18 June.[124] By 1823, the Marshalls were advertising their 'original peristrephic panorama of twelve views of these ever-memorable battles, painted on ten thousand square feet of canvas'.[125]

The ever-expanding canvas and forays into theatricality provided peristrephic panoramas with their answer to traditional panoramas' claims of true immersion. 'The figures, the size of life, and accompanied by a full military band', insisted the Marshalls in 1824, 'produces a complete sensation of reality, and gives the most perfect idea of the progress of those victories'.[126] Tied into those claims, however, as they were with the 360-degree panoramas, was the crucial question of accuracy. In their *Waterloo Catalogue* and longer-form advertisements, the Marshalls reassured their public that 'drawings had been made on the spot' and 'the utmost attention has been paid to the relative situations of the armies, the correctness of events, and the propriety of costume, the whole having been painted from information received from the Adjutant-General's Office at Paris, and under the immediate direction of Lord Fitzroy Somerset, (Military Secretary and Aide-de-Camp to the Duke of Wellington) and Col. Francis Ponsonby, both which Officers bore distinguished parts in the battle'.[127] As in Leicester Square, Pall Mall, Piccadilly, and Baker Street, military attendance played a significant role in the legitimization of peristrephic panoramas wherever they were displayed. The *Glasgow Herald* reported in 1820 that 'several officers who were at the Battle of Waterloo have lately visited the Panorama in the Assembly Rooms, and expressed their high opinion of the accuracy of this painting.... This gives fresh proof of the merits of this exhibition.'[128]

The Messrs Marshall went out of their way to garner such attendance and plaudits. For the second anniversary of Waterloo in 1817, they festooned the painting with laurels and promised 'Every effort exerted to render the Exhibition more than unusually interesting.'[129] For the fifth anniversary in 1820, the 80th Regiment of Foot (the Staffordshire Volunteers) lent their own regimental band to the panorama then in Edinburgh and a 'great crowd was drawn together' in the evening to witness the festivities.[130] Sixteen months later Norwich's Waterloo veterans were invited to attend the noon showing of the panorama for free, on

---

[124] *Description of Messrs. Marshall's Grand Historical Peristrephic Painting*, 5, 29; *The Hull Packet and Original Weekly Commercial, Literary and General Advertiser*, 2 September 1817.

[125] *The Examiner*, 7 December 1823, p. 15; *Morning Post*, 24 February 1824, p. 1.

[126] *Morning Post*, 24 February 1824, p. 1.

[127] *The Hull Packet and Original Weekly Commercial, Literary and General Advertiser*, 2 September 1817; *Description of Messrs. Marshall's Grand Historical Peristrephic Painting*, iv. See also *Glasgow Herald*, 17 November 1820, p. 3; *Aberdeen Journal*, 14 March 1821, p. 2; *Bury and Norwich Post*, 4 July 1821, p. 2; *Norfolk Chronicle*, 1 September 1821, p. 3; *Stamford Mercury*, 1 March 1820, p. 3.

[128] *Glasgow Herald*, 17 November 1820, p. 2.   [129] *The Leeds Mercury*, 14 June 1817.

[130] Some young boys attempted to start a riot. *Caledonian Mercury*, 22 June 1820, p. 3; Milkes, 'A Battle's Legacy', 371–2.

the condition that they wear their Waterloo medals.[131] Deciding to make a day of it, 'nearly 200 Waterloo men went in procession, and were highly gratified with the accurate detail ... of the events of those memorable engagements'.[132] Pleased with the results, the Messrs Marshall repeated the same trick in Glasgow in 1825.[133] Visits from regular veterans were worth celebrating. The greatest encomium, however, came from the presence of Wellington himself, who attended the 1823–4 run of Marshalls' peristrephic panorama at London's Spring Gardens.[134] The next year, when the panorama returned to Edinburgh, the advertisements touted that it 'was twice visited by his Grace the Duke of Wellington, besides many other distinguished officers who shared in the fatigues of that ever-memorable day, and who expressed their entire approbation of the accuracy of the different views'.[135]

Thus far we have limited our discussion to successful exhibitions that, through a mixture of entrepreneurial pomp and military deference, managed to capture both the imaginations of the civilian population and the approval of Waterloo's veterans. To highlight how crucial that approval was, however, we must now turn to the rather sad story of William Siborne's model of the Battle of Waterloo.[136] Siborne, the son of a captain in the 9th (East Norfolk) Regiment of Foot who was wounded at the Battle of Nivelle, graduated from the Royal Military College, Sandhurst, in 1814 and joined his father's regiment.[137] Although he missed Waterloo, Siborne did serve with the army of occupation for two years before being put on half-pay when his regiment was reduced in 1817. He served in a variety of military odd jobs and published two works on topographical surveying and drawing before being commissioned in 1830 by Lord Hill, then serving as commander-in-chief, 'to undertake the construction of a model of the Battle of Waterloo' as a 'national military work'.[138] Siborne was granted a leave of absence from his military duties to complete the task and spent eight months surveying the battlefield in minute detail while living in the farm of La Haye Sainte, which had served as the foremost bulwark of Wellington's centre and had seen some of the most intense fighting during the battle.[139]

Having gained a detailed understanding of the ground, Siborne then set out to map the movements of the armies upon it. He applied to government sources for

---

[131] *Norfolk Chronicle*, 29 September 1821, p. 2.

[132] *Bath Chronicle and Weekly Gazette*, 24 October 1822, p. 3.

[133] Shaw, *Waterloo and the Romantic Imagination*, 84.   [134] *The Times*, 2 December 1823, p. 2.

[135] *Caledonian Mercury*, 21 February 1825.

[136] The spelling of Siborne's last name varies between Siborn, Sibourne, and Siborne depending on the source. This work will use Siborne, as that has become the historiographical standard. See, for example, William Siborne to Parliament, 24 May 1841, Waterloo Correspondence vol. v, British Library, 290. Balen, *A Model Victory*; Hofschroer, *Wellington's Smallest Victory*.

[137] *Oxford Dictionary of National Biography* online, entry 'William Siborne' [Siborn].

[138] William Siborne to Parliament, 24 May 1841, Waterloo Correspondence vol. V, British Library, 290.

[139] *Oxford Dictionary of National Biography* online, entry 'William Siborne' [Siborn].

the official versions of events and corresponded with hundreds of officers who had been present. To streamline this process, he had lithographed questionnaires printed, with space for officer's answers, and included blank maps of the Waterloo battleground for them to fill in what details they could about the movements of their regiments and those around them.[140] His focus was palpably to obtain as accurate an image of the battle as he could, to the point where he engaged in multiple rounds of correspondence with certain officers, seeking clarifications and reassuring them that he 'consider[s] all communications made to [him] by Officers respecting Waterloo as *strictly confidential*, and that, although it is my wish when returning thanks generally, in a preface, to name a few whose aid may have been important, I shall never, either in representing, or in describing any particular fact, bring forward the name of any officer in support of such fact'.[141] The correspondence Siborne conducted with allied officers remains the largest collection of first-person Waterloo narratives ever compiled, and is a testament to Siborne's work.

Armed with this near-encyclopedic knowledge of the battle and the battlefield, Siborne began his model. Deciding that a scale of 9 feet to the mile would best capture the battle, he built it in thirty-nine detailed sections which, when assembled, measured 21 feet 4 inches by 19 feet 9 inches. He then populated this 417 square foot model with 80,000 0.39-inch figures, roughly one for every two soldiers present at the battle.[142] Unfortunately, in the middle of constructing this vast representation, Siborne's luck ran out. In 1833, the new, post-Great Reform Act British government informed him that they were no longer willing to pay the £1,400 then estimated to finish the work, but if he completed the work on his own he would not have to pay back the £380 already advanced to him.[143] For the next sixteen years, Siborne worked on and tried desperately to pay for his model. He sought out subscribers multiple times, gaining some limited success, but never enough to pay off his debts.[144] He took inspiration from the other

[140] See, for example, William Siborne to Major Doherty, 10 November 1834; William Siborne to Major Walcott, 11 November 1834; William Siborne to Captain Enoch, 2 December 1834; William Siborne to Lieutenant Colonel Childers, 27 December 1834, Waterloo Correspondence, British Library, vol. IV, 209, 211, vol. II, 24, 209.

[141] William Siborne to Shaw Kennedy, 3 April 1836, Waterloo Correspondence vol. IV, British Library, 68. Emphasis in original.

[142] For the physical details of the model, see William Siborne, 'Model of the field of Waterloo with troops positioned as at 19.45 hours', 18 June 1815, London, National Army Museum, NAM. 1975-05-56-1/, <https://collection.nam.ac.uk/detail.php?acc=1975-05-56-1%2F>. He subsequently created another model centered around the charge of the British Heavy Cavalry at 1:30pm. It shows a smaller portion of the field but is on a much larger scale. 'Royal Armouries Stories: Model maker and Historian, London, Leeds, and Fareham, Royal Armouries, <https://royalarmouries.org/stories/our-collection/model-maker-and-historian/>.

[143] William Siborne to Viscount Howick, 2 January 1836, Waterloo Correspondence vol. IV, British Library, 122.

[144] Subscription proposal, January 1834; Colonel Bowles to William Siborne, 18 March 1846, Waterloo Correspondence, British Library, vols I and VI.

entrepreneurs and showmen discussed in this chapter and exhibited it publicly all over Great Britain (including at the Egyptian Hall).[145] It proved a draw, but not one sufficient to extricate him from his financial distress. Indeed, the costs of transporting and properly displaying it were so high 'that the receipts barely sufficed to cover such expenditure'.[146] He also repeatedly tried to sell it to the Royal Dublin Society and to both the War Office and the Ordnance Department as an educational tool.[147]

The original cancellation of his project by the government was pure bad luck, but Siborne was also frustrated by his own determination that his model should be as accurate as possible. Early in the process of designing it, he decided that the model should depict the field at 7 p.m., traditionally regarded as the climax of the battle.[148] It was at 7 p.m. that the French Imperial Guard crested the British-held ridge and were checked and subsequently defeated by the allied infantry. It is a justifiably celebrated moment in British military history, and one that is directly responsible for the ceremonial headwear of the Guards regiments, in imitation of those worn by the French Imperial Guard.[149] Unfortunately, by 7 p.m. the Prussians were also present on the battlefield and although Siborne's model limits their presence and influence (he did not go to anywhere near the same level of trouble contacting Prussian officers as he did British), many British officers still objected.[150] Captain John Kincaid (last encountered in Chapter 1) can be taken as speaking for many of the objecting officers when he wrote, in a letter to Siborne, that the model 'gives an equal division of the glory to a Power that did not taste our equal division in the labour'.[151]

The objection of ordinary officers was bad enough, but what was especially damning was the silence emanating from Apsley House. Wellington was, as we have seen, the ultimate arbiter of legitimacy when it came to Waterloo, and his lack of approval was especially problematic for a work that Siborne was desperately trying to sell to the nation as an educational tool. Whether Wellington went

[145] Pamphlet advertising Siborne's model at the Egyptian Hall, October 1838, London Play Places 11 (24), John Johnson Collection, Bodleian Library, University of Oxford.

[146] William Siborne petition to Parliament, 24 May 1841, Waterloo Correspondence, British Library, vol. V, 290.

[147] William Siborne to Edward Hardman, 10 September 1841; L. Sullivan to William Siborne, 20 March 1841; G. Murray to William Siborne, 24 November 1841, Waterloo Correspondence, British Library, vol. V, 288, 293.

[148] William Siborne to Major Doherty, 10 November 1834, Waterloo Correspondence, British Library, vol. IV, 209.

[149] The First Foot Guards were renamed the Grenadier Guards and provided with bearskin caps after the battle, and the headgear was extended to the other Foot Guard regiments in 1831.

[150] William Siborne, Model of the field of Waterloo with troops positioned as at 19.45 hours, 18 June 1815, London, National Army Museum, NAM. 1975-05-56-1/, <https://collection.nam.ac.uk/detail.php?acc=1975-05-56-1%2F>.

[151] John Kincaid to William Siborne, 2 May 1839, Waterloo Correspondence, British Library, vol. V, 29.

out of his way to sabotage Siborne's work, as certain scholars have suggested, or merely stepped aside and let his silence tell its own story is unclear, but Wellington does not appear on any of the subscriber lists, and Siborne unquestionably would have found life easier with Wellington's support.[152] That Siborne's depiction of the battle was objectionable to some in power, and that he knew it, is indicated by the postscript he added to his 1841 petition to Parliament. The petition, which makes it clear that the model had long since become a millstone around Siborne's neck, hopes Parliament 'may condescend to direct that the model be deposited in the British Museum, the Tower, or in any other public building, as the property of the nation, granting at the same time to your Petitioner such amount of compensation as to your Honorable House he may appear to deserve'.[153] In a postscript, added later on another sheet of paper, possibly in response to feedback from his allies in Parliament, Siborne, who at this point was one of the leading experts on Waterloo, strikes his colours:

> he would humbly venture to suggest that a Committee of military officers should be appointed to inspect the model at the time of its being deposited in the room selected for its reception, in order to ascertain whether any alterations might be advisable as regards the distribution of the troops, with a view to render the representation which it affords of the Battle, as accurate as possible, and that your Petitioner should be required to carry any alterations so proposed with effect.[154]

This admission is remarkable, as it effectively surrenders his own expertise, bought with eleven years of research, to a committee. Siborne is suggesting a peer-review of memory and, in the process, acknowledging that the appearance of accuracy is sometimes more important than accuracy itself. In 1841, despite the creeping nationalization of the memory of Waterloo, it was still the veteran officers who were the arbiters of that accuracy, especially when it came to exhibitions that sought to educate as well as entertain.

It should be noted that not all officers agreed with Wellington and Kincaid. Siborne found an unlikely ally in Lieutenant Colonel Jonathan Leach who, in his fourth book, *Rambles Along the Styx*, praised Siborne's models for their accuracy, especially compared to the popular panoramas that

> may answer equally well as representations of one fight as of another; Wagram or Waterloo,—Salamanca or Austerlitz,—Jena or Talavera. Lines and squares of

---

[152] Hofschroer, *Wellington's Smallest Victory*; List of Subscribers to Siborne's work, Waterloo Correspondence, British Library, vol. VI.

[153] William Siborne petition to Parliament, 24 May 1841, Waterloo Correspondence, British Library, vol. V, 290.

[154] Postscript to William Siborne petition to Parliament, 24 May 1841, Waterloo Correspondence, British Library, vol. V, 292.

Infantry blazing away in every direction; *here* into the ranks of friends, *there* into those of their enemies; Highlanders placed in the foreground, and playing first fiddle in battles wherein not a Highland Regiment happened to be present; cavalry charging to the right, left, and front simultaneously, without any apparent motive, and the Artillery discharging salvos of round and grape shot *ad libitum*; oftentimes in any and every direction but the right one.[155]

Leach's preference for Siborne's models is clear, as is the implication that the accuracy of those models, created by 'a gallant officer, at great expense of time and money', is far superior to anything produced by civilians for the general populace's entertainment.[156] Leach closes his recommendation with an excoriation of the government and its decision to not buy the models for the £4,000 pounds Siborne owed, and praises the efforts of those who have started a subscription to rescue Siborne from his debt and purchase for 'the British public … a most valuable and faithful representation of that great and decisive battle'.[157]

The model now resides in the National Army Museum, having been purchased by subscription by the regiments present at Waterloo two years after Siborne's death. His greater legacy, however, takes the form of paper rather than lead soldiers. In 1844 Siborne published his two-volume *History of the War in France and Belgium in 1815*, which remains in print and was, for many years, the standard work on Waterloo. In addition, Siborne's second son, Major General Herbert Taylor Siborne, edited a selection of his father's Waterloo correspondence and published it under the title *Waterloo Letters*.[158]

Siborne's mixed success, especially compared with the huge crowds and near-universal approbation garnered by Bullock, Barker, Burford, and the Messrs Marshall, demonstrates that a certain level of panache and showmanship was required to truly capture the imagination of the British public. It also illustrates that while accuracy was important, it was, in fact, the perception of accuracy imparted by the attendance of Waterloo veterans, especially the well-known ones, that was truly crucial. Relics were in many ways a safer bet, as provenance could be more definitively proven, and provided less of a threat to certain nationally accepted narratives. For representation exhibitions to truly succeed, therefore, they needed a very traditional form of legitimacy and approval imparted through attendance. There is no question that Siborne put more work and research into the accuracy of his model than Barker or the Marshalls put into their panoramas,

---

[155] Jonathan Leach, *Rambles Along the Styx* (London: T. and W. Boone, 1847), 130–1. Leach uses the plural because Siborne created two models, see note 142.

[156] Leach, *Rambles Along the Styx*, 130.   [157] Leach, *Rambles Along the Styx*, 131.

[158] *Oxford Dictionary of National Biography* online, entry William Siborne [Siborn].

and yet Barker retired early a rich man, while Siborne died with his model still haunting his every move. There is also no question that Wellington and his officers knew exactly what they were doing. In 1840, the Countess of Wilton asked him why he had never seen Siborne's model. The duke responded that he 'was unwilling to give any Sanction to the truth of such a representation in this Model, which must have resulted from my visiting it' and thus remained silent and absent.[159]

[159] Arthur Wellesley, 1st Duke of Wellington, to Mary, Countess of Wilton, 23 April 1840 in Arthur Wellesley, Seventh Duke of Wellington, ed., *Wellington and his Friends* (London: Macmillan, 1965), 134.

5

'Grand Military and National Spectacle'

Waterloo on Stage and Canvas

In the small hours of the morning on 4 November 1846, the Garrick Theatre on Leman Street in London's East End was consumed by fire. The accepted cause of the fire was the wadding from a cannon fired during the previous evening's performance of the *Battle of Waterloo*. The wadding, the London papers posited, had been fired from the cannon and lodged in one of the theatre's scenic flats, where it smouldered until it set the flat itself on fire.[1] Thirty-one years after the Chateau Hougoumont burned, the Battle of Waterloo had claimed another building. The fact that the Garrick Theatre had put on the show thirty-one years after the battle, and not on the anniversary but in November, illustrates just how deeply Waterloo had become embedded in Britain's cultural fabric. Depictions of Waterloo were not limited to annual celebrations and exhibitions, but frequently made their way into other forms of popular entertainment and culture.

This chapter examines several of these, most notably *The Battle of Waterloo* (1824) hippodrama at Astley's Royal Amphitheatre, and four paintings: Joseph Mallord William Turner's *The Field of Waterloo* (1818), Sir Thomas Lawrence's *Portrait of the Duke of Wellington, in the dress that he wore, and on the horse he rode at the battle of Waterloo* (1818), Jan Willem Pieneman's *The Battle of Waterloo* (1824), and William Salter's *The Waterloo Banquet, 1836* (1840/1). Some measure of the impact of these pieces can be taken from their longevity. Astley's *The Battle of Waterloo* ran intermittently for three decades, was immortalized in William Makepeace Thackeray's *The Newcomes*, and one character proved so popular that she was later imported into another play.[2] Pieneman's *The Battle of Waterloo* proved extraordinarily popular when it was exhibited and now hangs in the Rijksmuseum. Finally, while neither Turner's *The Field of Waterloo* nor Salter's *The Waterloo Banquet, 1836* sold immediately, they did achieve lasting success. The Turner is now an integral part of the Tate Britain's

---

[1] 'Destruction of the Garrick Theatre by Fire', *The Standard*, 4 November 1846, p. 2; 'Destruction of the Garrick Theatre by Fire', *Morning Chronicle*, 5 November 1846, p. 5; 'Destruction of the Garrick Theatre by Fire', *Morning Post*, 5 November 1846, p. 6.
[2] 'Astley's Royal Amphitheatre', *The Times*, 17 February 1844, p. 6; J. H. Amherst, *Ireland as it is* (New York: Samuel French, 1865).

Who Owned Waterloo? Battle, Memory, and Myth in British History, 1815–1852. Luke Reynolds, Oxford University Press.
© Luke Reynolds 2022. DOI: 10.1093/oso/9780192864994.003.0006

'Walk Through British Art', and the Salter hangs in Apsley House's Portico Drawing Room, right next to the gallery it depicts.

All the works considered here were produced for entertainment and profit, but the motives for their creation ran deeper. Astley's *The Battle of Waterloo* was a commemorative celebration that, while adding fictional heroes and comic relief, kept the military conflict at its centre. Like its main rival, Vauxhall's military fete, and the various Waterloo exhibitions, Astley's went out of its way to emphasize the authenticity of its depictions and sought out the attendance and approval of veterans to prove its legitimacy. Turner's *The Field of Waterloo* takes a different approach. Inspired by Byron, the painting is about as explicitly anti-war as a depiction of a victory can get. Its dark and sombre atmosphere, which sets aside the individuality of the Waterloo veterans in favour of an overall mood, is presented as a contrast to the other four pieces, all of which sought the approval (and in some cases explicit patronage) of the Duke of Wellington and other senior officers. Wellington and his cadre used their approval (and the access that came with it) to shape how they and Waterloo were depicted, thus retaining some ownership of the battle and its memory in a field that was entirely dominated by civilian creators.

This chapter focuses on a hippodrama and four paintings rather than references to Waterloo in more canonical novels for two reasons. First, military victories were not centrepieces in novels to the extent they were on stage. While military men were regular characters in the novels of British authors from Jane Austen to Benjamin Disraeli and were skewered in print by *Punch*, Charles Dickens, and Thackeray as regularly as they were in the prints of George Cruikshank and William Heath, Waterloo and the other battles they fought were the province of histories and memoirs, not novels and short stories.[3] Waterloo novels were instead, much like the genre of battle painting discussed later in the chapter, the province of France. It was in a France still in some ways recovering from the fallout of the Napoleonic era that writers from Stendhal to Victor Hugo seized upon Waterloo as a romantic military tragedy—the final glorious defeat of a man who, just like the heroes of antiquity, was too great for the world to accept. Stendhal's *The Charterhouse of Parma* (1839), Erckmann-Chatrian's *Waterloo*

---

[3] See Louise Carter, 'Scarlet Fever: Female Enthusiasm for Men in Uniform', in Kevin Linch and Matthew McCormack, eds, *Britain's Soldiers: Rethinking War and Society, 1715–1815* (Liverpool: Liverpool University Press, 2014); Edward Copeland, *The Silver Fork Novel: Fashionable Fiction in the Age of Reform* (Cambridge: Cambridge University Press, 2012); Scott Hughes Myerly, '"The Eye Must Entrap the Mind": Army Spectacle and Paradigm in Nineteenth-Century Britain', *Journal of Social History* 26, no. 1 (Autumn 1992): 105–31; Gordon N. Ray, 'Thackeray's "Book of Snobs"', *Nineteenth-Century Fiction* 10, no. 1 (June 1955): 22–33; Philip Shaw, *Waterloo and the Romantic Imagination* (London: Palgrave Macmillan, 2002); Luke Reynolds, '"The Exquisite *Militaire*:" The Army Officer, Fashion, and Satire in the Aftermath of Waterloo', in Andrew Bamford, ed., *Celebrating 100 Years of Army Historical Research: Selected Proceedings of the SAHR Centenary Conference* (Warwick: Helion & Company, forthcoming). This is one area where the traditional British preference for the navy is not evident—Trafalgar was equally neglected.

(1864), and Hugo's *Les Misérables* (1862) are all, in their own ways, attempts to process the cultural impact of the defeat while not only embellishing the Napoleonic legend, but also celebrating the soldiers of France for whom, in the words of Hugo, 'the whole plain is a sepulcher'.[4]

There are, naturally, exceptions to this rule, the most significant being *Vanity Fair* (1848). Thackeray's best-known work boasts a number of military characters and features the Battle of Waterloo at nearly the exact centre of the story. While Thackeray eschews the detailed description that some other fictional accounts provide, the battle and its consequences serve as an effective meditation on the disruptive nature of war to individuals, society, and the Regency period as a whole. Waterloo affects every major character, providing a universal moment in a novel originally subtitled '*Pen and Pencil Sketches of English Society*', and sets in motion events that usher the story towards its denouement.[5] It would, therefore, be a logical addition to this chapter. However, that brings us to the second reason: those English works that do feature Waterloo prominently have attracted extensive scholarly attention. *Vanity Fair* is Thackeray's most written-about work, and several scholars have already discussed it in a military context.[6] Rather than repeat this scholarship, this chapter will instead focus on the hippodrama and paintings listed above, which have not received the attention they deserve.

Battles and military themes were quite popular within British theatrical circles, especially during the wars themselves. An examination of plays produced between 1800 and 1850 reveals that there were 150 plays centred on specific battles or campaigns. Of these, fifty-three drew their inspiration from the Napoleonic Wars.[7] Many of these productions were temporary in nature—designed to capitalize on the most recent victory and be forgotten with news of the next one.[8] The battles of Trafalgar, Talavera, Salamanca, Vittoria, and Waterloo and the sieges of Flushing and Badajoz all had theatrical spectacles marking them within a year of

---

[4] Victor Hugo, *Les Misérables* (London: George Routledge and Sons, 1887), II: 25; Alan Forrest, *Waterloo* (Oxford: Oxford University Press, 2015), 142–6.

[5] William Makepeace Thackeray, *Vanity Fair: Pen and Pencil Sketches of English Society* (London: Punch Office, 1847).

[6] See Ian Ousby, 'Carlyle, Thackeray, and Victorian Heroism', *The Yearbook of English Studies* 12 (1982): 152–68; Julian Jimenez Heffernan, 'Lying Epitaphs: "Vanity Fair", Waterloo, and the Cult of the Dead', *Victorian Literature and Culture* 40, no. 1 (2012): 25–45; Edward Adams, *Liberal Epic: The Victorian Practice of History from Gibbon to Churchill* (Charlottesville: University of Virginia Press, 2011), chapter 3; Alexandra Mullen, 'Vanity Fair and Vexation of Spirit', *The Hudson Review* 54, no. 4 (Winter 2002): 581–9; Robert E. Lougy, 'Vision and Satire: The Warped Looking Glass in Vanity Fair', *PMLA* 90, no. 2 (March 1975): 256–69; Russell A. Fraser, 'Pernicious Casuistry: A Study of Character in Vanity Fair', *Nineteenth-Century Fiction* 12, no. 2 (September 1957): 137–47.

[7] See Appendix for a complete list of military subject plays. 'Hand-List of Plays, 1800–1850', in Allardyce Nicoll, *A History of English Drama, 1600–1900* (Cambridge: Cambridge University Press, 1955), IV: 245–643.

[8] For the British theatre as propaganda during the Napoleonic Wars, see Susan Valladares, *Staging the Peninsular War: English Theatres 1807–1815* (London: Routledge, 2016); Gillian Russell, *The Theatres of War: Performance, Politics, and Society 1793–1815* (Oxford: Clarendon Press, 1995).

the actual event, and there is little evidence that these were ever revived.[9] As the Napoleonic Wars retreated into memory, theatres moved away from current events and towards more pastoral or fantastic themes, often looking to antiquity or beyond Europe. When performances did touch on military themes or involve military individuals after 1815, they were more likely to take their inspiration from medieval and ancient history than they were from the army's relatively recent victories.[10] In 1824, however, Astley's Royal Amphitheatre opened their 'unprecedentedly magnificent representation' of Waterloo for the first time, an exception to the usual theatrical fare that was to become extremely popular.[11]

The 1824 *Battle of Waterloo* was not the first tribute to the victory to grace the London stage. Ten productions that involved the battle appeared between 1815 and 1850, with the first premièring on 15 November 1815, less than five months after the battle itself. Several of the productions were not battle spectacles, but were more traditional performances set around the battle, and boasting titles such as *La Vivandière; or, The Eve of Waterloo* or *The Duke's Coat; or, The Night After the Battle*.[12] What set Astley's *The Battle of Waterloo* apart was its success. Written by J. H. Amherst and with battle and set-piece choreography by Andrew Ducrow, Europe's premier equestrian performer, the spectacle was specifically written to take advantage of Astley's unique design.[13] The Royal Amphitheatre was a permanent circus located in Lambeth. Famous for its horse and acrobatic shows it featured, rather than a traditional stage, a 42-foot ring, surrounded by seats.[14] The spectacle was divided into three acts, each ending with a battle scene. The first of these was the Bridge at Marchienne, from which the advancing French evicted the Prussians on 15 June on their way towards Brussels. The second was the crossroads at Quatre Bras, south of Waterloo, which the allied army held against the French on 16 June but which prevented Wellington from coming to the aid of Blücher at Ligny. The final climax was set around Mont St Jean, on the French side of the valley in which the Battle of Waterloo was fought, towards the close of the

[9] Trafalgar and Waterloo were the only battles of the war commemorated extensively after 1815. In 1828, however, Astley's did produce a show called *Buonaparte's Fatalities* that consisted of portions of older spectacles. 'Hand-List of Plays', IV: 437.

[10] 72 of the 150 military plays were based on wars that preceded the Napoleonic Wars, while 13 drew on mythological or fictional conflicts. See Appendix; The Marcus Stone Collection, London, Victoria & Albert Museum Theatre and Performance, THM/234/8/1–8.

[11] 'Multiple Advertisements and Notices', *Morning Post*, 10 June 1824, p. 1; George Speaight, *Juvenile Drama: The History of the English Toy Theatre* (London: Macdonald & Co., 1946), 70; Scott Hughes Myerly, *British Military Spectacle: From the Napoleonic Wars Through the Crimea* (Cambridge, Mass.: Harvard University Press, 1996), 145.

[12] Appendix section B.

[13] For further details on the action, see A. H. Saxon, *Enter Foot and Horse: A History of the Hippodrama in England and France* (New Haven: Yale University Press, 1968), 138–40; for Ducrow, see A. H. Saxon, *The Life and Art of Andrew Ducrow* (Hamden: Archon Books, 1978).

[14] A traditional stage could be erected if necessary. The influence of Astley's can be judged by the fact that its ring size became the international standard for circuses. Richard D. Altick, *The Shows of London* (Cambridge, Mass.: Belknap Press, 1978), 119, 176.

day on 18 June.[15] The advertising for the show made much of its authenticity, proudly informing potential audience members that 'the infantry movements [were] by picked Waterloo men' and the backdrops and scenery had been painted on the field itself by the theatre's artists.[16] Amherst made sure to include several well-known individuals from the battle, including Napoleon, Wellington, and Blücher, along with a number of their generals. William Davis, then the owner and manager of Astley's, played Prince Blücher, and Ducrow played the Duke of Brunswick, whose death at the Battle of Quatre Bras served as the second-act finale.[17] If any of the historic figures could be said to be the lead, it would be Napoleon, who was written in a sympathetic light.[18] He was played by a Mr Gomersall, who received top billing for the role and whose likeness to, and performance as, the former emperor was praised by nearly everyone from theatrical critics to Thackeray.[19] Wellington was of course represented, although in much more of a cameo role than Napoleon, and spoke largely in patriotic quotations.[20]

In addition to the household names, the show also included several fictional characters for the audience to sympathize and identify with. These included the fiery Prussian wife Phedora (played by the well-known actress and equestrian Mrs Makeen), who followed the Prussian army to war to see justice done for Napoleon's depredations.[21] Seeking to balance both Phedora and the violence of the battle scenes, Amherst, the playwright, took the stage in the form of the half-French comic relief, Monsieur Maladroit, who ensures he speaks the language of every army engaged in a battle, so he can claim protection from any of them.[22] Romance was introduced by the British hero Standfast, a corporal in the

---

[15] J. H. Amherst, *The Battle of Waterloo, A Grand Military Melo-Drama in Three Acts* (London: Duncombe, 1824), 11–13, 23–4, 36.

[16] 'Davis's Royal Amphitheatre', *The Times*, 20 April 1824, p. 2; Brenda Assael, *The Circus and Victorian Society* (Charlottesville: University of Virginia Press, 2005), 53.

[17] Saxon, *Enter Foot and Horse*, 138–9.

[18] For an examination of Napoleon in British post-war theatre, see Stuart Semmel, *Napoleon and the British* (New Haven: Yale University Press, 2004), chapter 8; Louis James, 'Inverted Emblems for Albion: Wellington and Napoleon on Stage', in Raphael Samuel, ed., *Patriotism: The Making and Unmaking of British National Identity* (London: Routledge, 1989), III: 243–51.

[19] Thackeray's Colonel Newcome 'was amazed—amazed, by Jove, sir—at the prodigious likeness of the principal actor to the Emperor Napoleon'. William Makepeace Thackeray, *The Newcomes* (London: J. M. Dent & Sons, Ltd., 1910), I: 170; Royal Amphitheatre (Astley's), 14 July 1828, The Marcus Stone Collection, London, Victoria & Albert Museum Theatre and Performance, THM/234/8/1, 376; Bonaparte, as performed by Mr Gomersal, The Marcus Stone Collection, London, Victoria & Albert Museum Theatre and Performance, THM/234/8/1, AST-85; 'Royal Amphitheatre', *The Drama; or, Theatrical Pocket Magazine* 6, no. 4 (June 1824): 201; Walter Macfarren, *Memories: An Autobiography* (London: The Walter Scott Publishing Co., Ltd., 1905), 25–6; T. Allson Brown, *History of the American Stage: Containing Biographical Sketches of Nearly Every Member of the Profession that has Appeared on the American Stage, from 1733 to 1870* (New York: Dick & Fitzgerald, 1870), 146.

[20] Amherst, *The Battle of Waterloo*, 24, 28; Assael, *The Circus and Victorian Society*, 55–7; Saxon, *Enter Foot and Horse*, 139.

[21] Amherst, *The Battle of Waterloo*, 2–5, 21–3; Saxon, *Enter Foot and Horse*, 138.

[22] Amherst, *The Battle of Waterloo*, 2, 10–11; Saxon, *Ducrow*, 165.

Highlanders, and his sweetheart, Mary, who dons a uniform of her own and masquerades as a male recruit to follow him to war.[23] Finally we have Molly Maloney, a comic version of the stock Mother Courage character, played in pantomime-dame style by a Mr Herring.[24] Maloney was undoubtedly meant to instil some more humour into the piece, but the character is meant to be laughed with, rather than at. She rescues Corporal Standfast at one point, and largely serves the same purpose here that Captains Gower, Fluellen, Macmorris, and Jamy do in Shakespeare's *Henry V*: reinforcing the British, rather than English, nature of the victory, thus allowing it to emphasize union.[25] The character proved to be so popular that Astley's occasionally had Herring back just to sing Molly's song, and Amherst used her as the inspiration for the character of Judy O'Trot in his 1857 play, *Ireland as it is*.[26]

Astley's *The Battle of Waterloo* opened on 19 April 1824 and ran for a remarkable 144 consecutive performances, with a potential total audience of between 288,000 and 360,000.[27] Britain's general and theatrical press confirmed the popularity illustrated by the length of the initial run. *The Drama* reported that 'the "Battle of Waterloo" together with the amazing horsemanship of Mr. Ducrow have drawn such fashionable and crowded audiences to this theatre, that all thought of producing further novelty has for the present been laid aside'.[28] *The Court* magazine went so far as to credit Ducrow's purchase of Astley's at the end of the 1824 season to the show's success.[29] *The Morning Post* agreed, occasionally listing the members of the social elite that had been seen there, and reporting that the spectacle 'continues to excite the attention of all classes... the curtain never rises without an overflow'.[30] Astley's range of ticket prices helped somewhat with that cross-class appeal: box seats were four shillings each, stalls were two shillings a seat, and one shilling would buy access to the gallery.[31]

[23] Amherst, *The Battle of Waterloo*, 13–15, 30–2; *Pollock's Characters & Scenes in the Battle of Waterloo* (London: B. Pollock), The Marcus Stone Collection, London, Victoria & Albert Museum Theatre and Performance, THM/234/8/1, AST-86–97.

[24] Amherst, *The Battle of Waterloo*, 2; Astley's, *The Drama*, 6 July 1831, quoted in *The Album of Literature and Amusement* (London: W. Strange, 1831), II: 31; 'Royal Amphitheatre', *The Drama; or, Theatrical Pocket Magazine* 6, no. 4 (June 1824): 201.

[25] 'Here's may English, Irish, and Scotch, nivir quarrel together except in perfect harmony, and may their only contest be who shall be the first to strike the foe, and the foremost to spare the foe who strikes to them,' Amherst, *The Battle of Waterloo*, 16, 32; Peta Tait, *Fighting Nature: Travelling Menageries, Animal Acts and War Shows* (Sydney: Sydney University Press, 2016), 40; For depictions of all the characters and their notable interactions, see *Pollock's Characters & Scenes in the Battle of Waterloo* (London: B. Pollock), The Marcus Stone Collection, London, Victoria & Albert Museum Theatre and Performance, THM/234/8/1, AST-86–97.

[26] 'Royal Amphitheatre', *The Times*, 15 August 1827, p. 2; Amherst, *Ireland as it is*.

[27] Saxon, *Enter Foot and Horse*, 137; Assael, *The Circus and Victorian Society*, 51–2.

[28] 'Royal Amphitheatre', *The Drama; or, Theatrical Pocket Magazine*, 6, no. 4 (June 1824): 201.

[29] 'The Late Mr. Ducrow', *The Court, Lady's Magazine, Monthly Critic and Museum*, April 1842, 333.

[30] *Morning Post*, 13 May 1824; *Morning Post*, 29 May 1824.

[31] 'Royal Amphitheatre', *Morning Post*, 25 July 1825, p. 1.

Crucially, given *The Battle of Waterloo*'s claims of authenticity, military audiences were just as taken with it as the civilian populace. Late in the 1824 run, the directors of the Military Asylum, Chelsea, decided the show would be an ideal entertainment for their young charges, and arranged, with the school's patron, the Duke of York, for 700 of them to attend.[32] Benson E. Hill, a former artillery officer turned writer, saw the show for the first time expecting 'much food for mirth; but was amazed at the accuracy with which the military evolutions were executed'.[33] So impressed was he that he maintained that any 'old soldier, on the 18th of June, not to have sought the field of Waterloo, as there represented, would have been insensible to Britain's glory'.[34] Nor was Hill the highest military authority to witness and approve of the spectacle. Wellington himself went twice during the 1824 run, as did the Marquess of Anglesey, and both 'expressed themselves highly pleased, with the mimic representation of that celebrated conflict'.[35] Indeed, Wellington so enjoyed himself that he went to see it again during the 1829 Waterloo anniversary performances, accompanying the Countess of Jersey and thirty children.[36] Astley's was quick to take advantage of this, opening their customary ad in *The Times* three days after Wellington's visit with an announcement that 'the grand entertainments produced on Monday last having been represented before his Grace the Duke of Wellington and a distinguished assemblage of rank and title, and honoured with repeated marks of approbation, will be repeated this evening, tomorrow, and Saturday'.[37]

Beginning in 1829, Astley's would supplement whatever shows or guest acts it had on around 18 June with 'the Battle of Waterloo, including three grand melee scenes of the advance of the French army and the Battles of Ligny and Quatre Bras'.[38] The show was short enough that it always ran alongside at least one other production, sometimes as the headline attraction and sometimes as the closing act.[39] The annual revival became enough of a tradition that the advertisements, instead of going into details, merely announced 'the grand military national spectacle of the Battle of Waterloo'.[40] *The Battle of Waterloo*, however, was sufficiently popular that it was revived at least twice between its debut in 1824

---

[32] The Military Asylum, Chelsea, was an orphanage for the children of soldiers who had been killed in action. *Morning Post*, 30 September 1824.

[33] Benson Earle Hill, *Playing About; or Theatrical Anecdotes and Adventures* (London: W. Sams, 1840), I: 234.

[34] Hill, *Playing About*, 234.

[35] 'Royal Amphitheatre', *The Drama; or, Theatrical Pocket Magazine* 6 no. 4 (June 1824): 201; *Morning Post*, 4 August 1824.

[36] Entry for 6 July 1829, Lord John Russell, ed., *Memoirs, Journal, and Correspondence of Thomas Moore* (Boston: Little Brown, 1853), VI: 61; *The Bury and Norwich Post: Or, Suffolk and Norfolk Telegraph, Essex, Cambridge, & Ely Intelligencer*, 15 July 1829.

[37] 'Astley's Royal Amphitheatre', *The Times*, 9 July 1829, p. 2. See also 'Royal Amphitheatre', *Morning Chronicle*, 14 July 1829.

[38] 'Anniversary of the Battle of Waterloo', *The Times*, 19 June 1829, p. 2.

[39] See, for example, *Morning Chronicle*, 30 August 1824; *Morning Post*, 7 September 1825.

[40] 'Astley's', *The Times*, 19 June 1834, p. 4.

and the start of this trend five years later.[41] The first revival opened on 25 July 1825, 'dedicated to his Grace the Duke of Wellington'.[42] Despite the original run having closed less than a year before, the revival proved popular. In late August, *The Morning Post* reported the debut of a new piece alongside *The Battle of Waterloo*, noting that 'the whole concluded with the favourite spectacle of *The Battle of Waterloo*. The house was crowded to an overflow.'[43] The 1825 revival eventually closed in early September.[44] Less than three years later, the show was revived again. On 14 July 1828, the Amphitheatre's poster announced that its production of *The Battle of Navarino* was to be briefly superseded by 'the Grand Military and National Spectacle of The Battle of Waterloo', neatly spiking the guns of Vauxhall Gardens (Figure 5.1).[45] 'The anxious enquiries that have been made by the numerous Visitors of Rank and Title', the poster informed its readers, 'in conjunction with many distinguished Military Officers who honor the Amphitheatre with their support, respecting the re-production of this National and Imposing Spectacle, have induced the Managers to get up the Work with all its extensive Martial Appurtenances with encreased effect than heretofore, and on a Scale of the utmost magnitude.'[46] Despite the poster's assurances that the 1828 revival would be brief, the show once again proved popular and was extended several times, finally closing on 20 September 1828.[47]

The success of Astley's *The Battle of Waterloo* was not limited to the capital. Word of mouth ensured demand for the show outside London. A variety of provincial theatres licensed the show from Amherst and Astley's, although as some of these were traditional theatres, some adaptation would have been required.[48] Within three years of its debut in London, the production had appeared at the Theatre-Royal, Bristol; the Theatre Royal, Hull; the Olympic Circus and Cooke's Royal Amphitheatre, Liverpool; and the Caledonian

---

[41] Saxon, *Ducrow*, 135.

[42] 'Royal Amphitheatre', *The Examiner*, 24 July 1825; 'Royal Amphitheatre', *Morning Post*, 25 July 1825, p. 1.

[43] 'Astley's', *Morning Post*, 23 August 1825.

[44] 'Royal Amphitheatre', *Morning Post*, 5 September 1825, p. 1; 'Royal Amphitheatre', *Morning Post*, 7 September 1825, p. 1.

[45] 'Royal Amphitheatre (Astley's)', 14 July 1828, The Marcus Stone Collection, London, Victoria & Albert Museum Theatre and Performance, THM/234/8/1, 376. It had, in fact, been in previews since the 10th. 'Royal Amphitheatre', *The Times*, 10 July 1828, p. 2.

[46] 'Royal Amphitheatre (Astley's)', 14 July 1828, The Marcus Stone Collection, London, Victoria & Albert Museum Theatre and Performance, THM/234/8/1, 376.

[47] 'Royal Amphitheatre', *The Times*, 28 July 1828, p. 2; 'Royal Amphitheatre', *The Times*, 9 August 1828, p. 2; 'Royal Amphitheatre', *The Times*, 8 September 1828, p. 2; 'Royal Amphitheatre', *The Times*, 19 September 1828, p. 2.

[48] Here, as in London, military patronage was sought and valued. See 'Advertisements & Notices', *Manchester Times*, 20 February 1850, 1; Assael, *The Circus and Victorian Society*, 54–5, 176 n. 46. For an example of the changes, see Lord Chamberlain's Plays. Vol. VII. April–May 1825, MS Add MS 42871, British Library, 249–91.

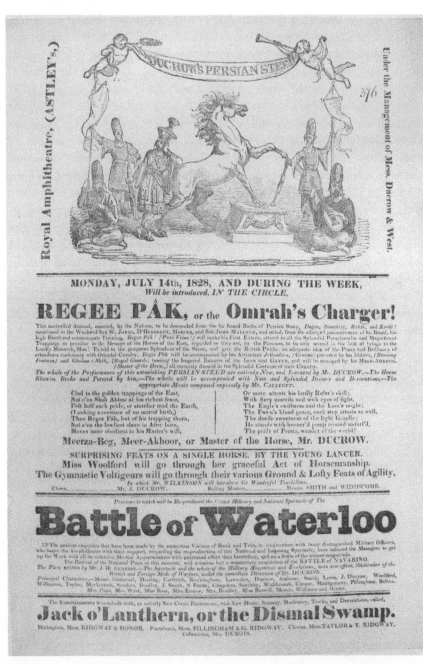

Figure 5.1 Royal Amphitheatre Poster from 14 July 1828. Royal Amphitheatre (Astley's), 14 July 1828, The Marcus Stone Collection, London, Victoria & Albert Museum Theatre and Performance, THM/234/8/1, 376. Courtesy of Victoria and Albert Museum, London. Photo by author.

Theatre, Edinburgh.[49] Further afield, Ducrow's company took the show to Dublin in 1825, and an American tour performed at New York's Bowery Theatre and Boston's National Theatre in the autumn of 1840 and the winter of 1841.[50]

Almost all of these touring productions were of shorter duration than the London runs, but were no less successful in attendance.[51] *The Bristol Mercury* informed its readers that the spectacle 'has attained a degree of popularity as unprecedented as the efforts by which it has been produced', and declared itself 'at a loss at what point to commence our approbation' of 'the most accurate display of military manœuvre ever beheld within the walls of any theatre'.[52] Further north, the production at the Olympic Circus, Liverpool, 'secured the greatest houses ever experienced at that theatre'.[53] The *Liverpool Mercury*, delighted by the 'splendour of the *materiel*, the beauty of the horses, and the strict fac-simile of all the performers to the original characters', posited that this theatrical interpretation of the battle 'is likely to prove as beneficial to [the Olympic Circus' owner], as the original was to Europe in general'.[54] Nor was the appeal purely patriotic in nature. In New York, *The Battle of Waterloo* proved successful enough to sustain a multi-month run and drove the theatre critic for the *Morning Herald* to blame it and similar equestrian spectacles for the decline in attendance of the 'legitimate' theatres.[55]

The Battle of Waterloo was so consistently popular that it outlived almost everyone who had been present at the actual battle. It was still being revived regularly in 1853, and in 1854, three decades after the show first opened, *The Times* was still using it as the benchmark of hippodrama in the capital, praising

[49] 'Theatre-Royal, Bristol', *The Bristol Mercury*, 22 November 1824; Lord Chamberlain's Plays. Vol. VII. April–May 1825, MS Add MS 42871, British Library, 249–50; 'Olympic Circus', *Liverpool Mercury etc.*, 31 December 1824; 'Public Amusements', *Liverpool Mercury etc.*, 23 February 1827; 'Caledonian Theatre', *Caledonian Mercury*, 9 May 1825.

[50] Dublin Theatre, *Morning Chronicle*, 26 January 1825; Saxon, *Ducrow*, 126–7; Assael, *The Circus and Victorian Society*, 52–3; Theatres, *Boston Courier*, 1 March 1841, p. 4.

[51] *The Battle of Waterloo* ran in Bristol 22 November–1 December 1824, in Liverpool 24 December 1824–28 January 1825 and again for a short time in February 1826 and 1827, in Edinburgh 14 May 1825–28 June 1825, in New York from November to December 1840, and in Boston for at least two weeks in March 1841. 'Theatre-Royal, Bristol', *The Bristol Mercury*, 15 November 1824; 'Theatre-Royal, Bristol', *The Bristol Mercury*, 29 November 1824; 'Olympic Circus', *Liverpool Mercury etc.*, 31 December 1824; 'Olympic Circus', *Liverpool Mercury etc.*, 28 January 1825; 'Olympic Circus', *Liverpool Mercury etc.*, 10 February 1826; 'Circus', *Liverpool Mercury etc.*, 17 February 1826; 'Public Amusements', *Liverpool Mercury etc.*, 23 February 1827; 'Caledonian Theatre', *Caledonian Mercury*, 9 May 1825; 'Caledonian Theatre', *Caledonian Mercury*, 2 July 1825; 'Theatricals', *Morning Herald*, 2 November 1840, p. 1; 'Theatricals', *Morning Herald*, 19 December 1840, p. 2; 'Theatres', *Boston Courier*, 1 March 1841, p. 4; 'National Theatre', *Bay State Democrat*, 12 March 1841, p. 3.

[52] Some of that accuracy may have been due to the theatre's management actively recruiting Waterloo veterans to perform. 'Theatre-Royal, Bristol', *The Bristol Mercury*, 8 November 1824; 'The Theatre', *The Bristol Mercury*, 29 November 1824.

[53] *Liverpool Mercury, etc.*, 31 December 1824.

[54] *Liverpool Mercury, etc.*, 7 January 1825; *Liverpool Mercury, etc.*, 14 January 1825.

[55] 'Theatricals', *Morning Herald*, 2 November 1840, p. 1; 'Theatricals', *Morning Herald*, 1 December 1840, p. 2; 'Bowery Theatre', *Morning Herald*, 3 December 1840, p. 3; 'Theatricals', *Morning Herald*, 19 December 1840, p. 2.

the new *Battle of Alma* as 'the best military spectacle that has been seen since the days of the *Battle of Waterloo*'.[56] *Punch* went a step further, using the show in 1853 as a comparison to the actual military manoeuvres organized at Chobham Camp, noting that 'Aides-de-Camp were now seen flying about in all directions with breathless speed, delivering "property" despatches, similar to those with which the gallant officers at Astley's are in the habit of prancing over the platformed planes of Waterloo'.[57] The last recorded revival of the hippodrama was in May 1869, for the centenary of Wellington's birth.[58] It ran for only a few weeks, despite the *Daily Express* declaring it 'worthy of the palmy days of Ducrow', but was brought back 'by special desire' for a matinee on 19 June, where 'the surviving veterans who fought on the 18th of June, 1815, [would] be present, by permission'.[59]

Part of the reason for the longevity of Astley's *Battle of Waterloo* may have been its merchandizing. The same year as it debuted at Astley's, William West, one of the most prolific publishers of juvenile dramas, announced a toy theatre version of the spectacle, entitled *Characters & Scenes in the Battle of Waterloo* (Figure 5.2).[60] Toy theatre took the popular stage hits of the day and miniaturized them. An artist was sent to a performance of the chosen production, where they sketched the scenic backgrounds and each major character in costume. The printers would then reproduce the characters on sheets, with each figure usually between two and a half and three inches high, and with the scenic backgrounds to match. For some of the more popular productions, like *The Battle of Waterloo*, West also published even smaller versions, with character models only measuring one inch.[61] *The Battle of Waterloo* featured twelve plates of characters, including over 170 figures, depicted either individually or in groups, and twelve scenes, ranging from barracks and encampments to Waterloo village and the battlefield itself.[62] *The Battle of Waterloo* proved so popular that it was published by six different printers and appears to have been available into the twentieth century, which may explain, along with the emerging popularity of toy soldiers, why the battle continued to

[56] 'Astley's Royal Amphitheatre', *The Times*, 12 July 1853, p. 4; 'Astley's Royal Amphitheatre', *The Times*, 6 August 1853, p. 5; 'Astley's Amphitheatre', *The Times*, 24 October 1854, p. 10. In 1864, *The Times* declared *The Battle of Waterloo* to be either the most or second most successful production in Astley's history. 'Astley's Theatre', *The Times*, 7 October 1864, p. 7.

[57] 'Civil (very civil) war at Chobham', *Punch Vol. XXV* (London: Punch Office, 1853), 3.

[58] 'Astley's Theatre Royal', *The Times*, 25 May 1869, p. 8.

[59] The *Daily Express*, quoted in 'Astley's Theatre Royal', *The Times*, 25 May 1869, p. 8; 'Astley's Theatre', *The Times*, 10 June 1869, p. 8; 'Astley's', *The Times*, 18 June 1869, p. 10; 'Astley's', *The Times*, 17 June 1869, p. 8.

[60] Speaight, *Juvenile Drama*, 214; *Pollock's Characters & Scenes in the Battle of Waterloo* (London: B. Pollock), The Marcus Stone Collection, London, Victoria & Albert Museum Theatre and Performance, THM/234/8/1, AST-86.

[61] Speaight, *Juvenile Drama*, 74–6.

[62] In the version held in the Marcus Stone Collection, the character sheets are black and white, while the backgrounds are in full colour. Other, more expensive versions were coloured throughout. *Pollock's Characters & Scenes in the Battle of Waterloo* (London: B. Pollock), The Marcus Stone Collection, London, Victoria & Albert Museum Theatre and Performance, THM/234/8/1, AST-86–97.

Figure 5.2 Frontispiece from Pollock's toy theatre version of *The Battle of Waterloo*. Anne S. K. Brown Military Collection, John Hay Library, Brown University, Providence.

have a cultural impact on generations who had not been alive when Wellington ordered the general advance.[63]

The wars of the second half of the long eighteenth century transformed art as much as they had other portions of culture. In Britain the genre of history painting had evolved from depictions of biblical, mythological, and classical events to representations of more recent victories and sacrifices. *Exemplum virtutis* paintings such as Benjamin West's *The Death of General Wolfe* (1770) or John Singleton Copley's *The Death of Major Peirson* (1783) combined Renaissance styles and poses with eighteenth- and nineteenth-century notions of heroism and hero worship and became hugely popular, as did vast canvases such as Copley's *Defeat of the Floating Batteries at Gibraltar* (1783–91).[64] While history painting was flourishing in Britain, however, its sub-genre, battle painting, remained a

[63] Speaight, *Juvenile Drama*, 237.
[64] Holger Hoock, *Empires of the Imagination: Politics, War, and the Arts in the British World, 1750–1850* (London: Profile Books, 2010), 94–6; Wendy Wassyng Roworth, 'The Evolution of History Painting: Masaniello's Revolt and Other Disasters in Seventeenth-Century Naples', *Art Bulletin* 75,

continental, especially French, speciality.[65] Napoleon, ever conscious of his image, had embraced battle painting as a form of national propaganda, while in Britain, the lack of such a style was held up as proof of their superior culture.[66] This presented something of a problem when it came to artistic commemoration of Waterloo. Some artists tried to correct this. Henry Alken exhibited his *Battle of Waterloo* at Messrs S. and J. Fuller's in Rathbone-place in 1816, while Dennis Dighton's *The Battle of Waterloo: General Advance of the British Lines*, William Findlater's *The Life Guards charging the Cuirassiers: The Battle of Waterloo* and Richard Ansdell's *The Battle of the Standard* were part of the Royal Academy's exhibitions in 1816, 1818, and 1848, respectively, but they were dismissed as popular works rather than truly artistic.[67] Financially, this was no bad thing, as the most successful British battle paintings of the time were at that point gener- ating a very tidy profit for their owners not at the Royal Academy, but half a mile to the west at The Panorama, Leicester Square. This dearth of battle painting in fine art, however, has resulted in a temporal gap, where the paintings we most associate with Waterloo, such as Elizabeth Thompson, Lady Butler's *Scotland Forever!* (1881) and *The 28th Regiment at Quatre Bras* (1875) were not painted until the late nineteenth century, and are closer, chronologically, to John Singer Sargent's *Gassed* (1918) than they are to Joseph Mallord William Turner's *The Field of Waterloo* (1818).

There were attempts to correct this national oversight in the case of Waterloo. The British Institution offered a thousand-guinea prize for the best sketch or painting of the Battle of Waterloo, with mixed results. *The Times* lamented that the collection 'betrays equal poverty of intellect and imagination in our native artists'.[68] The *Annals of Fine Arts* was more sanguine, applauding the Institution's

no. 2 (June 1993): 219–34; Michael Putter, '"A Very Naïve and Completely New Manner": Pieneman, History Painting and the Exhibitions of the Battle of Waterloo', *The Rijksmuseum Bulletin* 63, no. 3 (2015): 196–227.
[65] David O'Brien, *After the Revolution: Antoine-Jean Gros, Painting and Propaganda Under Napoleon* (University Park, Pa: Penn State University Press, 2006); Todd Porterfield and Susan Locke Siegfried, *Staging Empire: Napoleon, Ingres, and David* (University Park, PA: Penn State University Press, 2006); Susan Locke Siegfried, 'Naked History: The Rhetoric of Military Painting in Postrevolutionary France', *Art Bulletin* 75, no. 2 (June 1993): 235–58.
[66] J. W. M. Hichberger, *Images of the Army: The Military in British Art, 1815–1914* (Manchester: Manchester University Press, 1988), 2.
[67] 'Battle of Waterloo', *Morning Post*, 12 January 1816, p. 1; 'The Battle of Waterloo', *Morning Post*, 23 March 1816, p. 1; *The Exhibition of the Royal Academy, M. DCCCXVIII* (London: B. McMillan, 1818), 15. *The Literary Panorama*, in reference to Dighton's painting declared 'here Art is foiled' while one guide to the 1848 Royal Academy exhibition dismissed *The Battle of the Standard* as 'mere portraiture' 'with very little taste'. 'Fine Arts: Exhibition of the Royal Academy', *The Literary Panorama, and National Register*, June 1816, 475; *Rosenberg's Guide to the Exhibitions of the Royal Academy and the Institution for the Free Exhibition of Modern Art* (London: H. Hurst, 1848), 18. Both Ansdell's and Findlater's paintings were, it should be noted, relatively well received by the press. 'The Fine Arts', *The London Literary Gazette and Journal of Belles Lettres, Arts, Sciences, etc.*, 20 March 1819, 185; 'The Exhibition of the Royal Academy, Trafalgar-Square', *The Era*, 14 May 1848, p. 10; 'Exhibition of the Liverpool Academy', *Liverpool Mercury*, 3 October, 1848, p. 4.
[68] 'The British Gallery', *The Times*, 3 February 1816, p. 3.

announcement that they were considering commissioning one or more of the winning artists to reproduce their battle paintings on 'a larger scale for some public building... a decision, which must serve to raise these important helpmates to a nation's fame, to a higher rank in England, than in any other nation in Europe'.[69] In the end, 1,800 guineas in prizes were distributed among four artists. It is telling, however, that the most significant prize went not to a strict depiction of the battle, but to an allegory of it.[70]

Nineteenth-century British history and battle paintings and their relation to both military and civilian society have all received a significant amount of scholarly attention, and as such does not need to be addressed at length here.[71] However, it is worth contrasting four notable works concerning Waterloo and the reactions they received: Turner's *The Field of Waterloo*, Lawrence's *Portrait of the Duke of Wellington, in the dress that he wore, and on the horse he rode at the battle of Waterloo*, Pieneman's *The Battle of Waterloo*, and Salter's *The Waterloo Banquet, 1836*, none of which have received sufficient attention from scholars.[72]

Joseph Mallord William Turner was already a well-established artist when he left Britain in August 1817 to visit Waterloo. It was only his second time leaving Britain, and the fact that he chose Waterloo and the Rhine as opposed to Rome or one of the other traditional artist pilgrimages illustrates how totally Waterloo had come to dominate the public consciousness. In addition to the general societal pressure, Turner had recently finished reading the newly published third canto of Lord Byron's *Childe Harold's Pilgrimage*, which made a compelling argument for visiting the area.[73] Turner took with him as a guide Charles Campbell's *The Traveller's Complete Guide to Belgium and Holland*, which had that year been

---

[69] 'Decision of the British Institution', *Annals of the Fine Arts for MDCCCXVI* (London: Sherwood, Neely, and Jones, 1817), I: 104–5.

[70] A. Cooper and L. Clennell each received 150 guineas, James Ward, RA, received the original 1,000 guineas for an allegorical depiction, and G. Jones was awarded another 500 guineas. 'Decision of the British Institution', *Annals of the Fine Arts for MDCCCXVI* (London: Sherwood, Neely, and Jones, 1817), I: 104–5.

[71] See, for example, Hichberger, *Images of the Army*; Hoock, *Empires of the Imagination*; Linda Colley, *Britons: Forging the Nation 1707–1837* (New Haven: Yale University Press, 2009), chapter 9; Michael Paris, *Warrior Nation: Images of War in British Popular Culture, 1850–2000* (London: Reaktion Books, 2000); Nicholas Tromans, *David Wilkie: The People's Painter* (Edinburgh: Edinburgh University Press, 2007), chapter 4.

[72] Turner's *The Field of Waterloo* has been largely ignored in favour of his other work, perhaps thanks to its lack of success at the time. Only one article discusses Lawrence's portraits of Wellington in detail, and that is chiefly interested in the relationship between painter and sitter. Susan Jenkins, 'Sir Thomas Lawrence and the Duke of Wellington: A Portraitist and his Sitter', *The British Art Journal* 8, no. 1 (Summer 2007): 63–7. Pieneman's painting is similarly neglected, with the exception of Putter, '"A Very Naïve and Completely New Manner"', 196–227. The only article dedicated to Salter's work examines it from a strictly militaria perspective. N. P. Dawnay and J. M. A. Tamplin, 'The Waterloo Banquet at Apsley House, 1836, by William Salter', *Journal of the Society for Army Historical Research* 49, no. 198 (Summer 1971): 63–76.

[73] Franny Moyle, *Turner: The Extraordinary Life and Momentous Times of J. M. W. Turner* (New York: Penguin Press, 2016), 290.

updated to include a guide to both the battle and the field of Waterloo.[74] The guidebook also contained excerpts from Walter Scott's *The Field of Waterloo*, Robert Southey's *The Poet's Pilgrimage to Waterloo*, and Lord Byron's *Childe Harold's Pilgrimage*, which fit nicely into Turner's inspirations for the trip.[75] Turner walked the battlefield in the manner recommended by Campbell, and produced seventeen sketches, supplemented by anecdotes gleaned from the on-site tour guides that, even in the span of two years, had become ubiquitous.[76] Upon his return to Britain, Turner set about turning the ideas contained in those seventeen sketches into larger pieces. The result was two watercolours, and the roughly five- by seven-foot oil painting entitled *The Field of Waterloo*.

   The Field of Waterloo (Figure 5.3) is a departure from every tradition of battle and commemorative painting. It shows the valley of Waterloo the night after the battle. The entire piece is oppressively dark, with only three sources of light: the burning Chateau Hougoumont, a distant flare, fired either to discourage looters or

Figure 5.3 *The Field of Waterloo*, exhibited 1818, Joseph Mallord William Turner. Accepted by the nation as part of the Turner Bequest 1856. Photo: Tate.

[74] Joseph Mallord William Turner, 'Itinerary Rhine Tour Sketchbook [Finberg CLIX]', in Helena Bonett, Ysanne Holt, Jennifer Mundy, eds, *The Camden Town Group in Context*, Tate Research Publication, May 2012, <https://www.tate.org.uk/art/research/group/65801?project=2>, accessed 23 August 2018, CLIX 101; Charles Campbell, *The Traveller's Complete Guide through Belgium & Holland; Containing Full Directions for Gentlemen, Lovers of the Fine Arts, and Travellers in General: With a Sketch of a Tour in Germany* (London: Sherwood, Neely, and Jones, 1817), chapter 4.

[75] Campbell, *The Traveller's Complete Guide through Belgium & Holland*, 62–4, 69.

[76] Joseph Mallord William Turner, 'Waterloo and the Rhine Sketchbook', London, Tate Britain, D12733-D12749, Turner Bequest CLX 17a–CLX 26.

to aid the Prussian army's night chase of Napoleon, and the torch held by the women in the foreground. At first glance there are only ten or twenty bodies on display, but a closer examination reveals that nearly the entire bottom left quarter of the painting is covered by bodies and the discarded detritus of war. The lack of illumination seems to provide a glimpse into the future of the fallen: forgotten, they will be absorbed by the earth. Turner envisioned the painting as an explicit indictment of the horrors of war and signalled his intention by displaying it with a quote from *Childe Harold's Pilgrimage*, which had done with verse what he was attempting with oils.

The Field of Waterloo made its public debut at the 1818 Royal Academy Exhibition, where it met with a mixed reception. The *Annals of the Fine Arts* dismissed it completely, stating that 'before we referred to the catalogue we really thought this was the representation of a drunken hubbub on an illumination night, and the host as far gone as his scuffling and scrambling guests, was, with his dame and kitchen wenches looking with torches for a lodger, and wondering what was the matter'.[77] The *Literary Chronicle* was briefer but equally damning, decrying it as an 'abortive attempt'.[78] Even some of those who had visited the battlefield as Turner had were puzzled. Henry Crabb Robinson, who had walked the field two months after the battle, when it still bore some of the detritus Turner included, described the painting as 'a strange incomprehensible jumble'.[79]

In contrast, *The Repository of Arts* recommended it to their readers, arguing that 'it possesses a strong claim to attention ... there is a good deal of grandeur in the effect of this picture as a whole, and the executive parts are handled with care and attention'.[80] Even they admitted, however, that '*The Field of Waterloo*, in the catalogue, gives a name to the picture which the subject, in the manner it is handled, would not suggest to the spectator. It is more an allegorical representation of "battles magnificently stern array," than any actual delineation of a particular battle.'[81] In the more general press, *The Sun* praised it as 'a terrific representation of the effects of war'.[82] *The Monthly Magazine* called it 'affecting' and insisted that it would 'be valued as long as [its] canvas endures'.[83] Unsurprisingly, *The Examiner*, traditionally anti-war, declared it a 'magical illustration of that principle of colour and claire obscure, which combines all their varieties of tint

---

[77] 'Review of the Exhibition at the Royal Academy', *Annals of the Fine Arts, for MDCCCXVIII* (London: Sherwood, Neely, and Jones, 1819), III: 299.

[78] *Literary Chronicle*, 22 June 1818, quoted in Martin Butlin and Evelyn Joll, *The Paintings of J. M. W. Turner* (New Haven: Yale University Press, 1984), 105.

[79] Henry Crabb Robinson, *Diary, Reminiscences, and Correspondence of Henry Crabb Robinson*, ed. Thomas Sadler (Boston: Houghton, Mifflin and Co., 1898), 387.

[80] 'Exhibition at the Royal Academy', *The Repository of Arts, Literature, Fashions, Manufacturers, &c.*, 1 June 1818, 365.

[81] 'Exhibition at the Royal Academy', *The Repository of Arts, Literature, Fashions, Manufacturers, &c.*, 1 June 1818, 365.

[82] *The Sun*, 15 May 1818, quoted in Butlin and Joll, *The Paintings of J. M. W. Turner*, 105.

[83] 'Varieties, Literary and Philosophical', *The Monthly Magazine*, 1 June 1818, 446–7.

and strength in exhibiting... when the wives and brothers and sons of the slain come, with anxious eyes and agonized hearts, to look in Ambition's charnel-house, after the slaughtered victims of legitimate and illegitimate selfishness and wickedness'.[84] Despite this praise, Turner's *The Field of Waterloo* did not sell.[85]

Debuting at the same exhibition was Sir Thomas Lawrence's *Portrait of the Duke of Wellington, in the dress that he wore, and on the horse he rode at the battle of Waterloo* (Figure 5.4).[86] This thirteen by eight foot equestrian portrait is representative of the more traditional British take on battle paintings—of the battle, but not depicting it.[87] Wellington is portrayed mounted on his favourite horse, Copenhagen, dressed in a plain blue coat and cloak, white breeches, and polished black boots. He is holding a telescope and Copenhagen's reins in one hand and is lifting his bicorn hat in the other. The background is dark and relatively anonymous, but Lawrence's use of light hints that Copenhagen stands at the edge of a ridge, from behind which a column of smoke rises in a way that is evocative of battle without actually depicting it. The darkness of the background is challenged by brighter clouds in the top left segment, suggesting clearer skies just out of view. Copenhagen is facing that way, and Wellington lifts his hat towards the light as it illuminates his face, the great man of history leading his country out of the darkness of war and into the light.

Lawrence was the ideal choice for such a piece. An artistic prodigy from a remarkably early age, in 1818 he was nearing the apogee of his meteoric rise. He had been appointed painter-in-ordinary to the court of George III in 1792 (at the age of 23), was elected a full member of the Royal Academy in 1794 (when he reached the required age of 25), was knighted in 1815 by his patron, the prince regent, and would be elected president of the Royal Academy in 1820.[88] Throughout his career, he was commissioned to paint Wellington seven times, although the last one was left unfinished when Lawrence died in 1830.[89] Of those seven, the 1818 equestrian portrait is the largest, and, thanks to its association with Waterloo, has the closest ties to history painting, a genre that Lawrence always desired to master.[90] That desire, according to Benjamin West, Lawrence's predecessor as president of the Royal Academy, only reinforced his portraiture. 'Do not confound his pictures with mere portraits,' West admonished a friend, 'painted as his are, they cease to be portraits in the ordinary sense; they rise to the dignity of

---

[84] 'Claire obscure' is the French term for chiaroscuro. 'Royal Academy Exhibition', *The Examiner*, 24 May 1818.

[85] Turner's other painting included in the exhibition, however, *Dort or Dordrecht: The Dort Packet Boat from Rotterdam Becalmed*, also a product of his trip to the Continent, did sell, for a landmark 500 guineas. Moyle, *Turner*, 297, 299.

[86] *The Exhibition of the Royal Academy*, 12.

[87] Kenneth Garlick, *Sir Thomas Lawrence: A Complete Catalogue of the Oil Paintings* (New York: New York University Press, 1989), 279.

[88] For a detailed summary of his life and work, see Garlick, *Sir Thomas Lawrence*, 11–29.

[89] Garlick, *Sir Thomas Lawrence*, 279–80.   [90] Garlick, *Sir Thomas Lawrence*, 18–19.

Figure 5.4 Thomas Lawrence, *Portrait of the Duke of Wellington, in the dress that he wore, and on the horse he rode at the Battle of Waterloo, 1818.* © Mark Fiennes Archive/Bridgeman Images.

history, and, like similar works of Titian and Vandyke, they may be said to be painted not alone to gratify friends and admirers in the present day, but rather for posterity.'[91]

The painting was commissioned by Henry, Earl Bathurst, who held the office of Secretary of State for War and the Colonies from 1812 to 1827 and worked closely with Wellington in the final years of the Peninsular War and throughout the Waterloo campaign and the occupation of France. There is some indication that Wellington resented the time it took to sit for portraits, even those painted by Lawrence, whom he evidently liked.[92] He clearly shared West's belief that Lawrence's paintings were as much for posterity as the present, however, and determined as he always was to curate his reputation and legacy, he went out of his way to ensure the success of this particular painting. In addition to dedicating the time required for Lawrence's sittings, Wellington loaned the artist the sword he had carried at Waterloo, which Lawrence used as a prop for the next twelve years.[93] Wellington also ensured that Lawrence had ample opportunities to properly capture Copenhagen, who at that time was in France with the army of occupation. Copenhagen was promptly dispatched across the channel, and Lawrence spent several mornings at Astley's watching the Amphitheatre's riding-master put him through his paces.[94] Lawrence and Wellington also exchanged letters to ensure Copenhagen's tack was depicted accurately.[95]

Lawrence's hard work and attention to detail paid off, and the painting was very well received. The Duchess of Wellington relayed to Lawrence that the duke thought it a better portrait than the one Lawrence had painted of Wellington for Viscount Castlereagh in 1814.[96] David Wilkie, who saw the painting in January 1818, recorded that 'it is one of those images of the Duke that is likely to supplant every other; and I should not be surprised if it were to become...common

---

[91] D. E. Williams, *The Life and Correspondence of Sir Thomas Lawrence, Kt.* (London: Henry Colburn and Richard Bentley, 1831), II: 6–7.

[92] Wellington commissioned over £1,500 worth of portraits from Lawrence and would routinely visit the artist's studio. Wellington was also instrumental in aiding Lawrence on his European tour in 1818. Jenkins, 'Sir Thomas Lawrence and the Duke of Wellington', 66; John Timbs, *Anecdote Lives of William Hogarth, Sir Joshua Reynolds, Thomas Gainsborough, Henry Fuseli, Sir Thomas Lawrence, and J. M. W. Turner* (London: Richard Bentley & Sons, 1881), 293; Harriet Arbuthnot, *The Journal of Mrs. Arbuthnot, 1820–1832*, ed. Francis Bamford & the Duke of Wellington (London: Macmillan & Co., 1950), II: 292, 347; Wellington to Lawrence, 16 September 1818, George Somes Layard, ed., *Sir Thomas Lawrence's Letter-Bag* (London: George Allen, 1906), 133; Lawrence to Joseph Farington, 17 September 1818, Layard, *Sir Thomas Lawrence's Letter-Bag*, 133–4; Elizabeth Croft, 'Recollections of the Artist', in Layard, *Sir Thomas Lawrence's Letter-Bag*, 270.

[93] The 'shabby looking old sabre' had to be reclaimed from Lawrence's studio shortly after his death. Croft, 'Recollections of the Artist', 287; Arbuthnot, *Journal*, II: 347; Lord Grantham to Archibald Keightley, 13 September 1831, Royal Academy Archive LAW/2/214.

[94] Lawrence made several sketches of Copenhagen, which were sold after the artist's death. Croft, 'Recollections of the Artist', 262; Wellington to Lawrence, 15 July 1817, Royal Academy Archive LAW/2/213; Lawrence to Farington, 31 July 1817, Royal Academy Archive, LAW/2/217.

[95] Wellington to Lawrence, 8 August 1817, Royal Academy Archive LAW/2/219.

[96] Duchess of Wellington to Lawrence, 8 July 1817, Royal Academy Archive LAW/2/211; Garlick, *Sir Thomas Lawrence*, 279.

throughout the country'.[97] *The Repository of Arts* praised the 'great grandeur' of the painting, but reserved some criticism for Copenhagen's 'forced and unnatural position'.[98] *The Examiner* had no such reservations, insisting that 'the sentiment of the picture is so raised above the accustomed style of Portraiture, that we doubt whether we ought not to place it in the class of Poetry'.[99] Unsurprisingly, those who had failed to see the merits of Turner's *Field of Waterloo* were won over by Lawrence's more traditional piece. The *Annals of the Fine Arts* agreed with *The Repository of Arts*' criticism of Lawrence's depiction of Copenhagen, but declared the overall portrait 'magnificent' and 'possessing many excellencies of colour, arrangement, drawing, and effect'.[100] By the same token Robinson closed his diary entry on the exhibition by declaring Lawrence's work 'a fine painting'.[101] The highest praise, however, came from Lawrence himself, who included the following inscription in Latin in the lower right corner of the painting: 'Arthur, Duke of Wellington, how he carried himself in the famous Battle of Waterloo, with his uniform, arms, horse and saddlecloth, faithfully portrayed by Thomas Lawrence, knight, easily the foremost amongst the painters of his age in the Year of Salvation 1818.'[102]

While both Turner's and Lawrence's paintings were darker than was traditional at that time, they are, as representations of Waterloo, diametric opposites.[103] Turner's work, redolent with atmosphere, is almost apocalyptic in nature. It eschews the individual for the landscape. The Chateau Hougoumont, scene of some of the hardest fighting on the day, is nearly hidden in flame and smoke, while the soldiers who cover the field literally fade into the background. Lawrence's equestrian portrait, in contrast, celebrates Wellington as the singular hero of the nation: a lone avatar of victory. He is remarkably clean, his white breeches unstained by the violence and chaos of one of nineteenth-century Europe's bloodiest battles; the implicit ridge in the background of the painting and his faithful Copenhagen serving to literally elevate him above the horror of war.

Lawrence was not the last painter to benefit from Wellington's determination to shape his own image. In February 1821, Jan Willem Pieneman travelled from the Netherlands to London on Wellington's invitation. Pieneman, a self-taught painter from Amsterdam who had risen to become Assistant Director of the Royal Cabinet of Paintings and a professor at the new Royal Academy of Fine Arts in Amsterdam, exploded onto the history painting scene with his *The Battle*

[97] Timbs, *Anecdote Lives*, 294.

[98] 'Exhibition at the Royal Academy', *The Repository of Arts, Literature, Fashions, Manufacturers, &c.*, 1 June 1818, 362.

[99] 'Royal Academy Exhibition', *The Examiner*, 24 May 1818.

[100] 'Review of the Exhibition at the Royal Academy', *Annals of the Fine Arts, for MDCCCXVIII* (London: Sherwood, Neely, and Jones, 1819), III: 297.

[101] Robinson, *Diary, Reminiscences, and Correspondence*, 387.

[102] Garlick, *Sir Thomas Lawrence*, 279.   [103] Timbs, *Anecdote Lives*, 294.

of Quatre Bras (1818). The painting, which started as an equestrian sketch of William Frederick, Prince of Orange (later William II), evolved into a full battle painting and became a phenomenon across the Netherlands, earning Pieneman a knighthood in the chivalric order of the Netherlands Lion. After the success of *Quatre Bras*, Waterloo was the next logical step, and Pieneman's British contacts suggested he travel to London to capture the likenesses of Wellington and other officers from life. Wellington, impressed by Pieneman's talent and recognizing an opportunity to further influence the artistic immortalization of Waterloo, leapt at the chance. Pieneman spent nearly four months in London and found Wellington to be an extremely effective patron. In addition to providing Pieneman with a temporary studio in Apsley House itself and posing for his own portrait, Wellington arranged for all of the other officers that Pieneman needed to paint to pose for the artist. Wellington even had Copenhagen brought from Stratfield Saye so that Pieneman could, like Lawrence, paint the horse from life.[104] Wellington also served, albeit temporarily, as Pieneman's patron in the original, monetary sense. Early in the artist's visit, Wellington laid claim to all of Pieneman's studies of the officers, eventually paying £417 18s. for them.[105] These provided Wellington with the foundation for another ambition—'a collection of the pictures of the principal officers whom I had the honour of commanding during the war'.[106]

Pieneman returned to the Netherlands on 30 May 1821 with at least thirteen portraits of British senior officers and, crucially, one of a horse. He supplemented these with another portrait of the Prince of Orange, who would also be featured in the painting, and set to work.[107] The painting took him nearly three years to complete. Eighteen and a half feet tall and twenty-seven feet long, Pieneman's *The Battle of Waterloo* is less a battle painting than it is a group portrait of over twenty-five significant figures, depicted life-sized, with the battle raging as the backdrop (Figure 5.5).[108] Wellington takes centre stage, surrounded by his staff and generals, while the Prince of Orange reclines in the foreground on a stretcher after being wounded. The painting features British, Dutch, King's German Legion, and even French soldiers, but despite it being set towards the end of the battle, there is not a single Prussian individual in it. From the start, Pieneman planned to exhibit the painting and rumours circulated that it was eventually destined for Stratfield Saye. In this case, however, Wellington was outmanoeuvred by an old ally. The Prince of Orange, upon seeing the completed painting for the first time,

[104] All details from Putter, '"A Very Naïve and Completely New Manner"'.
[105] Evelyn Wellington, *A Descriptive and Historical Catalogue of the Collection of Pictures and Sculpture at Apsley House, London* (London: Longmans, Green, and Co., 1901), II: 288.
[106] Wellington to Berkely Paget, 15 December 1832, Quoted in Wellington, *Catalogue of Pictures and Sculpture at Apsley House*, II: 274.
[107] Putter, '"A Very Naïve and Completely New Manner"', 216.
[108] 'Battle of Waterloo', *The Times*, 18 June 1825, p. 1.

Figure 5.5 Jan Willem Pieneman, *The Battle of Waterloo*, 1824. Rijksmuseum, Amsterdam.

immediately offered Pieneman 40,000 guilders for it, a price that his father, William I, eventually ended up paying as a gift to his son.[109] Pieneman, delighted with the sum, still insisted it should tour before the prince took ownership, and so preparations began for its display in London.

In January 1825 'public curiosity was excited ... by preparations for erecting a Temple' in Hyde Park to house and display the painting.[110] *The Battle of Waterloo* was so large that no suitable indoor space could be found, and so, with the continued support of Wellington and the permission of both the king and his Office of Woods, a purpose-built temporary gallery was constructed on the site of the Old Riding House near Grosvenor Gate.[111] The painting opened to the public in early May 1825 after a private viewing for the press that was graced by the presence of many of the painting's 'distinguished conquerors', who praised the 'faithful hand of the artist in many of the details of the battle'.[112]

London's artistic press was not as unified in their praise as Wellington's officers. *The Literary Gazette*, in addition to objecting to the ugliness of the building, lamented that such effort was being undertaken on behalf of a foreign artist. Even

---

[109] Putter, '"A Very Naïve and Completely New Manner"', 218–19.

[110] Hyde Park, *Morning Post*, 28 January 1825.

[111] Wellington to Mrs Arbuthnot, 7 September 1824 in Arthur Wellesley, Seventh Duke of Wellington, ed., *Wellington and his Friends* (London: Macmillan, 1965), 49–50; Temporary exhibition building for a picture of the Battle of Waterloo, 1825, London, National Archives, WORK 16/26/5.

[112] The Arts, *Morning Post*, 9 May 1825; *Morning Post*, 11 May 1825.

they could not deny the impact of the piece itself, however, begrudgingly admit-ting that 'it is a great work; and has, with some glaring defects, very considerable talent'.[113] *The New Monthly Magazine* was more positive, declaring it 'without exception, the best work on a large scale that we remember to have seen exhibited by a foreigner in this country, or indeed on the continent'.[114] Despite the apparent danger of supporting a foreign artist, London society privileged the view of Wellington and his officers over the press and flocked to Hyde Park, paying a shilling for admission and another shilling for the description/guide.[115] The painting's military bona fides were further burnished on the tenth anniversary of the battle, when the admission fee was waived for any veteran of the battle, 'provided they bring their medal in uniform, or certificate of discharge out of uniform', a decision *The Morning Post* declared 'highly creditable to those who agreed to grant the privilege to the brave fellows'.[116] Thanks to its implicit military backing, its privileging of the British and Dutch perspectives over the Prussian, its artistic merits, and its nearly panoramic size, Pieneman's painting remained popular through the rest of 1825. The advertisements for the exhibition in the days following Christmas 1825 assured the public that 'a good fire [was] con-stantly kept', a necessity in a temporary building that had been designed for a British summer.[117] It is unclear when it finally closed, but reports indicate that it was still on view in March 1826, ten months after it had first opened.[118]

William Salter's *The Waterloo Banquet, 1836*, completed in 1840, seeks to strike a balance between the interpretations of the three previous paintings discussed (Figure 5.6). It is closest conceptually to Pieneman's, reflecting the fact that Wellington once again lent his aid to the artist. Wellington, unsurprisingly, is centred in the work, but he shares the glory with nearly eighty identifiable officers—a significant increase from the roughly twenty-seven in Pieneman's vast canvas. The painting-lined walls of Apsley House's picture gallery are a far cry from the chaotic and muddy valley of Waterloo, but in addition to capturing the details of the banquet, moving the setting from the field of battle to Apsley House implicitly limits that glory to the men in the room, maintaining their elite status and ownership of the victory.

According to anecdotal legend, Salter happened to be riding in Hyde Park on 18 June and caught a glimpse of the banquet through the large windows of the gallery. Immediately seeing the potential for a painting depicting the event, he

---

[113] 'The Battle of Waterloo', *The Literary Gazette and Journal of the Belles Lettres*, 14 May 1825, p. 315–16.
[114] 'The Battle of Waterloo', *The New Monthly Magazine*, 1 July 1825, p. 302.
[115] 'Battle of Waterloo', *The Times*, 18 June 1825, p. 1.
[116] 'Anniversary of the Battle of Waterloo', *Morning Post*, 14 June 1825, p. 1; *Morning Post*, 15 June 1825, p. 3.
[117] 'Battle of Waterloo', *Morning Post*, 27 December 1825, p. 1; 'Battle of Waterloo', *Morning Post*, 29 December 1825, p. 1.
[118] *Morning Post*, 28 March 1826.

Figure 5.6 William Salter, *The Waterloo Banquet, 1836*, 1840, Apsley House, London, © Stratfield Saye Preservation Trust.

applied to his patron, Lady Burghersh, who, fortuitously, was Wellington's niece. She agreed to contact her uncle, who immediately refused, citing the complicated nature of the painting and Salter's youth (he was in his early thirties at the time). Burghersh persisted, however, and eventually Wellington was persuaded.[119] Once he was convinced, Wellington took great interest in the painting and went out of his way to aid Salter and ensure its success. He clearly saw it as an opportunity to present a more carefully curated view of his veterans to the British public. *The Times*, in their review of the painting, noted that 'the noble owner of Apsley-house has furnished the artist with every facility'.[120] He granted Salter access to Apsley House's picture gallery and collections of plate and china so that he could paint 'the splendid plateau which ornaments the table, the furniture, and the pictures which adorn the noble apartment' from life, to guarantee their accuracy.[121] It is also safe to assume he encouraged Salter's plan to paint individual studies of all the attendees before attempting the overall work, and his approval may have been one of the reasons why all but two of the seventy-eight officers depicted in the painting sat for individual studies in uniform.[122] In addition, Wellington turned a blind eye

[119] John Timbs, *Wellingtonia: Anecdotes, Maxims, and Characteristics of the Duke of Wellington* (London: Ingram, Cooke, and Co., 1852), 134–5.

[120] 'The Picture of the Waterloo Banquet', *The Times*, 7 May 1841, p. 5.

[121] 'The Picture of the Waterloo Banquet', *The Times*, 7 May 1841, p. 5.

[122] Although every individual that was included had a vested interest in a good likeness. The two not painted from life were Earl Bathurst and Lord Robert Manners. 'Our Weekly Gossip', *The Athenæum*, 1 May 1841, 342; Dawnay and Tamplin, 'The Waterloo Banquet at Apsley House, 1836, by William Salter'.

to the one glaring inaccuracy of the painting: the inclusion of several civilians, both male and female, standing by the picture gallery's door. These included Salter himself and the proprietor of Salter's gallery, F. G. Moon, along with Lady Burghersh and several of Wellington's other female relatives.[123] After the painting's completion, but before it was exhibited, Wellington increased public interest by visiting the artist's studio with several fashionable friends to inspect the work, which was reported in *The Times'* Court Circular.[124] This visit inspired another one by Prince Adolphus, Duke of Cambridge, and his son Prince George, which was also reported and no doubt encouraged further excitement.[125]

The excitement was justified. *The Morning Post* declared the finished work 'splendid', while *The Athenæum* commended Salter, 'who has embodied a scene that Posterity will regard with interest even greater than ours'.[126] *The Times* was perhaps the most effusive, informing its readers that it was 'a picture of very rare merit', before praising Salter for his skill. It is not an easy feat to depict a banquet with over eighty guests 'without the heads being distorted or twisted on the shoulders ... without forcing [the subjects] into attitudes, and torturing the limbs to a subserviency of his effects'.[127] 'The picture is strictly an historical one,' *The Times* concluded, 'and will long remain a document of one of the greatest events in modern history. The subject is one that interests every Briton, and has been treated by the artist in the way it deserves.'[128] *The Times*'s prediction that the painting's subject would interest the general populace proved correct. The six foot two inches by eleven foot painting, along with the portrait sketches, were exhibited for over a month at Moon's gallery in Threadneedle Street, and were sufficiently popular that Moon took advantage of the anniversary of Waterloo to move the exhibition to a more centrally located gallery on Regent Street in St James's for a week.[129] It was also immediately announced that there would be an engraving of the piece available for purchase by the general public.[130] The full painting, along with the studies, was exhibited again for the thirtieth

---

[123] Dawnay and Tamplin, 'The Waterloo Banquet at Apsley House, 1836, by William Salter', 63, fig. 6.

[124] 'Court Circular', *The Times*, 2 February 1841, p. 5. Wellington was sufficiently pleased with Salter that he sat for him again a few years later. Lord Gerald Wellesley and John Steegman, *The Iconography of the First Duke of Wellington* (London: Dent, 1935), 45.

[125] 'Court Circular', *The Times*, 8 April 1841, p. 3.

[126] 'Mr. Salter's Waterloo Banquet Picture', *Morning Post*, 19 June 1841; 'Our Weekly Gossip', *The Athenæum*, 1 May 1841, 342.

[127] 'The Picture of the Waterloo Banquet', *The Times*, 7 May 1841, p. 5.

[128] 'The Picture of the Waterloo Banquet', *The Times*, 7 May 1841, p. 5.

[129] 'The Waterloo Banquet Picture', *The Times*, 18 June 1841, p. 12; 'Mr. Salter's Waterloo Banquet Picture', *Morning Post*, 19 June 1841; 'The Waterloo Banquet Picture', *The Times*, 19 June 1841, p. 4; 'The Waterloo Banquet Picture', *The Times*, 26 June 1841, p. 4.

[130] 'The Picture of the Waterloo Banquet', *The Times*, 7 May 1841, p. 5; Dawnay and Tamplin, 'The Waterloo Banquet at Apsley House, 1836, by William Salter', 63.

anniversary of Waterloo in 1845.[131] The individual studies also garnered some interest. They were roughly twenty by seventeen inches and were mostly three-quarter-length portraits. Two sets were made—one for Salter's reference and for display with the completed piece, and one so that each sitter could buy their own sketch.[132] A single study of Major-General Lygon, CB, appeared in the 1842 Royal Academy Exhibition, where it was lamented that Salter had not contributed more work.[133]

In 1846, William Greatbach finished the engraving of the piece and Moon promptly started printing. Prices ranged from £15 15s. for the rarer pre-lettered proofs to £10 10s. for the standard print, and each print included a key so that each person present could be identified.[134] Sales of the twenty-four and half inch by forty-four inch engraving were good, and were no doubt helped by *The Times*'s repeated praise.[135] The paper reported that 'the general effect is spirited, it possesses the energy of truth, and is wholly devoid of the scenic absurdities of theatrical representation and exaggerated outline, although some awkwardness in the positions of the guests could not be avoided. The engraving is in the line manner, and is brilliant, flowing, and defined.'[136] Rare proofs of the engraving became popular collector's items, and several art auction notices over the next few years specifically mention them.[137] Despite the interest in the engravings, the original painting remained unsold until 1852, when it was purchased by a Mr Mackenzie, a friend of Salter's.[138] It remained in the Mackenzie family until the mid-twentieth century, when the original purchaser's grandson, a major, bequeathed it to the 8th Duke of Wellington.[139]

Waterloo veterans were not the only members of the establishment who attempted to use art and spectacle to shape national memory. The prince regent (later George IV) spent several fortunes rebuilding several royal palaces and portions of London in an effort not only to convert the British metropolis into an imperial capital but also to permanently tie himself to the victory over Napoleon.[140] One of the most obvious manifestations of this was Windsor Castle's Waterloo

---

[131] The notices for this brief exhibition were cleverly placed directly above the notices for the popular Waterloo fete at Vauxhall Gardens. 'Waterloo Banquet', *The Times*, 17 June 1845, p. 5; 'Waterloo Banquet', *The Times*, 18 June 1845, p. 4.

[132] Dawnay and Tamplin, 'The Waterloo Banquet at Apsley House, 1836, by William Salter', 64–5.

[133] 'The Royal Academy Exhibition', *The Times*, 6 May 1842, p. 9.

[134] The Waterloo Banquet at Apsley House subscription pamphlet, Yale Center for British Art, New Haven, Rare Books and Manuscripts, ND497.S44 W38 1846 Box; Dawnay and Tamplin, 'The Waterloo Banquet at Apsley House, 1836, by William Salter', 65.

[135] Dawnay and Tamplin, 'The Waterloo Banquet at Apsley House, 1836, by William Salter', 65.

[136] 'The Waterloo Banquet', *The Times*, 6 April 1846, p. 6.

[137] See 'Sales by Auction', *The Times*, 5 June 1847, p. 10; 'Sales by Auction', *The Times*, 22 December 1847, p. 8; 'Sales by Auction', *The Times*, 30 August 1849, p. 8.

[138] Dawnay and Tamplin, 'The Waterloo Banquet at Apsley House, 1836, by William Salter', 65.

[139] It is currently on display in the public rooms of Apsley House. The collection of the single studies is in the possession of the National Portrait Gallery.

[140] Hoock, *Empires of the Imagination*, chapter 9.

Chamber. Designed by Sir Jeffry Wyatville, George IV imagined the chamber as a gallery of heroes of the late war, with himself permanently ensconced at the centre. He commissioned Sir Thomas Lawrence to embark on a European tour to paint the sovereigns, generals, and statesmen of the Quintuple Alliance. The result was a remarkable collection of portraits which included two emperors, four kings, seven princes, and a pope. One end of the chamber was (and remains) dominated by a full-length portrait of Wellington, but with the exception of him, Field Marshall Prince Blücher, and the various royals who also held military rank, the chamber was notably short of battlefield generals. George IV was determined to be the star of the show and crafted the chamber's portraits around his own grandiose ideas of his military as well as civil leadership. It was only after George IV's death that portraits were added of Britain's non-royal generals, such as the Marquess of Anglesey, Rowland, Viscount Hill, Sir James Kempt, and Sir Thomas Picton, the highest-ranking British casualty of Waterloo.[141]

As George IV's attempts show, there remained power in cultural representation. The flattering depiction of Wellington and his officers on the stage, in art, or even in wax could balance the criticisms levelled at them for their political stances or their defence of the army's purchase and punishment systems. These flattering depictions, when not motivated by sheer patriotism or conservative ideology, could be encouraged by senior officers via direct patronage or with donations of their time and presence. As with the exhibitions discussed in the previous chapter, approval of the battle's veterans, whether in the form of just attendance or more overt patronage, generated publicity and helped boost sales. This led to a symbiotic relationship. Veterans, led by Wellington, embraced this opportunity to retain some claim to ownership and shape the depictions of the battle, thus influencing the national memory of the victory in cooperation with, rather than in challenge to, the civilian creators and curators that dominated British popular culture. Those civilian creators and curators in turn gained legitimacy and, with it, increased profits. And there were profits to be had. All of the works discussed here illustrate the continued presence of the Battle of Waterloo in the cultural fabric of Britain. Even as newspapers declared that 'London is sick to death of Waterloo' and that 'people ... would now almost as soon wish to be in such a battle itself, as to visit representations of it', plays, paintings, annual commemorations, and exhibitions continued to merit media coverage and draw significant crowds.[142]

---

[141] Hoock, *Empires of the Imagination*, 359–61.

[142] William T. Whitley, *Art of England 1821–1837* (Cambridge: Cambridge University Press, 1930), 96; 'Ramas', *The Literary Gazette and Journal of the Belles Lettres*, 17 April 1824, p. 254.

6

'To commemorate the English character'

Monuments and Material Culture

In a letter to Francis Leggatt Chantrey published in the *Annals of the Fine Arts* in 1816, one resident of London put forward his thoughts on the Metropolis's proposed Waterloo Monument.[1] This resident, named John Galt, opined that the Duke of Wellington should not dominate the monument, as the palace voted to him in thanks by Parliament 'should be considered as the tribute due to his Grace's share in the victory, and the Monument as that which is to be paid to the Army'. This placed Galt in a difficult situation, as it eliminated several of the more common forms of monument. He dismissed the pillar as too focused on a singular individual, and likewise the triumphal arch which, he reminds his readers, originally 'marked the way by which the hero was conducted into the Capitol'. If a 'singular colossal statue' was settled on, it had to be allegorical, but here again difficulties presented themselves, as 'allegories, by requiring explanations, are liable to be misunderstood'. Finally Galt settled on a vast sarcophagus, 70 feet square, placed on a 100-foot square pedestal, the whole monument rising 200 feet into the London sky. Both pedestal and sarcophagus would be decorated with bas-reliefs, highlighting the greatness of both the triumph and the sacrifice required to gain it, while inside the sarcophagus tablets would list the names of fallen soldiers by regiment, 'while statues and busts of the officers, to be placed there by their friends, would appropriately furnish this solemn apartment'.[2]

Galt was far from the only person considering the wider implications of an official monument to Waterloo. The painter and dramatist Prince Hoare the Younger debated with the architect and surveyor Ignatius Bonomi whether the monument should properly celebrate the 'peace of the world', the 'people of England', or even the 'Majesty of National Virtue'.[3] Robert Smirke declared that it had to privilege Britain's 'benevolent and liberal feeling' and the 'sobriety of our

---

[1] Chantrey was one of the leading portrait sculptors of the day, notable for his successes on both sides of the Atlantic. See *Citizens and Kings: Portraits in the Age of Revolution, 1760–1830* (London: Royal Academy of Arts, 2007), 302.

[2] 'Letter I. Of a Series on Monumental Sculpture and Architecture, addressed to F. L. Chantrey, Esq. Sculptor. By John Galt, Esq.', *Annals of the Fine Arts* (London: Sherwood, Neely, and Jones, 1817), I: 66–9.

[3] Prince Hoare to Ignatius Bonomi, 10 April 1816, Cambridge University Library, University of Cambridge, Cambridge, UK, Add. 9389/6/H/16. Quoted in Holger Hoock, *Empires of the Imagination: Politics, War, and the Arts in the British World, 1750–1850* (London: Profile Books, 2010), 362.

Who Owned Waterloo? Battle, Memory, and Myth in British History, 1815–1852. Luke Reynolds, Oxford University Press.
© Luke Reynolds 2022. DOI: 10.1093/oso/9780192864994.003.0007

national character', even as 'Publius' insisted the monument had to, above all, deliver a 'perpetual assurance of patriotism [and] a perpetual warning to tyranny'.[4] These artistic questions were soon complicated by political and financial ones: why Waterloo instead of another battle or the Napoleonic Wars in general? What about the navy? And, always, what about the cost? Because these were multi-year projects there was ample time for politics, finance, or even lethargy to interfere, and all of them did. The result was that the truly lasting physical commemorations to Waterloo came in the form of namings and privately funded structures, while the best known and publicly funded monuments were, just as Galt had feared, dedicated to individuals, most notably the Duke of Wellington. Wellington, in this case perhaps above all others, became the avatar of British victory in the Napoleonic Wars, and celebrations of the man bypassed the traditional questions of picking specific battles or privileging one branch of service over another. The only hero who could come close to Wellington in the public imagination was Admiral Nelson, and he received his own share of statues, columns, and monuments, which both celebrated his accomplishments and reinforced Britain's continued sense of itself as the foremost naval power in the world.

The choice to ignore the artistic debate on the meaning of commemoration left monuments, in the design phase and once erected, vulnerable to the dangers of domestic politics and personal agendas. Despite the pride the British felt for their achievement at Waterloo, inevitably it was politics and finance that came to dominate the permanent physical commemoration of the victory. Monuments to individuals could be justified as celebrations of their life's work and dedication, which allowed those financing and building such tributes to avoid picking sides in international and service political disagreements. As Lord Carlisle, the Lord Lieutenant of Ireland, put it when considering what battles to immortalize on the Wellington Testimonial in Dublin, 'one licking of the French will be quite enough, especially in these days of close alliance'.[5] The embodiment of victory in a 'Great Man' allowed the celebration of military victories without publicly illustrating their cost or violence, encouraged the burgeoning mania for hero worship, and met with approval from a monarchy that was itself learning to manipulate such monuments and embodiments.[6] An inevitable corollary of this, of course, was the use of these monuments as tools of domestic political agendas. The Dublin Wellington Testimonial and the Wellington Column in Trim reinforced Wellington's Irish birth and heritage, while the Wellington statues in Edinburgh

[4] Royal Institute of British Architects, London, UK, MSS SmK2/17, quoted in Holger Hoock, *The King's Artists: The Royal Academy of Arts and the Politics of British Culture 1760–1840* (Oxford: Clarendon Press, 2003), 275–6; 'Publius, Letter I on the Waterloo Monument', *Annals of the Fine Arts* (London: Sherwood, Neely, and Jones, 1818), II: 146.

[5] Quoted in P. F. Garnett, 'The Wellington Testimonial', *Dublin Historical Record* 13, no. 2 (June–August 1952): 59.

[6] For nineteenth-century British hero worship, see Chapter 3. For the monarchy's embracing of embodiment, see Hoock, *Empires of the Imagination*, chapter 9.

and Glasgow were open attempts to celebrate and preserve Tory influence in Scotland.[7] Not all monuments were so successful, however. The 1822 Wellington Monument scandalized London with its nearly nude depiction of Achilles, while the 1846 equestrian statue of the duke was widely criticized for both the committee's corruption when choosing a sculptor and its final placement on the Pimlico/ Wellington Arch.[8] Across the Irish Sea, cursed by poorly managed finances and tied inextricably to Wellington's own politics, the Wellington Testimonial in Dublin took longer to construct than the Revolutionary and Napoleonic Wars took to fight.[9]

The popularity of Wellington as a subject and the central location of many of these monuments has resulted in them receiving a significant amount of scholarly attention. In addition to scholarship dedicated to the individual structures and works of art, they have been discussed at length in the various military, political, and cultural biographies of Wellington himself.[10] Instead of retreading this ground, this chapter will adopt a wider lens in its consideration of monuments and physical commemoration. The first half of the chapter will focus on the most common form of semi-permanent commemoration throughout Great Britain: the naming of establishments, buildings, streets, and even conveyances. It will start with the opening of the best-known example of this phenomenon: London's

[7] Garnett, 'The Wellington Testimonial'; J. E. Cookson, 'The Edinburgh and Glasgow Duke of Wellington Statues: Early Nineteenth-Century Unionist Nationalism as a Tory Project', *The Scottish Historical Review* 83, no. 215 (April 2004): 23–40. Coverage of the Wellington Testimonial highlighted that the entire cost of the project (£20,000) was 'raised from private funds, and every subscriber an Irishman'. 'The Wellington Testimonial', *Morning Post*, 18 August 1818, p. 3.

[8] See 'Statue to the Duke of Wellington in Hyde Park', *The Gentleman's Magazine: and Historical Chronicle* (London: John Nichols and Son, 1822), XCII: 70–1; George Cruikshank, *Making Decent!!* (London: The British Museum, 1822, BM Satires 1868,0808.8555); George Cruikshank, *Backside & Front View of the Ladies Fancy-Man, Paddy Carey O'Killus, Esq.*, 1822, Washington DC, Library of Congress, PC 1–14376; F. Darrell Munsell, *The Victorian Controversy Surrounding the Wellington War Memorial: The Archduke of Hyde Park Corner* (Lewiston: The Edwin Mellen Press, 1991); John Physick, *The Wellington Monument* (London: Her Majesty's Stationary Office, 1970). According to legend, Wellington's statue looked so ridiculous on the arch that a French officer upon seeing it for the first time declared, 'Nous sommes vengés.' H. V. Morton, *In Search of London* (Cambridge: Da Capo Press, 2002), 316.

[9] The project ran out of money in 1819. Wellington's support of Catholic Emancipation prompted the creation of an Emancipation Testimonial Fund that aimed to finish it, but financial goodwill evaporated following Wellington's opposition of the Great Reform Act in 1832. The testimonial was finally finished in 1861, forty-four years after the first stone was laid. By then it was not a testimonial, but a memorial, and it never received the equestrian statue of the duke nor the two guardian lions that were planned. Garnett, 'The Wellington Testimonial', 50, 54–6, 61; 'The Wellington Testimonial', *Morning Post*, 18 August 1818, p. 3.

[10] Garnett, 'The Wellington Testimonial'; Cookson, 'The Edinburgh and Glasgow Duke of Wellington Statues'; Munsell, *The Victorian Controversy Surrounding the Wellington War Memorial*; Physick, *The Wellington Monument*; R. E. Foster, *Wellington and Waterloo: The Duke, The Battle and Posterity, 1815–2015* (Staplehurst: Spellmount, 2014); Rory Muir, *Wellington: Waterloo and the Fortunes of Peace, 1814–1852* (New Haven: Yale University Press, 2015); Neville Thompson, *Wellington After Waterloo* (London: Routledge & Kegan Paul, Ltd, 1986). See also Alison Willow Yarrington, 'The Commemoration of the Hero 1800–1864: Monuments to the British Victors of the Napoleonic Wars', Ph.D. dissertation, University of Cambridge, 1980.

Waterloo Bridge. From there it will cast a wider net to encompass hotels, pubs, streets, and towns, all named for Waterloo. The second half of the chapter discusses physical commemoration on a more personal level, examining Waterloo in widespread material culture. Starting with the official governmental and unofficial collectors' medals, it then moves into commemorations in fashion and everyday goods such as snuff, games, and household items. Through this eclectic focus, it will argue that Waterloo itself received both more and less commemoration than is generally believed. By the strict standard of dedicated monuments, Waterloo remains virtually unmarked within Britain. By turning away from the statues of Wellington, however, and instead examining more utilitarian (and inevitably proletarian) constructions, a very different picture of commemoration appears. The naming of utilitarian structures such as bridges, pubs, hotels, and even streets and neighbourhoods after Waterloo and the creation of Waterloo souvenirs and merchandise available to the general populace served not only as an effective form of permanent (or at least semi-permanent) commemoration, but also as an extremely effective, widespread, and almost entirely uncontested form of nationalization. Waterloo remained something to be celebrated and commemorated but was divorced from the 'Great Men' of the battle and sometimes even the ordinary soldiers themselves.

This trajectory further highlights the progressive nationalization Waterloo underwent in Britain in the first half of the nineteenth century. The rhetoric and celebrations surrounding the opening of Waterloo Bridge reinforced British ownership of Waterloo, deliberately privileging British achievements over those of her allies, and positioning the bridge as grander and better constructed than anything like it on the Continent. The naming of businesses and streets by individuals and local governmental organizations, as well as individual commemoration of Waterloo through souvenirs, took that nationalization beyond international rivalries and towards the kind of national and civilian ownership and curation discussed in earlier chapters. It is no accident that this form of commemoration reinforced British beliefs in their own national superiority: a bridge, hotel, neighbourhood, or even schooner bearing the name Waterloo was seen as a much more tasteful and utilitarian expression of national pride than the gaudy columns and triumphal arches favoured by the continental powers.

In an excoriating letter published in the 16 January 1816 issue of *Cobbett's Weekly Political Register*, the editor, William Cobbett, took London's 'Boroughmongers' to task for their lack of promised monuments. 'What are become of your intended *Pillars* and *Triumphal Arches?* Early in 1816 you talked very big on this subject. You voted millions ... to build a brace or two of "solemn temples" with "cloud-capp'd" towers. In sober sadness, tho', are all these really sunk down into a "*Waterloo Bridge*," built by private speculators? Your folly marks you out for the contempt of mankind: your injustice and cruelty for its hatred.'[11] Cobbett's scorn may appear overly vitriolic, but his surprise was warranted. News of the Battle of Waterloo had been greeted across Britain with calls for permanent monuments to the triumph. Precisely two weeks after the battle, the House of Commons unanimously passed a call to the prince regent 'that he will be graciously pleased to give directions that a National Monument be erected in honour of the splendid victory of Waterloo, and to commemorate the fame of the Officers and Men of the British Army, who fell gloriously upon the 16th and 18th of the present month...and to assure his Royal Highness that this House will make good the expense attending the same'.[12]

Suggestions for said 'National Monument' poured in, ranging from calls for a traditional column or obelisk to more creative ideas. These included two crescent-shaped barracks in Regent's Park named respectively Waterloo and La Belle Alliance; the creation of a home for the widows of the battle, funded by the sale of patriotic works from the country's great artists; or a British Pantheon with 'ample space for a Memorial either by painting, statuary, or inscription of every individual whereof the army was composed'.[13] Benjamin Dean Wyatt, the architect who would redesign Apsley house for Wellington and create the Waterloo Gallery, proposed a giant tiered pyramid, as tall as St Paul's Cathedral and filling all of what is now Trafalgar Square, with a step for every year of the conflict, going so far as to try and enlist the prince regent's backing by sending him a watercolour of the design (Figure 6.1).[14] One of the most ambitious plans, put forward by the artist Andrew Robertson, combined several of these ideas. It called for an entire complex to be erected on and around Primrose Hill, containing an asylum, palaces for the prince regent and the Duke of Wellington, and, at its centre, a rebuilt Parthenon, celebrating both the army and the navy and incorporating the portions of the original Parthenon already in British possession.[15] Between these structures would be a 'cemetery for those who fought in the war' and pleasure grounds laid out 'for fêtes to celebrate the battle of Waterloo, and one other victory each year in rotation on its anniversary'.[16]

---

[11] Emphasis in original. 'To the Boroughmongers', *Cobbett's Weekly Political Register* 34, no. 17, 16 January 1816, 536.

[12] House of Commons Debate, 29 June 1815, Historic Hansard, vol. 31, columns 1048–57. <https://api.parliament.uk/historic-hansard/commons/1815/jun/29/address-for-a-national-monument-and>. There is some evidence that the budget proposed was up to £500,000. Frederic Wordsworth Haydon, ed., *Benjamin Robert Haydon: Correspondence and Table-Talk* (London: Chatto and Windus, 1876), 92.

[13] 'Monument of Waterloo', *Morning Post*, 29 July 1815, p. 4; 'The Fine Arts and Waterloo', *Morning Post*, 2 January 1816, p. 3; 'Waterloo Monument', *The Times*, 19 January 1816, p. 3.

[14] Felix Barker and Ralph Hyde, *London as it Might Have Been* (London: John Murray, 1982), 68–9.

[15] Andrew Robertson to John Ewen, 22 May 1816, *Letters and Papers of Andrew Robertson, A.M.*, ed. Emily Robertson (London: Eyre and Spottiswoode, 1895), 280.

[16] Andrew Robertson to John Ewen, 22 May 1816 and 24 July 1816, *Letters and Papers of Andrew Robertson*, 280–1. For further examples of some of the more ambitious plans, including several illustrations, see Barker and Hyde, *London as it Might Have Been*, 68–72.

Figure 6.1 After Benjamin Dean Wyatt, *Design for a pyramid commemorating the Napoleonic Wars*, 1815. Royal Collection Trust/© Her Majesty Queen Elizabeth II 2021.

The Times, with less ambition but foresight bordering on the supernatural, suggested a 'large Triumphal Arch ... surmounted with an equestrian statue of the great Conqueror ... placed at a principle entrance into the metropolis (Hyde-park corner, for instance)'.[17] Their suggestion not only anticipated the construction of the Pimlico/Wellington Arch in the 1820s and the addition of an equestrian statue of Wellington in 1846, but also the British press's tendency to use their coverage of monuments to remind their readers of national superiority. The editorial concluded with the argument that an arch 'would be a perpetual record before the eyes of all classes of people, telling it's tale plainly, with less ostentation, but with far more effect, than the laboured and boasting Column in Paris'.[18] Outside the capital, several privately funded 'boasting Columns' were already in the works. Within two months of the battle, the foundations had been laid for a monumental pillar located on Penhil-heuch Hill (Peniel Heugh) in Roxburghshire in the Scottish Borders, 'dedicated to the Duke of Wellington and the British army, by the Marquis of Lothian and his tenants', while a subscription was started soon

---

[17] 'London, Monday, June 26, 1815', *The Times*, 26 June 1815, p. 3.
[18] 'London, Monday, June 26, 1815', *The Times*, 26 June 1815, p. 3. This is most likely a reference to the Vendôme Column erected by Napoleon to celebrate his victory at Austerlitz. *The Times* conveniently forgot to mention the Arc de Triomphe du Carrousel, also erected by Napoleon between 1806 and 1808 to celebrate his victories.

after for 'the erection of a Column or Monument' to be placed on Blackdown Hill, two miles south of the Somerset town of Wellington.[19]

Despite unsolicited suggestions and multiple private ventures, however, no official or public monument was finalized in the heady months immediately following the victory. It took until January 1816 for announcements to appear in the popular press, calling for the artists of the United Kingdom to submit their 'models and designs for [a] National Monument' by 1 May.[20] Even as the first designs were being submitted, Robert Stewart, Viscount Castlereagh, then leader of the House of Commons in Lord Liverpool's Tory government, discovered that Parliament's original unanimity had fractured. Objections to the cost and demands for a similar monument to the naval victory at Trafalgar had emerged, as had voices arguing that it would be more fitting for the government to raise a monument (one MP suggested a church) to the general service of the army and navy over the past quarter-century of war rather than celebrating specific victories.[21] After Castlereagh promised an equally magnificent monument to Trafalgar and reassured the House that neither would cost the £2 million that one MP feared, both monuments were left in the theoretically safe hands of the Committee of Taste.[22] Roughly 200 designs were submitted over the next year before the committee finally unanimously selected the proposal submitted by William Wilkins and John P. Gandy in early 1817.[23] With an estimated budget of £180,000, Wilkins's and Gandy's design called for a heavily embellished 'ornamental tower of 3 orders of columns', rising some 280 feet, surrounded by a 'circular colonnade'.[24] It was to be built in the circle where Portland Place met

---

[19] *Caledonian Mercury*, 24 July 1815, p. 3; 'Waterloo Monument', *Morning Post*, 20 January 1816, p. 3. According to local legend, a more arboreal tribute was created at Longueville House in County Cork, Ireland, where two lines of oak trees were planted, supposedly in the same positions as the allied and French armies on the morning of 18 June. However, I can find no definitive proof that this is so. Social and Architectural History of Longueville, Longueville House, <https://www.longuevillehouse. ie/longueville-house-environmental-practice-and-ethos-copy1.html>.

[20] *Morning Chronicle*, 15 January 1816, p. 1; *Morning Post*, 16 January 1816, p. 1.

[21] In this certain Members of Parliament were remarkably prescient, as an almost identical controversy would emerge over the Waterloo Medal and the Military General Service Medal. 'Parliamentary Intelligence', *The Times*, 6 February 1816, p. 2.

[22] In fact, the Chancellor of the Exchequer insisted that the combined bill for both monuments had to be under £300,000. Committee of Taste to the Lords Commissioners of His Majesty's Treasury, 4 April 1818, Treasury Long Papers bundle 519: National Monuments, London, National Archives, T 1/4029.6968. The Committee of Taste had been established in 1802 to curate the monuments placed in St Paul's Cathedral. 'Parliamentary Intelligence', *The Times*, 6 February 1816, p. 2; 'National Monuments', *Royal Cornwall Gazette*, 14 June 1817, p. 4; Foster, *Wellington and Waterloo*, 98–9.

[23] William Wilkins and John P. Gandy to the Lords Commissioners of His Majesty's Treasury, 20 December 1827, Treasury Long Papers bundle 519: National Monuments, London, National Archives, T 1/4029.6968; *The Times*, 30 May 1817, p. 2. Models were to be sent to the British Gallery, Pall Mall, while designs were destined for the Army Pay Office, Whitehall. *Morning Post*, 2 February 1816, p. 1.

[24] William Wilkins and John P. Gandy to the Lords Commissioners of His Majesty's Treasury, 20 December 1827, Treasury Long Papers bundle 519: National Monuments, London, National Archives, T 1/4029.6968; *The Times*, 6 June 1817, p. 3. This left only £120,000 for the Trafalgar Monument.

the New Road (Park Crescent/Park Square today), facing Regent's Park, while the Trafalgar Monument, of equal height, was to be placed in Greenwich, the Navy's spiritual home in London.[25] Work, reported the *Royal Cornwall Gazette*, was to begin immediately, in an attempt to employ the 'multitude of workmen in the Metropolis, at present without the means of gaining their subsistence'.[26]

These grand promises and good intentions notwithstanding, the work never began. Neither monument was ever built and there remains no definitive record as to why.[27] Even Wilkins and Gandy had no idea, stating in an 1827 attempt to recoup their losses from the failed project that they simply learned 'that the intention of building these monuments having been abandoned through various causes'.[28] Some scholars have argued the plans failed for financial reasons, or that peace brought new priorities, while others suggest disagreements over design.[29] Whatever the cause, the result of this failure was that the first widely celebrated permanent and public monument to the Battle of Waterloo on British soil was not a soaring column, faux-classical temple, giant pyramid, or ornamental tower, but a much-needed, relatively plain bridge across the Thames, privately funded and approved when Napoleon was still feared across Europe and the village of Waterloo was just one more stop on the Brussels to Namur road.[30]

The first stone of what was then called the Strand Bridge was laid on 11 October 1811 and the bridge was more than half finished when news of the Battle of

---

[25] Despite being of equal height, the Trafalgar Monument, designed by Robert Smirke, was simpler. It comprised 'a plain octangular structure, 45 feet in diameter at the base, raised upon a magnificent flight of steps, and surmounted with a naval coronet'. *The Times*, 3 June 1817, p. 3; *The Times*, 6 June 1817, p. 3; 'National Monuments', *Royal Cornwall Gazette*, 14 June 1817, p. 4.

[26] Some of whom, almost certainly, were discharged soldiers. 'National Monuments', *Royal Cornwall Gazette*, 14 June 1817, p. 4.

[27] Foster, *Wellington and Waterloo*, 100.

[28] William Wilkins and John P. Gandy to the Lords Commissioners of His Majesty's Treasury, 20 December 1827, Treasury Long Papers bundle 519: National Monuments, London, National Archives, T 1/4029.6968.

[29] Hoock, *Empires of the Imagination*, 362; Hoock, *The King's Artists*, 275; Elisa Milkes, 'A Battle's Legacy: Waterloo in Nineteenth Century Britain', Ph.D. dissertation, Yale University, 2002, chapter 6; Yarrington, 'The Commemoration of the Hero', chapter 6; J. W. M. Hichberger, *Images of the Army: The Military in British Art, 1815–1914* (Manchester: Manchester University Press, 1988), 11–12; There is only one mention of the monuments in the British press after June 1817, and that was by a regular letter-writer to *The Times*, Septimus, who mentions them in passing in October 1819, more as an abstract concept than a reality. 'To the Editor of The Times', *The Times*, 27 October 1819, p. 3. Hoping to fill the gap, the architect Samuel Benwell submitted a fresh idea to the Duke of York in 1820, while the artist John Martin exhibited a design for a triumphal arch over Portland Place at the Royal Academy's summer exhibition the same year. Samuel Benwell, *Design for a monument to commemorate the Battle of Waterloo* (London: S. Benwell, 1820); John Martin, View of a design for a national monument, 1820, London, The British Museum, 1867,0309.1706. By January 1824 it seems that there was general acknowledgement that they would never be built, as a statue of the late Prince Edward, Duke of Kent and Strathearn, was erected on Park Crescent, Portland Place, instead. *Cumberland's Lives & Portraits of Public Characters* (London: John Cumberland, 1828), III, entry for Edward Augustus Duke of Kent.

[30] Waterloo Bridge cannot claim to be the first public monument to Waterloo, as Waterloo Place, discussed later in the chapter, had opened two months earlier.

Waterloo reached London.[31] As it was the most sizeable public structure then being constructed (its nature as a privately funded toll bridge notwithstanding) 'the natural and patriotic desire of commemorating, in the most noble public manner, the ever-memorable victory of Waterloo, afforded a fine opportunity for changing its appellation from that of the street merely into which it opens'.[32] The name was changed by act of Parliament in 1816, thus cementing the bridge as the best-known early public monument to the battle.[33]

Throughout the nineteenth century, London bridge openings followed a pattern marked by grand processions across the new bridge, the shutting down of nearly all commerce on the Thames, and Londoners' general delight in witnessing (and thus participating in) the spectacle. The opening of Waterloo Bridge was marked by all of these characteristics: the river and the portions of the city that overlooked it were packed, flags flew from every tall structure, and an amphibious procession headed by the prince regent was meticulously choreographed to declare the bridge open.[34] Replace the prince regent with his younger brother William IV, however, and that description works just as well for the opening of the New London Bridge in 1831 as it does for the opening of Waterloo Bridge in 1817.[35] As spectacular as the opening was, we must explore what precisely put 'Waterloo' in Waterloo Bridge.

The most obvious connection to the battle was the date chosen for the formal opening: 18 June 1817, the second anniversary of the Battle of Waterloo. Beyond the choice of date, other references to the battle were incorporated into the ceremony. The royal standard and flags of Britain and London were supplemented by those of Britain's Waterloo allies: Prussia, the Netherlands, and the flag of the House of Orange. Despite this nod to diplomacy, the flags of the allies were decisively outnumbered.[36] The contributions of Britain's allies were already being deliberately diminished in the eyes of the British public during the early years of Waterloo's transformation into a solely national victory. All nineteenth-

---

[31] Waterloo Bridge is located almost precisely halfway between Westminster Bridge and Blackfriars Bridge. *Descriptions to the Plates of Thames Scenery. Engraved by W. B. Cooke & G. Cooke, from the Original Drawings by Eminent Artists* (London: John Murray, 1818), no page numbers, entry for Waterloo Bridge; *Leigh's New Picture of London: Or, a View of the Political, Religious, Medical, Literary, Municipal, Commercial, and Moral State of the British Metropolis* (London: Samuel Leigh, 1820), 268; *London and its Environs; or, the General Ambulator and Pocket Companion for the* Tour of the Metropolis and its Vicinity (London: Scatcherd and Letterman, 1820), 73–4; Samuel Smiles, *Lives of Engineers* (London: John Murray, 1874), 267.

[32] 'Waterloo-Bridge', *The Times*, 19 June 1817, p. 3.   [33] *Leigh's New Picture of London*, 268.

[34] 'Opening of Waterloo Bridge', *Morning Chronicle*, 19 June 1817, p. 3; 'Waterloo-Bridge', *The Times*, 19 June 1817, p. 3.

[35] For comparison, see 'Opening of the New London Bridge', *The Times*, 2 August 1831, p. 3; 'Opening of London Bridge', *Morning Post*, 2 August 1831, p. 3. The Southwark Bridge was also opened by 'Grand Procession' in 1819. 'Southwark Bridge', *Morning Post*, 17 March 1819, p. 4.

[36] Waterloo Bridge alone flew eighteen flags. 'London, Thursday 19 June', *Norfolk Chronicle*, 21 June 1817, p. 2; R. Ackermann, *His Royal Highness The Prince Regent's, the Duke of Wellington's, &c. &c. first Visit to Waterloo Bridge on the 18th June, 1817*, 1817, London, The British Museum, Prints & Drawings, R, 9.39.

century public events in Britain graced by the monarchy incorporated some military element, if only in a security and support role, but the Waterloo Bridge opening, as befitting its namesake, was more militaristic than most. The opening was preceded by 'a party of the Horse Guards', 'all Waterloo men ... in gay and gallant uniform', wearing their Waterloo Medals and laurel wreaths, taking 'possession of the bridge'.[37] They were soon joined by the band and an honour guard of the Foot Guards and a detachment of the Royal Horse Artillery with twenty field guns.[38] Those field pieces were supplemented by 'a large cannon, taken at the great battle ... placed on some flag stones on the Bridge'.[39] The firepower was not just for display, but to provide ceremonial cover fire for the prince regent and his party, who made their way from Fife House in Whitehall to the bridge on the royal barge.[40] The barrage covered the barge's entire trip down the Thames, firing off a grand total of 202 shots—one for every enemy gun captured on the field of Waterloo.[41] Upon arriving at the bridge, the party ascended the stairs and were greeted by the bridge's construction committee, paid their tolls (one penny per foot passenger), and walked across the bridge. The prince regent obviously took centre stage, but he was accompanied on one side by his brother Field Marshal the Duke of York, commander-in-chief of the forces, and on the other by Field Marshal the Duke of Wellington. He was also surrounded fore and aft by military might, in the form of a guard of honour that preceded him and a collection of 'other great military characters and Officers of State', following in his wake.[42] Having crossed the bridge the prince regent and his party descended again to their barge and returned to Whitehall, once more saluted by the guns of the Royal Horse Artillery and the captured cannon.[43] With the royal party safely returned to Whitehall the military retreated, taking their cannon with them, and London's newest bridge was thrown open to the paying public at seven that same evening.[44]

[37] 'Opening of Waterloo Bridge', Morning Chronicle, 19 June 1817, p. 3; 'Opening of Waterloo Bridge', Lancaster Gazetter, 21 June 1817, p. 2.

[38] 'Waterloo Bridge', Northampton Mercury, 21 June 1817, p. 2.

[39] 'Topographical Outline of the Ancient and Present state of the Savoy', La Belle Assemblée; For July, 1817, no. 95, 21.

[40] 'Waterloo-Bridge', The Times, 19 June 1817, p. 3; 'Topographical Outline of the Ancient and Present state of the Savoy', La Belle Assemblée; For July, 1817, no. 95, 21; 'Opening of Waterloo Bridge', Morning Chronicle, 19 June 1817, p. 3.

[41] 'Opening of Waterloo Bridge', Morning Chronicle, 19 June 1817, p. 3; Descriptions to the Plates of Thames Scenery, no page numbers, entry for Waterloo Bridge.

[42] The Picture of London for 1820 (London: Longman, Hurst, Rees, Orme, and Brown, 1820), 190; 'Topographical Outline of the Ancient and Present state of the Savoy', La Belle Assemblée; For July, 1817, no. 95, 21; 'Waterloo-Bridge', The Times, 10 June 1817, p. 3; 'Opening of Waterloo Bridge', Morning Chronicle, 19 June 1817, p. 3.

[43] 'Waterloo-Bridge', The Times, 19 June 1817, p. 3; 'Opening of Waterloo Bridge', Morning Chronicle, 19 June 1817, p. 3.

[44] 'Waterloo-Bridge', The Times, 19 June 1817, p. 3; 'Opening of Waterloo Bridge', Morning Chronicle, 19 June 1817, p. 3; 'London, Thursday June 19', Norfolk Chronicle, 21 June 1817, p. 2; 'Waterloo Bridge', Morning Post, 18 June 1817, p. 1; 'Waterloo Bridge', Morning Chronicle, 18 June

Among the first to use the bridge were those returning home after the Waterloo Day revels. In addition to the Grand Ball at Almack's and the first Vauxhall Waterloo fete, the Royal Circus and Surrey Theatre recognized the opportunity presented by the opening of Waterloo Bridge.[45] Located on what is now St George's Circus, less than a mile south of the bridge, the management hoped the new Thames crossing would lure fashionable theatregoers from the West End to their performances. Taking advantage of its history as a hippodrome, they offered the London public 'a new occasional Burletta Spectacle, under the title of *Waterloo Bridge*, or *The Anniversary.*—In the course of the Piece will be introduced a View, from Somerset House Terrace, of Four Principle Arches of the New Bridge, with the Grand Processional Cavalcade.' Here again the connection to the battle was made clear, not only with the alternative title/subtitle, '*The Anniversary*', but also by the management's decision to conclude the performance 'with a Magnificent Panorama... of The Battle of Waterloo, as the climax of the contest'.[46] The strategy was a success, as the *Morning Post* reported on 21 June that 'the anniversary of Waterloo has not been celebrated any where with more spirit than at the Surrey Theatre, which distinguished itself by the production of a Piece on the subject ... [which was] received with universal and reiterated plaudits'.[47]

While the Surrey Theatre seems to have been the only institution to construct a replica of Waterloo Bridge for their stage, their spectacle was not the only attempt to commemorate the opening of the bridge. In honour of the day, the prince regent commissioned Thomas Wyon Jr., Chief Engraver of the Royal Mint and designer of the Waterloo Medal, to create a new medal, with the prince's likeness on the obverse and the standard of the United Kingdom on the reverse.[48] This medal, struck from the silver remaining from the production of the Waterloo Medal, was presented by the prince to 'every Proprietor' of the bridge as well as, in all likelihood, many of the notable figures who attended the opening ceremony.[49] For those lacking the social connections to obtain a medal, the printmaker and publisher Rudolph Ackermann offered a commemorative print, *His Royal Highness The Prince Regent's, the Duke of Wellington's, &c. &c. first Visit to Waterloo Bridge on the 18th June, 1817* (Figure 6.2). Priced at 4s. in colour, the seven and a half by eleven and a half inch print boasted a dramatic view of the

---

1817, p. 1. The prince regent journeyed onward from Whitehall to Windsor, to attend 'the grand Ball and Supper given by the Officers of the Royal Horse Guards in honour of the victory of Waterloo' discussed in Chapter 3. 'Opening of Waterloo Bridge', *Morning Chronicle*, 19 June 1817, p. 3.

[45] 'Fashionable World', *Morning Post*, 16 June 1817, p. 3.

[46] 'Royal Circus and Surrey Theatre', *Morning Post*, 18 June 1817, p. 1; 'Positively for Two Nights Only', *Morning Chronicle*, 16 June 1817, p. 3.

[47] *Morning Post*, 21 June 1817, p. 2.

[48] 'Memoir of the late Thomas Wyon, Jun. Esq.', *The Gentleman's Magazine*, February 1818, p. 183; Leonard Forrer, *Biographical Dictionary of Medallists* (London: Spink & Son, Ltd, 1916), VI: 647.

[49] *The Repertory of Arts, Manufactures, and Agriculture* (London: J. Wyatt, 1817), II: XXXI, 85; Daniel Fearon, *Spink's Catalogue of British Commemorative Medals: 1588 to the Present Day, with Valuations* (Exeter: Webb & Bower, 1984), 60.

Figure 6.2 Rudolph Ackermann, *His Royal Highness The Prince Regent's, the Duke of Wellington's, &c. &c. first Visit to Waterloo Bridge on the 18th June, 1817*, 1817. Anne S. K. Brown Military Collection, John Hay Library, Brown University, Providence.

bridge from Somerset House.[50] Here again we find the connection to Waterloo emphasized through military spectacle and national pride. The foreground of the print is centred on the prince regent, the Duke of York, and the Duke of Wellington (distinguished by his nose), all in military uniform and surrounded by the Foot and Horse Guards. The flags of Britain fly proudly across the centre of the image, heavily outnumbering those of their allies, while the smoke of the Royal Horse Artillery can be seen rising from the centre spans. Spectators, brightly dressed in the foreground and an anonymous grey crowd everywhere else, fill the entire bridge, the banks of the Thames, and hang from the balconies of Somerset House. While Waterloo Bridge takes centre stage, it is the ceremony itself that is highlighted, with people, uniforms, and national pride superseding the architectural facets of the bridge. Indeed, if one is looking for a view of the complete bridge, the print does a much better job highlighting Westminster Bridge than it does Waterloo Bridge.

Britain's newspapers were quick to realize that the bridge's association with the battle allowed them a chance not only to exponentially reinforce national pride by

---

[50] Rudolph Ackermann, *His Royal Highness The Prince Regent's, the Duke of Wellington's, &c. &c. first Visit to Waterloo Bridge on the 18th June, 1817*, 1817, London, The British Museum, Prints & Drawings, R, 9.39; 'Works lately published by R. Ackermann', *The Quarterly Review*, October 1817, back matter.

celebrating bridge and battle simultaneously but also to praise their own national taste in eschewing the continental (read: French) fondness for ornamental pillars and arches for something of such great public utility. The magazine *La Belle Assemblée* compared the bridge with the Temple of Solomon and lauded it as 'the greatest, and...most permanent structure in the kingdom; well suited to com-memorate a victory, where the two greatest Captains of the age met to decide a contest that had lasted a quarter of a century'.[51] It was 'a model of national taste and grandeur', enthused *Trewman's Exeter Flying Post*, 'rising, like another Phœnix, to commemorate the last and grand achievement of British valour'.[52] Not to be outdone by the provincial and periodical press, one visual guide to London thundered that the bridge was 'framed to perpetuate through many an age the renown of that well fought field whose title it bears, by its masterly construc-tion, the durability of its materials, and the excellence of its workmanship: for what mind can anticipate the period when this stupendous chain of arches will yield to the ravages of time, whose power it seems to hold in stern defiance?'[53]

While some (such as the letter published in *Cobbett's Weekly Political Register* that opens this section) questioned why a bridge should commemorate such a victory, *The Times* insisted that its very purpose elevated the commemoration: 'No mode of perpetuating great deeds by works of art is more consistent with good taste than where such works combine, in a high degree, what is ornamental with what is useful. Monuments of this kind have stronger claims on public respect than the costly construction of pillars, obelisks, and towers.'[54] *Cobbett's Weekly Political Register* was forced to agree, and even they started using the bridge as an allegorical stand-in for the battle. In an October 1819 editorial addressed to Sir Robert Peel, *Cobbett's* argued that it was not Britain's military but financial might that had won the war, and that 'it ought not to be called "Waterloo Bridge;" but "Paper-money Bridge"'.[55]

Of course, such allegorical associations encouraged many publications to com-pare Waterloo Bridge to various bridges constructed in the French capital, with the same outcome as the battle for which the bridge was named. The technique used to shore up the bridge arches during construction had been employed on the Pont de Neuilly and several publications were delighted to report that the centres of Waterloo Bridge had dropped one inch when the supports were removed, versus eighteen inches in Paris.[56] *The Times* recognized that the most effective

---

[51] 'Topographical Outline of the Ancient and Present state of the Savoy', *La Belle Assemblée; For July, 1817*, no. 95, p. 19.

[52] 'Waterloo Bridge', *Trewman's Exeter Flying Post*, 19 June 1817, p. 3.

[53] The first Waterloo Bridge was severely damaged in 1884 and was demolished in the 1930s. *Descriptions to the Plates of Thames Scenery*, no page numbers, entry for Waterloo Bridge.

[54] 'Waterloo-Bridge', *The Times*, 19 June 1817, p. 3.

[55] 'To Sir Robert Peel', *Cobbett's Weekly Political Register* 35, no. 8, 9 October 1819, p. 233.

[56] *Leigh's New Picture of London*, 269–70; *London and its Environs*, 75; *Descriptions to the Plates of Thames Scenery*, no page numbers, entry for Waterloo Bridge.

comparison would not be to the Pont de Neuilly or the other new Parisian bridges, but to the Pont de Jena and the Pont d'Austerlitz, both constructed explicitly to honour French victories in the Napoleonic Wars. Despite the decisiveness of those victories, *The Times* was not impressed. 'Those bridges,' they declared, 'however elegant and convenient, are but trifles in civil architecture and engineering when compared with that which opened yesterday.'[57]

Despite the pomp of its opening, Waterloo Bridge was just one of many businesses, structures, and thoroughfares to be named in honour of the victory. On 27 December 1815, a little over six months after the Battle of Waterloo, a notification appeared on the front page of *The Morning Post*. J. Rowe, a former waiter at Watier's Gambling Club, 'beg[ged] leave most respectfully to inform the Nobility' that he had opened the Waterloo Hotel at 91 Jermyn Street, 'where every accommodation will be rendered, and the strictest attention paid, to those families and Gentlemen who may please to honour him with their favours'.[58] The hotel became an instant success, making regular appearances in the society columns of the *Morning Post*, the *Morning Chronicle*, and *The Times*.[59] Unsurprisingly, it was particularly favoured by military men travelling through London on their way to and from postings, especially during the years of the allied army of occupation of France.[60] It proved successful with civilians as well, serving as the London address of several lords and MPs, perhaps lured by the 'sumptuous' breakfasts it was known for.[61]

Mr Rowe's establishment on Jermyn Street may have been the first, but it was by no means the only Waterloo Hotel. Six months later, on the first anniversary of the battle, Thomas Roberts, late of the Bell and Antelope Inn, Holywell, threw open the doors of the Royal Waterloo Hotel on Crosby Sea Bank, some five miles north of Liverpool.[62] The Royal Waterloo Hotel had, like Waterloo Bridge, been

---

[57] 'Waterloo-Bridge', *The Times*, 19 June 1817, p. 3.

[58] *Morning Post*, 27 December 1815, p. 1. Watier's, known affectionately as the Dandies Club, was a short-lived gentlemen's club much in favour with the prince regent and his set, including Beau Brummell and Captain Rees Howell Gronow.

[59] See, for example, 'Fashionable World', *Morning Post*, 23 January 1816, p. 3; 'Mirror of Fashion', *Morning Chronicle*, 15 April 1816, p. 3; 'On Saturday Evening', *The Times*, 16 December 1818, p. 2.

[60] 'Fashionable World', *Morning Post*, 25 March 1816, p. 3; 'Fashionable Parties', *Morning Chronicle*, 5 August 1816, p. 3; 'Mirror of Fashion', *Morning Chronicle*, 12 August 1816, p. 3; 'Fashionable World', *Morning Post*, 26 August 1816, p. 3; 'Mirror of Fashion', *Morning Chronicle*, 3 October 1816, p. 2; 'Mirror of Fashion', *Morning Chronicle*, 26 October 1816, p. 2; 'Mirror of Fashion', *Morning Chronicle*, 20 November 1816, p. 3; 'Mirror of Fashion', *Morning Chronicle*, 9 September 1817, p. 3.

[61] *Transactions of the Society, Instituted at London, for the Encouragement of Arts, Manufactures, and Commerce* (London: Society for the Encouragement of Arts, Manufactures, and Commerce, 1821); *The Royal Kalendar: and Court and City Register, for England, Scotland, Ireland, and the Colonies, for the Year 1825* (London: William March & Son, 1825), 53; *The Royal Kalendar: and Court and City Register, for England, Scotland, Ireland, and the Colonies, for the Year 1840* (London: Suttaby & Co., 1840), 77. For the breakfasts, see Anglicanus, *View of the Character, Position, and Prospects of the Edinburgh Bible Society* (Edinburgh: Brown & Wardlaw, 1827), 46.

[62] *Chester Chronicle*, 7 June 1816, p. 1; *Chester Chronicle*, 14 June 1816, p. 2; *Liverpool Mercury*, 14 June 1816, p. 1.

planned before the battle, as the 'fine hard sands', clean air, and plentiful sea bathing were already attracting well-to-do Liverpudlians, but the victory proved too much of a lure, and so the Crosby Seabank Hotel became the Royal Waterloo Hotel.[63] Reading the anniversary mood with the skill of a seasoned publican, Mr Roberts debuted his hotel with a public dinner to celebrate 'the Splendid Victory of Waterloo'. Tickets were a guinea apiece, and transport was provided to and from Liverpool via the Leeds and Liverpool Canal Packet.[64] The *Liverpool Mercury* declared the event a great success, reporting that 'a greatly respectable party of Gentlemen assembled ... the dinner was very elegant and prepared with much taste by Mr. Roberts ... the wines were excellent, [and] the evening was spent with the greatest harmony and good humour. The party separated, highly delighted with the entertainment, and agreed to meet annually to celebrate the memorable day.'[65]

While the dinners were not hosted every year, the launch and occasional celebrations had the desired effect, and the Royal Waterloo Hotel and Crosby Sea Bank became a popular destination.[66] In 1817 a light post coach route was established between Liverpool and Crosby; christened 'The Waterloo', it completed the hour and a half trip each way daily.[67] Between the Waterloo Coach and the various canal and coastal packets, Crosby Sea Bank was an ideally situated coastal escape and began to expand, growing sufficiently that a new name was sought to differentiate it from Crosby.[68] Unsurprisingly, the area became known as Waterloo, an epithet the residents encouraged by naming a variety of streets after locations and heroes of the battle.[69] In 1841 the Liverpool merchant William Potter sought to take the connection even further by building a coastal estate with buildings that were replicas of notable buildings from the battlefield itself. While his business encountered financial problems before his plan was completed, Potter's Barn Park still houses a red sandstone gate house, coach house, and stables that closely resemble portions of the walled farmhouse of La Haye Sainte.[70]

[63] Thomas Baines, *History of the Commerce and Town of Liverpool, and of the Rise of Manufacturing Industry in the Adjoining Counties* (London: Longman, Brown, Green, and Longmans, 1852), 567–8. According to local legend, the first stone of the hotel was laid on 18 June 1815. 'The Battle of Waterloo: Merseyside township celebrates battle's bicentennial', *Liverpool Echo*, 12 June 2015, <https://www.liverpoolecho.co.uk/news/nostalgia/battle-waterloo-merseyside-township-celebrates-9400012>.

[64] *Liverpool Mercury*, 14 June 1816, p. 1.   [65] *Liverpool Mercury*, 21 June 1816, p. 6.

[66] So popular that, when a local railway was discussed in 1848, it was suggested that the Liverpool to Waterloo be prioritized as that route would help fund the rest of the project. 'Liverpool, Crosby, and Southport Railway', *Liverpool Mercury*, 4 January 1848, p. 5. 'Varieties, Local', *Liverpool Mercury*, 21 June 1822, p. 6; 'The Eighteenth of June', *Liverpool Mercury*, 20 June 1823, p. 8.

[67] *Liverpool Mercury*, 5 September 1817, p. 2. This was not the only coach named after the battle. See *Morning Post*, 5 February 1816, p. 1; William Parson and William White, *History, Directory, and Gazetteer of the Counties of Durham and Northumberland* (Leeds: Edward Waines and Son, 1827), I: 134.

[68] To meet growing demand, the hotel was expanded in 1821. *Liverpool Mercury*, 20 July 1821, p. 5.

[69] Richard Pollard and Nikolaus Pevsner, *Lancashire, Liverpool, and the South West* (New Haven: Yale University Press, 2006), 644.

[70] Pollard and Pevsner, *Lancashire, Liverpool, and the South West*, 579; Waterloo Heritage Trail pamphlet (London: Historic England, n.d.).

At least eight Waterloo Hotels operated across Great Britain between 1815 and 1850. In addition to the discussed hotels in London and Crosby Sea Bank/Waterloo, Waterloo Hotels were opened in Edinburgh, Durham, Leominster, Runcorn, and the Blyth suburb of Waterloo (which sought to be Northumberland's answer to Crosby).[71] Not content with the Royal Waterloo Hotel five miles to their north, Liverpool opened a Waterloo Hotel of its own on Ranelagh Street, which became a centre for the local horse racing scene, sponsoring the annual Waterloo Cup.[72] As popular as Waterloo hotels were, however, they were eclipsed by Waterloo inns, pubs, and taverns. At least forty of these sprang up in the years following the battle. Public establishments bearing the name Waterloo opened in the urban centres of London, Liverpool, Manchester, Sheffield, Birmingham, Glasgow, and Durham and across the country from north Wales to the Isle of Wight to the port cities of the north-east.[73] Arguably the most famous of these was the Heroes of Waterloo Inn in

[71] The Edinburgh Waterloo Hotel was purpose built and purported to cost between £22,000 and £30,000. 'Improvements in Edinburgh', *The Scots Magazine*, 1 March 1818, p. 88; *The Scots Magazine*, 1 October 1818, p. 84; *Morning Post*, 24 September 1823, p. 1; *Caledonian Mercury*, 15 June 1826, p. 3; J. Stark, *Picture of Edinburgh: Containing a Description of the City and its Environs* (Edinburgh: John Anderson, 1831), 90; Lord and Lady Stewart, *Morning Post*, 18 May 1819, p. 3; *Lancaster Gazetter*, 11 September 1819, p. 1; *The Publications of the Surtees Society* (Newcastle: J. Blackwell and Co., 1837), I: 261; *Leigh's New Pocket Road-Book of England and Wales* (London: Leigh and Son, 1837), 11; Samuel Bagshaw, *History, Gazetteer, and Directory of the County Palatine of Chester* (Sheffield: George Ridge, 1850), 576; Parson and White, *History of Durham and Northumberland*, I: 411–12; *Pigot and Co.'s National Commercial Directory for 1828–9* (London: J. Pigot & Co., 1829), 578; *The Jurist: Containing Reports of Cases Determined in Law and in Equity; and a General Digest of all the Cases Published and Statutes Passed during the Year 1840* (London: S. Sweet, 1841), IV: 712, 782.
[72] *Caledonian Mercury*, 27 May 1820, p. 2; *Liverpool Mercury*, 14 July 1820, p. 1; T. B. Johnson, ed., Sportsman's Cabinet and Town and Country Magazine (London: Sherwood, Gilbert, & Piper, 1833), I: 216, 223–4; George Rapalje, *A Narrative of Excursions, Voyages, and Travels, Performed at Different Periods in America, Europe, Asia, and Africa* (New York, West & Trow, 1834), 58; Boleyne Reeves, ed., *Coluburn's Kalendar of Amusements in Town and Country, for 1840* (London: Henry Colburn, 1840), 69; Delabere P. Blaine, *An Encyclopædia of Rural Sports* (London: Longman, Brown, Green, and Longmans, 1852), 588. Racing was not the only sport that honoured Waterloo. In the 1830s and 1840s cricket and rowing clubs called the Waterloo Club emerged. 'Cricket', *Leicester Chronicle*, 31 August 1839, p. 2; 'Sporting Intelligence', *Newcastle Journal*, 3 September 1842, p. 3; 'Aquatics', *The Era*, 28 July 1844, p. 12; 'Cricket', *The Era*, 11 August 1844, p. 7; 'Cricket', *Nottinghamshire Guardian*, 4 September 1851, p. 8.
[73] 'Scotch Bankrupts', *Caledonian Mercury*, 16 January 1817, p. 4; *Hampshire Courier*, 1 April 1816, p. 1; *Hampshire Telegraph and Sussex Chronicle*, 27 April 1818, p. 3; *Stamford Mercury*, 8 January 1819, pp. 2–3; *Liverpool Mercury*, 6 August 1819, p. 1; *Liverpool Mercury*, 24 September 1819, p. 1; *Newcastle Courant*, 20 February 1819, p. 3; 'Winchester, Saturday 10 March 1819', *Hampshire Telegraph and Sussex Chronicle*, 22 March 1819, p. 4; *Stamford Mercury*, 15 October 1819, p. 1; *Chester Chronicle*, 14 January 1820, p. 4; *Liverpool Mercury*, 14 April 1820, p. 1; *Liverpool Mercury*, 8 December 1820, p. '5; 'Lancaster, December 16, 1820, Married', *Lancaster Gazetter*, 16 December 1820, p. 3; 'Coroner's Inquest', *Morning Chronicle*, 25 April 1821, p. 3; *Berrow's Worcester Journal*, 28 March 1822, p. 2; *Berrow's Worcester Journal*, 16 May 1822, p. 2; 'Births, Deaths, Marriages and Obituaries', *Norfolk Chronicle*, 24 August 1822, p. 2; 'Loyal Orange Association', *Norfolk Chronicle*, 17 July 1824, p. 2; *Leeds Mercury*, 6 November 1824, p. 2; *Yorkshire Gazette*, 26 March 1825, p. 3; *Chester Chronicle*, 8 July 1825, p. 3; 'Died', *Jackson's Oxford Journal*, 8 October 1825, p. 3; 'Married', *Manchester Courier and Lancashire General Advertiser*, 28 January 1826, p. 3; 'Trial of Henry Childe', *Birmingham Gazette*, 3 April 1826, p. 2; 'Grand Procession', *Birmingham Gazette*, 27 November 1826, p. 1; *North Wales Chronicle*, 3 January 1828, p. 3; 'Marriages', *Sheffield Independent*, 13 September 1828, p. 3; Edward Baines, *History, Directory and Gazetteer, of the County of York* (Leeds: Edward Baines, 1822), I: 326,

Bere Forrest, Hampshire, eight miles north of Portsmouth, which opened shortly after the battle and took its name from it.[74] Local legend is divided on whether the name comes from a number of soldiers who had disembarked at Portsmouth and decided to break their journey north at the newly opened inn or if the name drew a number of veterans of the battle who decided to settle there, but the inn gave its name to the village of Waterloo that grew up around it.[75] The name was eventually changed to Waterlooville to avoid confusion with the Merseyside resort, but the town's identity remains linked to the battle, with the inn marking the anniversary with a dinner for many years.[76]

Commemoration of Waterloo was not limited to the hospitality industry. Numerous buildings and businesses were also named in the victory's honour. Stockport's pubs were supplied by the city's Waterloo Brewery, Sunderland offered the Waterloo Baths, Bradford's cloth was produced in the Waterloo Mill, Cork's glass in the Waterloo Glass House Company, Londoners danced in the Royal Waterloo Assembly Rooms, and industrialization came to the town of Andover in Hampshire in the form of the Waterloo Iron Works.[77] Waterloo became such a popular name for private houses and cottages that Mr Thomas Parker, one of the characters in Jane Austen's unfinished novel *Sanditon*, laments that he and his wife Mary named their house Trafalgar House, 'for Waterloo is more the thing now'.[78] He consoles himself, however, that 'Waterloo is in reserve... for a little crescent'.[79] Sanditon may have been fictional, but Waterloo Crescent was real. On 18 June 1817, the Town Steward of Truro, accompanied by the Corporation, laid the foundation stone for Wellington House, the centrepiece of the planned

489; Edward Baines, *History, Directory, and Gazetteer of the County Palatine of Lancaster* (Liverpool: William Wales & Co., 1824–1825), I: 605, II: 325; Parson & White, *History of Durham and Northumberland*, I: 221, 260, 271, 288, 297, 352, 412; *Pigot and Co.'s National Commercial Directory for 1828–9*, 578, 1147; Bagshaw, *History of Chester*, 98, 105, 114, 226, 242, 295, 689; *Slater's (Late Pigot & Co.) Royal National and Commercial Directory and Topography* (Manchester: Isaac Slater, 1852), Berkshire 51, Hampshire 33, 64, 123, Huntingdonshire, 6, Norfolk 88.

[74] *Hampshire Courier*, 1 April 1816, p. 1; *Hampshire Telegraph and Sussex Chronicle*, 20 March 1820, p. 1; *Hampshire Telegraph and Sussex Chronicle*, 17 January 1831, p. 4.

[75] Foster, *Wellington and Waterloo*, 98; Steve Jones, *The Early History of Waterlooville 1810–1910 and a History of the Forest of Bere* (Havant: Havant History Booklets, 2005), 22–3; Steve Jones, *The Public Houses and Inns of Waterlooville, Cowplain, Lovedean, Purbrook and Widley* (Havant: Havant History Booklets, 2005), 9.

[76] Jones, *The Public Houses and Inns of Waterlooville, Cowplain, Lovedean, Purbrook and Widley*, 9.

[77] Bagshaw, *History of Chester*, 294; Parson and White, *History of Durham and Northumberland*, I: 352; *Bradford Observer*, 18 June 1840, p. 2; Michael Seymour Dudley Westropp, *Irish Glass: An Account of Glass-Making in Ireland from the XVIth Century to the Present Day* (Philadelphia: J. B. Lippincott Company, 1921), 121–5; *Morning Post*, 2 June 1818, p. 1; *Slater's Commercial Directory*, Hampshire 9; L. T. C. Rolt, *Waterloo Ironworks: A History of Taskers of Andover, 1809–1968* (New York: A. M. Kelley, 1969).

[78] Jane Austen, *Lady Susan, The Watsons, Sanditon*, ed. Margaret Drabble (London: Penguin Books, 1974), 169; William White, *History, Gazetteer, and Directory of Norfolk* (Sheffield: Robert Leader, 1836), 399; Bagshaw, *History of Chester*, 250, 576; *History, Gazetteer, and Directory of Cambridgeshire* (Peterborough: Robert Gardner, 1851), xiv; *Slater's Commercial Directory*, Berkshire 19, 34, 57, Huntingdonshire 15.

[79] Austen, *Lady Susan, The Watsons, Sanditon*, 169.

fifteen-house 'addition to the beauty of this town', to commemorate 'England's triumph and Europe's deliverance', named, naturally, Waterloo Crescent.[80]

It is unclear if Austen was directly inspired by Truro, or if she was simply using *Sanditon* to comment on a national trend, for streets were just as popular as other forms of commemoration. London and Edinburgh led the way with their fashionable Waterloo Places. Conceived by the prince regent's favourite architect, John Nash, London's Waterloo Place formed the final, crucial piece of the imperial metropolis' new triumphal thoroughfare: a direct challenge to the boulevards of the continental capitals (and especially Paris). Starting at the new Regent's Park, this grand avenue moved south all the way to St James's Park, Pall Mall, Piccadilly Circus, and the Strand, in the process providing a clear delineation between the fashionable West End and the less salubrious Soho. Waterloo Place was the final portion of this route, running straight from Piccadilly Circus to the grand entrance of the regent's residence, Carlton House, south of Pall Mall. The implication was clear: Waterloo was one of the capstones of Britain's new imperial glory. This was reinforced by Waterloo Place opening for carriages for the first time on 21 April 1817 for one of the prince regent's levees at Carlton House, when it was used as the final approach by those attending the levee.[81] Carlton House was demolished in 1826 when the former prince regent (now George IV) and John Nash turned their attention to Windsor Castle and the new Buckingham Palace, but Waterloo Place retained its triumphal and fashionable appeal, housing various memorials, a number of grand town houses, the United Service Club (also designed by Nash), Decimus Burton's Athenaeum Club, and Waterloo Gardens.[82]

Edinburgh's Waterloo Place was also the final portion of a grand thoroughfare, connecting the fashionable Princes Street of Edinburgh's New Town to the Great London Road (also known as the Great North Road). While the entire project was not completed and opened until 1819, the street connecting Princes St to the new construction began in 1815 and was thus named Waterloo Place in honour of the victory.[83] The new road was anchored by the Waterloo Hotel, Tavern, and Coffee Room, conveniently located right where the Great London Road joins one of Edinburgh's main shopping and business thoroughfares. The 'elegan[t]' buildings surrounding it became mercantile offices and Edinburgh's main post office.[84] Other cities and towns soon followed the example set by London, Edinburgh,

[80] 'Waterloo Crescent', *Royal Cornwall Gazette*, 11 October 1817, p. 2.

[81] They were greeted by an honour guard of the Third Foot (Scots) Guard, commanded by Lt Colonel Douglas Mercer, a Waterloo veteran, along with the bands of the Third Foot (Scots) Guards and the Life Guards. 'Fashionable World', *Morning Post*, 22 April 1817, p. 3.

[82] Hoock, *Empires of the Imagination*, 365–6. Waterloo Place was also extended and now provides direct pedestrian access to The Mall and St James's Park via a wide stairway.

[83] 'Regent Bridge, Edinburgh', *The Mirror of Literature, Amusement, and Instruction*, 9 August 1828, pp. 81–2.

[84] Stark, *Picture of Edinburgh*, 46; *The Scots Magazine*, 1 October 1818, p. 84; *Caledonian Mercury*, 15 June 1826, p. 3.

and Truro. There exist records of at least fifteen Waterloo Places across Britain, along with Waterloo Streets, Courts, Roads, Squares, and Terraces.[85]

The use of naming as a form of public commemoration was not limited to Great Britain. Upper and Lower Canada each acquired a town named Waterloo in the 1820s.[86] An 1848 geographical dictionary of Australia lists three Waterloos (two in New South Wales and one in Western Australia), plus Waterloo Bay (now Elliston), Waterloo Plains, and Waterloo Point.[87] In Sierra Leone the city of Waterloo was founded in 1819, while the idea of naming the city after the battle may have been inspired by an anniversary dinner held the year before.[88] Nor was the idea exclusive to the British Empire. On 22 October 1815 Berlin renamed *Rondell* square *Belle-Alliance-Platz*, while the Russian Empire rechristened King George Island off the coast of Antarctica *Ватерлоо* (or *Vaterloo*).[89] Despite having been at war with Great Britain until four months before the battle, the United States was also seduced by the name. An 1831 list of United States post offices reveals Waterloos in New York, Pennsylvania, Maryland, North Carolina, South Carolina, Alabama, Indiana, and Illinois.[90] New York City also boasted an outdoor eatery known as Waterloo Gardens in 1825, although, as one English visitor noted, the name was probably chosen to serve 'as a magnet... to attract the contents of Johnny Bull's purse', rather than out of any desire to commemorate the battle.[91]

---

[85] 'Exeter, Wednesday, 12 March', *Trewman's Exeter Flying Post*, 13 March 1817, p. 4; Baines, *History of York*, I: 36, II: 72, 516; Baines, *History of Lancaster*, I: 259, II: 216, 425, 558–9; Parson and White, *History of Durham and Northumberland*, I: clxi, 285, 354, 499; *Pigot and Co.'s National Commercial Directory for 1828–9*, 672, 1147; William West, *The History, Topography and Directory of Warwickshire* (Birmingham: R. Wrightson, 1830), 214, 308; William White, *History, Gazetteer, and Directory of Nottinghamshire* (Sheffield: Robert Leader, 1832), 215; William White, *History, Gazetteer, and Directory of Staffordshire* (Sheffield: Robert Leader, 1834), 580–8; William White, *History, Gazetteer, and Directory of the West-Riding of Yorkshire* (Sheffield: Robert Leader, 1837), I: 530; *Pigot and Co.'s National Commercial Directory of the Whole of Scotland and of the Isle of Man* (London: J. Pigot & Co., 1837), 189, 492; William White, *History, Gazetteer, and Directory of Leicestershire, and the Small County of Rutland* (Sheffield: Robert Leader, 1846), 129, 143, 171, 173, 196; William Whellan and Co., *History, Gazetteer, and Directory of Northamptonshire* (London: Whittaker and Co., 1849), 174–82; Bagshaw, *History of Chester*, 223, 263, 576, 681; *Slater's Commercial Directory*, Berkshire 24, 26, 34, Hampshire 48, 87–8, Lincolnshire 23.

[86] *Sketches of Upper Canada* (Simpkin & Marshall, 1822), 382, 477 ; *The Canadian Biographical Dictionary and Portrait Gallery of Eminent and Self-Made Men* (Chicago: American Biographical Publishing Company, 1881), II: 185.

[87] William Henry Wells, *A Geographical Dictionary or Gazetteer of the Australian Colonies* (Sydney: W. & F. Ford, 1848), 415.

[88] *Proceedings of the Church Missionary Society for Africa and the East. Twenty-First Year, 1820–1821* (London: R. Watts, 1821), 233; 'Sierra Leone', *Morning Post*, 25 August 1818, p. 2.

[89] In 1947 *Belle-Alliance-Platz* was renamed *Mehringplatz* in honour of the publicist Franz Mehring. Alessandro Barbero, *The Battle: A New History of Waterloo*, trans. John Cullen (New York: Walker & Company, 2005), 313.

[90] *Table of The Post Offices in the United States* (Washington: Duff Green, 1831), 349.

[91] Joseph Pickering, *Emigration or No Emigration* (London: Longman, Rees, Orme, Brown, and Green, 1830), 31.

While the original monuments commissioned by Parliament never materialized on British soil, several government-funded commemorations did appear. The first of these took the form of HMS *Waterloo*, a third-rate ship of the line of 84 guns. Originally commissioned as HMS *Talavera* after the 1809 victory in the Peninsular War, it was renamed for Waterloo in the summer of 1817, and a full-length sculpture of Wellington was added as her figurehead.[92] She was launched in Portsmouth on 16 October 1818 before an estimated crowd of 20,000 spectators. 'A great number of ladies and gentlemen were launched in her', reported *The Times* and 'the harbour was covered with noblemen and gentlemen's pleasure-boats of all descriptions'.[93] HMS *Waterloo* served for six years before being renamed HMS *Bellerophon* and being assigned to an experimental squadron.[94] On Waterloo Day 1833, the navy again honoured the army, this time at Chatham, with the launch of the second HMS *Waterloo*, a 120-gun first-rate ship of the line. The launch once again attracted a large crowd, both on land and in private yachts, and this time was supplemented with a fireworks display and a re-enactment of the battle by detachments of four regiments on the heights overlooking Chatham.[95]

The most widespread government commemoration came the same year as the launch of the first HMS *Waterloo* in the form of the Church Building Act. Inspired by the prince regent's command that Parliament direct

> particular attention to the deficiency, which has so long existed, in the number of places of public worship belonging to the established church, when compared with the increased and increasing population of the country. [W]ith a just sense of the many blessings which this country, by the favour of Divine Providence, has enjoyed, and with the conviction that the religious and moral habits of the people are the most sure and firm foundation of national prosperity,

Parliament created the Church Building Commission and funded it to the tune of £1 million.[96] It proved a sufficient success that an additional £500,000 was voted in

---

[92] 'Shipping Intelligence', *Royal Cornwall Gazette*, 23 August 1817, p. 4; 'The Waterloo', *The Times*, 19 October 1818, p. 3.

[93] 'The Waterloo', *The Times*, 19 October 1818, p. 3.

[94] Brian Lavery, *The Ship of the Line Volume 1: The Development of the Battlefleet 1650–1850* (London: Conway Maritime Press, 2003), 187.

[95] 'Launch of the Waterloo', *The Times*, 19 June 1833, p. 5. The navy was not alone in this: there is evidence of multiple steam packets, coastal traders, and schooners named *Waterloo*. 'Coast List', *Royal Cornwall Gazette*, 19 July 1817, p. 3; 'Plymouth', *Royal Cornwall Gazette*, 16 August 1817, p. 3; *Royal Cornwall Gazette*, 23 August 1817, p. 3; 'Plymouth', *Royal Cornwall Gazette*, 27 September 1817, p. 3; 'Penzance', *Royal Cornwall Gazette*, 25 October 1817, p. 3; *Caledonian Mercury*, 27 May 1820, p. 2; Baines, *History of Lancaster*, I: 460–2.

[96] Building of New Churches, House of Commons Debate, 16 March 1818, Historic Hansard, vol. 37, columns 1116–31. <https://api.parliament.uk/historic-hansard/commons/1818/mar/16/building-of-new-churches>.

1824 and the Commission eventually constructed over 600 churches, thirty-eight in London alone.[97] Because of the prince regent's deliberate tying of the construction to the blessings (and triumphs) of the country and because several MPs argued that these churches should take the place of the proposed monuments, these churches became known in the press and to the general populace as 'Waterloo churches'.[98]

This association of Waterloo with houses of worship was not universally welcomed. The *Berkshire Chronicle*, in noting the construction of one of the new churches in the forest of Bere, stated that 'this will be in very bad taste: surely a temple dedicated to the God of Peace, ought to have no association with one of the most bloody battles in the history of the world'.[99] Others, however, embraced the connection. In a sermon preached on Waterloo Day 1819 to raise money for a proposed monumental church in Edinburgh, the Reverend John Somerville, minister of the Scottish village of Currie, demanded to know if 'any thing be imagined more fit, or more appropriate?—a temple to God, and a monument to men, recording your gratitude to both'.[100] Somerville backed his claim with the evidence of the Old Testament's Israelites (a favourite comparison of nineteenth-century British preachers) as well as Greece and Rome, and insisted it was their duty, as both Scotsmen and Britons, to ensure Waterloo was remembered forever.[101] 'When we shall sleep in the dust,' he promised, 'the future sons of Scotland, as they journey from every quarter of the land to visit our capital, shall point to the monument of the brave as they pass, and ask their fathers, saying, What mean ye by these stones? And then shall they say unto them, That these stones are for a sign and memorial for ever, of the gratitude of this nation to God, and to their countrymen.'[102]

For all the vainglorious promises of a never-built ornamental tower or the successful efforts of the Church Building Commission, the most ground-breaking

---

[97] M. H. Port, *600 New Churches: The Church Building Commission 1818–1856* (Reading: Spire Books, 2006); Alan Forrest, *Waterloo* (Oxford: Oxford University Press, 2015), 108; Hoock, *Empires of the Imagination*, 354; Ben Weinreb, Christopher Hibbert, Julia Keay, and John Keay, *The London Encyclopaedia* (London: Macmillan, 2008), 992.

[98] Building of New Churches, House of Commons Debate, 16 March 1818, Historic Hansard, vol. 37, columns 1116–17, 1128. <https://api.parliament.uk/historic-hansard/commons/1818/mar/16/build ing-of-new-churches>. Yarrington, 'The Commemoration of the Hero', 213. For the press referring to these new houses of worship as Waterloo Churches, see *Morning Chronicle*, 12 September 1822, p. 1; *Hampshire Telegraph and Sussex Chronicle*, 17 January 1831, p. 4.

[99] 'Basingstoke, Feb. 12', *Berkshire Chronicle*, 21 February 1829, p. 3.

[100] John Somerville, *National Gratitude: A Sermon* (Edinburgh: Macredie, Skelly, & Co., 1819), 30.

[101] George Croly, Rector of St Stephen Walbrook in the City of London declared in a sermon preached before the Lord Bishop of London in St Paul's Cathedral in 1838 that 'the British empire, through the Established Church, has been constituted by Providence the heir to the duties, the privileges, and the promises of Israel'. George Croly, *The Reformation a Direct Gift of Divine Providence: A Sermon* (London: James Duncan, 1838), 44; John Wolffe, 'British Sermons on National Events', in Robert H. Ellison, ed., *A New History of the Sermon: The Nineteenth Century* (Leiden: Brill, 2010), 181–206.

[102] Capitalization reproduced from the original. Somerville, *National Gratitude*, 32.

governmental commemoration was a one-and-a-half-inch silver disc. The Waterloo Medal was announced in a memorandum from Horse Guards published in the 23 April 1816 issue of *The London Gazette* 'in commemoration of the brilliant and decisive victory of Waterloo, a medal shall be conferred upon every Officer, Non-Commissioned Officer, and Soldier of the British Army present upon that memorable occasion'.[103] The medal was designed by Thomas Wyon Jr., before he designed the Waterloo Bridge medal and just after he finished the newly issued silver currency.[104] The medal featured the bust of the prince regent, bedecked with laurels and marked 'George P. Regent' on the obverse and the figure of Victory on the reverse, seated on a plinth marked 'Waterloo' with 'Wellington' curved around the top of the medal over her head. It was suspended on a crimson ribbon with blue edges, and the memorandum that created it forbade the wearing of the ribbon without the medal attached.[105] The medal represents three British army firsts: it was the first campaign or battle medal issued to all soldiers present at an action, regardless of rank; it was the first campaign medal to be issued to the next-of-kin of those killed in action; and it was the first medal where the recipient's name, rank, and regiment were impressed into the edge of the medal by machine.[106] It was the first of these three that proved controversial.

Campaign medals were not a new idea; they were common practice on the Continent and the East India Company issued them to its forces.[107] The general view of these in the United Kingdom, as reported by a Victorian coin expert, was that 'English military pride had hitherto rebelled against the practice common in Continental armies, of conferring medals and distinctions on every man, or every regiment, who had simply done their duty in their respective services'.[108] Waterloo, however, was significant enough to prove an exception, especially since the idea for the medal came from Wellington himself and the prince regent rather liked the idea of a medal with his head on it.[109] The problem was that, despite Waterloo's unique status, once Horse Guards started issuing campaign medals, soldiers who risked their lives in other less geopolitically significant but equally dangerous campaigns wanted that acknowledgement. Almost all future

---

[103] In fact, any British soldier or member of the King's German Legion who was present at the battles of Ligny, Quatre Bras, or Waterloo was eligible. Over 37,000 were struck. 'Memorandum', *The London Gazette*, 23 April 1816, p. 749.

[104] Lawrence L. Gordon, *British Battles and Medals* (Aldershot: Gale and Polden, 1962), 52; *Oxford Dictionary of National Biography* online, entry 'Wyon family'.

[105] W. S. W. Vaux, 'On English and Foreign Waterloo Medals', in W. S. W. Vaux et al., eds, *The Numismatic Chronicle and Journal of the Numismatic Society* (London: John Russell Smith, 1869), IX: 109–10; 'Memorandum', *The London Gazette*, 23 April 1816, p. 749. Victory's pose was heavily influenced by a fifth century stater from the Greek city state of Elis. Forrer, *Biographical Dictionary of Medallists*, VI: 647–648.

[106] Gordon, *British Battles and Medals*, 52.

[107] The medal awarded for the capture of Seringapatam and the Fourth Anglo-Mysore War in 1799 may have been the first medal the Duke of Wellington, then Sir Arthur Wellesley, ever received.

[108] Vaux, 'On English and Foreign Waterloo Medals', 111.

[109] Gordon, *British Battles and Medals*, 52; Vaux, 'On English and Foreign Waterloo Medals', 110.

conflicts in which the British army was involved resulted in a campaign medal, and the next significant European conflict, the Crimean War, was the origin of the Victoria Cross, Britain's highest award for gallantry.[110]

In 1816, however, the debate over medals focused not on the future, but on the past. After Napoleon's first abdication in 1814, the veteran British army that had fought across the Iberian Peninsula was broken up, with many regiments being sent to North America for the tail end of the War of 1812, or to far-flung portions of the empire. A large portion of the British forces at Waterloo were new recruits, as there had not been time since Napoleon's return to recall the veteran battalions. This unfortunate concatenation of geography and military planning led to the sight of relatively new recruits, some with under a year of service, proudly wearing the Waterloo Medal, while veterans who had served through all six years of the Peninsular War were bare chested. It was inevitable that calls began to emerge for a similar medal to be awarded to all Peninsular veterans. There were medals produced for the Peninsular War, but as a soldier had to command a battalion or corps during an engagement to be eligible, the lowest ranking British soldier to be awarded one was a captain.[111] The solution to this quandary came (although not until 1847) with the Military General Service Medal, which was awarded (only upon application) to anyone who had served in a major battle with the British army between the years 1793 and 1814.[112]

As he was suggesting the Waterloo Medal for all ranks, Wellington also suggested the idea of a grand commemorative medal, originally planned to be of solid gold, that was destined only for the allied monarchs, ministers, and generals. The prince regent, who seized on anything that might associate him with the glory of Napoleon's defeat, expanded the idea to three versions of the same medal: in gold, to be distributed as Wellington had envisioned, in silver for lesser dignitaries, and in bronze, available for purchase by the public.[113] The Royal Mint held a design competition in 1816 and settled on a proposed design by John Flaxman, but was overruled by the prince regent, who preferred a classical design by

[110] See John Glanfield, *Bravest of the Brave: The Story of the Victoria Cross* (Stroud: Sutton Publishing, 2005).

[111] 'Horse Guards, October 7, 1813', *The London Gazette*, 5 October 1813, p. 1985; Gordon, *British Battles and Medals*, 48–51; Stanley Currie Johnson, *The Medal Collector; A Guide to Naval, Military, Air-Force and Civil Medals and Ribbons* (London: H. Jenkins, 1921), 52–7.

[112] A total of 26,091 were awarded. For those who earned both the Waterloo Medal and the MGSM, they became a matched set, and there is evidence that the MGSM was added to portraits years after they were painted. Gordon, *British Battles and Medals*, 25; Vaux, 'On English and Foreign Waterloo Medals', 111–12; The portrait of Colonel Thomas Wildman by James Lonsdale shows the subject in uniform and sporting both the Waterloo Medal and the MGSM, despite the fact that the MGSM was not awarded until 1847 and the artist died in 1839. In this case the MGSM is not pinned next to the Waterloo medal, but is instead worn on the pelisse, where, presumably, it was easier to add it later. Thomas Wildman by James Lonsdale, Art UK, <http://artuk.org/discover/artworks/thomas-wildman-17871859–47850.>.

[113] A limited number of the silver medals would also be purchasable. 'The Great Waterloo Medal', *The Art Journal*, 1 November 1849, 333–4.

Benedetto Pistrucci, an Italian engraver who had risen to prominence in France towards the end of the Napoleonic Wars before moving to Britain in December 1815 (Figure 6.3).[114]

Pistrucci's design was a then unprecedented 5.5 inches in diameter and depicted at its centre the busts of the kings of Britain, Austria, Russia, and Prussia. The allied sovereigns were surrounded by sixty classical figures, all allegorical in nature. Apollo is depicted in his chariot at the top of the medal, restoring the day to Europe, and his chariot is followed by a rainbow zephyr, scattering flowers onto the earth as a sign of peace. He is heading towards two youths representing the constellation Gemini, the dominant astrological sign on 18 June. Gemini, depicted as the usual figures of Castor and Pollux bearing spears, also represent Wellington and Blücher reaching their apotheosis. Power is represented as a large man with a club sitting beneath an oak tree, but is, by his placement behind the sovereigns, subservient to Justice, who sits with all four of the sovereigns facing her, indicating the chosen direction of Europe.[115] Justice sits with a palm in one hand, ready to reward virtue, and a sword in the other, to punish crime. Along the bottom of the medal flees Night, banished by Apollo's light; finally, to her right the Furies gather under Power, while on her left the Fates look to Justice for guidance. The centre of the medal's reverse is dominated by two riding figures, classically dressed but wielding the batons of field marshals and again representing Wellington and Blücher. Wellington charges ahead while Blücher gallops to his aid, while between them the winged figure of victory holds their reins. Above them, on the top of the medal's reverse, Jupiter, mounted in his chariot, stands in victory at the culmination of the battle of the Giants, nineteen of whose tumbling, defeated bodies form the rest of the medal's reverse border, each representing a year of war.[116]

Upon the selection of his design in 1819, Pistrucci successfully lobbied for a total fee of £3,500, payable as he progressed, arguing that the medal represented the labour of thirty ordinary medals, for which he was charging £105 at the time.[117] His estimate of the work involved was accurate, as he did not deliver the dies until 1844, at which point the only original planned recipient still alive was the Duke of Wellington.[118] The challenges did not end with the delivery of the finished dies. The dies for the medal had to be hardened before the medals could be struck, but this process had never been performed on a die of this scale before.

---

[114] G. P. Dyer and P. P. Gaspar, 'Reform, the New Technology and Tower Hill, 1700–1966', in C. E. Challis, ed., *A New History of the Royal Mint* (Cambridge: Cambridge University Press, 1992), 478; *Oxford Dictionary of National Biography* online, entry Benedetto Pistrucci.

[115] The figure with the club connoting power may be Hercules.

[116] All details of the medal taken from 'The Great Waterloo Medal', *The Art Journal*, 1 November 1849, pp. 333–4.

[117] *Oxford Dictionary of National Biography* online, entry Benedetto Pistrucci.

[118] Dies of the Pistrucci Waterloo Medal, Age of Revolution <https://ageofrevolution.org/200-object/dies-of-the-pistrucci-waterloo-medal/>.

Figure 6.3 The obverse and reverse dies for the Pistrucci Waterloo Medal. The Royal Mint Museum.

Instead of potentially ruining them, the dies were kept as-is, with a few medals being produced in silver via the newly discovered process of electrotyping.[119]

Commemorative medals were not limited to official sources and many, as in the arts and publishing, took advantage of the public's interest in Waterloo and other British victories.[120] Of these, James Mudie's set presents an excellent example. Mudie was indirectly connected with the Napoleonic Wars, having served as an officer in the Marines from 1799 to 1810. He suffered from bouts of ill health and never saw combat, but did serve as a recruitment officer before debts and various other activities caused him to be dismissed from the service.[121] Inspired by a set commissioned by Napoleon in Paris, Mudie decided to create a 'grand series of national medals' commemorating recent achievements in British history.[122] Debuted in 1819, Mudie's set comprised forty medals and could be purchased in bronze (half a guinea each or 20 guineas for the set), silver (one guinea each or 40 guineas for the set), or gold (15 guineas each or 600 guineas for the set).[123] Mudie's published records for the medal series list 259 subscribers in Britain, India, and the United States, including twenty-two current or former officers in the armed forces. The army was represented by nine general officers, led by the Duke of Wellington and the Marquess of Anglesey.[124] Mudie employed a variety of engravers over the course of the forty medals, the majority from France, but the collection boasts several engravings each by Thomas Webb, William Wyon, and George Mills.[125]

Each medal was roughly 1.6 inches in diameter and depicted a notable moment in British history, often a battle, while the reverse usually featured the bust of a significant figure from that event. The treatment of these events varied based on the artist's preferences. Some are depicted with a modicum of realism, considering the medium, while others are fully allegorical in nature. The medals ranged, chronologically, from the British settlement of Bombay in 1602 to the establishment of a constitution for the Ionian Islands in 1817. Of the forty medals, fifteen are directly related to the Peninsular War, five represent the aftermath and

[119] *Oxford Dictionary of National Biography* online, entry Benedetto Pistrucci; Dies of the Pistrucci Waterloo Medal, Age of Revolution <https://ageofrevolution.org/200-object/dies-of-the-pistrucci-waterloo-medal/>.

[120] See Timothy Alborn, *All That Glittered: Britain's Most Precious Metal from Adam Smith to the Gold Rush* (Oxford: Oxford University Press, 2019), chapter 9.

[121] Bernard T. Dowd and Averil F. Fink, 'Mudie, James (1779–1852)', *Australian Dictionary of Biography*, National Centre of Biography, Australian National University, 1967, <http://adb.anu.edu.au/biography/mudie-james-2487/text3345>.

[122] *An Historical and Critical Account of A Grand Series of National Medals* (London: Henry Colburn and Co., 1820).

[123] 'Insolvent Debtors' Court', *The Times*, 28 August 1821, p. 3; 'Grand Series of National Medals', *The Leeds Mercury*, 27 March 1819, p. 1; *Historical and Critical Account of A Grand Series of National Medals*, x.

[124] *Historical and Critical Account of A Grand Series of National Medals*, v–ix.

[125] *Historical and Critical Account of A Grand Series of National Medals*, xvi; 'Mr. Mudie's Grand Series of Medals', *The Gentleman's Magazine*, November 1817, 444.

the Congress of Vienna, and six represent the Battle of Waterloo and its aftermath. Of the subscribers to Mundie's complete series, ten had the satisfaction of seeing themselves depicted as busts within the collection.[126] The Duke of Wellington was by far the most portrayed figure in the series; various busts of him (both in uniform and classically depicted) are on eight of the medals (e.g., see Figure 7.4).[127] In 1820, as a supplement to the medals (and his income), Mudie published a companion book, with detailed descriptions of the events, figures, and the medals themselves, as well of plates illustrating the obverse and reverse of each one.

Mudie was not the only entrepreneur to take advantage of the desire to commemorate Waterloo in the form of souvenirs and merchandise. David Bray, an ironmonger with a foundry on Cranbourn Street, just off Leicester Square, developed a Wellington door knocker (Figure 6.4), 'every knock [of which] brings home to the bosom the recollection of the heroic deeds achieved at Waterloo, and the final downfal [sic] of the enemy of the rights and liberties of mankind'.[128] Originally developed following Napoleon's first exile in 1814, the Wellington door knocker found popularity in the wave of national pride that swept the country following Waterloo, when the Morning Post declared it 'one of the most ingenious and pleasing inventions of the present day'.[129] Available in 'Brass, Bronzed, or Japan' the door knocker took the form of Wellington's hand grasping his field marshal's baton from which hung a wreath of laurel leaves.[130] The hand was attached to the door and the baton acted as the pivot point, allowing visitors to swing the laurel wreath up and down. At the bottom centre of the wreath, serving as the striker, was a lion's head.

Original advertising copy indicates that the knocker was intended to be sold with a strike plate in the form of a French eagle so that each strike reaffirmed the defeat of French imperial ambitions by the British lion.[131] The knocker seems to have made Bray's name, as advertisements for unrelated products noted that his 'much admired Wellington Door Knocker' could be had at the same address.[132]

Nor were the displays limited to the exterior of houses. The potteries of Britain leapt to the task of producing commemorative pieces, the cheaper ones often using recycled art from Peninsular victories.[133] At the higher end of the market, Spode,

[126] The subscribers who were also portrayed were: George IV, the Duke of York, the Duke of Wellington, the Marquess of Anglesey, the Earl St Vincent, Lord Beresford, Lord Exmouth, Lord Hill, Lord Lynedock, and Sir Sidney Smith. *Historical and Critical Account of A Grand Series of National Medals.*
[127] *Historical and Critical Account of A Grand Series of National Medals.*
[128] 'Hebdomadary', *Morning Post*, 16 January 1816, p. 4.
[129] 'Hebdomadary', *Morning Post*, 16 January 1816, p. 4; *Morning Post*, 17 June 1817, p. 1.
[130] *Morning Post*, 19 May 1814, p. 1.   [131] *Morning Post*, 19 May 1814, p. 1.
[132] *Morning Post*, 13 June 1818, p. 1.
[133] See Miranda Goodby, 'Wellington and Waterloo in Commemorative Ceramics', in Andrew Watts and Emma Tyler, eds, *Fortunes of War: The West Midlands at the Time of Waterloo* (Warwickshire: West Midlands History Ltd: 2015), 46–8.

Figure 6.4 Wellington Door Knocker. Charles Graham Architectural Antiques and Fireplaces, Leicestershire.

the well-known producer of blue underglaze patterns, honoured the victory with a Waterloo pattern, which first appeared in 1818.[134] Despite the name, this was in fact a more general military collection, possibly inspired by the porcelain service gifted to Wellington by the King of Prussia. The pattern featured a surround of laurel wreaths and rosettes of flags, weapons, and armour, while at the centre of each piece was a depiction of a battle from the Napoleonic Wars, culminating, of course, with Waterloo. The pattern proved popular enough that it remained in production to at least the 1830s.[135]

Fashionable gentlemen did not need to resort to ironmongery or china to pay tribute to Wellington and Waterloo but could instead opt to don what would become one of the duke's more lasting legacies: the Wellington boot. Wellington boots were modified versions of Hessian boots, knee-high leather boots decorated with ornamental tassels and sometimes braid along the top, that were worn over breeches or trousers. Wellington had commissioned them from his shoe and bootmaker for the Waterloo campaign, instructing him to make a pair of Hessian boots with an even top, a slightly shorter leg, and without the decoration,

[134] Llewellyn Jewitt, *The Ceramic Art of Great Britain from Pre-Historic Times Down to the Present Day* (London: Virtue and Co., Ltd, 1878), II: 184.
[135] Sydney B. Williams, *Antique Blue and White Spode* (London: B. T. Batsford, Ltd, 1943), 189, figure 95.

so that they could be worn either inside or outside of legwear.[136] Hessian boots had been popular with both military and civilian dandies, but from 1815 on, they were abandoned by the British population in favour of the footwear that bore the name and approval of their new national hero.[137] As an 1847 history of boots and shoes put it, 'the Wellington is unquestionably the most gentlemanly thing of its kind, and all the attempts... to rival it, most signally fail'.[138]

Men were not alone in aping the styles of Napoleonic heroes; military influence can also be seen in women's fashion. In the late eighteenth century, it became fashionable for society ladies to commission female versions of the uniforms of the regiments their husbands commanded.[139] By the Napoleonic Wars, military touches had crept into more general fashion. The pelisse, a short, fur trimmed (or lined) jacket worn over the left shoulder of hussar uniforms, was adopted into women's wear, where it was lengthened and worn as a coat. It retained touches of its military origins until the 1830s, however, in its frogging, braid trim, and occasional fur lining.

For those who wanted to supplement their pelisses with even more patriotic *élan*, a new colour was available: Waterloo blue. Waterloo blue first appeared shortly after the battle in 1815, often advertised explicitly for pelisses, but soon

---

[136] Matthew McCormack, 'Boots, Material Culture and Georgian Masculinities', *Social History* 42, no. 4 (2017): 475; 'The Street Companion; or the Young Man's Guide and the Old Man's Comfort, in the Choice of Shoes', *The London Magazine and Review*, 1 January 1825, pp. 75–6; John O'Sullivan, *The Art and Mystery of the Gentle Craft, Being an Essay on the Practice and Principles of Boot and Shoe Making, and Cutting* (London: Mr Mason, 1834), 14; Wellington to George Hoby, 11 April 1815, quoted in Elizabeth Longford, *Wellington: The Years of the Sword* (New York: Harper and Row, 1969), 409. Wellington boots were made in leather until the 1850s, when vulcanized rubber was invented; from then on, the utilitarian and waterproof rubber Wellington boot increased in popularity, eventually totally eclipsing the leather original.

[137] The term 'Wellington boots' first appeared in advertising in 1814, but the popularity of the term exploded following Waterloo. 'Advertising and Notices', *The Norfolk Chronicle and Norwich Gazette*, 5 November 1814. In February of 1815, a letter-writer to *Cobbett's Weekly Political Register* lamented the social airs of the country's large farmers, providing as one example 'the young gentleman, the farmer's son, instead of thick high shoes well studded with hobnails, with a smock frock, and carter's whip on his shoulder, now sports his military-cut-upper-coat of superfine, lined with silk, his Wellington boots, his jimmy rattan, and his bit of blood'. 'Cheap Corn', *Cobbett's Weekly Political Register* 25 February 1815; 'The Reformed Dandy: A True Story', *The Repository of Arts, Literature, Fashions, Manufactures, &c.* 6, no. 35 (1 November 1818): 282. This trend was even more marked in Prussia, where Wellington demi-boots, Wellington slippers, and Prince Blucher demi-boots became popular in the immediate aftermath of Waterloo. 'Fashions for November', *Wright's Leeds Intelligencer*, 6 November 1815; 'Berlin Fashions', *Royal Cornwall Gazette, Falmouth Packet & Plymouth Journal*, 11 November 1815; 'Parisian Fashions', *The Cheltenham Chronicle and Gloucestershire Advertiser*, 14 January 1819, p. 4. At least one City boot maker tried to start a trend in Wellington shoes as well as Wellington boots. *Morning Post*, 19 September 1816, p. 1. Among certain circles, they remained associated with the military. An article in *Cobbett's Weekly Political Register* refers to officers as 'flashy blades in whiskers and in Wellington-boots'. 'To the Lord Chancellor', *Cobbett's Weekly Political Register*, 9 June 1821. In modern scholarship, Christopher Breward declared them 'a virtual national costume after the victory of Waterloo'. Christopher Breward, 'Men in Heels: From Power to Perversity', in Helen Persson, ed., *Shoes: Pleasure and Pain* (London: V&A Publishing, 2015), 137.

[138] J. Sparkes Hall, *The Book of Feet: A History of Boots and Shoes* (New York: William H. Graham, 1847), 125.

[139] See the portrait of Lady Worsley by Sir Joshua Reynolds, Leeds, Harewood House.

became a popular choice for a variety of cloths and uses.[140] In her 1835 novel *Chances and Changes*, Elizabeth Strutt recorded that soon after the battle 'every beau was parading Bond-street, in Wellington boots; every belle was dressed in Waterloo blue'.[141] Elizabeth Grant noticed the same phenomenon, much to her dismay. She recorded in her memoirs that 'we were inundated this whole winter [of 1816] with a deluge of a dull ugly colour called Waterloo blue', which she describes as a 'vile indigo' that 'none of us were sufficiently patriotic to deform ourselves by wearing'.[142] She and her set seem to have been alone in their view, for in the spring of 1817 the *Morning Post* reported that Waterloo blue was one of the two most popular colours for day dresses, while by 1823 it was once again popular for pelisses, silk dresses, and velvet reticules.[143] Several novels also mention the colour, including Lady Lytton Bulwer's *Cheveley*, where a bridegroom sports a Waterloo blue cravat that draws admiration.[144] Its popularity was also boosted by reports in the fashionable press of several society ladies incorporating the colour into their court dress between 1824 and 1843.[145] Nor was it used exclusively for clothes. It became a popular colour for dining sets, draperies, furniture, book bindings, and especially vehicles, most notably coaches.[146]

Importantly, Waterloo blue retained its connection to the battle and was used to symbolically acknowledge the victory and authority. In 1823, when the Drury Lane Theatre was preparing for a visit from George IV, the royal box was 'hung

---

[140] *Caledonian Mercury*, 25 November 1815, p. 1.

[141] Elizabeth Strutt, *Chances and Changes: A Domestic Story* (London: Smith, Elder and Co., 1836), II: 150.

[142] Lady Strachey, ed., *Memoirs of a Highland Lady: The Autobiography of Elizabeth Grant of Rothiemurchus afterwards Mrs. Smith of Baltiboys, 1797–1830* (New York: Longmans, Green, and Co., 1899), 278.

[143] 'The Parks', *Morning Post*, 21 April 1817, p. 3; 'London Female Fashions for October', *Morning Chronicle*, 1 October 1823, p. 4; 'Female Fashions', *Morning Post*, 1 December 1823, p. 3. This trend continued into 1824. 'The Park', *Morning Post*, 10 May 1824, p. 3.

[144] Lady Lytton Bulwer, *Cheveley; or, The Man of Honour* (London: Edward Bull, 1839), II: 172. See also Erskine Neale, *The Living and the Dead* (London: Charles Knight, 1827), 284; Orlo Williams, *Lamb's Friend the Census-Taker: Life and Letters of John Rickman* (Boston: Houghton Mifflin Company, 1912), 126.

[145] 'His Majesty's Drawing Room', *Morning Chronicle*, 21 May 1824, p. 2; 'The Queen's Birthday', *Morning Post*, 25 February 1832, p. 3; 'Drawing-Room at the Castle', *Freeman's Journal*, 13 March 1841, p. 3; 'Fashionable World', *Morning Post*, 30 June 1843, p. 6. It only makes one appearance in men's court dress, in the form of a Waterloo blue velvet coat sported by Lord Sondes at a costume ball given by Victoria in 1845. 'Fashionable World', *Morning Post*, 9 June 1845, pp. 4–5.

[146] *Hull Packet*, 10 March 1818, p. 2; *Liverpool Mercury*, 5 November 1819, p. 5; *Morning Post*, 15 May 1822, p. 1; *Berrow's Worcester Journal*, 31 October 1822, p. 2; *The Ipswich Journal*, 22 February 1823, p. 3; *Caledonian Mercury*, 3 May 1823, p. 1; *Derby Mercury*, 12 November 1823, p. 3; *Derby Mercury*, 28 April 1824, p. 3; *Berrow's Worcester Journal*, 23 December 1824, p. 2; *Stamford Mercury*, 2 September 1825, p. 3; *Manchester Courier and Lancashire General Advertiser*, 14 January 1832, p. 2; *Reading Mercury*, 13 August 1832, p. 3; *Morning Post*, 2 July 1834, p. 1; *Manchester Courier and Lancashire General Advertiser*, 16 August 1834, p. 2; *Leeds Intelligencer*, 8 July 1837, p. 4; 'Arrival of Her Majesty at Windsor', *Morning Post*, 23 August 1837, p. 3; *Morning Post*, 12 July 1838, p. 6; *Morning Post*, 14 July 1838, p. 1; *Morning Chronicle*, 1 September 1842, p. 1; *Morning Chronicle*, 24 January 1845, p. 8; *Stamford Mercury*, 8 December 1848, p. 3.

with Waterloo blue draperies, ornamented with fringe in imitation of gold lace'.[147] In 1826, the state carriage of the Senior Sheriff of the City of London was painted Waterloo blue, while in 1848, the state liveries for the City's Lord Mayor's Day featured Waterloo Blue coats.[148] At the Calne election in 1830, the band wore Waterloo blue favours in honour of one of the candidates, Colonel Edward Cheney, CB, who had commanded the Second Dragoons (Scot's Greys) at the end of the battle.[149] The Hampshire Friendly Society, who boasted the Duke of Wellington as their patron, wore medals bearing his likeness on Waterloo blue ribands, as did the Blandford Tradesmen's Friendly and Benefit Society, who could boast no such patron, but did host their annual festival on 18 June.[150] Waterloo blue also continued the traditional association with conservatism in some areas. The Blackburn Operative Conservative Association paraded under three banners, one of which was Waterloo blue with a white Persian border, while Edward Litton, the Conservative MP for Coleraine in County Londonderry, was greeted upon his arrival in that constituency with five flags, the second of which was Waterloo blue silk and bore the words 'The Queen and Constitution'.[151]

While there was no reason why Waterloo blue could not be employed in children's clothes, children received their own forms of physical commemoration. M. Dunnett, proprietor of Dunnett's Toy and Tunbridge Ware Repository located on the corner of Paternoster Row and Cheapside, offered 'The Battle of Waterloo, or British Game of Chess'.[152] Released just in time for Christmas 1817 and costing 18s., the game, M. Dunnett informed his customers, 'has already been favoured with a very extensive sale, and will be found upon trial well worth Public Patronage'.[153] Sadly, no further details exist concerning the game, but as it seems to have been largely paper in construction, it is likely no copies survive.[154] In 1845 a puzzle was released which featured a spiral made up of Wellington's notable victories, with Waterloo forming the grand centrepiece.[155]

---

[147] 'His Majesty's Visit to Drury-Lane Theatre', *Morning Chronicle*, 2 December 1823, p. 3.

[148] The Junior Sheriff's state carriage was lined in Waterloo blue. 'The New Sheriff's State Equipages', *Morning Post*, 26 September 1826, p. 2; 'Court Circular', *Morning Chronicle*, 8 November 1848, p. 4.

[149] *Calne, Devizes and Wiltshire Gazette*, 5 August 1830, p. 3.

[150] 'Localities and Generalities', *Berkshire Chronicle*, 11 October 1828, p. 4; 'Local Intelligence', *Salisbury and Winchester Journal*, 18 May 1835, p. 3; 'Odiham', *Reading Mercury*, 17 June 1848, p. 2; 'Odiham', *Reading Mercury*, 1 June 1850, p. 2.

[151] 'Blackburn, Wednesday, October 12, 1836', *Blackburn Standard*, 12 October 1836, p. 9; 'Coleraine', *The Standard*, 14 July 1837, p. 3. The Bell Club in Wilton and the Odiham chapter of the Hampshire Friendly Society also paraded under Waterloo blue banners, while the Senior Society in Wrexham sported Waterloo blue collars. 'Salisbury', *Salisbury and Winchester Journal*, 22 June 1840, p. 4; 'Odiham', *Reading Mercury*, 1 June 1850, p. 2; 'Wrexham', *North Wales Chronicle*, 23 April 1844, p. 3.

[152] *Morning Chronicle*, 6 December 1817, p. 1.

[153] *The Times*, 8 December 1817, p. 1; 'List of New Works', *The British Review, and London Critical Journal* (London: Baldwin, Cradock, and Joy, 1818), XI: 280.

[154] *The British Review* lists it as being offered 'On a sheet'. 'List of New Works', *The British Review*, XI: 280.

[155] Linda Hannas, *The English Jigsaw Puzzle, 1760–1890: With a Descriptive Check-list of Puzzles in the Museums of Great Britain and the Author's Collection* (London: Wayland, 1972), 99.

In addition to house furnishings, fashion, and games, the horticulturists and botanists of Britain went out of their way to ensure that a number of plants would bear the name of the battle. One 1839 treatise on flowers lists seven carnations, three pinks (another type of dianthus), four auriculas, two polyanthi, a tulip, and a hyacinth all named Waterloo.[156] For those who preferred edible commemoration, there was the New Waterloo, 'one of the largest and tallest of the marrow peas', and the Waterloo variety of the cherry tree, praised for its tender pulp.[157]

In the winter of 1815, Poole & Co., London tobacconists (not to be confused with the Savile Row tailor of the same name), offered their 'Waterloo Mixture... a composition, exclusively their own, composed of some of the finest genuine Foreign Snuff'.[158] It proved so popular that, in an advertisement early in 1816, the company stressed that the blend was exclusive to them, as 'the celebrity the Waterloo Mixture has acquired [has] induced several persons to offer for sale a spurious article, under that name'.[159] Their advertising continued this trend through the winter and a year later they still noted they were the 'sole proprietors of the Waterloo Mixture'.[160] The snuff became recognizable enough to be parodied. In September of 1818, the *Morning Chronicle* ran the 'Diary of a Modern Dandy', in it, the anonymous dandy notes that a snuff expert 'has invented a new *mixture*, Wellington's and Blucher's, which he has named, in honour of the meeting of the two heroes, after the battle of Waterloo—*La belle Alliance*—a good bit—*not to be sneezed at*'.[161] In 1832 *The Examiner*'s explicitly political column 'The Political Examiner' featured a poem entitled 'The Phantom Duke' that parodied Wellington's defeat at the hands of the 1832 Representation of the People (Great Reform) Act. Among its grisly description of the duke the poem declares, 'A human skull for a snuff-box shows, | And with pinches of gunpowder tickles his nose— | Waterloo mixture—treble strong'.[162]

The political editor of *The Examiner* was not the only Briton disturbed by this glorification of a battle that, though a victory, resulted in a great deal of death and suffering. The criticism and satire of the Battle of Waterloo, the men (mainly officers) who fought it, and the nationalization and commemoration of it was relatively common among reformers and radicals. The most cutting satire of all came in the form of parody monuments and medals suggested after the St Peter's

---

[156] Thomas Hogg, *A Practical Treatise on the Culture of the Carnation, Pink, Auricula, Polyanthus, Ranunculus, Tulip, Hyacinth, Rose, and Other Flowers* (London: Whittaker & Co., 1839), 91, 93–5, 97, 107, 117–18, 157, 162, 187, 194, 209.

[157] George Duff, *The Vegetable Garden* (Dublin: James Charles), 91; Patrick Neill, *The Fruit, Flower, and Kitchen Garden* (Philadelphia: Henry Carey Baird, 1851), 122.

[158] *Morning Post*, 11 January 1816, p. 1.   [159] *Morning Post*, 11 January 1816, p. 1.

[160] *Morning Post*, 3 February 1816, p. 2; *Morning Post*, 7 February 1816, p. 1; *Morning Post*, 20 January 1817, p. 1.

[161] Emphasis in original. 'Diary of a Modern Dandy', *Morning Chronicle*, 8 September 1818, p. 3.

[162] 'The Phantom Duke', *The Examiner*, 27 May 1832, p. 3.

Fields Massacre (Peterloo) on 16 August 1819.[163] In the same article where he first coined the term Peterloo (a portmanteau combining St Peter's Field and Waterloo), James Wroe, editor of *The Manchester Observer*, skewered the Waterloo Medal. 'It is rumoured that orders have been sent to an eminent artist for a design, to be engraved for a medal, in commemoration of Peter Loo Victory.'[164] In 1821, the radical writer and publisher William Hone and the satirical printmaker George Cruikshank produced a potential design for the medal in their parody broadsheet *A Slap at Slop and the Bridge-Street Gang* (Figure 6.5). The medal featured a border of skulls and crossbones and at its centre a faceless member of the Manchester and Salford Yeomanry, with the accoutrements of a butcher worn over his uniform, raising an axe to strike down a kneeling and begging protester, while another body lay at his feet. In the description that accompanied their design, Hone and Cruikshank further strengthened the Waterloo connection by suggesting the medals be cast from brass produced by melting down the trumpet of Edward Meagher, the Manchester and Salford Yeomanry's trumpeter, just as campaign medals were sometimes made from the metal of captured cannons.[165] The proposed medal also drew connections between the working class protesters and African slaves by explicitly referencing the antislavery medallions that had become popular across the late eighteenth and early nineteenth century Atlantic World.[166] The pose of the kneeling protester begging for mercy on the Peterloo Medal echoes that of the slave on Wedgewood's original design, and it bore the same question on its reverse that was often found on the medallions, 'Am I not a man and a brother?', here answered 'No!... you are a poor weaver!'[167]

Hone and Cruikshank did not stop at the medal, also parodying the various monuments to Waterloo discussed at the beginning of this chapter. Peterloo, Hone informs his readers in *A Slap at Slop and the Bridge-Street Gang*, 'has been called a *battle*, but erroneously; for, the multitude was *unarmed*, and made no resistance to the heroes *armed*; there was no contest—it was a *victory*; and has

---

[163] For the definitive account of Peterloo, see Robert Poole, *Peterloo* (Oxford: Oxford University Press, 2019).

[164] 'Manchester Political Meeting', *The Manchester Observer*, 21 August 1819, p. 7.

[165] William Hone and George Cruikshank, *A Slap at Slop and the Bridge-Street Gang*, 1821, London, British Library, 806.k.1.(124.).

[166] See Mary Guyatt, 'The Wedgewood Slave Medallion: Values in Eighteenth-Century Design', *Journal of Design History* 13, no. 2 (2000): 93–105. Marcus Wood has argued that it equally could have been a criticism of abolitionists, who were often lambasted by radicals for using slavery as a way of ignoring the poor conditions present in their own country. 'How it was read,' he concludes, 'would finally have depended upon the political sympathies of the viewer.' Marcus Wood, *Blind Memory: Visual Representations of Slavery in England and America, 1780–1865* (Manchester: Manchester University Press, 2000), 171–2.

[167] William Hone and George Cruikshank, *A Slap at Slop and the Bridge-Street Gang*, 1821, London, British Library, 806.k.1.(124.).

Figure 6.5 Hone and Cruikshank's proposed design for a Peterloo Medal. William Hone and George Cruikshank, 'A Slap at Slop and the Bridge Street Gang', in *Facetiæ and Miscellanies* (London: William Hone, 1827), 36. Duke University Library via archive.org.

accordingly been celebrated in triumph'.[168] The monument is therefore simply titled *Victory at Peterloo* (Figure 6.5), in honour of an 'event...more important in its consequences than the Battle of Waterloo'.[169] The monument takes the form of a traditional equestrian statue of another faceless member of the Manchester and Salford Yeomanry (identified by the 'MYC' above a crown and the initials 'GR' on the saddle cloth), with his sabre raised to cut down into the mother and infant who, along with several other civilians, are being trampled by his horse's hooves. The plinth is decorated with fifteen skulls to represent the massacre's casualties and is flanked by shackles to mark those who were arrested and imprisoned in the aftermath. The sides of the plinth were to be decorated with 'the names of the officers and privates successfully engaged...the names of the persons killed, and of the six hundred maimed and wounded in the attack and pursuit; also the names

---

[168] William Hone and George Cruikshank, *A Slap at Slop and the Bridge Street Gang* (London: William Hone, 1822), 35.

[169] Hone and Cruikshank, *A Slap at Slop*, 35.

MANCHESTER AUGUST 16ᵗ. 1819.

Figure 6.6 *Victory of Peterloo*, William Hone and George Cruikshank, 'A Slap at Slop and the Bridge Street Gang', in *Facetiæ and Miscellanies* (London: William Hone, 1827), 35. Duke University Library via archive.org.

of the captures, who are still prisoners in His Majesty's gaols; with the letter of thanks, addressed to the victors, by His Majesty's Command.'[170] The plinth's final

---

[170] By 1821, when *A Slap at Slop and the Bridge-Street Gang* was published, the prince regent had ascended to the throne as George IV. Hone and Cruikshank, *A Slap at Slop*, 35.

side was decorated with a crown surrounded by knives and bayonets, all pointing outwards to symbolize the traditionally feared relationship between the monarchy and the military. Along the bottom an inscription simply read 'Manchester, August 16. 1819.'[171]

Peterloo also saw non-satirical commemorations that echo those generated by Waterloo. Physical tokens of commemoration were relatively common. Several actual Peterloo Medals were produced, probably to be sold to raise funds for the benefit of the day's victims, and there is evidence that Henry Hunt, the radical orator and politician and one of the speakers arrested at Peterloo, carried one for several years.[172] Unsurprisingly, it bears little resemblance to the satirical design proposed by Hone and Cruikshank, and instead shows the cavalry riding through the crowd, sabres aloft. A similar image, although larger in scale, was produced on commemorative handkerchiefs, which featured readable banners among the crowd and a decorative border listing the demands of the reformers and radicals who had gathered on 16 August.[173] Finally, as with Waterloo, Peterloo attracted its share of literary commemorations, ranging from Hone's 1819 satirical children's pamphlet *The Political House that Jack Built* to Percy Bysshe Shelley's *The Masque of Anarchy*.[174]

The multiple layers of allegory incorporated in the various Peterloo satires illustrate just how far into daily life and culture commemoration of Waterloo had penetrated. Wroe, Cruikshank, Hone, and the political editor of *The Examiner* did not bother to explain the references because they knew they did not have to. They had more faith in the public than John Galt—the letter-writer at the beginning of this chapter—did when he insisted that allegory always needed explanation and even then would be misunderstood.[175]

Almost no purpose-built monuments to the battle existed by the time of the Duke of Wellington's death in 1852. Instead, physical commemoration had taken a more utilitarian and individual route. Waterloo was more than just a household name. It could be the name of your street, the name of the coach that carried your mail, the tavern where you drank, the snuff you took, or the game your child

---

[171] George Cruikshank and William Hone, *Victory of Peterloo*, 1821, London, The British Museum, BM Satires 14209, 1870,1008.1321.3.

[172] Peterloo Commemorative Medal, Manchester, People's History Museum, NMLH.2018.197; Medal, 1819, London, The British Museum, M.5625; 'Awful Event!!', *Morning Post*, 29 March 1830; Philip Attwood and Felicity Powell, *Medals of Dishonour* (London: British Museum Press, 2009), 65.

[173] A Representation of the Manchester Reform Meeting Dispersed by the Civil and Military Power. Augt. 16th. 1819, 1819, London, The British Museum, 1893,0106.39. For other examples of ephemera, see Hunt and Liberty Beaker, 1819, London, The British Museum, 2009,8031.1; Peterloo Commemorative Jug, Manchester, People's History Museum, HMLH.1995.91.3.

[174] William Hone, *The Political House that Jack Built* (London: William Hone, 1819); Percy Bysshe Shelley, *The Masque of Anarchy* (London: Edward Moxon, 1832); Marcus Wood, *Radical Satire and Print Culture, 1790–1822* (Oxford: Clarendon Press, 1994), chapter 5; John Gardner, *Poetry and Popular Protest: Peterloo, Cato Street and the Queen Caroline Controversy* (Basingstoke: Palgrave Macmillan, 2011), chapter 4.

[175] Letter I, *Annals of the Fine Arts*, I: 67.

played. Waterloo had been comprehensively nationalized. Its memory was largely curated by civilians and its permanent physical commemorations, be they bridges, hotels, roads, or place names, reflect that.

In contrast to the dearth of explicit, traditional monuments to Waterloo by 1852, eight separate monuments stood to Wellington, and another two were being constructed. This may seem odd, given the vitriol he inspired in certain circles, but Wellington, as we have seen, proved adept at managing his own image. He remained for some the reviled Tory Iron Duke, but for most people, including many that had been granted the franchise by the Great Reform Act that he had opposed, he was above all the avatar of Britain's victory: the 'Conqueror of the World's Conqueror'. As we move forward to consider Wellington's funeral and the near-universal outpouring of grief, it is important to remember this. National memory is not just based on remembrance; it is also based on forgetting at convenient times. By 1852, and when faced with the loss of so prominent a figure, the vitriol of Peterloo and the Great Reform Act were forgotten or put aside in favour of national pride. In this, Waterloo superseded Wellington and even those who despised Wellington the prime minister mourned the loss of Wellington the field marshal.

Epilogue

'The last great Englishman is low': The Funeral of the Duke of Wellington

The 18th of November 1852 dawned over London with angry skies after a night of rain, as 18th of June 1815 had some thirty-seven years before over the Netherlands. The rain of the night of 17 and 18 November, like the rain of the night of 17 and 18 June, fell on thousands of people who resigned themselves to a wet night as the price for being where they needed to be. Several regiments of infantry, cavalry, and artillery gathered on Horse Guards Parade, Birdcage Walk, and in St James's Park in the sodden pre-dawn, while civilians watched the sun rise over London from prime positions along the Mall, Piccadilly, St James's, Pall Mall, the Strand, Fleet Street, and Ludgate Hill, which they had claimed the day before and defended throughout the rain-lashed night. By the time the minute guns started firing at around eight in the morning, one and a half million people were gathered between Hyde Park Corner and St Paul's Cathedral to pay their last respects to the commander of those soaked men thirty-seven years before who had turned the village of Waterloo into a British household name.[1]

The funeral of the Duke of Wellington was a national spectacle of mourning on a scale not seen since the funeral of Admiral Nelson, some forty-six years before. It eclipsed the funerals of three of the four monarchs Wellington served and was by far the largest granted a former Prime Minister until Sir Winston Churchill's in 1965.[2] Given its size, it is unsurprising that the funeral of the Duke of Wellington has attracted a fair amount of scholarly attention.[3] Beyond its size and splendour, Wellington's funeral (and the duke's death) is of particular interest to this book as

---

[1] Minute guns are cannon fired every minute to mark the funeral of a senior military officer. 'The Funeral of the Duke of Wellington', *The Times*, 19 November 1852, p. 5; 'The Grand State Funeral of Arthur Duke of Wellington', *Illustrated London News*, 27 November 1852, pp. 473–4.

[2] David Cannadine, 'The Context, Performance and Meaning of Ritual: The British Monarchy and the "Invention of Tradition", c.1820–1977', in Eric Hobsbawm and Terence Ranger, eds, *The Invention of Tradition* (Cambridge: Cambridge University Press, 1983), 116.

[3] Peter W. Sinnema, *The Wake of Wellington: Englishness in 1852* (Athens: Ohio University Press, 2006); Cornelia D. J. Pearsall, 'Burying the Duke: Victorian Mourning and the Funeral of the Duke of Wellington', *Victorian Literature and Culture* 27, no. 2 (1999): 365–93; James Stevens Curl, *The Victorian Celebration of Death* (Stroud: Sutton Publishing Ltd., 2004), chapter 7; Harry Garlick, *The Final Curtain: State Funerals and the Theatre of Power* (Amsterdam: Rodopi, 1999), chapter 4; John Morley, *Death, Heaven and the Victorians* (Pittsburgh: University of Pittsburgh Press, 1971), chapter 7; Matthias Range, *British Royal and State Funerals: Music and Ceremonial since Elizabeth I*

Who Owned Waterloo? Battle, Memory, and Myth in British History, 1815–1852. Luke Reynolds, Oxford University Press.
© Luke Reynolds 2022. DOI: 10.1093/oso/9780192864994.003.0008

it presents the apogee of several of the themes discussed in the previous six chapters. In the two months between Wellington's death on 14 September and his funeral on 18 November, and especially at the funeral itself, we find examples of the nationalization not only of his victories, but also of the grief at his passing. We find spectacle, some of it artistic, some of it military, but all dominated, one way or another, by the civilian sphere. Finally, those two months saw a significant outpouring of books, poems, and souvenirs that built on, and were reminiscent of, the publications and ephemera produced in connection to Waterloo over the previous three decades.

The procession deliberately highlighted Wellington's influence across all aspects of British society.[4] It was, unsurprisingly, dominated by the military. The procession contained seven battalions of infantry, including two that Wellington had been colonel of, and the 33rd (First Yorkshire West Riding) Regiment of Foot, which he had commanded in Flanders and India early in his career, and which was renamed the 33rd (The Duke of Wellington's) Regiment of Foot by royal decree in 1853.[5] The cavalry were represented by eight squadrons, three drawn from the Household Cavalry, comprising a total of 640 swords.[6] Mixed in with the cavalry were seventeen guns—nine from the Royal Artillery's field batteries, and eight from the Royal Horse Artillery. The military provided 'martial and solemn' music, in the form of sixteen regimental bands sprinkled throughout the procession, the majority of which played the Dead March from George Frideric Handel's oratorio *Saul*.[7] The military presence was further supplemented by eighty-three Chelsea Pensioners (one for each year of Wellington's life); three infantrymen and three artillerymen from the East India Company's

(Woodbridge: The Boydell Press, 2016), chapter 6; R. E. Foster, '"Bury the Great Duke": Thoughts on Wellington's Passing', in C. M. Woolgar, ed., *Wellington Studies V* (Southampton: University of Southampton, 2013), 299–328.

[4] All procession details taken from 'Programme of the Procession from the Horse Guards to St Paul's Cathedral', *Morning Post*, 18 November 1852, p. 5; 'The Funeral of the Duke of Wellington', *The Times*, 19 November 1852, p. 5; 'The Funeral Procession', *Daily News*, 19 November 1852; 'The Grand State Funeral of Arthur Duke of Wellington', *Illustrated London News*, 27 November 1852, pp. 478–9; *Official Programme of the Public Funeral of the Late Field-Marshal, Arthur Duke of Wellington, K.G., as Issued by the Authority of the Earl-Marshal* (London: N. Pearce, 1852).

[5] The two infantry regiments Wellington had served as colonel of were the Rifle Brigade and the Grenadier Guards. Wellington served as colonel-in-chief of the Rifle Brigade from 1820 and colonel of the Grenadier Guards from 1827. Upon his death in 1852, Prince Albert took over as colonel of both regiments.

[6] 'The Grand State Funeral of Arthur Duke of Wellington', *Illustrated London News*, 27 November 1852, p. 474.

[7] While reports indicate that the bands played the Dead March repeatedly, some variation also shone through. The band of the 33rd began their march with the German Hymn, which Wellington had remarked on the beauty of in the aftermath of Waterloo and marked their arrival at Buckingham Palace with a roll of muffled drums. When the bands of the Guards Regiments passed Apsley House, they also substituted music for a long roll of their muffled drums. The Band of the 93rd Highlanders, the last band in the procession, switched to 'Adeste Fideles' as they marched up the Strand. 'The Funeral of the Duke of Wellington', *The Times*, 19 November 1852, p. 5; 'The Funeral Procession', *Daily News*, 19 November 1852; 'The Grandtate Funeral of Arthur Duke of Wellington', *Illustrated London News*, 27 November 1852, p. 474.

army, each pair representing one of the three presidencies; and ten men from every regiment in the service (a captain, a junior officer, a sergeant, a corporal, and six soldiers), who marched together in a remarkably diverse battalion of detachments. Europe's militaries were represented by seven mourning coaches from Spain, Russia, Prussia, Portugal, the Netherlands, Hanover, and Great Britain, each carrying one of Wellington's field marshal batons, borne by a senior officer of that country supported by two juniors.[8]

Intermingled with the military was the civilian side of British society. Large portions of both Houses of Parliament attended the funeral, although they did not participate in the procession, preferring to take private steamboats along the Thames from Parliament to St Paul's.[9] Six members of the cabinet, however, did take part in the procession, where they were joined by the Speaker of the House of Commons, the Lord High Chancellor representing the House of Lords, several high-ranking judges, clergy, ministers of the crown, and other members of the Civil Service, London, and Home Counties governments. Each rank of the Order of the Bath was represented by a carriage carrying four members, 'being one of each class from the Army, one from the Navy, one from the East India Company's Service, and one from the Civil Service'.[10] The queen and the royal family were represented by Prince Albert, although several empty royal coaches were added to the procession as a mark of respect, and the court was well represented by such luminaries as the Earl Marshal of England, the Lord Great Chamberlain, and the Lord Privy Seal. Unsurprisingly, the College of Arms played a major role in the organization of the procession and the funeral, and a number of their officers participated. To honour Wellington's eighteen years of service as the Chancellor of the University of Oxford, a delegation of dons, comprising two coaches, participated in the procession, as did the Lieutenant and Deputy-Lieutenant of Dover Castle and the Captains of Deal, Walmer, Sandgate, and Sandown Castles in acknowledgement of Wellington's twenty-three year tenure as Lord Warden of the Cinque Ports. These deputations were joined by carriages from the Merchant Tailor's Company, the East India Company, and the Corporation of Trinity House. Finally, the City of London contributed nine coaches' worth of sheriffs, aldermen, and dignitaries, including the Lord Mayor, on foot and carrying the City Sword, all of whom joined the procession after it had passed through Temple Bar and officially entered the City of London itself.

At the centre of the procession, surrounded by the cream of the British army and civil society, was the scarlet and gold coffin of the Duke of Wellington, carried on an £11,000 funeral car so large and elaborate that it 'seemed ... like a moving

---

[8] Only Austria refused to send a general officer to bear their baton.
[9] 'Funeral of the Duke of Wellington', The Times, 18 November 1852, p. 5.
[10] 'The Funeral Procession', Daily News, 19 November 1852.

Figure 7.1 *The Funeral Car of Field-Marshal Arthur, First Duke of Wellington, Album of illustrations of imperial & royal state carriages together with other carriages of deceased statesmen; and the funeral cars of Wellington and Nelson also the four original locomotive engines used on railways in England* (London: Worshipful Company of Coach Makers and Coach Harness Makers, 1899), figure 13. Science, Industry and Business Library: General Collection, The New York Public Library. New York Public Library Digital Collections.

temple' (Figure 7.1).[11] Twenty-seven feet long and ten feet wide, this six-wheeled, ten to eleven ton 'gigantic vehicle' was drawn by twelve large black horses, clothed in black velvet caparisons with Wellington's arms embroidered upon them and headpieces surmounted by black plumes, harnessed in four rows of three abreast.[12] The three-tiered design, by Richard Redgrave, Art-Superintendent, was personally approved by both Queen Victoria and Prince Albert.[13] The bottom tier, the wheels, and the duke's crest on the front were cast entirely out of bronze from enemy cannon captured by Wellington's armies.[14] From this base rose 'a rich

[11] 'The Duke of Wellington's Funeral', *Illustrated London News*, 20 November 1852, p. 431; 'The Grand State Funeral of Arthur Duke of Wellington', *Illustrated London News*, 27 November 1852, p. 475. This is roughly the equivalent of £1 million to £1.5 million today. Relative Value, MeasuringWorth, 2019, <https://www.measuringworth.com/calculators/ukcompare/relativevalue.php>.

[12] Each set of three horses was led by a sergeant of the Royal Horse Artillery. 'The Funeral of the Duke of Wellington', *The Times*, 19 November 1852, p. 5; 'Official Account of the Funeral Car of the Duke of Wellington', *Illustrated London News*, 20 November 1852, p. 439.

[13] 'Official Account of the Funeral Car of the Duke of Wellington', *Illustrated London News*, 20 November 1852, p. 439; Pearsall, 'Burying the Duke', p. 370.

[14] F. J. Rowe and W. T. Webb, *Selections from Tennyson with Introduction and Notes* (London: Macmillan and Co., 1890), 142 n. 55; W. T. Meloy, *Wanderings in Europe* (Chicago: La Monte, O'Donnell & Co., 1892), 199; *Official Programme of the Public Funeral of the Late Field-Marshal, Arthur Duke of Wellington*, 5.

pediment of gilding, in the panels of which' were engraved the names of twenty-four of Wellington's victories, from Ahmednuggur (1803) to Waterloo.[15] This pediment was flanked on the front and sides by rosettes of arms and armour, also taken as trophies, union flags, and surmounted by representations of Wellington's 'Ducal coronets and batons'.[16] Placed on this pediment was the bier, its handles almost as long as the car itself, and draped in a black velvet pall, finished with a two-foot deep fringe of silver and embroidered alternately with Wellington's arms and his crossed field-marshal's batons, a laurel border, and the legend 'Blessed are the dead that die in the Lord.'[17] On the bier rested the coffin, upon which was laid Wellington's hat and sword, the whole shaded by a 'superb canopy of silver tissue, after an Indian pattern', 'with pendent cords and tassels of the richest and most costly description', suspended by four halberds hung with real laurel.[18]

The route of the procession was also designed to highlight the various aspects of Wellington's legacy (Figure 7.2).[19] The procession gathered at Horse Guards Parade, the administrative home of the British army, and directly under the windows of the office Wellington occupied when he served as commander-in-chief. From there the procession moved north along Horse Guards Parade before turning left onto the Mall, echoing the evening promenades of London's fashionable set. The cortège passed Buckingham Palace, where the royal standard flew at half-mast and Queen Victoria and her family watched from the balconies, before turning up Constitution Hill. It passed under the Wellington Arch and turned right onto Piccadilly, passing the honour guard of Light Dragoons positioned in front of a darkened Apsley House, the metal shutters which had earned Wellington the sobriquet of 'the Iron Duke' closed. It continued down Piccadilly, passing the great mansions, some of which were dark in mourning while others were packed with well-to-do spectators. The procession then turned right down St James's Street, passing St James's Palace before turning left onto Pall Mall. This detour through St James's, chosen to allow Queen Victoria and her family, who had moved from Buckingham Palace to St James's Palace after the cortège had turned up Constitution Hill, another look, also meant that the procession passed through the heart of London's 'clubland'. The fashionable institutions that lined St James's and Pall Mall, several of whom (most notably the Army and Navy Club and the Carlton Club) could claim Wellington as a founding member and patron, were

[15] 'The Funeral of the Duke of Wellington', *The Times*, 19 November 1852, p. 5; 'Official Account of the Funeral Car of the Duke of Wellington', *Illustrated London News*, 20 November 1852, p. 439.
[16] 'The Funeral of the Duke of Wellington', *The Times*, 19 November 1852, p. 5; 'Official Account of the Funeral Car of the Duke of Wellington', *Illustrated London News*, 20 November 1852, p. 439.
[17] 'The Funeral of the Duke of Wellington', *The Times*, 19 November 1852, p. 5; 'Official Account of the Funeral Car of the Duke of Wellington', *Illustrated London News*, 20 November 1852, p. 439.
[18] 'The Duke of Wellington's Funeral', *Illustrated London News*, 20 November 1852, p. 431; 'The Funeral of the Duke of Wellington', *The Times*, 18 November 1852, p. 5; 'Official Account of the Funeral Car of the Duke of Wellington', *Illustrated London News*, 20 November 1852, p. 439.
[19] Details of the route taken from 'The Grand State Funeral of Arthur Duke of Wellington', *Illustrated London News*, 27 November 1852, pp. 473–9; 'The Funeral of the Duke of Wellington', *The Times*, 19 November 1852, p. 5; 'The Funeral Procession', *Daily News*, 19 November 1852.

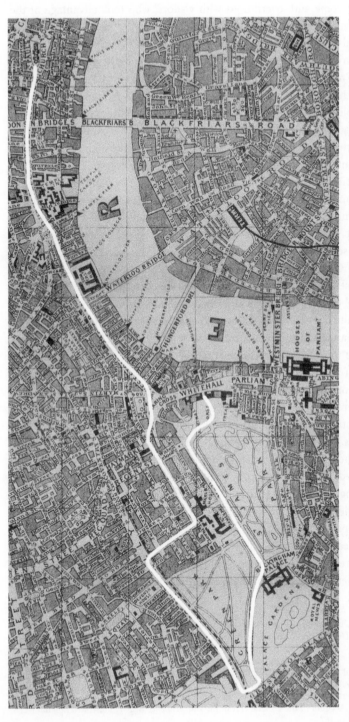

Figure 7.2 The route of the Duke of Wellington's funeral procession, from Horse Guards Parade to St Paul's Cathedral. Detail from *Reynolds's Map of Modern London* (London: James Reynolds, 1857). The Lionel Pincus and Princess Firyal Map Division, The New York Public Library. Route added by Lawrence Gullo.

draped in black crêpe and 'overflowed with visitors' who took advantage of the opportunity to view the procession in comfort.[20]

This detour also allowed the cortège to pass Waterloo Place, now marked by a troop of the 4th (Royal Irish) Dragoon Guards, before moving from Pall Mall into Charing Cross and on to the Strand. This route, from Pall Mall to the Strand, meant the procession passed the foot of Nelson's Column in Trafalgar Square, a notable visual tribute to Wellington's naval counterpart in the canon of British martial heroes. As the procession passed into the Strand, *The Times* noted that 'a new phase in the character of the funeral pageant and its reception became apparent. The demonstrations of respect became parochial, and the churches formed the great centres for spectators.'[21] St Martin's-in-the-Fields, St Mary-le-Strand, St Clement Danes, and St Dunstan's now anchored the multitudes of middle-class mourners the way the mansions of Piccadilly and the clubs of St James's had their aristocratic and genteel counterparts. The procession paused at Temple Bar, the grand arch that marked the western entrance to the City of London, which had been decorated over the preceding days to demonstrate 'the respect which the City entertains for the memory of the Great Duke' (Figure 7.3).[22] It was entirely swathed in 'velvet and black cloth draped with white fringe', which was punctuated by several laureled monograms of the letters A and W, from which hung the symbols of several of his chivalric orders.[23] At the top of the lower arch was the City's coat of arms, while from each column of the upper arch were suspended crests of shields surmounted with the flags of the European nations that had appointed Wellington field marshal. The entire structure was topped by 'four conspicuous Roman urns, surrounding a still larger one in the centre, with twelve funeral flambeaus'.[24] As grand as it was, the archway of Temple Bar still limited the space over the roadway, and the funeral car paused before it so that the canopy over the coffin could be lowered, allowing the car to pass. 'Thus,' one observer noted, 'the old Duke of Wellington, even after death, did homage to the ancient laws of this country, and the representative of military power bowed for the last time to salute the civil power.'[25]

Having entered the City, the professions took the place of religion as the Strand became Fleet Street and the cortège passed the Inns of Court and the City's coffee houses, publishers, and other businesses. Here the crowds grew even larger,

---

[20] The Carlton Club was one of the few exceptions to this and remained as dark as Apsley House. 'The Funeral of the Duke of Wellington', *The Times*, 19 November 1852, p. 5; 'The Grand State Funeral of Arthur Duke of Wellington', *Illustrated London News*, 27 November 1852, p. 475.

[21] 'The Funeral of the Duke of Wellington', *The Times*, 19 November 1852, p. 5.

[22] 'The Funeral of the Duke of Wellington', *The Times*, 19 November 1852, p. 5.

[23] 'The Funeral Procession', *Daily News*, 19 November 1852.

[24] 'The Funeral Procession', *Daily News*, 19 November 1852.

[25] 'A Foreigner's Account of the Funeral (From the *Independence Belge*)', *Illustrated London News*, 27 November 1852, p. 467.

Figure 7.3 Thomas H. Ellis, *Funeral Car of the Late Field Marshal Duke of Wellington*, 1852. London, The British Museum, 1880,1113.2986 © The Trustees of the British Museum.

extending as far south as Blackfriars Bridge and necessitating the squadron of the Royal Regiment of Horse Guards (The Blues) that formed the procession's rearguard to turn and block Temple Bar once the cortège had passed through to stop the crowd following. The procession continued along Fleet Street as it became Ludgate Hill, passing Old Bailey, before the professions surrendered the nature of the pageant once again to the military. No spectators were allowed on Ludgate Hill east of Creed and Ave Maria Lanes, and as the battalions that led the procession entered this area of relative calm, they moved out of the march to line the route, providing a final guard of honour as the funeral car made its way past.[26]

St Paul's Cathedral's doors opened at seven in the morning, and from that point on, there was a steady influx of mourners, each bearing a numbered, stamped, and printed ticket, issued by the office of the earl marshal, which specified the area of

---

[26] 'Programme of the Procession from the Horse Guards to St Paul's Cathedral', *Morning Post*, 18 November 1852, p. 5.

the cathedral in which they were to take their place.[27] By the time the last person was seated and the funeral service itself was ready to begin, over 17,000 people, including numerous foreign dignitaries and representatives of every aspect of British life, were crammed into 'the great cathedral of Protestant Europe'.[28] There they waited for an hour, the great doors open to the November cold, thanks to a malfunction in the machinery built in to the funeral car that prevented the transfer of the bier to the smaller cart used for the funeral service itself. Once the funeral car was persuaded to surrender the 'mortal remains of the hero', the funeral proceeded without delay, and culminated in the lowering of the coffin directly into the crypt.[29] Unfortunately, as Nelson's tomb was located directly under the dome in the crypt, this meant that Wellington's coffin came to rest directly on top of his naval counterpart. It remained there for over a year before it was moved to its final resting place: a tomb of rare luxullianite granite, located several yards east of Nelson.[30]

This was not, it should be noted, the only time the funeral car had caused trouble. The final design had been approved only three weeks before the funeral, and different portions of it had been cast in London, Sheffield, Birmingham, and Pimlico.[31] The result was that it was still being assembled on the morning of the 18th.[32] Once it was assembled, its enormous weight cracked pavements along the route, and it brought the procession to a halt when it stuck fast on the turning from Horse Guards into the Mall.[33] Its size also required the removal of a large portion of the railing around St Paul's to allow it entrance into the churchyard.[34] Most dangerously, when travelling downhill along St James's 'a body of police was employed, who, by means of ropes fastened to the back of the car, prevented it from attaining a velocity which might have been fatal to the horses nearest to the ponderous machine'.[35]

Despite these setbacks, the funeral was considered a great success. *The Times* informed their readers that 'the spectacle was such as none of us can ever hope...

---

[27] Invitations to the Funeral of the Late Field Marshal the Duke of Wellington, Montreal, Rare Books, Special Collections & Archives, McGill University Library, MS662, Wellington Collection, C2; 'The Funeral of the Duke of Wellington', *The Times*, 19 November 1852, p. 5.

[28] 'The Grand State Funeral of Arthur Duke of Wellington', *Illustrated London News*, 27 November 1852, p. 475; 'Funeral of the Duke of Wellington', *The Times*, 18 November 1852, p. 5.

[29] 'The Grand State Funeral of Arthur Duke of Wellington', *Illustrated London News*, 27 November 1852, p. 474.

[30] Pearsall, 'Burying the Duke', 383–4.

[31] 'Official Account of the Funeral Car of the Duke of Wellington', *Illustrated London News*, 20 November 1852, p. 439.

[32] 'Funeral of the Duke of Wellington', *The Times*, 18 November 1852, p. 5.

[33] 'The Grand State Funeral of Arthur Duke of Wellington', *Illustrated London News*, 27 November 1852, p. 474; 'The Funeral of the Duke of Wellington', *The Times*, 19 November 1852, p. 5; 'The Funeral Procession', *Daily News*, 19 November 1852; Pearsall, 'Burying the Duke', 378.

[34] 'The Funeral of the Duke of Wellington', *The Times*, 19 November 1852, p. 5.

[35] 'The Grand State Funeral of Arthur Duke of Wellington', *Illustrated London News*, 27 November 1852, p. 475.

to see the like of again', while *The Illustrated London News* declared it 'one of the most impressive ceremonials ever witnessed in this country', which may have 'surpassed in significant grandeur any similar tribute of greatness ever offered in the world'.[36] There was an undeniable military air to portions of the proceedings. Tribute was paid to Wellington's military victories and the roughly 5,000 soldiers who took part in the funeral, and several papers took the opportunity to sprinkle in some military language.[37] *The Times* noted that the choir of St Paul's had to call in 'reinforcements of picked men from the Chapel Royal, Westminster Abbey, &c.' and that the area around the cathedral had 'become a garrison. St Paul's is invested', while the *Daily News* sardonically excused the panicked galloping of the procession's commander, the Duke of Cambridge, by explaining that 'it was his royal highness's first battle, and he was naturally nervous'.[38]

As with the annual celebrations of the Battle of Waterloo, however, much of the language used to describe the funeral emphasized the national, rather than military, nature of the loss. Prince Albert, who was heavily involved in the planning of the funeral, conceived of it not only as fitting farewell to a hero of the nation, but also as an opportunity to demonstrate British achievement to the world: a Great Exhibition in mourning.[39] The funeral car was one of the best demonstrations of this philosophy, as it united British industry and art, and drew on talent from across Great Britain. 'In no other country but England could a work of the kind have been accomplished with such marvellous expedition,' declared *The Times*, 'as a whole, [it] will justly be regarded as one of our finest artistic productions.'[40]

British papers had always made sure to mention the crowds that attended various Waterloo exhibitions and commemorations. Now, in keeping with that, it was the size of the funeral's civilian crowd, rather than the serried ranks of soldiers or the wonders of the ten-ton funeral car, that the press held up as evidence of the truly national nature of the funeral. 'A million and a half of people beheld and participated in the ceremonial,' *The Times* reported on 19 November, 'which was national in the truest and largest sense of the word.'[41] The turnout was impressive. An 'enormous tide of country visitors' flowed into the capital, many taking advantage of special 'Funeral Trains', organized so that individuals from

---

[36] 'The Funeral of the Duke of Wellington', *The Times*, 19 November 1852, p. 5; 'The Duke of Wellington's Funeral', *Illustrated London News*, 20 November 1852, p. 431.

[37] 'The Grand State Funeral of Arthur Duke of Wellington', *Illustrated London News*, 27 November 1852, pp. 474–5.

[38] 'Funeral of the Duke of Wellington', *The Times*, 18 November 1852, p. 5; 'The Funeral of the Duke of Wellington', *The Times*, 19 November 1852, p. 5; 'The Funeral Procession', *Daily News*, 19 November 1852.

[39] Pearsall, 'Burying the Duke', 370.

[40] 'Funeral of the Duke of Wellington', *The Times*, 18 November 1852, p. 5.

[41] 'The Funeral of the Duke of Wellington', *The Times*, 19 November 1852, p. 5.

'the extremities of the kingdom' could make their way into and out of London.[42] Along the route of the funeral procession, and on any roads that intersected it, the crush of people became so great that 'A midge could not find a passage between the dense mass of human beings' and the gas lamps remained lit throughout the day as their custodians could not reach them to turn them off.[43] In Piccadilly, just past where the procession turned down St James's, 'wagons, carts, coaches, and omnibuses' were converted into impromptu viewing platforms 'to give their occupants a more commanding view'.[44] More traditional—but just as temporary—viewing platforms were erected in front of any building along the route that was set at all back from the road.[45] Building sites became temporary galleries, and every upper-storey window 'had people thrust from them eagerly gazing' down.[46] Along the Strand and in the City, shopkeepers converted their ground-floor shop windows into still more seating, and 'inclosed numbers of full-grown people, compressing themselves for the occasion into the dimensions of charity-school children', 'producing the effect of the benches of an amphitheatre indefinitely elongated'.[47] For the brave, the roofs offered excellent viewing, and some spectators sat on chimney pots or took advantage of awnings erected by building owners 'to protect those who stand upon the tiles or leads from the weather'.[48] It was, as *The Times* put it, 'as if the whole world had assembled to witness the ceremonial, for the people were everywhere—built into the walls, swarming the streets, and clustered like hives on every projection and parapet'.[49]

For the popular press, this turnout was the greatest tribute to Wellington. A reporter for *The Illustrated London News*, in summarizing the honours heaped on Wellington, insisted that 'there remained yet but one form in which this gratitude and veneration could give itself expression ... and that last sad resource was on Thursday exhausted by the hundreds of thousands who attended to do honour to the remains of Wellington'.[50] The *Daily News* felt that 'the immense mass of people present appeared to be as much a part of the ceremonial as any

[42] 'Funeral of the Duke of Wellington', *The Times*, 20 November 1852, p. 5; 'A Foreigner's Account of the Funeral (From the *Independence Belge*)', *Illustrated London News*, 27 November 1852, p. 467.

[43] 'The Funeral Procession', *Daily News*, 19 November 1852; 'The Funeral of the Duke of Wellington', *The Times*, 19 November 1852, p. 5.

[44] 'The Funeral of the Duke of Wellington', *The Times*, 19 November 1852, p. 5.

[45] 'The Funeral Procession', *Daily News*, 19 November 1852.

[46] 'The Funeral Procession', *Daily News*, 19 November 1852; 'The Funeral of the Duke of Wellington', *The Times*, 19 November 1852, p. 5.

[47] 'The Funeral of the Duke of Wellington', *The Times*, 19 November 1852, p. 5; 'The Duke of Wellington's Funeral', *Illustrated London News*, 20 November 1852, p. 431.

[48] 'The Funeral of the Duke of Wellington', *The Times*, 19 November 1852, p. 5; 'The Funeral Procession', *Daily News*, 19 November 1852. The use of roofs as viewing platforms caused the one casualty of the day, when a gentleman fell from the roof of Drummond's Bank in Charing Cross. He was rushed to Charing Cross Hospital but died half an hour after arriving.

[49] 'The Funeral of the Duke of Wellington', *The Times*, 19 November 1852, p. 5.

[50] 'The Duke of Wellington's Funeral', *Illustrated London News*, 20 November 1852, p. 431.

portion of the official programme'.[51] *The Times* was even more eulogistic, informing their readers early in their coverage that they sought

> to give some idea, not of the pageant itself... but rather of the public reception
> which it experienced on its way, and of the unexampled spectacle which the
> streets of this metropolis exhibited throughout the day. Words are, we feel,
> completely powerless to convey anything like a just idea of a demonstration so
> marvellous. On no occasion in modern times has such a concourse of people
> been gathered together, and never probably has the sublimity which is expressed
> by the presence of the masses been so transcendently displayed.

They concluded in much the same vein, declaring that 'the great distinguishing
feature of yesterday's ceremonial remains, however. The funeral pomp, splendid
as it was, is nothing, but the million and a half of mourners will be remembered as
a historic fact—a shining proof that we have not forgotten to value patriotism, and
that the memory of him who on so many fields defended the liberties of his
country is embalmed in the hearts of her people.'[52]

Nor was the impact of such a display lost on foreigners who witnessed it. One
Belgian observer, writing in *L'Indépendence Belge*, dismissed the military portions
of the procession as 'altogether miscarried' and 'very poor', but 'the national
demonstration—the English demonstration—it was universal; and, under this
point of view, it was indeed magnificent.... It is this universal concurrence of a
whole nation which appear[ed] to [him] the most striking trait of this solemn
funeral.'[53] He was equally impressed by the work stoppages that allowed so many
people to make their way into the capital on a Thursday.[54] He insisted that the
greatest tribute 'this business-like nation' could give their fallen hero was 'to have
suspended all occupation for a whole day, that day not being a Sunday'.[55]

A similar message of unifying and universal grief was preached from the pulpits
of British churches. The Reverend Charles Overton, preaching in Cottingham
Church on the outskirts of Hull on the day of Wellington's funeral, reminded his
parishioners that 'all of England, and the inhabitants of Great Britain... at this
time, mingle, and suspend, and for a while forget, every other consideration, as
they unite as one man, to *do honor* to the illustrious Duke *at his death*'.[56] Three
days later and over 150 miles to the south, the Reverend Charles Heathcote

---

[51] 'The Funeral Procession', *Daily News*, 19 November 1852.

[52] 'The Funeral of the Duke of Wellington', *The Times*, 19 November 1852, p. 5.

[53] 'A Foreigner's Account of the Funeral (From the *Independence Belge*)', *Illustrated London News*, 27 November 1852, p. 467.

[54] For a summary of how the funeral was marked outside of London, see 'Funeral of the Duke of Wellington', *The Times*, 20 November 1852, p. 5.

[55] 'A Foreigner's Account of the Funeral (From the *Independence Belge*)', *Illustrated London News*, 27 November 1852, p. 467.

[56] Charles Overton, *The Burial of Wellington: A Sermon* (Hull: John Mozley Stark, 1853), 4–5.

elaborated on the same theme in a sermon preached to the congregation of St Thomas's, Stamford Hill. He insisted that the spectacle 'was no vain and empty show...it was not the elevation of one party over another in the person of its chief; it was not a tribute offered by the majority of a *divided* people;—an entire nation's heart was in that pageantry, and was the soul of it'. 'Let a man consider', he invited any who doubted him, 'how personal interest, the prejudice of party, private as well as public prepossessions prevent the possibility...of thousands, and ten-thousands, and ten-times ten-thousands, uniting in heart, as well as in tongue, in the public honouring of one and the same man.'[57]

The prioritization of the national nature of the outpouring of grief at Wellington's funeral was not the only connection between his death and the culture of spectacle, memorialization, and celebration that emerged around the Battle of Waterloo in the nearly four decades since the victory. Indeed, the two months between Wellington's death and his funeral saw almost every aspect of Waterloo memory discussed in this book repurposed to one extent or another. The collecting impulse that had guaranteed a continual trade in Waterloo relics now turned to Wellingtonian relics, both of the duke's life and of the funeral itself. New commemorative items and souvenirs, often closely resembling those produced to mark the victory, were offered up for sale. London benefited from the same surge in tourism that Waterloo had seen, with Londoners taking equal advantage of the influx that their counterparts in Brussels and Waterloo had of a generation of British visitors. St Paul's position as a site of national pilgrimage was reinforced, in both the immediate aftermath of the funeral and the years to come. Brand new sculptures and paintings of Wellington and notable moments from his life were put on display, alongside old favourites that had earned devoted followings in the previous four decades, with prints and copies of all offered for sale. Similarly, exhibitions new and old involving Wellington and Waterloo were opened or revived. Memoirs of Wellington's life and collections of the many anecdotes that surrounded his legend were added to shelves already groaning with soldiers' memoirs and civilian histories of Waterloo, while commemorative compositions, both musical and verse, surged in popularity.

While not as grisly or numerous as the buttons, bullets, bones, and other trappings of war that could be purchased on a visit to Waterloo, Wellington's death produced its own forms of relics. Piper Brothers & Co. published the official souvenir programme of the procession and funeral, by authority of the earl marshal, complete with an 'authorized representation of the car'.[58] *The Illustrated London News* also published two souvenir issues for the funeral, containing special

---

[57] Charles J. Heathcote, *A Sermon Preached on the Sunday After the Funeral of the Duke of Wellington* (Hackney: John Coventry, 1852), 4.

[58] Official Programme of the of the Funeral of the Duke of Wellington, Montreal, Rare Books, Special Collections & Archives, McGill University Library, MS662, Wellington Collection, C2.

Wellington supplements and each boasting special large engravings, which together sold over two million copies.[59] Invariably, many who possessed autographs or letters signed by Wellington offered them at high prices, while locks of both his hair and Copenhagen's (some genuine, others no doubt not), and even a waistcoat 'in good preservation, worn by his Grace some years back', were also available for the right price.[60] Further relics appeared a decade later when, on 30 December 1862, the Office of Works held an auction of 'the valuable trappings, funeral furniture, and equipments', that had taken centre stage at Wellington's funeral. The items up for auction included the embroidered velvet pall and a variety of other decorations.[61] The funeral also renewed interest in the more famous battlefield relics. *The Illustrated London News* ran a story on the Wellington Elm and its fate in their second commemorative funeral issue.[62]

As commemorative objects celebrating Waterloo had supplemented relics and served the same purpose for those who could not visit the battlefield, the passing of Wellington prompted the creation of new commemorative items. A new medal marking Wellington's life and death was struck by Pinches Mint and sold by Mr Mitchell of Old Bond Street, which bore a notable resemblance to several of the commemorative medals produced by James Mudie in 1819. The medal featured Count D'Orsay's portrait of Wellington on the obverse and the duke's birth and death dates, surrounded by a laurel wreath, on its reverse (Figure 7.4).[63] P. G. Dodd, a goldsmith, offered 'striking likenesses, in cameo and intaglio jewelry, of every description' starting at 2s. 6d. and going up to 10s.[64] For those who preferred to honour Wellington with décor rather than jewellery, *The Illustrated London News* noted that his death and funeral had prompted the creation and sale of 'scores of busts and portraits of the great Commander', and reported on which were the most lifelike and had earned the patronage of Queen Victoria, the second Duke of Wellington, and Viscount Hardinge.[65] These pieces would have made excellent companions to the various prints and other artistic pieces that had been popular in the years following Waterloo. There were also much more bizarre souvenirs to be found, as is illustrated by the advertisements in the 16 November

[59] 'Wellington Supplement', *Illustrated London News*, 20 November 1852, pp. 441–56; 'Wellington Supplement', *Illustrated London News*, 27 November 1852, pp. 473–88; Pearsall, 'Burying the Duke', 365.
[60] *The Times*, 16 November 1852, p. 1; *The Times*, 13 November 1852, p. 1; *The Times*, 15 November 1852, p. 2; *The Times*, 17 November 1852, p. 1.
[61] Funeral of the Duke of Wellington, 1852–1854, London, National Archives, WORK 21/41; Pearsall, 'Burying the Duke', 389.
[62] 'The Wellington Tree on the Field of Waterloo', *Illustrated London News*, 27 November 1852, p. 469.
[63] 'Medal of the Late Duke of Wellington', *Illustrated London News*, 20 November 1852, pp. 429–30.
[64] 'The Striking Likenesses', *The Times*, 16 November 1852, p. 1.
[65] 'Bust of the Duke of Wellington. By Adams', *Illustrated London News*, 27 November 1852, p. 462; 'Portraits, Statues, and Memorials of the Duke of Wellington', *Illustrated London News*, 20 November 1852, p. 446.

Figure 7.4 'Medal of the Late Duke of Wellington, by Pinches', *Illustrated London News*, 20 November 1852, p. 429. General Research Division, The New York Public Library. New York Public Library Digital Collections; The reverse of Medal 35, obverse of Medal 22, and the reverse of Medal 10, James Mudie, *An Historical and Critical Account of a Grand Series of National Medals* (London: Henry Colburn and Co., 1820), Beinecke Rare Book and Manuscript Library, Yale University.

issue of *The Times* offering 'Duke of Wellington's Funeral Wine' and 'Wellington Funeral Cake', both of which readers were urged to put in orders for early, 'owing to the immense demand' for such 'delicious article[s]'.[66]

Londoners, like the residents of Waterloo, were not above using their geographical location for profit, although instead of relics of the battle found by scouring the field, Londoners offered space and views. In the days leading up to the funeral, *The Times* boasted over a column of advertisements offering seats and rooms with a view of the procession.[67] Demand became so high that *The Illustrated London News* reported individual seats going for up to three guineas, while one individual seeking to rent an entire first floor 'in the line of procession, with two or three large windows' refused to pay more than twenty guineas.[68] For those who preferred not to take their chances with small ads, the Wellington

[66] 'Duke of Wellington's Funeral Wine', *The Times*, 16 November 1852, p. 1; 'Wellington Funeral Cake', *The Times*, 16 November 1852, p. 1.

[67] *The Times*, 13 November 1852, p. 1; *The Times*, 15 November 1852, p. 2; *The Times*, 16 November 1852, p. 1; *The Times*, 17 November 1852, p. 1.

[68] 'The Grand State Funeral of Arthur Duke of Wellington', *Illustrated London News*, 27 November 1852, p. 475; 'The Duke's Funeral—Wanted', *The Times*, 16 November 1852, p. 1.

Funeral Agency offered 'seats along the entire line of Procession' which could be obtained by visiting their office off the Strand.[69]

Wellington's funeral also produced its own forms of tourism, analogous, on a smaller scale, to Waterloo becoming a fixture on any tour of the Low Countries. We have already discussed the hordes of people from all over the country who descended on London to witness the funeral, but Wellingtonian thanatourism went beyond that one day. The lying in state at Chelsea Hospital which preceded the funeral attracted an 'undistinguished multitude, in a torrent, which continued to roll on irresistibly and without pause throughout' the five days it was open to the public, with *The Times* estimating that 65,000 mourners attended on the last day alone.[70] Once Wellington's coffin had been placed in its sarcophagus, the crypt of St Paul's experienced the same influx of visitors that had flowed to the Waterloo village church or the chapel at Hougoumont. The demand to see Wellington's final resting place grew so large that St Paul's was forced to install gas lighting to properly illuminate the crypt, replacing the 'ghostly light of a lantern' that had long guided visitors to Nelson's tomb.[71]

St Paul's had also seen an increase in visitors immediately after the funeral. Just as those not invited to the annual Waterloo banquet had sought admission to Apsley House earlier in the day to see the dinner service laid out in the portrait gallery, many who had not secured seats for the funeral in St Paul's sought to see the cathedral the following days. The demand was so great that *The Times* reported on 20 November that 'the Cathedral is to be thrown open to the public next week, in order to give those who were not present at the funeral an opportunity of seeing the manner in which it has been fitted up'.[72] The cathedral was opened from noon until 8 p.m. on Monday 22 November, and from 8 a.m. to 8 p.m. for the rest of the week. The number of visitors was limited to 700 per hour. To ensure that no more than that would be admitted, tickets issued by the Excise Office or the Office of Works were required for entry.[73] The same demand prompted the funeral car to be placed in Marlborough House, where *The Times* theorized 'it will probably in a few days be exhibited to the public'.[74] The Office of Works eventually offered the car to St Paul's, where it was displayed in the crypt alongside the tomb of the man it had carried. Up until 1871, the car was 'drawn' by

---

[69] By Authority. The Duke of Wellington's Funeral, Montreal, Rare Books, Special Collections & Archives, McGill University Library, MS662, Wellington Collection, C2.

[70] 'Funeral of the Duke of Wellington', *The Times*, 18 November 1852, p. 5; 'The Lying in State at Chelsea Hospital', *Illustrated London News*, 20 November 1852, pp. 428–30.

[71] The funeral itself had prompted the installation of gas lighting in the area under the dome. George Leonard Prestige, *St. Paul's in its Glory: A Candid History of the Cathedral, 1831–1911* (London: S.P.C.K., 1955), 41–2.

[72] 'Funeral of the Duke of Wellington', *The Times*, 20 November 1852, p. 5.

[73] 'Funeral of the Duke of Wellington', *The Times*, 20 November 1852, p. 5.

[74] 'Funeral of the Duke of Wellington', *The Times*, 20 November 1852, p. 5.

three wicker horses, but these were removed when they decayed, and thereafter it was presented in solitary splendour.[75]

Less than a year after the Great Exhibition, London was perhaps more exhibition mad in 1852 than it had been in the first flush of Waterloo exhibitions in the teens and twenties, and impresarios saw opportunity in the national mourning. The Gallery of Illustration's 'Grand Moving Diorama' of Wellington's campaigns from India to Waterloo, which had opened in May 1852, added three new scenes within a month of Wellington's death.[76] These comprised two views of the exterior of Walmer Castle, and a life-size view of 'the room in which the Duke breathed his last'.[77] With these additions, the exhibition changed its name from 'The Wellington Campaigns' to 'Life of Wellington', and claimed the honour not only of the 'presences of Her Majesty, the Royal Family, and the late Duke', but also of being 'the only complete diorama of His Grace's career ever exhibited'.[78] Not to be outdone, the Leicester Square Panorama offered, beginning the day before the funeral, the 'last opportunity of viewing Burford's Celebrated Historical Picture of the glorious Battle of Waterloo' in the large rotunda.[79] While it was the 1842 edition, rather than the 1816 original, potential visitors were assured that the panorama was based on 'drawings taken on the spot immediately after the Battle, completed under the authority of Officers at Head-Quarters at Paris; and frequently visited and approved of by the late lamented Duke of Wellington'.[80] It once again proved hugely popular: despite claims that it would only be open a few weeks, it remained on display until 19 March 1853.[81]

Madame Tussaud's adopted a similar strategy, switching their advertising in early October from their new additions of Benjamin Disraeli and the queens of Henry VIII to 'Arthur Wellesley, the great Duke of Wellington, taken from life during his frequent visits to the Napoleon Relics at Madame Tussaud's' while quoting the *Evening Sun*'s declaration that 'if this figure alone constituted the whole of the Exhibition it would well repay the trouble of a visit'.[82] Not content with merely altering their advertising, Tussaud's opened a new room in December 1852. Opposite the entrance of the exhibition, the new room contained a 'magnificent shrine or memorial, in honour of the late illustrious Wellington'.[83]

[75] Prestige, *St. Paul's in its Glory*, 78–9; Pearsall, 'Burying the Duke', 389. In 1981, the car was transferred to Stratfield Saye, the country seat of the Dukes of Wellington, where it remains.

[76] *The Times*, 12 May 1852, p. 1.

[77] 'Gallery of Illustration', *The Times*, 16 October 1852, p. 8.

[78] *The Times*, 25 September 1852, p. 1; *The Times*, 21 October 1852, p. 4; *Illustrated London News*, 13 November 1852, p. 407. Scenes of 'the Lying in State, Funeral Procession, and the Interior of St Paul's' were added after the funeral. *The Times*, 21 December 1852, p. 1.

[79] *Illustrated London News*, 13 November 1852, p. 407; *The Times*, 16 November 1852, p. 1.

[80] *Illustrated London News*, 13 November 1852, p. 407.

[81] *The Times*, 12 March 1853, p. 1. The Gallery of Illustration's Life of Wellington lasted a bit longer, closing on 11 June 1853. *The Times*, 4 June 1853, p. 1.

[82] *The Times*, 4 October 1852, p. 4; *The Times*, 25 September 1852, p. 1.

[83] *The Times*, 21 December 1851, p. 1.

The shrine, much like that of Napoleon found further into the exhibit, depicted the duke lying in state on a tented couch covered with the mantle of the Order of the Garter, in a field marshal's uniform, 'bearing the various Orders of Knighthood' and 'surrounded by emblems of his dignity'. The shrine was paired with Hayter's painting of the duke visiting Napoleon and was presented as a 'National Subject...a sight which cannot be seen without vibrating in every British heart'.[84]

The arts had commemorated Waterloo with paintings, plays, poetry, and musical compositions, almost entirely created and curated by civilians. Here again, Wellington's passing aped Waterloo commemoration. We have already mentioned the significant number of statues, busts, and paintings that were offered to the public between his death and funeral. These were supplemented by paintings of Wellington and significant moments in his career, most notably Waterloo, that were once again displayed to the public by owners eager to profit from this fresh interest. The same columns in *The Times* that held ads for seats overlooking the funeral procession route also contained notices informing the public that they had only a few days to see these works, almost all of which seemed to be 'the most characteristic portrait hitherto taken of the illustrious deceased', or 'a perfect realization of life'.[85] Nor was it only the decorative arts that offered up tributes. Despite the constant use of Handel's Dead March during the funeral procession, Sir Henry R. Bishop offered the public a specially composed funeral march for piano, duet, or military band.[86] Several other composers presented their own musical tributes, with titles such as 'Mourn for the Mighty Dead', 'The Flag is Half-Mast High', and 'The Hero's Burial'.[87]

On the literary side, we can see aspects of the histories of Waterloo and the memoirs of the soldiers who fought there in the publications of such works as John Timbs's *Wellingtoniana: Anecdotes, Maxims, and Characteristics of the Duke of Wellington* and the *Memoir of the Duke of Wellington*, published by Longman and Co. as part of the Traveller's Library series, both of which sought to summarize Wellington's life and capitalize on public interest in the duke following his death.[88] Nor was instinct limited to new publications. *The Battle of Waterloo*, the

---

[84] *Biographical and Descriptive Sketches of the Distinguished Characters which compose the Unrivalled Exhibition and Historical Gallery of Madame Tussaud and Sons* (London: G. Cole, 1862), 3.

[85] 'For Three Days Only', *The Times*, 16 November 1852, p. 1; 'The Grand National Painting', *The Times*, 15 November 1852, p. 2. See also *The Times*, 13 November 1852, p. 1; *The Times*, 15 November 1852, p. 2; *The Times*, 16 November 1852, p. 1; *The Times*, 17 November 1852, p. 1; *Illustrated London News*, 20 November 1852, p. 455; Invitation to See The Meeting of Field Marshal Blücher and the Duke of Wellington, Montreal, Rare Books, Special Collections & Archives, McGill University Library, MS662, Wellington Collection, C2.

[86] 'Wellington's Funeral March', *Illustrated London News*, 27 November 1852, p. 471.

[87] 'New Music, &c., The Flag is Half-Mast High, The Hero's Burial', *Illustrated London News*, 20 November 1852, p. 455.

[88] John Timbs, *Wellingtoniana: Anecdotes, Maxims, and Characteristics of the Duke of Wellington* (London: Ingram, Cooke, and Co., 1852); 'Memoir of the Duke of Wellington', *The Times*, 6 November 1852, p. 4.

first civilian history written of the battle and one of the most popular, was reprinted in an expanded eleventh edition to commemorate the duke's death.[89] For more religious readers, the publisher John Snow offered *Wellington and Victory*, a discourse on the duke and religion by Revd A. Morton Brown, LL.D.[90] More than sixty sermons preached to mark Wellington's death or funeral were also published, including *Greatness, Godliness, Glory*; *'The Lord Gave, and the Lord Hath Taken Away'*; *'Iron and Clay'*; *The Last Conqueror*; and *Wellington and War*, the last authored by the celebrated dissenter reverend, Christopher Newman Hall.[91] The language of these sermons echoed that used in the sermons preached in the immediate aftermath of Waterloo, emphasizing the divine gift of victory and Britain's place as God's chosen nation.[92] For those who preferred their reading material to be aesthetic rather than spiritual, publishing met memorabilia in *The Wellington Souvenir*, which offered 'the life and deeds of the great Duke ... chronicled in letters of gold, and splendidly illustrated; forming an appropriate memento, or an elegant present', which could be purchased in bookshops across the country for 2*s.* 6*d.*[93]

Despite this grandiose offering, the most notable and lasting literary tribute came from the pen of the Poet Laureate, Alfred, Lord Tennyson. *Ode on the Death of the Duke of Wellington* is a nine-strophe tribute in the form of a Horatian ode. Its most popular and effective section is strophe VI, which takes the form of a dialogue between Tennyson, speaking for Britain, and the shade of Nelson, who demands to know 'Who is he that commeth, like an honour'd guest, ... With a nation weeping, and breaking on my rest?' Tennyson explains to Nelson,

> Mighty seaman, this is he
> Was great by land as thou by sea.
> Thine island loves thee well, thou famous man,
> The greatest sailor since our world began.
> Now, to the roll of muffled drums,
> To thee the greatest soldier comes.

[89] *The Battle of Waterloo, with those of Ligny and Quatre Bras, Described by eye-witnesses and by the series of official accounts published by authority*, 11th edn (London: L. Booth, 1852).

[90] 'New Books, &c.', *Illustrated London News*, 27 November 1852, p. 471; A. Morton Brown, *Wellington and Victory; or, Christians More Than Conquerors. A Discourse Occasioned by the Death of the Duke of Wellington* (London: John Snow, 1852).

[91] D. J. Harrison, *Greatness, Godliness, Glory. A Sermon on the Death of the Duke of Wellington* (London: T. Hatchard, 1852); C. A. I. Smith, *'The Lord Gave, and the Lord Hath Taken Away.' A Sermon Preached in the Old Church, Macclesfield* (London: T. Hatchard, 1852); J. De Kewer Williams, *'Iron and Clay.' A Funeral Sermon for the Duke of Wellington* (London: John Snow, 1852); Joseph Sortain, *The Last Conqueror. A Sermon, Occassioned by the Death of the Duke of Wellington* (Brighton: Robert Folthorp, 1852); Newman Hall, *Wellington and War* (London: John Snow, 1852). The British Library catalogue contains 68 sermons explicitly preached and published for Wellington's death or funeral.

[92] They also emphasized that Waterloo was a British victory. See Smith, *'The Lord Gave, and the Lord Hath Taken Away'*, 12–14.

[93] 'New Books, &c.', *Illustrated London News*, 27 November 1852, p. 471.

Listing Wellington's achievements, from his victory 'against the myriads of Assaye' to 'that world's-earthquake, Waterloo!', Tennyson beseeches Nelson, 'If love of country move thee there at all, | Be glad, because his bones are laid by thine!', and urges Britain, 'in full acclaim...With honour, honour, honour, honour to him, | Eternal honour to his name.'[94] The image of Britain's two great martial heroes, each the avatar of their respective service branch, who had only met once in life, meeting again below St Paul's proved irresistible, and even those critics who considered the entire poem to be below Tennyson's usual standards praised that particular strophe. The populace agreed. Despite receiving a mixed reception from critics, it was extensively republished and plagiarized in papers across the country and went through multiple editions between its original publication in 1852 and 1855, when what scholars consider the definitive version was published.[95]

Even as their chief was being entombed and honoured, the veteran officers of Waterloo received a small amount of his glory through transference. Wellington's British field marshal's baton was 'borne on a black velvet cushion...by the Marquis of Anglesey, K.G.—Supported by Colonel the Duke of Richmond, K.G., and Major-General the Duke of Cleveland, K.G.'[96] In the cathedral, the standard or pennon was borne by Major-General Sir Harry Smith, the guidon by General Sir Howard Douglas, the banner of Wellesley by Lieutenant-General Lord Saltoun, and the great banner of the United Kingdom by Lieutenant-General Sir James Macdonell. The ten bannerols which flanked the pallbearers and the coffin were carried by Lieutenant-General Sir William Napier, Lieutenant-General Sir George Scovell, Lieutenant-General Sir Willoughby Cotton, Lieutenant-General Lord Charles Manners, Lieutenant-General Sir John Wilson, Major-General Lord Sandys, Lieutenant-General Sir Frederick Stovin, Lieutenant-General Sir George Berkeley, Lieutenant-General Sir Arthur Clifton, and Lieutenant-General Sir Thomas McMahon. Finally, there were the eight pallbearers themselves, General Viscount Combermere, General Marquess of Londonderry, General Sir Peregrine Maitland, General Viscount Hardinge, Lieutenant-General Lord Seaton, Lieutenant-General Sir Alexander Woodford, Lieutenant-General Viscount Gough, and Lieutenant-General Sir Charles Napier. In addition to honouring Wellington and receiving a portion of his national glory reflected back upon them, these twenty-five officers represent the army's involvement with Waterloo commemoration in the thirty-seven years since the battle. Among them, we find twelve officers who were guests at Wellington's Waterloo banquet (several of them over ten times), eight of whom were immortalized at that event by William Salter,

[94] Alfred Tennyson, *Ode on the Death of the Duke of Wellington* (London: Edward Moxon, 1852), 9–11.
[95] For a history of the *Ode* and its reception, see Edgar F. Shannon, Jr, 'The History of a Poem: Tennyson's "Ode on the Death of the Duke of Wellington"', *Studies in Bibliography* 13 (1960): 149–77.
[96] 'Funeral of the Duke of Wellington', *The Times*, 18 November 1852, p. 5.

and three officers who are depicted in Jan Willem Pieneman's *Battle of Waterloo*. There is little doubt that almost all of them, at one point or another, attended Vauxhall's fete, Astley's hippodrama, or one of the various exhibitions. Many more, not officially involved in the funeral, took their seats in St Paul's to bid a final farewell to the man who had commanded them. Drawing their inspiration from the coverage of the Waterloo banquet, *The Illustrated London News* published a list of the surviving Waterloo officers, declaring, 'now that the chief of that compact band that fought and bled on the field of Waterloo has been consigned to the tomb, a list of the survivors of that glorious battle may be interesting'.[97]

While the honours associated with the funeral must have been gratifying in a melancholy way, the entombment of Wellington also symbolized the beginning of the end of the commemoration of Waterloo as a lived event rather than an abstract cultural memory. As *The Economist* pointed out in their coverage of the procession, 'of the many hundred thousand who lined the streets yesterday comparatively few, the bulk being young…know much of Wellington. His victories were achieved before they were born.'[98] All knew the name Waterloo, but the nationalization of that victory was complete. The word Waterloo was just as likely to conjure up images of a busy rail terminus, a grand Georgian bridge, or a dozen streets, squares, or businesses as it was a blood-soaked ridge or the shattered yard at Hougoumont. What would be the last Waterloo banquet had occurred three months before Wellington's death, and with the ending of that tradition, one of the last reminders that Waterloo had been won by named individuals was gone. Waterloo became something experienced exclusively via abstract remembrance and national curation: it was taught in schools, viewed in paintings, and seen in plays and events, all produced by people who had either never been to Waterloo, or had only visited as tourists, and increasingly had not been alive on 18 June 1815.

Between 1815 and 1852, cultural ownership of Waterloo evolved in several ways and was never simple. Different groups owned or presented legitimate claims to ownership of different portions of Waterloo remembrance at different times. What is perhaps most interesting is the number of cases where multiple groups cooperated to further their respective claims. The alliance of veteran officers and civilian artists remains the best example of this. Drawing inspiration from the royal family and upper echelon of British society, the veteran officers, led by Wellington, effectively weaponized patronage. By cooperating with artists such as David Wilkie, Sir Thomas Lawrence, Jan Willem Pieneman, and William Salter, and by publicly approving and patronizing exhibitions and artistic productions, the veterans shaped the public's perception of both Waterloo and the men who fought it and lent what clout they could to those efforts as partial arbiters of

---

[97] 'The Surviving Waterloo Officers', *Illustrated London News*, 20 November 1852, p. 426.
[98] 'Wellington's Funeral', *The Economist*, 20 November 1852, p. 1287.

Waterloo legitimacy. We also see this in the wave of memoirs published in the 1830s, where veteran authors occasionally challenged critics but more commonly worked with Britain's publishers to their mutual benefit. By consciously limiting their narratives to their own eyewitness experience, the veterans supplemented rather than challenged other histories while emphasizing their own place on the battlefield and in the victory. In addition, they reminded readers that Waterloo was only one part of their larger service while simultaneously ensuring that their accounts would continue to shape civilian histories and views of the battle, even after their deaths.

A version of this can also be seen in annual commemorations, where military parades and Wellington's Waterloo banquet rubbed shoulders with Vauxhall's fete, special performances, and provincial balls. Even events that were, at their heart, very limited elitist gatherings or purely military spectacles were eagerly co-opted as national celebrations by the press and crowds of civilians treating them as entertainment for their benefit. This co-option was furthered by the adoption of Wellington and Waterloo as conservative icons, expanding Waterloo into a political victory as well as a military one and fostering a slew of new civilian meetings and banquets. Within the lifetimes of many veterans, 18 June had become a national holiday celebrated without any acknowledgement of the date's original significance.

In other spheres, ownership was claimed in unexpected ways. The battlefield itself became a major tourist destination, but it was of particular importance to the rising British middle class, determined to invent their own international traditions and prove their loyalty to their nation. Closer to home, the same impulses that drove people to visit Waterloo and be seen to visit Waterloo resulted in the production and consumption of Waterloo-linked material culture and the enduring popularity of exhibitions that allowed one to experience Waterloo without leaving the United Kingdom. Following the same impulses, individuals and local governments took commemoration into their own hands via the naming of businesses, locations, and infrastructure, until Waterloo was quite literally a household name. In response to this nationalization, radicals claimed Waterloo for their own purposes, co-opting the name and the very language of commemoration.

Despite these examples of contested ownership, by the time of Wellington's death in 1852 Waterloo was fully enshrined in the nation's collective memory as a cultural and, above all, national phenomenon. The same was not the case for the other nations that had fought there. People in every country involved in the Waterloo campaign marked the battle in some way, but none with the all-encompassing drive of Great Britain.[99] For Prussia, Waterloo paled in comparison

---

[99] For a more detailed overview of commemoration beyond the English Channel, see Alan Forrest, *Waterloo* (Oxford: Oxford University Press, 2015), chapters 7 and 8.

to the 1813 Battle of Leipzig, which pushed Napoleon's control back to the Rhine, thus bringing the Wars of Liberation to their promised conclusion. Berlin boasted a *Belle-Alliance-Platz* from 1815 until 1947 and Prussia erected a monument to their fallen soldiers on the battlefield in 1819 but Waterloo could never match Leipzig in either glory or significance. The German state that most avidly celebrated Waterloo was, of course, Hanover, who saw the battle as a way to emphasize their link with Britain and the service of so many Hanoverians in the King's German Legion. Hanover was the first country after Britain to place a monument on the battlefield itself in 1818 and also erected both a victory column in the city of Hanover and a triumphal gate in Osnabrück. When the monarchies of Great Britain and Hanover split in 1837, however, the significance of Waterloo as a unifying moment began to fade.

For the Netherlands, Waterloo commemoration was, above all, dynastic. As we have seen with the construction of the Waterloo Mound and Jan Willem Pieneman's paintings, William I seized the opportunity presented by the battle to paint his son, the Prince of Orange, as a war hero not only for the Dutch but also for the Belgians, many of whom were unhappy with their relatively new status as subjects of the House of Orange. Much of this state-sponsored commemoration was, inevitably, eliminated after Belgium's independence in 1830, while the new nation grappled with complications presented by Waterloo's continued popularity as a tourist destination and the enduringly pro-French outlook of the Catholic and francophone portions of its population. Finally we come to France itself, where Waterloo's memory became a different kind of battlefield, one where pro-Napoleonic and Revolutionary forces faced off against royalists and conservatives who, in turn, painted the battle as either a 'glorious defeat' of the avatar of liberty and progress or confirmation that Napoleon was nothing but a petty tyrant who had sacrificed a generation of Frenchmen to his own ambition. In the end, French commemoration of the battle came to focus on the patriotism and heroism of the rank-and-file soldiers of France, symbolized by the last stand of the Old Imperial Guard and their almost-certainly apocryphal claim (traditionally credited to Pierre Cambronne, their commander at the time) that 'the Guard dies but does not surrender!'[100]

Britain was therefore unique, not only in its nearly four decades of commemoration, but also for the ever broadening and national nature of its celebrations. For several generations of Britons, Waterloo was remembered not just as a battle, but as a series of carefully curated spectacles, ephemera, and works of art. One of the best indications of the lasting cultural legacy of Waterloo came not in 1852, however, but 163 years later, with the bicentenary of the battle in 2015. With the

---

[100] Forrest, *Waterloo*, chapter 7; Brian Joseph Martin, *Napoleonic Friendship: Military Fraternity, Intimacy & Sexuality in Nineteenth Century France* (Durham: University of New Hampshire Press, 2011).

centennial of the battle in 1915 significantly dampened by the First World War, the bicentennial took on a special allure.[101] The year 2015 saw, as historical anniversaries often do, a significant jump in new scholarship about Waterloo, including several of the works cited in this book. It also saw a variety of reprints of primary sources, most notably Charlotte Waldie's *The Battle of Waterloo*. Along with this boom in printing came other forms of historical commemoration, drawn from the battle's cultural memory. Apsley House recreated the Waterloo banquet, hosted this time by the 9th Duke of Wellington and attended by the descendants of a number of original attendees along with the Prince of Wales and the Duchess of Cornwall.[102] Apsley House also paid homage to the tradition of visitors seeking a glimpse of the arrangements, and throughout the summer of 2015 the portrait gallery was laid out as a banquet hall. Nor was Apsley House alone in their celebrations. The towns of Waterloo in Merseyside and Waterlooville in Hampshire joined their bicentennials to that of the battle and celebrated both in a series of festivals and events.[103]

While neither the Leicester Square panorama nor Madame Tussaud's Waterloo exhibitions survived to be reopened in 2015, several museums stepped into the gap. Both Apsley House and Wellington Arch hosted temporary exhibitions and lecture series on the battle and Wellington, complete with various relics. The Royal Green Jackets (Rifles) Museum in Winchester took the opportunity to open a new Waterloo Room, anchored by a large model of the battle. In Edinburgh, the colours carried by the 3rd Battalion of the 1st Regiment of Foot (Royal Scots) at Waterloo were put on display one final time before being placed permanently in storage.[104] As for material culture and ephemera, the Royal Mint also decided to get in on the action, not only issuing a commemorative £5 coin, but also finally producing Pistrucci's medal in its original glory.[105] Even the Nelson Society was

---

[101] For a discussion of the plans for the centenary in 1915, see Timothy Fitzpatrick, *The Long Shadow of Waterloo: Myths, Memories, and Debates* (Philadelphia: Casemate, 2019), chapter 7.

[102] Carolyn Hart, 'Recreating the Duke of Wellington's Victory Banquet, 200 Years on', *The Telegraph*, 28 May 2015. <https://www.telegraph.co.uk/foodanddrink/recipes/11630938/Recreating-the-Duke-of-Wellingtons-victory-banquet-200-years-on.html>; 'The Duke of Wellington's Waterloo Banquet', *The Court Jeweller*, 20 June 2015, <http://www.thecourtjeweller.com/2015/06/the-duke-of-wellingtons-waterloo-banquet.html>. Jane Branfield, Archivist, Stratfield Saye House, email to author, 15 June 2021.

[103] 'The Battle of Waterloo: Merseyside township celebrates battle's bicentennial', *Liverpool Echo*, 12 June 2015, <https://www.liverpoolecho.co.uk/news/nostalgia/battle-waterloo-merseyside-township-celebrates-9400012>; Jones, *The Public Houses and Inns of Waterlooville, Cowplain, Lovedean, Purbrook and Widley*, 9; Waterlooville 200, <https://www.waterlooville200.org/>. The Royal Waterloo Hotel, now simply the Royal Hotel, in Crosby Sea Bank/Waterloo, followed suit the next year, reviving their tradition of annual dinners with a banquet that simultaneously celebrated the hotel's 200th anniversary and the battle's 201st. Iain Brodie Browne, The Royal Hotel (200th anniversary), The Mayoral Blog, 19 June 2016, <http://themayoralblog.blogspot.com/2016/06/theroyal-hotel-200th-anniversary.html>.

[104] All of these exhibits were attended by the author.

[105] 'The Royal Mint marks 200 years since the Battle of Waterloo', The Royal Mint, 8 June 2015, <https://www.royalmint.com/aboutus/news/the-battle-of-waterloo-200/>; The Pistrucci Waterloo Silver Medal 2015, The Royal Mint, <http://www.royalmint.com/shop/The_Pistrucci_Waterloo_Silver_Medal_2015>.

caught up in the excitement, and staged a performance of Amherst's *The Battle of Waterloo* at the Old Royal Naval College in Greenwich using Pollock's Toy Theatre backdrops and figures.[106]

The centrepiece of the bicentennial was, of course, Waterloo itself. Stretching over four days from 18 June to 21 June and boasting two days of re-enactment and separate living history bivouacs/camps for the allied and French armies, Waterloo 200 drew 6,200 re-enactors (roughly twice the number that attend in a normal year) from across Europe and as far afield as Canada and over 100,000 attendees.[107] This multinational army descended on Belgium, many of them following the traditional route of travelling to Brussels and then journeying south to the village of Waterloo and on to the battlefield. They toured the field, shopped in the bivouacs and museums, and watched the re-enactments, either from the comfort of purpose-built bleachers or from the top of the Lion Mound, which has become one of the favourite viewing platforms for all Waterloo re-enactments.

While the re-enactment formed the lion's share of the programming on 19 and 20 June, the anniversary of the battle itself, 18 June, was marked by a multimedia spectacle christened *Inferno*. The brainchild of Belgian designer and spectacle creator Luc Petit, *Inferno* centred around twelve tableaux telling the story of the battle. Employing a 450-foot long stage, a giant lion's head, vast projection screens, pyrotechnics, and a cast of several hundred including re-enactors, dancers, singers, and musicians, *Inferno* sought to eschew recreation or re-enactment in favour of 'a poetic interpretation' of the battle.[108] Poetic interpretation aside, however, it can be argued that *Inferno* was, in fact, just as accurate a re-enactment as the two days of battle that followed it. In its attempts to capture the spirit and memory of Waterloo on stage before an audience of thousands of paying guests, *Inferno* was a re-enactment of the various cultural commemorations discussed in this book. Even two centuries after the last shot was fired, Waterloo could not escape its own spectacle.

---

[106] Waterloo Flyer, The Nelson Society, 19 November 2015, <https://nelson-society.com/waterloo-flyer-pdf>.

[107] All information on the Waterloo 200 re-enactment drawn from Robert Wilde-Evans, aide-de-camp to the allied commander-in-chief during the re-enactments, email to author, 31 August 2020; Ashley Wilde-Evans, email to author, 24 August 2020; <http://www.waterloo2015.org>; Bob Schulman, Waterloo: 200 Years Later, Napoleon to Lose Again, Huffpost, 7 June 2015, <https://www.huffpost.com/entry/waterloo-200-years-later_b_7531278>. There are also innumerable personal blog posts covering the re-enactment.

[108] *Inferno*, <http://inferno2015.prezly.com/inferno-a-poetic-interpretation-of-the-battle-of-waterloo-in-twelve-tableaux-in-which-the-imagination-plays-a-central-role>, archived 26 June 2015, <https://web.archive.org/web/20150626122329/http://inferno2015.prezly.com/inferno-a-poetic-interpretation-of-the-battle-of-waterloo-in-twelve-tableaux-in-which-the-imagination-plays-a-central-role#>.

Military plays and Hippodramas before and after Waterloo

NB: The date in parentheses is the date of the event being dramatized

A. Pre-Revolutionary/Napoleonic Wars

Title	Date first performed
The Battle of Sedgemoor (1685)	02/1837
The Battle of Bothwell Brig (bridge 1679)	03/05/1832
Ethelstan; or, the Battle of Brunanburh (937)	08/1841
The Battle of Bothwell Brigg (1679)	22/05/1820
Marmion; or, The Battle of Flodden Field (1513)	12/06/1848
King Harold; or, The Battle of Hastings (1066)	16/09/1839
Chevy Chase; or, The Battle of Otterburn (1388)	23/04/1832
Peter the Great; or, The Battle of Pultawa (Poltava 1709)	21/02/1829
King Stephen; or, The Battle of Lincoln (1141)	08/1822
Alfred the Great; or, The Battle of Eddington (878)	16/10/1823
The Battle of Agincourt; or, The Fight of St. Crispin's Day (1415)	15/9/1834
The Battle of Agincourt; or, The Parricide (1415)	02/06/1825
The Battle of Barnet; or, The Last of the Barons (1471)	24/10/1845
The Battle of Blenheim; or, the Horse of the Disinherited (1704)	20/09/1841
The Battle of Bosworth Field (1485)	16/02/1824
The Battle of Bosworth Field; or, The Life and Death of Richard III (1485)	29/01/1827
The Battle of Cronstad (Kronstadt 1790)	02/12/1828
The Battle of Hexham; or, Days of Yore (1464)	17/08/1812
The Battle of Pultawa; or, The King and the Czar (Poltava 1709)	23/02/1829
The Battle of Worcester; or, King Charles in the Royal Oak (1651)	18/04/1825
Brian Boroihme, the Victorious; or, The Battle of Clontarffe (Clontarf 1014)	28/02/1820
Charles XII and Peter the Great; or, The Battle of Pultawa (Poltava 1709)	26/05/1828
The Death of Caesar; or, The Battle of Philippi (42 BCE)	26/12/1823
Edward the Black Prince; or, The Battle of Cressy (Crecy 1346)	09/11/1807
Edward the Black Prince; or, The Hero of England (Crecy 1346)	07/01/1805
England's Monarch; or, The Battle of Worcester and the Royal Oak (1651)	24/07/1843
Harry of England; or, The Battle of Agincourt (1415)	16/05/1842
The Invasion of England by William the Conqueror; or, The Battle of Hastings (1066)	08/04/1844

Title	Date first performed
King Charles II; or, The Battle of Worchester (1651)	11/08/1821
King Richard III; or, The Battle of Bosworth Field (1485)	26/12/1812
The Last of the Barons; or, Warwick the King Maker and the Battle of Barnet (1471)	10/11/1845
The Life and Death of King Richard III; or, The Battle of Bosworth Field (1485)	16/02/1813
Marmion; or, The Battle of Flodden Field (1513)	25/10/1810
Marmion; or, The Battle of Flodden Field (1513)	24/03/1811
Perkin Warbeck; or, The Battle of Garra-Muir (~1497)	23/05/1836
Robert the Bruce; or, the Battle of Bannockburn (1314)	24/05/1819
The Siege of Londonderry and the Battle of the Boyne (1690)	22/05/1820
The Victories of Edward the Black Prince; or, The Battlefield (~1346)	01/04/1839
The White Rose and the Red Rose; or, The Battle of Bosworth Field (1485)	10/08/1835
Jane of the Hatchet; or, The Siege of Beauvais (1472)	20/07/1840
Charles the Bold; or, the Siege of Nantz (1477)	15/06/1815
The Ethiop; or, The Siege of Granada (1482–92)	1801
The Siege of Gibraltar (1779–83)	29/04/1805
The Siege of Rochelle (1627–28)	23/09/1835
The Siege of Carthage (149 BCE)	08/1819
The Siege of Valencia (1065)	08/1823
The Siege of St Quentin; or, Spanish Heroism (1557)	10/11/1808
The Siege of Berwick; or, The Brothers Devoted (1296, 1318, or 1333)	08/1818
Wallace the Brave; or, The Siege of Perth (~1297–1305)	12/1819
The Siege of Bradford (1643)	08/1821
Charles XII; or, The Siege of Stralsund (1711–15)	11/12/1828
The Siege of Corinth (146 BCE)	08/11/1836
The King and the Duke; or, The Siege of Alençon (1049–51)	08/02/1839
The Russian Impostor; or, The Siege of Smolensko (1632–3)	22/07/1809
The Siege of Cuzco (1536–7)	08/1800
Charles the Terrible; or, the Siege of Nancy (1477)	26/12/1821
Jane of Flanders; or, The Siege of Hennebonne (1342)	08/1801
Katizka; or, The Siege of Dresden (1760)	29/03/1848
Leila, the Maid of the Alhambra; or, The Siege of Granada (1482–92)	22/10/1838
The Siege of Belgrade (1789)	17/04/1828
The Siege of Calais (1346–7)	22/09/1832
The Siege of Danzig; or, The Polish Patriot (could be various. Probably 1734)	05/06/1837
The Siege of Gibraltar; or, General Elliot in 1782 (1782)	20/04/1835
The Siege of Jerusalem; or, The Camp of the Wilderness (70 CE)	20/04/1835
The Siege of Lynn (King's Lynn 1643)	08/05/1838
Stanislaus; or, The Siege of Dantsic (Danzig 1734)	08/09/1832
The Victories of Joan of Arc; or, The Siege of Orleans (1428–9)	04/11/1839
T. Gwenllian; or, The Siege of Kidwelly (~1403)	08/1841
The Siege of Vienne (Vienna 1529)	08/1838
The Siege of Liverpool; or, The Days of Prince Rupert (~1644)	28/04/1830
The Covenanters; or, The Battle of Drumclog (1679)	08/03/1825
The Partisans; or, The War of Paris in 1649 (1649)	21/05/1829
The Spy of the Neutral Ground; or, The American War of 1780 (1780)	27/09/1825

B. Revolutionary and Napoleonic Wars

Land

Title	Date first performed
The Battle of Waterloo (1815)	19/4/1824
The Battle of Salamanca (1812)	24/8/1812
The Battle of Televera (Talavera 1809)	21/08/1809
The Battle of Vittoria (1813)	10/07/1813
The Battle of Waterloo (1815)	15/11/1815
The Battle of Waterloo (1815)	25/04/1825
The Duke; or, the Night before the Battle (1815)[1]	01/07/1837
The Duke's Coat; or, The Night after the Battle (1815)	03/05/1824
The Duke's Coat; or, The Night after Waterloo (1815)[2]	06/09/1815
The Night After the Battle; or, The Emperor and the Page (1815)[3]	08/10/1823
Buonaparte's Invasion of Russia; or, The Conflagration of Moscow (1812)	04/04/1825
The Siege of Ancona (1815)	08/1846
The Siege of Sarragossa; or, Spanish Patriots in 1808 (1808)	18/01/1813
The Siege, Storming and Taking of Badajoz (1812)	04/05/1812
The Passage of the Deserts; or, The French in Egypt and the Siege of Acra (1799)	16/04/1838
The Siege of Acre; or, Britons in the East (1799)	26/01/1824
Sir Sidney Smith; or, The Siege of Acre (1799)	30/08/1830
Napoleon Buonaparte, Captain of Artillery, General and First Consul, Emperor and Exile	16/05/1831
Napoleon; or, The Emperor and the Soldier	15/09/1828
The Abdication of Ferdinand; or, Napoleon at Bayonne (1808)	08/1809
Napoleon; or, the Victim of Ambition	21/05/1831
Napoleon Bonaparte, General, Consul and Emperor	23/7/1821
Napoleon's Glory; or, Wonders in St. Helena	08/12/1840
Napoleon Bonaparte; or, The Deserter and his Dog	07/1840
Vittoria; or, Wellington's Laurels	12/07/1813
The Wars of Wellington	31/03/1834
John Bull and Buonaparte; or, A Meeting at Dover	08/08/1803
Buonaparte Burnt Out; or, The Allies Victorious	18/10/1813
Buonaparte's Destiny	31/01/1831
Buonaparte's Fatalities[4]	15/09/1828
The Champ de Mai; or, The Hundred Days of Buonaparte	20/09/1824
The Little Corporall or, Buonaparte at the Military School at Brienne	26/05/1831
Forget me not! Or, The Flower of Waterloo	23/06/1817
Waterloo Bridge; or, the Anniversary	18/06/1817
La Vivandière; or, The Eve of Waterloo	02/07/1845

[1] Assuming this is a reference to Waterloo.
[2] Full title: *The Duke's Coat; or, The Night after Waterloo. A Dramatick Anecdote*; prepared for Representation at the Theatre-Royal, Lyceum, and Interdicted by the Licenser of Plays. 8° 1815. L. 106 M. [29/8/1815; licence refused]. [This play was advertised at the Lyceum on 6/9/1815.]
[3] Assuming this is a reference to Waterloo.
[4] This was made up from previous spectacles at the Royal Amphitheatre.

Title	Date first performed
The Horrors of War; or, Sixteen Years Since	16/11/1831
Wars in Spain	15/08/1844
The Comrades, an Anecdote of the Spanish War	20/03/1848
The French War; or, The Soldier's Bride	23/04/1832
The Wars in Spain	15/05/1837

Sea

Title	Date first performed
The Battle of the Nile (1798)	28/03/1815
The Battle of Trafalgar (1805)	14/04/1806
The Battle of Trafalgar; or, The Death of Nelson (1805)	14/04/1806
The Siege of Flushing (1809)	28/08/1809
The Victory and Death of Lord Viscount Nelson (1805)	11/11/1805
Nelson's Glory	07/11/1805
Nelson; or, The Life of a Sailor	19/11/1827
Ben Brace; or, the Last of Lord Nelson's Agamemnon	06/06/1836
National Gratitude; or, Nelson's Funeral	15/05/1806
The Naval Victory and Triumph of Lord Nelson	07/12/1805
Nelson's Arrival in the Elysian Fields	18/01/1806
Trafalgar; or, The Last Days of Nelson	12/06/1849
Trafalgar; or, The Sailor's Play	08/1807

C. Post-Napoleonic Wars

Title	Date first performed
The Battle of Navarino; or, The Arab of the Red Desert (1827)	26/05/1828
The Chinese War; or, The Conquest of Amoy by British Arms (1841)[5]	27/05/1844
The French Spy; or, The Siege of Constantina (1836)	04/12/1837
The Siege of Antwerp; or, The Inundation (1832)	14/01/1833
The Conquest of Scinde; or, The Siege of Hyderabad (1843)	28/07/1845
The Burmese War; or, Our Victories in the East (1824–6)	27/03/1826
The Siege of Missolonghi; or, The Massacre of the Greeks (1825–6)	10/07/1826
The Siege of Moultan (1848–9)	1849
The Sikh's Invasion; or, The War in India (1845–6)	01/06/1846
The War in Syria; or, The Bombardment and Capture of St. Jean d'Acre (1821 or 1832)	07/12/1840
Wars of the Punjab (1845–6)	01/10/1846
The Afghanistan War; or, the Revolt at Cabul and British Triumphs in India (1839–42)	24/04/1843

---

[5] This may have covered more than just that battle in the First Opium War. It was also known as *Wars in China; or, The Battle of Ching Ho*.

D. Fictional/Unknown

Title	Date first performed
'Blood will have Blood!' or, The Battle of the Bridges	10/06/1811
The Eve of Battle	07/10/1844
The Battle of Luncarty; or, The Valiant Hays Triumphant over the Danish Invaders (990)	12/1804
The Siege of Isca; or, The Battles of the West	10/05/1810
The Battle of the Amazons (classical Greek myth)	12/02/1848
The Yellow Admiral; or, The Perils of the Battle and the Breeze	12/05/1845
Melodrame Mad! Or, The Siege of Troy	21/06/1819
Tekeli; or, the Siege of Montgatz	24/11/1806
The Giant Horse; or, The Siege of Troy	08/04/1833
The Siege of Abydos; or, The Pirate of the Isles	15/03/1844
The Siege of Montgatz; or, The Mill of Keben	27/09/1824
Zembuca and the Net-maker of Persia; or, The Siege of Estakhar	21/09/1835
The Siege of Troy; or, The Great Horse of Greece	08/1840

Select Bibliography

For reasons of space, a complete bibliography could not be included in this manuscript. The full bibliography for this book can be found at <https://www.lukealreynolds.com/who-owned-waterloo>

Adams, Edward. *Liberal Epic: The Victorian Practice of History from Gibbon to Churchill.* Charlottesville: University of Virginia Press, 2011.

Agazarian, Dory. 'Buying Time: Consuming Urban Pasts in Nineteenth-Century Britain'. Ph.D. Dissertation, The Graduate Center, City University of New York, 2018.

Aguirre, Robert. *Informal Empire: Mexico and Central America in Victorian Culture.* Minneapolis: University of Minnesota Press, 2004.

Alborn, Timothy. *All That Glittered: Britain's Most Precious Metal from Adam Smith to the Gold Rush.* Oxford: Oxford University Press, 2019.

Altick, Richard D. *The Shows of London.* Cambridge: The Belknap Press, 1978.

Amigoni, David, ed. *Life Writing and Victorian Culture.* Farnham: Ashgate, 2006.

Ashplant, Timothy G., Graham Dawson, and Michael Roper, eds. *Commemorating War: The Politics of Memory.* London: Routledge, 2000.

Assael, Brenda. *The Circus and Victorian Society.* Charlottesville: University of Virginia Press, 2005.

Assman, Aleida. *Cultural Memory and Western Civilization: Arts of Memory.* Cambridge: Cambridge University Press, 2013.

Assman, Aleida. 'Transformations between History and Memory'. *Social Research* 72, no. 1 (Spring 2008): 49–72.

Assmann, Jan and John Czaplicka. 'Collective Memory and Cultural Identity'. *New German Critique* 65 (Spring–Summer 1995): 125–33.

Auslander, Leora and Tara Zahra, eds. *Objects of War: The Material Culture of Conflict & Displacement.* Ithaca, NY: Cornell University Press, 2018.

Bainbridge, Simon. *British Poetry and the Revolutionary and Napoleonic Wars: Visions of Conflict.* Oxford: Oxford University Press, 2003.

Balen, Malcolm. *A Model Victory: Waterloo and the Battle for History.* London: Harper Perennial, 2006.

Barbero, Alessandro. *The Battle: A New History of Waterloo.* Translated by John Cullen. New York: Walker & Company, 2005.

Bayly, C. A. *Imperial Meridian: The British Empire and the World 1780–1830.* London: Longman, 1989.

Bell, David. *The First Total War: Napoleon's Europe and the Birth of Warfare as we Know it.* New York: Mariner, 2007.

Bennett, Tony. *The Birth of the Museum: History, Theory, Politics.* London: Routledge, 1995.

Berger, Stefan, Mark Donovan, and Kevin Passmore. *Writing National Histories: Western Europe since 1800.* London: Routledge, 1999.

Berger, Stefan, Linas Eriksonas, and Andrew Mycock, eds. *Narrating the Nation: Representations in History, Media, and the Arts.* New York: Berghahn, 2008.

Best, Geoffrey. *War and Society in Revolutionary Europe, 1770–1870*. Leicester: Leicester University Press, 1982.

Billig, Michael. *Banal Nationalism*. London: Sage, 1995.

Black, Barbara J. *On Exhibit: Victorians and their Museums*. Charlottesville: University Press of Virginia, 2000.

Black, Jeremy. *The Battle of Waterloo*. New York: Random House, 2010.

Black, Jeremy. *Britain as a Military Power: 1688–1815*. London: University College London Press, 1999.

Black, Jeremy. *European Warfare: 1660–1815*. London: University College London Press, 1994.

Black, Jeremy. *War and the Cultural Turn*. Cambridge: Polity Press, 2012.

Black, Jeremy. *Western Warfare, 1775–1882*. Bloomington: Indiana University Press, 2001.

Bonehill, John and Geoff Quilley, eds. *Conflicting Visions: War and Visual Culture in Britain and France c.1700–1830*. Aldershot: Ashgate, 2005.

Booth, Michael. *Victorian Spectacular Theatre 1850–1910*. Boston: Routledge & Kegan Paul, 1981.

Bourdieu, Pierre. 'The Forms of Capital'. In John G. Richardson, ed., *Handbook of Theory and Research for the Sociology of Education*, 241–60. Westport, Conn.: Greenwood Press, 1986.

Bowen, H. V. *War and British Society, 1688–1815*. Cambridge: Cambridge University Press, 1998.

Bratton, J. S., Richard Allen Cave, Breandan Gregory, Heidi J. Holder, and Michael Pickering. *Acts of Supremacy: The British Empire and the Stage, 1790–1930*. Manchester: Manchester University Press, 1991.

Breward, Christopher. 'Men in Heels: From Power to Perversity'. In Helen Persson, ed., *Shoes: Pleasure and Pain*, 128–39. London: V&A Publishing, 2015.

Brewer, John. '"The Most Polite Age and the Most Vicious": Attitudes Towards Culture as a Commodity, 1660–1800'. In Ann Bermingham and John Brewer, eds, *The Consumption of Culture, 1660–1800: Image, Object, Text*. London: Routledge, 1997.

Brewer, John. *The Sinews of Power: War, Money and the English State, 1688–1783*. Cambridge, Mass.: Harvard University Press, 1988.

Briggs, Asa. *The Age of Improvement, 1783–1867*. Harlow: Pearson, 1959.

Briggs, Asa. *Victorian Cities*. London: Penguin, 1990.

Briggs, Asa. *Victorian Things*. Chicago: University of Chicago Press, 1989.

Bryant, Julius. *Apsley House: The Wellington Collection*. London: English Heritage, 2015.

Buzzard, James. *The Beaten Path: European Tourism, Literature, and the Ways to 'Culture', 1800–1918*. Oxford: Oxford University Press, 1993.

Cannadine, David. *Aspects of Aristocracy: Grandeur and Decline in Modern Britain*. New Haven: Yale University Press, 1994.

Cannadine, David. *The Decline and Fall of the British Aristocracy*. New York: Vintage Books, 1990.

Cannadine, David. *Ornamentalism: How the British Saw Their Empire*. Oxford: Oxford University Press, 2001.

Cannadine, David. *The Rise and Fall of Class in Britain*. New York: Columbia University Press, 1999.

Cashin, Joan E., ed. *War Matters: Material Culture in the Civil War Era*. Chapel Hill: University of North Carolina Press, 2018.

Cathcart, Brian. *The News from Waterloo: The Race to Tell Britain of Wellington's Victory*. London: Faber & Faber, 2015.

Chambers, Thomas A. *Memories of War: Visiting Battlegrounds and Bonefields in the Early American Republic*. Ithaca, NY: Cornell University Press, 2012.

Chase, Karen and Michael Levenson. *The Spectacle of Intimacy: A Public Life for the Victorian Family*. Princeton: Princeton University Press, 2000.

Citizens and Kings: Portraits in the Age of Revolution, 1760–1830. London: Royal Academy of Arts, 2007.

Clark, Christopher. *Iron Kingdom: The Rise and Downfall of Prussia, 1600–1947*. Cambridge: Belknap Press, 2006.

Clark, Christopher. 'The Wars of Liberation in Prussian Memory: Reflections on the Memorialization of War in Early Nineteenth-Century Germany'. *The Journal of Modern History* 68, no. 3 (September 1996): 550–76.

Clark, G.Kitson. *The Making of Victorian England*. New York: Atheneum, 1972.

Clark, Samuel. *Distributing Status: The Evolution of State Honours in Western Europe*. Montreal: McGill-Queen's University Press, 2017.

Clarke, Stephen. *How the French Won Waterloo (or Think They Did)*. London: Cornerstone Publishing, 2015.

Claro, Lyndsey Rago. 'Pieces of History: The Past and Popular Culture in Victorian Britain, 1837–1882'. Ph.D. dissertation, University of Delaware, 2011.

Clayton, Tim. *Waterloo: Four Days that Changed Europe's Destiny*. London: Little Brown, 2014.

Coke, David and Alan Borg. *Vauxhall Gardens: A History*. New Haven: Yale University Press/Paul Mellon Centre for Studies in British Art, 2011.

Colby, Reginald. *The Waterloo Despatch: The Story of the Duke of Wellington's Official Despatch on the Battle of Waterloo and its Journey to London*. London: Her Majesty's Stationery Office, 1965.

Colley, Linda. *Britons: Forging the Nation 1707–1837*. New Haven: Yale University Press, 2009.

Confino, Alon. 'Collective Memory and Cultural History: Problems of Method'. *American Historical Review* 102, no. 5 (December 1997): 1386–403.

Conlin, Jonathan, ed. *The Pleasure Garden, from Vauxhall to Coney Island*. Philadelphia: University of Pennsylvania Press, 2013.

Conlin, Jonathan. 'Vauxhall Revisited: The Afterlife of a London Pleasure Garden, 1770–1859'. *Journal of British Studies* 45, no. 4 (October 2006): 718–43.

Cookson, J. E. 'The Edinburgh and Glasgow Duke of Wellington Statues: Early Nineteenth-Century Unionist Nationalism as a Tory Project'. *The Scottish Historical Review* 83, no. 215 (April 2004): 23–40.

Corfield, Penelope J. *Vauxhall and the Invention of Urban Pleasure Gardens*. London: History and Social Action Publications, 2008.

Cornwell, Bernard. *Waterloo: The History of Four Days, Three Armies and Three Battles*. London: William Collins, 2015.

Corrigan, Gordon. *Waterloo: Wellington, Napoleon, and the Battle that Saved Europe*. New York: Pegasus Books, 2014.

Corrigan, Gordon. *Wellington: A Military Life*. London: Bloomsbury Academic, 2006.

Coss, Edward J. *All for the King's Shilling: The British Soldier Under Wellington, 1808–1814*. Norman: University of Oklahoma Press, 2010.

Craig, Gordon A. *The Politics of the Prussian Army 1640–1945*. New York: Oxford University Press, 1964.

Crane, David. *Went the Day Well? Witnessing Waterloo*. New York: Alfred A. Knopf, 2015.

Cronin, Richard. *Paper Pellets: British Literary Culture after Waterloo*. Oxford: Oxford University Press, 2010.

Curl, James Stevens. *The Victorian Celebration of Death*. Stroud: Sutton Publishing Ltd, 2004.

Dawnay, N. P. and J. M. A. Tamplin. 'The Waterloo Banquet at Apsley House, 1836, by William Salter'. *Journal of the Society for Army Historical Research* 44 no. 198 (Summer 1971): 63–76.

de Bolla, Peter. 'The Visibility of Visuality: Vauxhall Gardens and the Siting of the Viewer'. In Stephen Meville and Bill Readings, eds. *Vision and Textuality*. Durham, NC: Duke University Press, 1995.

Dudink, Stefan and Karen Hagemann. 'Masculinity in Politics and War in the Age of Democratic Revolutions, 1750–1850'. In Stefan Dudink, Karen Hagemann, and John Tosh, eds, *Masculinities in Politics and War: Gendering Modern History*, 3–21. Manchester: Manchester University Press, 2004.

Eley, Geoff. 'Some Thoughts on German Militarism'. In Klaus-Jürgen Müller and Eckardt Opitz, eds, *Militär und Militarismus in der Weimarer Republik*, 223–35. Düsseldorf: Droste, 1978.

Emsley, Clive. *British Society and the French Wars, 1793–1815*. London: Macmillan, 1979.

Epstein, James A. *Radical Expression: Political Language, Ritual, and Symbol in England, 1790–1850*. Oxford: Oxford University Press, 1994.

Erll, Astrid and Ansgar Nünning, eds. *Cultural Memory Studies: An International and Interdisciplinary Handbook*. Berlin: Walter de Gruyter, 2008.

Fauret, Mary A. *War at a Distance: Romanticism and the Making of Modern Wartime*. Princeton: Princeton University Press, 2010.

Fitzpatrick, Timothy. *The Long Shadow of Waterloo: Myths, Memories, and Debates*. Oxford: Casemate, 2019.

Forrest, Alan, *Waterloo*. Oxford: Oxford University Press, 2015.

Forrest, Alan, Karen Hagemann, and Jane Randall, eds. *Soldiers, Citizens and Civilians: Experiences & Perceptions of the Revolutionary and Napoleonic Wars*. London: Palgrave Macmillan, 2009.

Forrest, Alan, Étienne François, and Karen Hagemann, eds. *War Memories: The Revolutionary and Napoleonic Wars in Modern European Culture*. Basingstoke: Palgrave Macmillan, 2012.

Forrest, Alan, Karen Hagemann, and Michael Rowe, eds. *War, Demobilization and Memory: The Legacy of War in the Era of Atlantic Revolutions*. Basingstoke: Palgrave Macmillan, 2016.

Foster, R. E. *Wellington and Waterloo: The Duke, the Battle and Posterity 1815–2015*. Staplehurst: Spellmount, 2014.

Foster, R. E. 'Food for Thought: The Waterloo Banquet'. *The Waterloo Journal* 35, no. 2 (Summer 2013): 13–17.

Foulkes, Nick. *Dancing into Battle: A Social History of the Battle of Waterloo*. London: Weidenfeld & Nicolson, 2006.

Francois, Pieter. 'If it's 1815, This Must be Belgium: The Origins of the Modern Travel Guide'. *Book History* 15 (2012): 71–92.

Francois, Pieter. '"The Best Way to See Waterloo is with your Eyes Shut": British "Histourism", Authenticity and Commercialism in the Mid-Nineteenth Century'. *Anthropological Journal of European Cultures* 22, no. 1 (2013): 25–41.

Fraser, Hilary. 'Writing the Past'. In Joanne Shattock, ed., *The Cambridge Companion to English Literature, 1830–1914*, 108–26. Cambridge: Cambridge University Press, 2010.

Frye, Northrop. *Anatomy of Criticism: Four Essays*. Princeton: Princeton University Press, 1957.

Fulford, Tim. 'Sighing for a Soldier: Jane Austen and Military Pride and Prejudice'. *Nineteenth Century Literature* 57, no. 2 (2002): 153–78.

Fussell, Paul. *The Great War and Modern Memory*. Oxford: Oxford University Press, 1975.

Fussell, Paul. *Wartime: Understanding and Behavior in the Second World War*. Oxford: Oxford University Press, 1989.

Gardener, John. *Poetry and Popular Protest: Peterloo, Cato Street and the Queen Caroline Controversy*. Basingstoke: Palgrave Macmillan, 2011.

Garlick, Harry. *The Final Curtain: State Funerals and the Theatre of Power*. Amsterdam: Rodopi, 1999.

Garnett, P. F. 'The Wellington Testimonial'. *Dublin Historical Record* 13, no. 2 (June–August, 1952): 48–61.

Gaulme, Dominique and François Gaulme. *Power & Style: A World History of Politics and Dress*. Paris: Flammarion, 2012.

Gitbels, Jolien. 'Tangible Memories: Waterloo Relics in the Nineteenth Century'. *The Rijksmuseum Bulletin* 63, no. 3 (2015): 228–57.

Glover, Gareth. *Waterloo in 100 Objects*. Stroud: The History Press, 2015.

Glover, Gareth. *Waterloo: The Defeat of Napoleon's Imperial Guard: Henry Clinton, the 2nd Division and the End of a 200-Year-Old Controversy*. London: Frontline Books, 2015.

Glover, Gareth, ed. *The Waterloo Archive, Volumes 1–6*. Barnsley: Frontline Books, 2010–14.

Greig, Matilda. *Dead Men Telling Tales: Napoleonic War Veterans and the Military Memoir Industry, 1808–1914*. Oxford: Oxford University Press, 2021.

Greig, Matilda, John-Erik Hansson, and Mikko Toivanen. 'Authorship in the Long Nineteenth Century: A Reappraisal'. *Nineteenth-Century Contexts* 41, no. 4 (2019): 369–76.

Guyatt, Mary. 'The Wedgewood Slave Medallion: Values in Eighteenth-Century Design'. *Journal of Design History* 13, no. 2 (2000): 93–105.

Halbwachs, Maurice. *On Collective Memory*. Edited and translated by Lewis A. Cosner. Chicago: University of Chicago Press, 1992.

Harari, Yuval Noah. 'Military Memoirs: A Historical Overview of the Genre from the Middle Ages to the Late Modern Era'. *War in History* 14, no. 3 (2007): 289–309.

Harari, Yuval Noah. *The Ultimate Experience: Battlefield Revelations and the Making of Modern War Culture 1450–2000*. London: Palgrave Macmillan, 2008.

Haynes, Christine. 'The Battle of the Mountains: Repatriating Folly in France in the Aftermath of the Napoleonic Wars'. *Historical Reflections/Réflexions historiques* 44, no. 3 (December 2018): 50–70.

Haynes, Christine. *Our Friends the Enemies: The Occupation of France after Napoleon*. Cambridge, Mass.: Harvard University Press, 2018.

Heinzen, Jasper. 'Transnational Affinities and Invented Traditions: The Napoleonic Wars in British and Hanoverian Memory, 1815–1915'. *The English Historical Review* 127, no. 529 (December 2012): 1404–34.

Herbert, Trevor and Helen Barlow. *Music & The British Military in the Long Nineteenth Century*. Oxford: Oxford University Press, 2013.

Hewitt, Martin. *The Victorian World*. London: Routledge, 2012.

Hichberger, J. W. M. *Images of the Army: The Military in British Art, 1815–1914*. Manchester: Manchester University Press, 1988.

Hobsbawm, Eric and Terence Ranger, eds. *The Invention of Tradition*. Cambridge: Cambridge University Press, 1983.

Hofschroer, Peter. *1815 The Waterloo Campaign: Wellington, His German Allies and the Battles of Ligny and Quatre Bras*. London: Greenhill Books, 1998.

Hofschroer, Peter. *1815 The Waterloo Campaign: The German Victory*. London: Greenhill Books, 1999.

Hofschroer, Peter. *Wellington's Smallest Victory: The Duke, the Model Maker, and the Secret of Waterloo*. London: Faber & Faber, 2004.

Holmes, Richard. *Redcoat: The British Soldier in the Age of Horse and Musket*. London: Harper Collins, 2001.

Holmes, Richard. *Wellington: The Iron Duke*. London: Harper Collins, 2003.

Hoock, Holger. *Empires of the Imagination: Politics, War, and Arts in the British World, 1750–1850*. London: Profile Books, 2010.

Hoock, Holger. *The King's Artists: The Royal Academy of Arts and the Politics of British Culture 1760–1840*. Oxford: Clarendon Press, 2003.

Hoock, Holger, ed., *History, Commemoration and National Preoccupation: Trafalgar 1805–2005*. Oxford: Oxford University Press, 2005.

Houghton, Walter E. *The Victorian Frame of Mind: 1830–1870*. New Haven: Yale University Press, 1985.

Huhtamo, Erkki. 'Penetrating the Peristrephic: An Unwritten Chapter in the History of the Panorama'. *Early Popular Visual Culture* 6, no. 3 (November 2008): 219–38.

Huhtamo, Erkki. *Illusions in Motion: Media Archaeology of the Moving Panorama and Related Spectacles*. Cambridge, Mass.: The MIT Press, 2013.

Hunt, Aeron. 'Ordinary Claims: War, Work, Service, and the Victorian Veteran'. *Victorian Studies* 61, no. 3 (Spring 2019): 395–418.

Hurl-Eamon, Jennine. *Marriage & the British Army in the Long Eighteenth Century*. Oxford: Oxford University Press, 2014.

Hynes, Samuel. *The Soldiers' Tale: Bearing Witness to Modern War*. New York: Penguin, 1998.

Hynes, Samuel. *A War Imagined: The First World War and English Culture*. London: Bodley Head, 1990.

Jackson, Lee. *Palaces of Pleasure: From Music Halls to the Seaside to Football. How the Victorians Invented Mass Entertainment*. New Haven: Yale University Press, 2019.

James, Leighton. 'Travel Writing and Encounters with National "Others" in the Napoleonic Wars'. *History Compass* 7, no. 4 (2009): 1246–58.

Jenkins, Susan. 'Sir Thomas Lawrence and the Duke of Wellington: A Portraitist and his Sitter'. *The British Art Journal* 8, no. 1 (Summer 2007): 63–7.

Johnston, Douglas M. *The Historical Foundations of World Order: The Tower and the Arena*. Leiden: Martinus Nijhoff Publishers, 2008.

Jones, Steven E. 'To Go Down, Bound: William Hone and the Materiality of Print Culture'. In Hermione de Almeida, ed., *Nature, Politics, and the Arts: Essays on Romantic Culture for Carl Woodring*, 63–81. Newark: University of Delaware Press, 2015.

Jurafsky, Dan. *The Language of Food: A Linguist Reads the Menu*. New York: W. W. Norton & Co., 2014.

Keegan, John. *The Face of Battle: A Study of Agincourt, Waterloo, and the Somme*. London: Penguin, 1976.

Keegan, John. *The Mask of Command: Alexander the Great, Wellington, Ulysses S. Grant, Hitler, and the Nature of Leadership*. London: Penguin, 1988.

Keen, Paul. *Literature, Commerce, and the Spectacle of Modernity, 1750–1800*. Cambridge: Cambridge University Press, 2012.

Keirstead, Christopher and Marysa Demoor, eds. 'Special Issue: Waterloo and its Afterlife in the Nineteenth-Century Periodical and Newspaper Press'. *Victorian Periodicals Review* 48, no. 4 (Winter 2015).

Keller, Ulrich. *The Ultimate Spectacle: A Visual History of the Crimean War*. New York: Routledge, 2001.

Kennedy, Catriona. 'John Bull into Battle: Military Masculinity and the British Army Officer during the Napoleonic Wars'. In Karen Hagemann, Gisela Mettele, and Jane Rendall, eds, *Gender, War and Politics: Transatlantic Perspectives, 1775–1830*, 127–46. Basingstoke: Palgrave Macmillan, 2010.

Kennedy, Catriona and Matthew McCormac, eds. *Soldiering in Britain and Ireland, 1750–1850: Men of Arms*. New York: Palgrave Macmillan, 2012.

Kriegel, Lara. *Grand Designs: Labor, Empire, and the Museum in Victorian Culture*. Durham, NC: Duke University Press, 2008.

Linch, Kevin. *Britain and Wellington's Army: Recruitment, Society, and Tradition, 1807–1815*. New York: Palgrave Macmillan, 2011.

Linch, Kevin and Matthew McCormack,,eds. *Britain's Soldiers: Rethinking War and Society, 1715–1815*. Liverpool: Liverpool University Press, 2014.

Longford, Elizabeth. *Wellington: The Years of the Sword*. New York: Harper & Row, 1970.

Longford, Elizabeth. *Wellington: Pillar of State*. New York: Harper & Row, 1972.

Luvaas, Jay. *The Education of an Army: British Military Thought, 1815–1940*. Chicago: University of Chicago Press, 1964.

McCormack, Matthew. *Embodying the Militia in Georgian England*. Oxford: Oxford University Press, 2015.

McCormack, Matthew. 'Boots, Material Culture and Georgian Masculinities'. *Social History* 42, no. 4 (2017): 461–79.

Mackenzie, John. *Orientalism: History, Theory and the Arts*. Manchester: Manchester University Press, 1995.

McKinney, Kayla Kreuger. 'Collecting Subjects/Objects: The Museum and Victorian Literature 1830–1914'. Ph.D. dissertation, West Virginia University, 2015.

Marcus, Sharon. 'Victorian Theatrics: Response'. *Victorian Studies* 54, no. 3 (Spring 2012): 438–50.

Markovits, Stephanie. *The Crimean War in the British Imagination*. Cambridge: Cambridge University Press, 2009.

Martin, Brian Joseph. *Napoleonic Friendship: Military Fraternity, Intimacy & Sexuality in Nineteenth Century France*. Durham, NC: University of New Hampshire Press, 2011.

Melman, Billie. *The Culture of History: English Uses of the Past, 1800–1953*. Oxford: Oxford University Press, 2006.

Mikaberidze, Alexander. *The Napoleonic Wars: A Global History*. Oxford: Oxford University Press, 2020.

Milkes, Elisa. 'A Battle's Legacy: Waterloo in Nineteenth Century Britain'. Ph.D. dissertation, Yale University, 2002.

Morley, John. *Death, Heaven and the Victorians*. Pittsburg: University of Pittsburg Press, 1971.

Mosse, George L. *Fallen Soldiers: Reshaping the Memory of the World Wars*. Oxford: Oxford University Press, 1990.

Muir, Rory. *Wellington: The Path to Victory, 1769–1814*. New Haven: Yale University Press, 2013.

Muir, Rory. *Wellington: Waterloo and the Fortunes of Peace, 1814–1852*. New Haven: Yale University Press, 2015.

Mullen, Richard and James Munson. *The Smell of the Continent: The British Discover Europe*. London: Macmillan, 2009.

Munsell, F. Darrell. *The Victorian Controversy Surrounding the Wellington War Memorial: The Archduke of Hyde Park Corner.* Lewiston, Pa: The Edwin Mellen Press, 1991.

Myerly, Scott Hughes. *British Military Spectacle from the Napoleonic Wars Through the Crimea.* Cambridge, Mass.: Harvard University Press, 1996.

Myerly, Scott Hughes. '"The Eye Must Entrap the Mind": Army Spectacle and Paradigm in Nineteenth-Century Britain'. *Journal of Social History* 26, no. 1 (Autumn, 1992): 105–31.

Navickas, Katrina. *Protest and the Politics of Space and Place, 1789–1848.* Manchester: Manchester University Press, 2016.

Nenadic, Stana. 'Romanticism and the Urge to Consume in the First Half of the Nineteenth Century'. In Maxine Berg and Helen Clifford, eds, *Consumers and Luxury: Consumer Culture in Europe, 1650–1850,* 208–27. Manchester: Manchester University Press, 1999.

Neumann, Dietrich. 'Instead of the Grand Tour: Travel Replacements in the Nineteenth Century'. *Perspecta* 41 (2008): 47–53.

Nicoll, Allardyce. *A History of English Drama, 1600–1900.* Cambridge: Cambridge University Press, 1955.

Nofi, Albert A. *The Waterloo Campaign: June 1815.* Cambridge: De Capo Press, 1998.

Oettermann, Stephan. *The Panorama: History of a Mass Medium.* Translated by Deborah Lucas Schneider. New York: Zone Books, 1997.

O'Hara, Glen. *Britain and the Sea Since 1600.* Basingstoke: Palgrave Macmillan, 2010.

O'Keeffe, Paul. *Waterloo: The Aftermath.* New York: Vintage Books, 2015.

Ousby, Ian. 'Carlyle, Thackeray, and Victorian Heroism'. *The Yearbook of English Studies* 12 (1982): 152–68.

Page, Anthony. *Britain and the Seventy Years War, 1744–1815: Enlightenment, Revolution and Empire.* New York: Palgrave, 2015.

Paris, Michael. *Warrior Nation: Images of War in British Popular Culture, 1850–2000.* London: Reaktion, 2000.

Pearsall, Cornelia D. J. 'Burying the Duke: Victorian Mourning and the Funeral of the Duke of Wellington'. *Victorian Literature and Culture* 27, no. 2 (1999): 365–93.

Pemble, John. *The Mediterranean Passion: Victorians and Edwardians in the South.* Oxford: Clarendon Press, 1987.

Physick, John. *The Wellington Monument.* London: Her Majesty's Stationery Office, 1970.

Pilbeam, Pamela. *Madame Tussaud and the History of Waxworks.* London: Hambledon and London, 2003.

Pimlott, John. *The Englishman's Holiday: A Social History.* London: Faber and Faber, 1947.

Poole, Robert. *Peterloo: The English Uprising.* Oxford: Oxford University Press, 2019.

Poole, Robert. *Return to Peterloo.* Manchester: Manchester Centre for Regional History, 2014.

Poole, Robert. 'The March to Peterloo: Politics and Festivity in Late Georgian England'. *Past & Present* 192 (August 2006): 109–53.

Pragnell, Hubert J. *The London Panoramas of Robert Barker and Thomas Girtin.* London: London Topographical Society, 1968.

Ramsey, Neil. *The Military Memoir and Romantic Literary Culture, 1780–1835.* Farnham: Ashgate, 2011.

Ramsey, Neil and Gillian Russell, eds. *Tracing War in British Enlightenment and Romantic Culture.* Basingstoke: Palgrave Macmillan, 2015.

Range, Matthias. *British Royal and State Funerals: Music and Ceremonial since Elizabeth I.* Woodbridge: The Boydell Press, 2016.

Read, Ronald. *Peterloo: The Massacre and its Background.* Manchester: Manchester University Press, 1958.

Reid, Robert. *The Peterloo Massacre*. London: Heinemann, 1989.

Reynolds, Luke. 'Serving His Country: Wellington's Waterloo Banquets, 1822–1852'. *Journal of Victorian Culture* 23, no. 2 (2018): 262–78.

Reynolds, Luke. '"There John Bull might be seen in all his glory": Cross-Channel Tourism and the British Army of Occupation in France, 1815–1818'. *Journal of Tourism History* 12, no. 2 (2020): 139–55.

Richards, Thomas. *The Commodity Culture of Victorian England: Advertising and Spectacle, 1851–1914*. Stanford, Calif.: Stanford University Press, 1990.

Russell, Gillian. *The Theatres of War: Performance, Politics, & Society, 1793–1815*. Oxford: Oxford University Press, 1995.

Said, Edward W. *Orientalism*. New York: Vintage Books, 1979.

Samuel, Raphael. *Theatres of Memory: Past and Present in Contemporary Culture*. London: Verso, 2012.

Samuel, Raphael, ed. *Patriotism: The Making and Unmaking of British National Identity*. London: Routledge, 1989.

Saxon, A. H. *Enter Foot and Horse: A History of the Hippodrama in England and France*. New Haven: Yale University Press, 1968.

Saxon, A. H. *The Life and Art of Andrew Ducrow*. Hamden: Archon Books, 1978.

Seaton, A. V. 'War and Thanatourism: Waterloo 1815–1914'. *Annals of Tourism Research* 26, no. 1 (1999): 130–58.

Semmel, Stuart. *Napoleon and the British*. New Haven: Yale University Press, 2004.

Semmel, Stuart. 'Reading the Tangible Past: British Tourism, Collecting, and Memory after Waterloo'. *Representations* 69 (2000): 9–37.

Shaw, Philip, ed. *Romantic Wars: Culture & Conflict, 1793–1822*. Farnham: Ashgate, 2000.

Shaw, Philip. *Waterloo and the Romantic Imagination*. New York: Palgrave, 2002.

Sinnema, Peter W. *The Wake of Wellington: Englishness in 1852*. Athens: Ohio University Press, 2006.

Smith, Leonard V. 'Paul Fussell's *The Great War and Modern Memory*: Twenty-Five Years Later'. *History and Theory* 40, no. 2 (May 2001): 241–60.

Speaight, George. *Juvenile Drama: The History of the English Toy Theatre*. London: Macdonald & Co., 1946.

Spencer-Smith, Jenny. *Portraits for a King: The British Military Paintings of A. J. Dubois Drahonet 1791–1834*. London: National Army Museum, 1990.

Spiers, Edward M. *Army and Society, 1815–1914*. London: Longman, 1980.

Strachan, Hew. *Clausewitz's On War: A Biography*. New York: Grove Press, 2007.

Strachan, Hew. *European Armies and the Conduct of War*. London: George Allen & Unwin, 1983.

Strachan, Hew. *From Waterloo to Balaclava: Tactics, Technology, and the British Army, 1815–1854*. Cambridge: Cambridge University Press, 1985.

Strachan, Hew. *Wellington's Legacy: The Reform of the British Army, 1830–54*. Manchester: Manchester University Press, 1984.

Strawson, John. *Beggars in Red: The British Army, 1789–1889*. Barnsley: Pen & Sword Military Classics, 2003.

Sullivan, Greg, ed. *Fighting History: 250 Years of British History Painting*. London: Tate Publishing, 2015.

Tait, Pela. *Fighting Nature: Travelling Menageries, Animal Acts and War Shows*. Sydney: Sydney University Press, 2016.

Thompson, Neville. *Wellington after Waterloo*. London: Routledge & Kegan Paul, 1986.

Tussaud, John Theodore. *The Romance of Madame Tussaud's*. New York: George H. Doran Company, 1920.

Uglow, Jenny. *In These Times: Living Through Napoleon's Wars, 1793–1815*. London: Faber & Faber, 2015.

Valladares, Susan. *Staging the Peninsular War: English Theatres 1807–1815*. London: Routledge, 2016.

Vernon, Alex, ed. *Arms and the Self: War, the Military, and Autobiographical Writing*. Kent, Oh.: Kent State University Press, 2005.

Walmsley, Robert. *Peterloo: The Case Reopened*. Manchester: Manchester University Press, 1969.

White, R. J. *Waterloo to Peterloo*. London: Penguin, 1968.

White-Spunner, Barney. *Of Living Valour: The Story of the Soldiers of Waterloo*. New York: Simon & Schuster, 2015.

Wilcox, Scott. 'The Panorama and Related Exhibitions in London'. M.Litt. thesis, University of Edinburgh, 1976.

Wilson, Kathleen, ed. *A New Imperial History: Culture, Identity and Modernity in Britain and the Empire, 1660–1840*. Cambridge: Cambridge University Press, 2004.

Wilson, Peter. 'European Warfare 1815–2000'. In Jeremy Black, ed., *War in the Modern World since 1815*, 192–216. New York: Routledge, 2003.

Winter, Jay. *Sites of Memory, Sites of Mourning: The Great War in European Cultural History*. Cambridge: Cambridge University Press, 1995.

Winter, Jay and Emmanual Sivan, eds. *War & Remembrance in the 20th Century*. Cambridge: Cambridge University Press, 2000.

Wintermute, Bobby A. and David J. Ulbrich. *Race and Gender in Modern Western Warfare*. Berlin: De Gruyter, 2018.

Wood, Gillen D'Arcy. *The Shock of the Real: Romanticism and Visual Culture, 1760–1860*. New York: Palgrave, 2001.

Wood, Marcus. *Blind Memory: Visual Representations of Slavery in England and America, 1780–1865*. Manchester: Manchester University Press, 2000.

Wood, Marcus. *Radical Satire and Print Culture, 1790–1822*. Oxford: Clarendon Press, 1994.

Wood, Marcus. 'Emancipation Art, Fanon, and the "Butchery of Freedom"'. In Brycchan Carey and Peter J. Kitson, eds, *Slavery and the Cultures of Abolition: Essays Marking the Bicentennial of the British Abolition Act of 1807*, 11–41. Cambridge: D. S. Brewer, 2007.

Woodring, Carl. 'Three Poets on Waterloo'. *The Wordsworth Circle* 18, no. 2 (Spring 1987): 54–7.

Woolgar, C. M., ed. *Wellington Studies V*. Southampton: Hartley Institute, University of Southampton, 2013.

Wright, Christine. *Wellington's Men in Australia: Peninsular Veterans and the Making of the British Empire c.1820–1840*. New York: Palgrave Macmillan, 2011.

Yagoda, Ben. *Memoir: A History*. New York: Riverhead Books, 2009.

Yarrington, Alison Willow. 'The Commemoration of the Hero 1800–1864: Monuments to the British Victors of the Napoleonic Wars'. Ph.D. dissertation, University of Cambridge, 1980.

Yates, Frances. *The Art of Memory*. London: Routledge and Kegan Paul, 1996.

Index

Note: Figures are indicated by an italic 'f', respectively, following the page number.

For the benefit of digital users, indexed terms that span two pages (e.g., 52–53) may, on occasion, appear on only one of those pages.

Adventures in the Rifle Brigade in the Peninsula, France, and the Netherlands from 1809-1815 30–5
Albert, Prince Consort 102–4, 108–11, 130–3, 214–16, 221
Anglesey, Henry Paget, Marquess of 108–9, 111–12, 129, 132–3, 139, 154, 167–9, 169f, 171–2, 171f, 173–4, 200, 201n. 126, 231–2
Leg of 61–3
Anton, James 38–9
Apsley House 86–7, 102, 105–6, 170–3, 171f, 216–18
Astley's Royal Amphitheatre 96, 96n. 137, 151–5

Barker Family 134–8
Bathurst, Henry, Earl 78–9, 166, 172n. 123
Battle of Waterloo (1815 publication) 18–21
Battle of Waterloo (1824 hippodrama) 9, 96–7, 100–1, 151–9, 156f
Toy theatre version of 158–9, 159f
Battle of Waterloo (1824 painting) 167–70, 169f
Belgium 44–5
Ownership of Waterloo 15–16, 20, 23, 26–7, 33, 40, 234
Blücher, Gebhard Leberecht von, Prince von Wahistatt 15–16, 33, 79n. 26, 80–1, 125n. 37, 128–9, 131, 151–2, 173–4, 198, 199f, 203n. 137
Bonaparte, Napoleon
Britain's fascination with 21–2, 54–6, 117, 128–9
British ownership of 22, 117, 130–1
Coach 124–8, 125f, 126f, 129–32
Depictions of 81–2, 125–7, 125f, 126f, 128–9, 131–2, 132f, 133n. 79, 151–2
Relics of 122–3, 131–2
Shrine of 130–2, 132f
Bullock's London Museum 124–5, 128
Bullock, William 124–8
Byron, Lord George Gordon 54–6, 63–4, 125–7, 161–3

Chelsea Pensioners reading the Waterloo Dispatch 16–17, 17f
Childe Harold's Pilgrimage 54–6, 161–3
Clarence, Duke of, *see* William IV
Copenhagen (horse) 9, 164, 165f, 166–8, 169f, 224–5
Cotton, Edward 56–8
Cruikshank, George 125–7, 125f, 206–10, 208f, 209f

Dance on the Nythe 89
Ducrow, Andrew 96, 96n. 137, 98–9, 151–3

Eaton, Charlotte (nee Waldie) 3, 18–21, 46–8
Egyptian Hall 100–1, 124–5, 128, 143–4
Eyewitness Narratives 13–14, 18–20, 30–2, 36–7, 41–2

Field of Waterloo (1815 poem) 53
Field of Waterloo (1818 painting) 161–4, 162f, 167
France
British Opinions of 24, 26–7, 40, 159–60, 178, 180–1, 186–8, 196–7, 201
Objections to Waterloo Commemoration 115
Ownership of Waterloo 149–50, 234

George IV 62–3, 83, 173–4, 183–6, 186f, 192, 196–8, 200, 201n. 126

Hand-Book for Travellers on the Continent 55–7
Hanover,
King's German Legion 23, 33–4
Ownership of Waterloo 15–16, 233–4
Hardinge, Henry Viscount 108–9, 111–12, 171–2, 171f, 225–6, 231–2
Hill, Rowland, Viscount 129, 131–3, 142, 167–9, 169f, 171–2, 171f, 173–4
Historical Account of the Campaign in the Netherlands in 1815 21–5
Historical accuracy 95–8, 120–4, 125n. 37, 129, 131, 133–9, 141–5, 151–2, 154, 157, 169–70, 174, 228

HMS *Bellerophon* 81–2, 117, 194
HMS *Waterloo* 194
Hone, William 206–10, 208*f*, 209*f*
Hougoumont, Chateau of 50–1, 63–4, 95–6,
    98–9, 162–3, 162*f*, 167

Ireland,
    Ownership of Waterloo 5, 37–8, 77–8, 143–4,
    176–7

Kincaid, Sir John 14–15, 29–30, 144

Lawrence, Sir Thomas 164–7, 173–4
Leach, Lieutenant Colonel Jonathan 35–6,
    145–6
Leicester Square Panorama 135–9, 137*f*, 228
Lion's Mound 69–71, 72*f*, 236

Madame Tussaud and Sons 128–32, 137*f*,
    228–9
Marshall, Messrs 134–5, 139–42
Military General Service Medal 197, 197n. 112
Mudford, William 21–5
Mudie, James 200–1, 225–6, 226*f*

Nelson, Admiral Lord Horatio 175–6, 212–13,
    218–20, 230–1
Netherlands 44–5
    Ownership of Waterloo 15–16, 20, 23, 26–7,
    33, 40, 69–71, 167–9, 183–4, 198, 234

*Ode on the Death of the Duke of
    Wellington* 230–1

Palmer, Alex 122–4
Paul's Letters to his Kinfolk 51–3
Percy, Henry 78–9
Peterloo, *see* St Peter's Fields Massacre
Pieneman, Jan Willem 167–70
Pistrucci, Benedetto 197–200
Poet's Pilgrimage to Waterloo 53–4
Prince of Orange, *see* William II of the
    Netherlands
Prussia
    Exclusion of from Waterloo memory 18,
    28–9, 80–1, 144–7, 168–9
    Ownership of Waterloo 15–16, 20, 23–4,
    26–7, 32–3, 36–7, 40, 111–12, 144, 183–4,
    198, 233–4

Raglan, Baron, *see* Somerset, Lord Fitzroy
*Retrospect of a Military Life during the Most
    Eventful Periods of the Last War* 38–43
Rough Sketches of the Life of an Old Soldier 35–8

Salter, William 170–3
Scotland,
    Ownership of Waterloo 5, 18, 37–8, 77–8,
    88–9, 134–5, 145–6, 176–7, 195
Scott, Sir Walter 51–3, 66
Siborne, Captain William 142–7
Somerset, Lord Fitzroy 99–100, 141, 167–9, 169*f*,
    171–2, 171*f*
Southey, Robert 53–4
St Peter's Fields Massacre 4–5, 206–10,
    208*f*, 209*f*

Thackeray, William Makepeace 71–3, 150–2,
    152n.19
Trafalgar, Battle of 149n. 3, 150–1, 151n. 9,
    181–2, 181n. 24, 182n. 25, 191–2, 240–1
Turner, Joseph Mallord William 161–4

United Kingdom
    Ownership of Waterloo 1–4, 13–14, 18, 23,
    25, 27–8, 32–4, 37–8, 40, 43–5, 69–73,
    112–14, 144–7, 170, 183–6, 188, 201,
    232–3
    See also Ireland and Scotland
Uxbridge, Earl of, *see* Anglesey, Henry Paget,
    Marquess of

Vauxhall Gardens 1, 9–10, 75, 83–4, 92–101, 95*f*
Veterans
    Attending commemorations 4, 81–4, 86–7,
    90–2, 99–100, 102, 108–9, 121, 133–9,
    141–2, 144–7, 154–5, 158, 169–70, 174,
    183–4, 231–3
    Employed by commemorations 4, 91–2, 96–7,
    101, 121, 123–4, 151–2, 182n. 26, 183–4,
    192n. 81
Victoria I 86–7, 112, 132–3, 214–18

Waldie, Charlotte, *See* Eaton, Charlotte
    (nee Waldie)
War of 1812 81–2
Waterloo
    As a conservative victory 3–4, 75, 78, 88–9,
    103–4, 106, 176–7, 204–5
    As a pilgrimage site 53–4, 58, 71, 72*f*
    As a religious victory 78–81, 88–9
    Banquet 75, 86, 102–15, 111*f*, 170–3, 171*f*,
    231–2
    Bicentennial 234–6
    Blue (colour used in fashion and décor) 203–5
    Cannon captured there used in
    commemorations 69n. 115, 183–4, 206–7,
    214–16
    Churches 181–2, 194–5

Clubs 81–2, 84–5, 87–9, 114, 190n. 72
Correct way of visiting 46–51, 55–6
Criticism of celebrations 4–5, 114–15, 195, 206–7
Early celebrations of 3, 78–82
Establishments, infrastructure, and locations named after 188–93
Field of 3, 49–50, 64
Laurels 66, 74–5, 83–4, 83n. 52, 86–8, 86n. 81, 87n. 82, 91–2, 100–1, 107, 114–15, 141–2, 183–4, 201–2, 202*f*, 214–16, 218, 225–6
Maying, *see* Dance on the Nythe
Medal 86–7, 90–2, 108–9, 141–2, 170, 185, 195–7
Model 142–7
Museum 122–4
Musical commemorations of 3, 82–3, 87–8, 94–5, 98, 100–1, 139–41
Panoramas 134–42, 137*f*, 185, 228
Pistrucci Medal 197–200, 199*f*
Pressure to visit 44–6, 71–3
Proposed monuments to 175–6, 178–82, 180*f*
Re-enactment 1, 95–9, 194, 236
Regatta 99–100
Relics 58–69, 122–3
Relief Fund 79–81, 117
Reviews 74–5, 77–8, 86–7, 91–2
Riots 8–9, 74–5, 85–6, 90
Sermons 80–2, 195
Snuff 206
Soldiers' correspondence 18, 20–1, 64
Teeth 66–7
Village of 46, 48–9, 65*f*
Waterloo Banquet, 1836 (1840/1 painting) 170–3, 171*f*
Waterloo Bridge 9, 178–9, 182–8, 186*f*

Wellington, Arthur Wellesley, Duke of,
    Attendance of Waterloo events 83, 86–7, 97–101, 139n. 111, 141–2, 154, 183–4, 228–9
    Boot 202–3, 203n. 137
    Correspondence to 88–9, 104–5
    Criticism of 55, 114, 206
    Depictions of 94–5, 100–1, 106–7, 128–9, 151–2, 164–74, 165*f*, 169*f*, 171*f*, 175–7, 180–1, 185–6, 186*f*, 198, 199*f*, 200–1, 202*f*, 211, 225–6, 228–9
    Door knocker 201, 202*f*
    Funeral car 214–16, 215*f*, 218–20, 219*f*, 221, 224–5, 227–8
    Similarities between funeral of and Waterloo commemoration 224–32
    Portrait of by Sir Thomas Lawrence 164–7, 165*f*
    Return visit to Waterloo 62–3, 69–70, 70n. 123
    Use of patronage to shape Waterloo memory 16–17, 17*f*, 129, 131–3, 132*f*, 139n. 111, 141–2, 144–7, 149, 166–74, 196–8, 200, 227–8
    Waterloo Dispatch 15–17
Wellington, Arthur Wellesley, Second Duke of 101–2, 225–6
Wellington Tree 58–61, 59*f*, 60*f*
William II of the Netherlands 26–7, 69–70, 86–7, 167–9, 234
William IV 86–7, 99–100, 108–9, 112
Windsor Castle,
    Commemorations located there 74–5, 83
    Waterloo Chamber 173–4
Wyon, Thomas Jr. 185–6, 195–6

York and Albany, Prince Frederick, Duke of 74–5, 81–2, 85–6, 154, 183–6, 186*f*